JUDICIAL CONVERGENCE AND FRAGMENTATION IN INTERNATIONAL HUMAN RIGHTS LAW

This book provides an innovative analysis of the complex issue of judicial convergence and fragmentation in international human rights law, moving the conversation forward from the assessment of the two phenomena and investigating their triggering factors. With a wide geographical focus that includes the most up-to-date case-law from the three main regional systems (the African, European and Inter-American) and the United Nations Human Rights Committee, the book confirms the predominant judicial convergence across international human rights law. On this basis, the book engages with an interdisciplinary investigation into the legal and non-legal factors that could explain both convergence and fragmentation, ranging from the use of judicial dialogue and the notions of necessity and proportionality, to the composition of the courts and the role of NGOs. The aim of this book is to provide the tools to understand the dynamics between human rights adjudicatory bodies and possibly foresee future instances of judicial fragmentation.

ELENA ABRUSCI is Lecturer in Law at Brunel University London. She has an interdisciplinary background in law and politics, and she has served as a policy advisor to the UK government and as a consultant to several UN agencies. Her current research focuses on regional human rights systems and emerging technologies.

CAMBRIDGE
UNIVERSITY PRESS

Shaftesbury Road, Cambridge CB2 8EA, United Kingdom

One Liberty Plaza, 20th Floor, New York, NY 10006, USA

477 Williamstown Road, Port Melbourne, VIC 3207, Australia

314–321, 3rd Floor, Plot 3, Splendor Forum, Jasola District Centre, New Delhi – 110025, India

103 Penang Road, #05–06/07, Visioncrest Commercial, Singapore 238467

Cambridge University Press is part of Cambridge University Press & Assessment, a department of the University of Cambridge.

We share the University's mission to contribute to society through the pursuit of education, learning and research at the highest international levels of excellence.

www.cambridge.org
Information on this title: www.cambridge.org/9781316514818

DOI: 10.1017/9781009090964

First published 2023

A catalogue record for this publication is available from the British Library.

ISBN 978-1-316-51481-8 Hardback

Contents

List of Figures — *page* xi
List of Tables — xiii
Foreword — xv
Acknowledgements — xix
Table of Cases — xxi
List of Abbreviations — xxxi

Introduction — 1
Methodology — 7
Structure — 9

PART I INTRODUCING AND ASSESSING FRAGMENTATION AND CONVERGENCE IN INTERNATIONAL HUMAN RIGHTS LAW

1 **Fragmentation and Convergence: Context and Definitions** — 13
Introduction — 13
1.1 Fragmentation in International Law — 14
1.2 Normative Fragmentation and Convergence in IHRL — 18
1.2.1 Defining Normative Fragmentation and Convergence — 18
1.2.2 The Proliferation of Human Rights Normative Frameworks — 21
1.2.2.1 International Instruments — 21
1.2.2.2 Regional Instruments — 23
1.2.3 Actual and Potential Normative Fragmentation in IHRL — 23
1.3 Judicial Fragmentation and Convergence in IHRL — 26

1.3.1 Defining Judicial Fragmentation and Convergence 27
1.3.2 The Proliferation of Human Rights Institutions 29
1.3.2.1 International Human Rights Institutions 30
1.3.2.2 European Human Rights Institutions 32
1.3.2.3 American Human Rights Institutions 34
1.3.2.4 African Human Rights Institutions 35
1.3.2.5 Other Regional and Sub-regional Human Rights Institutions 36
1.4 Fragmentation and Convergence versus Relativism and Universality: A Reconciling Understanding 37
1.4.1 The Debate on Universality and Relativism of Human Rights 37
1.4.2 What Is the Relationship between Convergence and Fragmentation and Universalisms and Relativism? 40
Conclusion 41

2 **Assessing and Exploring Judicial Fragmentation in International Human Rights Law** 42
Introduction 42
2.1 Assessing Judicial Fragmentation in IHRL 42
2.1.1 The Right to Life 45
2.1.2 The Prohibition of Torture, Cruel, Inhuman and Degrading Treatments 49
2.1.3 The Right to Liberty and Security 51
2.1.4 The Freedom of Expression 53
2.1.5 The Freedom of Assembly 57
2.1.6 Discrimination Based on Sexual Orientation 58
2.1.7 The Absence of Fragmentation Explained by the Difference in the Cases 60
2.1.8 Concluding Observations 64
2.2 Analysing Judicial Fragmentation in IHRL 64
2.2.1 Freedom to Manifest Religion 65
2.2.2 Indigenous Property Rights 77
2.2.3 The Right to Marry for Same-Sex Couples and the Recognition of the Change of Gender Identity 87
Conclusion 92

PART II FACTORS EXPLAINING JUDICIAL CONVERGENCE AND FRAGMENTATION

3 **The Theory of Treaty Interpretation and Judicial Dialogue** 97
Introduction 97
3.1 The Theory of Treaty Interpretation: Substantial Convergence of Interpretation Methods 97
3.1.1 Interpretation Clauses 101
3.2 Judicial Dialogue 103
3.2.1 Definition, Features and Challenges 104
3.2.1.1 Why Engage in Judicial Dialogue? 105
3.2.1.2 Why Not Engage in Judicial Dialogue? 107
3.2.1.3 Concluding Observations 108
3.2.2 Judicial Dialogue in the Practice of Human Rights Bodies: Fostering Convergence 110
3.2.2.1 The Inter-American Court of Human Rights 110
3.2.2.2 The African Bodies 114
3.2.2.3 The European Court of Human Rights 121
3.2.2.4 The Human Rights Committee 124
3.2.3 The Lack of Judicial Dialogue between Human Rights Bodies: Triggering Fragmentation 126
3.2.3.1 Indigenous Peoples' Rights 126
3.2.3.2 Freedom of Religion 128
3.2.4 When Judicial Dialogue Is Not Enough for Ensuring Convergence 130
3.2.4.1 Enforced Disappearances 130
3.2.4.2 Right to Marry for Same-Sex Couples 132
Conclusion 134

4 **The Composition of the Courts and Other Adjudicative Bodies and the Role of Their Secretariats** 135
Introduction 135
4.1 The Composition of the Bodies 136
4.1.1 Rules and Procedures on the Composition of the Bodies 137
4.1.2 Who Are the Judges? 140
4.1.2.1 The Educational Background 141
4.1.2.2 The Professional Background 144

4.1.2.3 Assessing the Impact of Personal Background on Separate Opinions 149
4.1.3 Concluding Observations 158
4.2 The Role of the Secretariat 160
4.3 The Role of Meetings between the Members of Human Rights Bodies 165
Conclusion 167

5 **Calibrating Judicial Scrutiny: The Notions of Necessity and Proportionality** 169
Introduction 169
5.1 The Principle of Necessity: A Tale of Convergence 170
5.1.1 The Principle of Necessity in International and Regional Instruments: A Fertile Ground for Fragmentation? 171
5.1.2 The Principle of 'Necessity' at the Adjudicatory Level: Towards Convergence 175
5.1.2.1 The Meaning of Necessity in IHRL 175
5.1.2.2 'Necessary' versus 'Necessary in a Democratic Society' 178
5.1.2.3 The Restriction of the Right to Life When 'Absolutely Necessary' 182
5.2 The Principle of Proportionality in the Case-Law of Regional Courts and the HRC 184
5.2.1 The European Court of Human Rights 185
5.2.2 The Human Rights Committee 188
5.2.3 The Inter-American Court of Human Rights 190
5.2.4 The African Commission and Court on Human and Peoples' Rights 192
Conclusion 193

6 **Deference, Subsidiarity and Regional Consensus: The Margin of Appreciation Doctrine** 196
Introduction 196
6.1 The Margin of Appreciation Doctrine before the ECtHR 199
6.1.1 Origins and Evolution 199
6.1.2 The Features of the MoA before the ECtHR 201
6.2 The IACtHR and the Conventionality Control Doctrine: Is There Room for Subsidiarity and Deference? 203
6.2.1 The IACtHR and the MoA 204

6.2.2 The IACtHR and the Conventionality Control Doctrine: The Rejection of the MoA 205
6.3 The Human Rights Committee: What Space for the MoA Doctrine? 208
6.4 The African Commission and Court: In Search of a MoA? 211
6.5 Explaining Deference and Subsidiarity Differences: The Politics of the Courts and Committee and Their Relationship with Member States 213
6.6 What Impact May the MoA Have on Fragmentation and Convergence? 216
6.6.1 Fostering Convergence 216
6.6.1.1 The ECtHR and HRC on the Restriction to Freedom of Expression for the Protection of Public Morals 217
6.6.1.2 The MoA in Defamation Cases 218
6.6.2 Triggering Fragmentation 221
6.6.2.1 The ECtHR and HRC on the Restriction to Freedom of Wearing Religious Attire 221
6.6.2.2 The ECtHR and IACtHR on the Restriction to Freedom of Expression for the Protection of Public Morals and Religion 224
Conclusion 225

7 Outside the Courtroom: The Role of NGOs and the Obstacles to Litigation 228
Introduction 228
7.1 The Role of Non-governmental Organisations 228
7.1.1 Litigation 230
7.1.1.1 Amicus Curiae 232
7.1.2 Lobbying and Other Ways of Participation 235
7.2 When the Case Does Not Reach the Courts 236
7.2.1 Use and Abuse of Friendly Settlements and Unilateral Declarations 238
7.2.2 When the Human Rights Bodies Induce the Applicant to Withdraw the Case 240
7.2.3 Availability of NGOs in Bringing a Specific Case in Front of the Court 241
Conclusion 243

Conclusions 244

Appendix 1 International and Regional Human Rights Instruments 255

Appendix 2 Comparative Table of Leading Cases 263

Index 269

Figures

1 Current members who received university education outside their continent (percentage). *page* 143

2 Current and total members with previous work experience in international organisations and courts, 2021 data (percentage). 146

3 Current and total members previously working in UNTBs or SPs, 2021 data (percentage). 146

4 Current members currently or previously working in academia with specialisation subjects (percentage). 148

Tables

1 Members' education *page* 142
2 Members' work experience (international organisations/courts) 145
3 Members' work experience (academia) 148

Foreword

It is a *lapalissade* that judicial fragmentation poses a serious threat to international law. This threat is particularly acute in the field of international human rights law. By undermining the universality of international law, judicial fragmentation encourages states not to comply with human rights judgments and recommendations, weakens the authority of human rights courts and bodies and ultimately decreases the level of protection of human rights worldwide.

In spite of this, we keep seeing contrasting judgments from international human rights courts and bodies on old and new issues. For example, the freedom to wear religious attire, and in particular the hijab or niqab, or the right to self-representation of lawyers in criminal procedure are still controversial matters on which the European Court of Human Rights and the United Nations Human Rights Committee seem not to be able to agree. All this shows that judicial convergence, when and where it happens, is limited in scope and, more importantly, precarious in nature. To make things even more complicated, the picture of international human rights law adjudication is continuously evolving and changing, with the African and the Inter-American human rights courts and commissions getting more and diversified cases and distancing themselves from their European older brother, which could ultimately lead to more cases of contrasting interpretations.

Considering the above, it is essential not to limit academic research to the analytical assessment of judicial convergence and fragmentation, but to reflect further on why they happen and how we could control them. And this is exactly what this book urges us to do. It investigates what could be the factors that contribute to these phenomena with the belief that only this critical methodology will provide us with the tools to monitor and promote the development of judicial convergence and anticipate and avoid future instances of fragmentation.

Several factors have contributed to fragmentation, but one surely stands out. The heavy use of the margin of appreciation doctrine by the European Court of Human Rights is damaging the predictability of case-law and thus tarnishing the reputation of the institution and the credibility of the entire European human rights protection system. When compared to the emerging conventionality control of the Inter-American Court of Human Rights, the doctrine of the margin of appreciation leaves much to be desired, leading to stark contrasting outcomes depending on the respondent state. Distorted by the margin of appreciation doctrine, the discretionary application of the necessity and proportionality tests only aggravates this intolerable situation, which at the end of the day gives the impression of a judicial practice with double or even triple standards. My separate opinion in *Hutchinson* v. *The United Kingdom* testifies to this evaluation.

To counter this unfortunate practice, judges, lawyers and scholars must be attentive and resolute. Judicial dialogue between human rights courts and bodies appears to be one of the strongest safeguards for convergence. During my time in Strasbourg, I tried to encourage the European Court to build a two-way street with other international, constitutional and supreme courts, conveying to them our own adjudicatory standards, but also profiting from their judicial best practices. I still remember vividly the exciting discussions held in Strasbourg on hot topics with fellow judges from all over the world, like the judges of the South African Constitutional Court, the Japanese Supreme Court or the Indian Supreme Court. By bringing to the same table African, American, Asian and European judges, my purpose was to achieve a solid common ground upon which a universal understanding of fundamental legal principles could be built. The Strasbourg Court should not be an isolated ivory tower, but an open platform of dialogue with other courts and bodies tasked with the protection of human rights.

As this book so well demonstrates, there is another preponderant element to consider in this context: the identity of the judges, commissioners and committee members who decide the cases and the role of the registry and secretariats. I met Elena Abrusci during an interview for her PhD thesis, on which this book is based, and I was captured by her intellectual curiosity into understanding how my professional background and personal beliefs could influence my adjudication and, consequently, the dynamics of the court to which I belonged. This is a fascinating and much needed take on a long-standing and unresolved issue, the independence of international judges, to which I have devoted my attention in an article published in the *Liber amicorum* to Vincent De Gaetano (Springer, 2019). As human rights judges, we are frequently called to the difficult task of interpreting broad and vague norms, and we need to acknowledge what the biases are that we bring with ourselves and consider whether and, and if yes, how they may factor into the decision. By so doing, these extrajudicial factors can be rationalised and ultimately utilised for the improvement of human rights adjudication.

With her bright insights and persuasive argumentation, Elena provides us with a magnificent book which is a very timely and extremely important study that fills an important gap in literature, encouraging the reader, the academic community and the human rights practitioner to go deeper into the study of judicial convergence and fragmentation. Being the fruit of a serious intellectual reflection on delicate legal problems and politically charged issues, the book benefits from a laborious, objective research that questions the personal, structural and systemic reasons behind human rights adjudication, offering a rigorous analysis and innovative perspective. My only hope is that the example of Elena will inspire other young researchers to devote themselves to scientific research on the role of people, and particularly judges, serving in international human rights courts and bodies. Ultimately this research will contribute to a better output of their work, which means providing victims of human rights violations with a better response from the international justice system.

Paulo Pinto de Albuquerque
Former ECHR Judge (2011–2020);
Full Professor, Catholic University Lisbon;
Doctorate honoris causa by Edge Hill University (UK)
and Kharkiv National Law University (Ukraine)

Acknowledgements

This book is based on my doctoral thesis, completed in 2018 at the University of Nottingham. I would like to express my sincere gratitude to my supervisors, Professor Marko Milanovic and Professor Sandesh Sivakumaran, for their guidance, support and inspiration. With kindness and patience, they taught me how to develop, express and defend my ideas, always motivating me to challenge myself, improve and become a better researcher. I could not have imagined better supervisors and mentors. I also wish to thank my examiners, Professor Liora Lazarus and Professor Dominic McGoldrick, for a stimulating viva and insightful feedback that significantly improved my work.

My sincere thanks go also to everyone who agreed to take part in the interviews for this book. In particular, I'm grateful to Judge Pinto de Albuquerque and Judge Karakas of the European Court of Human Rights and the other judges of the Court, the members of the Human Rights Committee, the legal officers of the registry of the European Court, the Inter-American Court of Human Rights and the Treaty Bodies' branch of the Office of the High Commissioner for Human Rights. I'm also grateful to Dr Eno, Mr Diallo and Ms Kakai, Registrar, Deputy-Registrar and Head of Legal Division, respectively, of the African Court on Human and Peoples' Rights. Together with the human rights litigators and staff from the NGOs that accepted my invite, their knowledge, experience and insightful perspective significantly enriched me and this book.

I owe my deepest gratitude also to Professor Andrea de Guttry, Professor Micaela Frulli and Dr Emanuele Sommario for showing me, a long time ago, the beauty of international law and human rights law; to Professor Aoife Nolan for introducing me to the regional human rights systems; to Professor Roxanna Althoz and Professor Jo Cavallaro for the insightful discussions on the Inter-American systems; to Professor Philippa Webb for inspiring me with her pioneering research on judicial fragmentation; to Professor Lorna McGregor for imparting wisdom and method into my research; to Professor Ahmed Shaheed for profound discussions on freedom of religion and to Professor Carla Ferstman for being a mentor and a friend, and for encouraging me to publish this book.

My heartfelt thanks to Tom Randall and Shaheer Anwarali of Cambridge University Press, who patiently guided me through the publishing journey, and to the five anonymous reviewers for their helpful comments and suggestions.

I also wish to thank all the colleagues and friends with whom I had the pleasure of discussing my work and from whom I learnt immensely: at the University of Nottingham, my comrades Daniela Mendez Royo, Ewa Kruszewska, Usmaan Siddiqui, Richard Mackenzie-Gray Scott, Astghik Solomoyan, Sebastian Barreto Cifuentes, Rossella Pulvirenti, Eleni Kaprou, Emma Luce Scali, Richard Watkins, Florelia Vallejo, David Alvarez and Mauro Pucheta; the extraordinary group of women at the University of Essex – Ronit Matar, Sabrina Rau, Ebba Lekvall, Johanna Hoekstra and Cristina Blanco; and finally, at Brunel University, my brilliant colleagues Professor Alexandra Xanthaki, Professor Javaid Rehman, Piero Sullo, Marcus de Matos, Colin Luoma, Ermioni Xanthopolus, Francesco De Pascalis and Eduardo Alvarez-Armas.

I'm also indebted to Elisa Cencig and Marina Petri for reading several drafts of this book and sharing with me the joys and pains of the last decade. Words cannot express how much your friendship means to me.

My thanks and love to Daniele for tireless evenings reading drafts, but also, more importantly, for being my rock even when we were oceans apart.

Finally, I'm eternally grateful to my family for being the real engine of my success. Thanks to my parents, Vania and Michele, and my sister Irene for being a continuous source of inspiration and for providing me with encouragement and support when I needed it the most. Without your unconditional love, I would not have achieved all this.

Table of Cases

AFRICAN COMMISSION ON HUMAN AND PEOPLES' RIGHTS

Article 19 v. Eritrea, Communication no 275/03, 27 May 2003
Centre for Minority Rights Development (Kenya) and Minority Rights Group International on behalf of Endorois Welfare Council v. Kenya, 25 November 2009
Constitutional Rights Project and Others v. Nigeria, Communication nos 140/94 and 145/95, November 1999
Courson v. Zimbabwe, 1995
Curtis Francis Doebbler v. Sudan, Communication no 236/2000, 2003
Doebbler v. Sudan, Communication no 236/00, 4 May 2003
Garreth Anver Prince v. South Africa, Communication no 255/02, 7 December 2004
Jawara v. The Gambia, Communication nos 147/95–149/96, 11 May 2000
Lawyers of Human Rights v. Swaziland, Communication no 251/02, 2 July 2005
Legal Resources Foundation v. Zambia, Communication no 211/98, 7 May 2001
Malawi African Association, Amnesty International, Ms Sarr Diop, Union interafricaine des droits de l'Homme and RADDHO, Collectif des veuves et ayants-Droit, Association mauritanienne des droits de l'Homme v. Mauritania, Communication nos 54/91–61/91–96/93–98/93–164/97–196/97–210/98, 11 May 2000
Mtikila v. Tanzania, Application nos 9/2011 and 11/2011, 2013
Purohit and Another v. The Gambia, Communication no 241/01, 29 May 2003
Scanlen and Holderness v. Zimbabwe, Communication no 297/05, 3 April 2009
Social and Economic Rights Action Centre (SERAC) and Another v. Nigeria, Communication no 155/96, 27 October 2001

Sudan Human Rights Organisation & Centre on Housing Rights and Evictions (COHRE) v. Sudan, Communication nos 279/03–296/05, 27 May 2009
Zimbabwe Lawyers for Human Rights & Associated Newspapers of Zimbabwe v. Zimbabwe, Communication no 284/03, 2009

AFRICAN COURT ON HUMAN AND PEOPLES' RIGHTS

African Commission on Human and Peoples' Rights v. Kenya, Application no 006/2012 (ACtHPR, 26 May 2017)
Ally Rajabu and Others v. Tanzania, Application no 007/2015 (ACtHPR, 28 November 2019)
Boubacar Sissoko and 74 Others v. Mali, Application no 037/2017 (ACtHPR, 25 September 2020)
Efoua Mbozo'o Samuel v. Pan African Parliament, Application no 010/2011 (ACtHPR, 30 September 2011)
Evodius Rutechura v. Tanzania, Application no 004/2016 (ACtHPR, 25 June 2021)
Fidele Mulindahabi v. Rwanda, Application no 004/2017 (ACtHPR, 26 June 2020)
Hongue Eric Noudehouenou v. Benin, Application no 003/2020 (ACtHPR, 4 December 2020)
Ingabire Victoire Umhoza v. Republic of Rwanda, Application no 3/2014, 24 November 2017
Jebra Kambole v. Tanzania, Application no 018/2018 (ACtHPR, 15 July 2020)
Kennedy Owino Onyachi and Others v. Tanzania, Application no 003/2015, 28 September 2017
Lohé Issa Konaté v. Burkina Faso, Application no 004/2013, 5 December 2014
Michelot Yogogombaye v. Senegal, Application no 001/2008 (ACtHPR, 15 December 2009)
Minani Evarist v. Tanzania, Application no 027/2015 (ACtHPR, 21 September 2018)
Mohamed Abubakari v. Tanzania, Application no 007/2013 (ACtHPR, 3 June 2016)
Sebastien Germain Marie Aikoue Ajavon v. Benin, Application no 013/2017 (ACtHPR, 28 November 2019)
Tanganyka Law Society v. United Republic of Tanzania, Application nos 9 and 11/2011, 14 June 2013
Yahaya Zumo Makame and 3 Others v. Tanzania, Application no 023/2016 (ACtHPR, 25 June 2021)

EUROPEAN COMMISSION OF HUMAN RIGHTS

G. and E. v. Norway, Application nos 9278/81, 9415/81, 1983
Paton v. United Kingdom Application no 8416/79, 1980

EUROPEAN COURT OF HUMAN RIGHTS

A and Others v. United Kingdom, Application no 3455/05, 19 February 2009
A.P., Garçon and Nicot v. France, Application no 79885/12, 6 April 2017
Airey v. Ireland, Application no 6289/73, 9 October 1979
Aksoy v. Turkey, Application no 21987/93, 18 December 1996
Aktas v. France, Application no 43563/08, 30 June 2009
Aldeguer Tomas v. Spain, Application no 35214/09, 14 June 2016
Aquilina v. Malta, Application no 25642/94, 29 April 1999
Assanidze v. Georgia, Application no 71503/03, 8 August 2004
Bayrak v. France, Application no 14308/08, 30 June 2009
Bazorkina v. Russia, Application no 69481/01, 27 July 2006
Bramelid and Malmström v. Sweden, Application nos 8588/79 and 8589/79, 1982
Brumarescu v. Romania, Application no 28342/95, 28 October 1999
Bukta v. Hungary, Application no 25691/04, 17 July 2007
Castells v. Spain, Application no 11798/85, 23 April 1992
Chauvy and Others v. France, Application no 64915/01, 28 September 2000
Christine Goodwin v. United Kingdom, Application no 28957/95, 11 July 2002
Cruz Varas and Others v. Sweden, Application no 15576/89, 20 February 1991
Cumhuriyet Vakfi and Others v. Turkey, Application no 28255/07, 8 October 2013
Dahlab v. Switzerland, Application no 42393/98, 15 February 2001
Demír and Baykara v. Turkey, Application no 34503/97, 12 November 2008
Dogru v. France, Application no 27058/05, 4 December 2008
Dudgeon v. United Kingdom, Application no 7525/76, 22 October 1981
Dzhambekova and Others v. Russia, Application nos 27283/03 and 35078/04, 11 May 2009
E.B. v. France, Application no 43546/02, 22 January 2008
Éva Molnár v. Hungary, Application no 10346/05, 7 January 2009
Evans v. United Kingdom, Application no 6339/05, 10 April 2007
Ezelin v. France, Application no 11800/85, 26 April 1991
Frette' v. France, Application no 3615/97, 26 February 2002
Gafgen v. Germany, Application no 22978/01, 1 June 2010
Gamaleddyn v. France, Application no 18527/08, 30 June 2009
Garaudy v. France, Application no 65831/01, 24 June 2003
Gas and Dubois v. France, Application no 25951/07, 15 March 2012
Ghazal v. France, Application no 29134/08, 30 June 2009
Golder v. UK, Application no 4451/70, 21 February 1975

Handölsdalen Sami Village and Others v. Sweden, Application no 39013/04, 30 March 2010
Handyside v. UK, Application no 5493/72, 7 December 1976
Hassan v. UK, Application no 29750/09, 16 September 2014
Hingitaq 53 and Others v. Denmark, Application no 18584/04, 12 January 2006.
Ilascu v. Moldova and Russia, Application no 48787/99, 8 July 2004
Ireland v. United Kingdom, Application no 5310/71, 18 January 1978
Isayeva v. Russia, Application no 57950/00, 24 February 2005
James, Wells and Lee v. the United Kingdom, Application nos 25119/09, 57715/09, 18 September 2012
Jasvir Singh v. France, Application no 25463/08, 30 June 2009
Karaduman v. Turkey, Application no 16278/90, 3 May 1993
Karner v. Austria, Application no 40016/98, 24 July 2013
Kervanci v. France, Application no 31645/04, 4 December 2008
Klass and Others v. Germany, Application no 5029/71, 6 September 1978
Kokkinakis v. Greece, Application no 14307/88, 25 May 1993
Kudla v. Poland, Application no 30210/96, 26 October 2000
L. v. Lithuania, Application no 27527/03, 11 September 2007
Lautsi v. Italy, Application no 30814/06, 18 March 2011
Leyla Şahin v. Turkey, Application no 44774/98, 10 November 2005
Ligens v. Austria, Application no 9851/82, 8 July 1986
Mamatkulov and Askarov v. Turkey, Application nos 46827/99 and 46951/99, 4 February 2005
Mann Singh v. France, Application no 24479/07, 11 June 2007
Marckx v. Belgium, Application no 6833/74, 13 June 1979
Mata Estevez v. Spain, Application no 56501/00, 10 May 2001
McCann and Others v. United Kingdom, Application no 18984/91, 27 September 1995
Morice v. France, Application no 29369/10, 23 April 2015
Müller and Others v. Switzerland, Application no 10737/84, 24 May 1988
Musikhanova and Others v. Russia, Application no 27243/03, 4 December 2008
Nachova and Others v. Bulgaria, Application nos 43577/98 and 43579/98, 6 July 2005
Niedbata v. Poland, Application no 27915/95, 4 July 2000
Oliari and Others v. Italy, Application nos 18766/11 and 36030/11, 21 July 2015
Otto-Preminger-Institut v. Austria, Application no 13470/87, 20 September 1994
Oya Ataman v. Turkey, Application no 74552/01, 5 December 2006
P. and S. v. Poland, Application no 57375/08, 30 October 2012
Peruzzi v. Italy, Application no 39294/09, 30 June 2015
Phull v. France, Application no 35753/03, 11 January 2005

Piermont v. France, Application nos 15773/89 and 15774/89, 27 April 1995
R.R. v. Poland, Application no 27617/04, 26 May 2011
Rees v. United Kingdom, Application no 9532/81, 17 October 1986
Ricci v. Italy, Application no 30210/06, 8 October 2013
S.A.S. *v. France*, Application no 43835/11, 1 July 2014
Saadi v. the United Kingdom, Application no 13229/03, 29 January 2008
Salguiero da Silva Mouta v. Portugal, Application no 33290/96, 21 March 2000
Schalk and Kopf v. Austria, Application no 30141/04, 22 November 2010
Schlumpf v. Switzerland, Application no 29002/06, 8 January 2009
Selçuk and Asker v. Turkey, Application nos 12/1997/796/998–999, 24 April 1998
Selmouni v. France, Application no 25803/94, 28 July 1999
Silverand Others v. United Kingdom, Application nos 5947/72, 205/73, 7107/75, 7113/75 and 7136/75, 24 September 1982
Sitaropoulos and Giakoumopolous v. Greece, Application no 42202/07, 15 March 2012
Smith Kline and French Laboratories v. the Netherlands, Application no 12633/87, 1990
Soering v. United Kingdom, Application no 14038/88, 7 July 1989
Stran Greek Refineries and Stratis Andreadis v. Greece (Merits), Application no 13427/87, 1994
Sunday Times v. United Kingdom, Application no 6538/74, 16 April 1979
Togcu v. Turkey, Application no 27601/95, 31 May 2005
Tolstoy Miloslavsky v. United Kingdom, Application no 18139/91, 18 February 2008
Tyrer v. United Kingdom, Application no 5856/72, 25 April 1978
Tysiaç v. Poland, Application no 5410/03, 20 March 2007
VO v. France, Application no 53924/00, 8 July 2004
Witzsch v. Germany, Application no 7485/03, 30 September 1999
X *and Others v. Austria*, Application no 19010/07, 19 February 2013
X *v. Federal Republic of Germany*, Application no 8410/78, 1979
X *v. United Kingdom*, Application no 7992/77, 12 July 1978
Z. *v. Finland*, Application no 627/811, 25 February 1999
Zaurbekova and Zauberkova v. Russia, Application no 27183/03, 22 January 2009

UN HUMAN RIGHTS COMMITTEE

Alphen v. The Netherlands, Communication no 305/1988, 23 July 1990
Arhuaco v. Colombia, Communication no 612/1995, 29 July 1997
Bautista v. Colombia, Communication no 563/993, 27 October 1995

Bikramjit Singh v. France, Communication no 1852/2008, 4 February 2013
Bwalya v. Zambia, Communication no 314/1988, 14 July 1993
Castañeda v. Mexico, Communication no 2022/2012, 18 July 2013
Faurisson v. France, Communication no 550/1993, 8 November 1996
Fedotova v. Russian Federation, Communication no 1932/2010, 2012
Gauthier v. Canada, Communication no 633/1995, 5 May 1999
Grille Motta v. Uruguay, Communication no 11/1977, 29 July 1980
Guerrero v. Colombia, Communication no 45/1979, 31 March 1982
Hertzber and Others v. Finland, Communication no 61/1979, 2 April 1982
Jarvinen v. Finland, Communication no 295/1988, 15 August 1990
Joslin v. New Zealand, Communication no 902/1999, 2003
Judge v. Canada, Communication no 829/1998, 8 August 2003
K.L. *v. Peru*, Communication no 1153/03, 24 October 2005
Kivenmaa v. Finland, Communication no 412/1990, 31 March 1994
Laptsevich v. Belarus, Communication no 780/1997, 20 March 2000
Laureano v. Peru, Communication no 540/1993, 16 April 1996
Lloyd Reece v. Jamaica, Communication no 796/98, 14 July 2003
LMR *v. Argentina*, Communication no 1608/07, 28 April 2011
Marquez de Morais v. Angola, Communication no 1128/02, 29 March 2005
Massera v. Uruguay, Communication no 5/1977, 15 August 1979
Mellet v. Ireland, Communication no 2324/13, 31 March 2016
Nurbek Toktakunov v. Kyrgyzstan, Communication no 1470/2006, 28 March 2011
Park v. Republic of Korea, Communication no 628/1995, 5 July 1996
Raihon Hudoyberganova v. Uzbekistan, Communication no 931/2000, 8 December 2004
Ranjit Singh v. France, Communication no 1876/2000, 11–29 July 2011
Rodríguez v. Uruguay, Communication no 322/1988, 9 August 1994
Singh Bhinder v. Canada, Communication no 208/1986, 9 November 1989
Sister Immaculate Joseph and Others v. Sri Lanka, Communication no 1249/2004, 21 October 2005
Kindler v. Canada, Communication no 470/1991, 30 July 1993
Toonen v. Australia, Communication no 488/1992, 1994
Unn and Ben Leirvag and Others v. Norway, Communication no 1155/2003, 23 November 2004
Thompson v. St. Vincent and the Grenadines, Communication no 806/1998, 18 October 2000
Taright v. Algeria, Communication no 1085/02, 15 March 2006
Earl Pratt and Ivan Morgan v. Jamaica, Communication no 210/1986, 24 March 1990
Van Alphen v. The Netherlands, Communication no 305/88, 23 July 1990

Vitaly Symonik v. Belarus, Communication no 1952/2010, 24 October 2014
Weiss v. Austria, Communication no 1086/2002, 2002
X v. Colombia, Communication no 1361/2005, 2007
Y.L. v. Canada, Communication no 112/1981, 8 April 1986
Young v. Australia, Communication no 941/2000, 2004
Zeljko Bodrozic v. Serbia and Montenegro, Communication no 1180/2003, 31 October 2005
Lansman et al. v. Finland, Communication no 511/1992, 11 June 1992
Prince v. South Africa, Communication no 1474/2006, 31 October 2007
Paez v. Colombia, Communication no 195/1985, 12 July 1990

INTER-AMERICAN COMMISSION ON HUMAN RIGHTS

Baby Boy v. United States, 6 March 1981
Maya indigenous communities of the Toledo District v. Belize, 12 October 2004
Ecuador v. Colombia, 21 October 2011

INTER-AMERICAN COURT OF HUMAN RIGHTS

Almonacid-Arellano v. Chile, 26 September 2006
Angel Alberto Duque v. Colombia, 26 February 2016
Artavia Murillo et al. ("in vitro fertilization") v. Costa Rica, 28 November 2012
Atala Riffo and Daughters v. Chile, 24 February 2012
Bámaca Velásquez v. Guatemala, 25 November 2000
Benavides-Cevallos v. Ecuador, 19 June 1998
Caesar v. Trinidad and Tobago, 11 March 2005
Canese v. Paraguay, 31 August 2004
Castillo Paez v. Peru, 3 November 1997
Chaparro Álvarez and Lapo Íñiguez v. Ecuador, 8 September 1998
Compulsory Membership in an Association Prescribed by Law for the Practice of Journalism, Advisory Opinion OC-5/85, 13 November 1985
Dacosta Cadogan v. Barbados, 24 September 2009
Escher et al. v. Brazil, 6 July 2009
Gangaram-Panday v. Suriname, 21 January 1994
Gelman v. Uruguay, 24 February 2011
Gomes Lund et al. v. Brazil, 24 November 2010
Gómez-Palomino v. Peru, 22 November 2005
Herrera Uloa v. Costa Rica, 2004
Hilaire, Constantine and Benjamin et al. v. Trinidad and Tobago, 21 June 2002
Identidad de género, e igualdad y no discriminación a parejas del mismo sexo, Opinión consultiva OC-24/17, 9 January 2018

Kichwa Indigenous People of Sarayaku v. Ecuador, 27 June 2012
Las Palmeras v. Colombia, 6 December 2001
Loyaza-Tamayo v. Peru, 17 September 1997
Mapiripan Massacre v. Colombia, 15 September 2005
Mayagna (Sumo) Awas Tingni Community v. Nicaragua, 31 August 2001
Memoli v. Argentina, 22 August 2013
Miguel Castro-Castro Prison v. Peru, 25 November 2006
Montero Aranguren et al. (Detention Center of Catia) v. Venezuela, 5 July 2006
Myrna Mack Chang v. Guatemala, Merits, 25 November 2003
Olmedo-Bustos et al. v. Chile (The Last Temptation of Christ case), 5 February 2001
Panigua Morales v. Guatemala, 8 March 1998
Proposed Amendments to the Naturalization Provisions of the Constitution of Costa Rica, Advisory Opinion OC-4/84, 19 January 1984
Saramaka People v. Suriname, 28 November 2007
Sawhoyamaxa Indigenous Community v. Paraguay, 29 March 2006
The Interpretation of the American Declaration of the Rights and Duties of Man within the framework of Article 64 of the American Convention on Human Rights, Advisory Opinion, 14 July 1989
The Right to Information on Consular Assistance in the Framework of the Guarantees of the due Process of Law, Advisory Opinion, 1 October 1999
Tibi v. Ecuador, 7 September 2004
Tristán Donoso v. Panama, 27 January 2009
Velasquez Rodriguez v. Honduras, 29 July 1988
Xákmok Kásek v. Paraguay, 24 August 2010
Yake Axa Indigenous Community v. Paraguay, 17 June 2005
Zembrano-Velez et al. v. Ecuador, 4 July 2007

INTERNATIONAL COURT OF JUSTICE

Case Concerning Military and Paramilitary Activities in and against Nicaragua (Nicaragua v. United States of America), 27 June 1986
Case Concerning the Application of the Convention on the Prevention and Punishment of the Crime of Genocide (Bosnia and Herzegovina v. Serbia and Montenegro), Judgment, 26 February 2007

INTERNATIONAL CRIMINAL TRIBUNAL FOR THE FORMER YUGOSLAVIA (ICTY)

The Prosecutor v. Duško Tadić, IT-94-1-A, 15 July 1999

UNITED KINGDOM COURTS

R v. Ministry of Defence, ex p Smith [1996] QB 517, 554.
R v. Ministry of Defence, ex p Smith [1996] QB 517UK
R (on the application of Daly) v. Secretary of State for the Home Department [2001] 2 AC 532

UNITED STATES OF AMERICA COURTS

Craig v. Boren, 429 US 190 210–211
US v. Carolene Products Co., 304 US 144, 152 (1938)

Abbreviations

ACHPR	African Charter on Human and Peoples' Rights
ACHR	American Convention on Human Rights
ACommHPR	African Commission on Human and Peoples' Rights
ACtHPR	African Court on Human and Peoples' Rights
ASEAN	Association of Southeast Asian Nations
AU	African Union
CAT	UN Committee against Torture
CEDAW	UN Committee on the Elimination of Discrimination against Women
CERD	UN Committee on the Elimination of Racial Discrimination
CESCR	UN Committee on Economic, Social and Cultural Rights
CoE	Council of Europe
CRC	UN Committee on the Rights of the Child
EACJ	East African Court of Justice
ECHR	European Convention on Human Rights
ECJ	European Court of Justice
ECommHR	European Commission of Human Rights
ECSR	European Committee of Social Rights
ECtHR	European Court of Human Rights
EU	European Union
GC	general comment
HRC	UN Human Rights Committee
IACommHR	Inter-American Commission on Human Rights
IACtHR	Inter-American Court of Human Rights
ICCPR	International Covenant on Civil and Political Rights
ICESCR	International Covenant on Economic, Social and Cultural Rights

ICJ	International Court of Justice
ICTY	International Criminal Tribunal for the Former Yugoslavia
IHRL	international human rights law
IL	international law
ILC	International Law Commission
ILO	International Labour Organization
MoA	margin of appreciation
OAS	Organization of American States
OHCHR	Office of the High Commissioner for Human Rights
SADC	Southern African Development Community
TB	UN Treaty Body
UDHR	Universal Declaration of Human Rights
UNDRIP	UN Declaration on the Rights of Indigenous Peoples
VCLT	Vienna Convention on the Law of Treaties

Introduction

In the past decades, the international human rights law system welcomed the proliferation of regional and international human rights adjudicatory bodies, as they meant better and closer protection of human rights for people worldwide. Yet, this proliferation also increased the likelihood of conflicting interpretations of fundamental rights and freedoms, which may trigger what we call judicial fragmentation. Judicial fragmentation, described as the situation where two judicial or quasi-judicial bodies issue contrasting judgments, is certainly a double-sided phenomenon. On the one hand, it can bring adverse consequences, such as reduced legitimacy of the adjudicatory bodies, lower protection of human rights and a threat to universality. On the other hand, fragmentation is a constant element in lawmaking and possibly the only way for the law to develop and adapt to new challenges. In 2006, the International Law Commission (ILC) published a report, which found that fragmentation was significantly threatening international law.[1] Following such a worrying alert, scholars have started investigating whether fragmentation was also affecting international human rights law (IHRL), reaching the initial

[1] Martti Koskenniemi and Paiivi Leino, 'Fragmentation of International Law? Postmodern Anxieties' (2002) 15 *Leiden Journal of International Law* 553; Pierre-Marie Dupuy, 'Un débat doctrinal à l'ere de la globalisation: Sur la fragmentation du droit international' (2007) 1 *European Journal of Legal Studies* 1; Tomer Broude, 'Keep Calm and Carry On: Martti Koskenniemi and the Fragmentation of International Law' (2013) 27(2) *Temple International & Comparative Law Journal* 272; Gerhard Hafner, 'Pros and Cons Ensuing from Fragmentation of International Law' (2004) 25 *Michigan Journal of International Law* 849; Pierre-Marie Dupuy, 'The Danger of Fragmentation or Unification of the International Legal System and the International Court of Justice' (1999) 31 *New York University Journal of International Law and Politics* 791. More recently, Mads Andenas and Eirik Bjorge (eds), *A Farewell to Fragmentation. Reassertion and Convergence in International Law* (Cambridge University Press, 2015).

conclusion that the situation was not as alarming as expected.[2] However, the phenomenon is complex and continuously evolving, also considering that some regional human rights systems have significantly expanded and grown in the last few years, likely offering a different picture. Moreover, very little has been said so far about the possible factors behind convergence and fragmentation and why these two phenomena arise. The aim of this book is exactly to fill this gap in literature by providing a better understanding of the current fragmentation and convergence in IHRL and identifying the triggering factors driving these phenomena. In particular, the book addresses two key questions: (1) is judicial fragmentation actually affecting IHRL or does convergence prevail, looking at the three regional human rights systems and the UN Human Rights Committee?; (2) what are the factors that can be identified as contributing to this situation?

The answer to the first question builds on what scholars have demonstrated so far and ensures that the recent development in case-law and approach of all regional human rights systems, including the African and the Inter-American ones, are taken into account. International human rights law certainly offers a fertile ground for fragmentation given the endless struggle between universality and cultural relativism, the high sensitivity of the issues related to many human rights norms and the determinant role of social, cultural, religious and historical concerns. The African Court on Human and Peoples' Rights (ACtHPR) has seen an incredible growth both in terms of judgments issued and complexity of its reasoning in the last ten years. Likewise, the Inter-American Court of Human Rights (IACtHR) has significantly expanded the range of rights and topics addressed in its judgments, facing for the first time new rights and issues. These developments urge a new assessment of the

[2] ibid. See also Marjan Ajevski (ed), *Fragmentation in International Human Rights Law* (Routledge, 2017); Carla M. Buckley, Alice Donald and Philip Leach (eds), *Towards Convergence in International Human Rights Law: Approaches of Regional and International Systems* (Brill-Nijhoff, 2017); Eva Brems and Saïla Ouald-Chaib (eds), *Fragmentation and Integration in Human Rights Law* (Edward Elgar, 2018); Lucas Lixinski, 'Choice of Forum in International Human Rights Adjudication and the Unity/Fragmentation Debate: Is Plurality the Way Ahead?' (2009) 9 *University College Dublin Law Review* 23; Anthony Cassimatis, 'International Humanitarian Law, International Human Rights Law, and Fragmentation of International Law' (2008) 56(3) *International & Comparative Law Quarterly* 623; Vassilis P. Tzevelekos, 'The Use of Article 31(3)(C) of the VCLT in the Case Law of the ECtHR: An Effective Anti-Fragmentation Tool or a Selective Loophole for the Reinforcement of Human Rights Teleology?' (2010) 31 *Michigan Journal of International Law* 621; Monica Pinto, 'Fragmentation or Unification among International Institutions: Human Rights Tribunals' (1999) 31 *Journal of International Law and Politics* 833; Siobhán McInerney-Lankford, 'Fragmentation of International Law Redux: The Case of Strasbourg' (2012) 32(3) *Oxford Journal of Legal Studies* 609.

judicial convergence and fragmentation picture in IHRL. Offering a new perspective and constantly looking at the three main regional human rights systems (the African, European and Inter-American), this book confirms that judicial convergence is predominant in international human rights law.

The ILC Report mentioned earlier certainly provided clarity on the definition and importance of fragmentation for international law, but it did not put an end to the debate on its merit. There is very little agreement among scholars on whether we should see fragmentation as a positive or negative phenomenon, in international law as in international human rights law. Indeed, fragmentation is so multifaceted that it is naturally subject to a wide range of different opinions. As described by Martineau, a historical overview of fragmentation highlights how the concept has been varyingly used and abused for political and functional purposes.[3] 'Over the last 150 years, international lawyers have had recourse to the language of fragmentation as an argument for criticism and contestation. Indeed, the development of international law through specialised mechanisms is sometimes seen as healthy pluralism ("diversification"), sometimes as a perilous division ("fragmentation")'.[4]

On the one hand, fragmentation as diversification and expansion of a legal system produces positive effects such as, according to Hefner, the elaboration of more specialised regimes capable of answering to specific needs of protection and regulations and the development of law for higher and more suitable standards for all parties.[5] Moreover, fragmentation is pluralism and this ensures the democratisation of the international law space, where different 'political' preferences can express themselves in the international arena.[6] Likewise, as Peters recalls, fragmentation also means competitive pressure on international courts and tribunals to improve their performance and be more effective.[7] In the specific context of IHRL, fragmentation could be considered advantageous for human rights users as it is a natural development of the law to address emerging needs, and thus an opportunity to increase the level of protection of human rights.[8]

3 Anne-Charlotte Martineau, 'The Rethoric of Fragmentation: Fear and Faith in International Law' (2009) 22 *Leiden Journal of International Law* 1.

4 ibid, 2.

5 Hafner, 'Pros and Cons Ensuing from Fragmentation of International Law', 859.

6 Hélène Ruiz Fabri, 'Jeux dans la fragmentation: la Convention sur la promotion et la protection de la diversité des expressions culturelles' (2007) 111 *Revue Général de Droit International Public* 1, 43–88 and Kerstin Blome et al. (eds), *Contested Regime Collisions: Norm Fragmentation in a World Society* (Cambridge University Press, 2016).

7 Anne Peters, 'The Refinement of International Law: From Fragmentation to Regime Interaction and Politicization' (2017) 15 *International Journal of Constitutional Law* 3, 680–681.

8 Brems and Ouald-Chaib (eds), *Fragmentation and Integration in Human Rights Law*, 3.

On the other hand, fragmentation as the proliferation of contrasting norms and regulatory frameworks can 'jeopardise' the credibility and authority of IL and IHRL, with specific regimes increasing the possibilities of frictions between them.[9] It can also threaten the coherence and unity of the IL and IHRL system.[10] Moreover, especially when arising from institutions with overlapping jurisdictions, fragmentation undermines legal certainty, which is a key safeguard of any rule of law system[11] and could encourage states not to comply with human rights judgments and recommendations.[12]

Some commentators stand for a middle position, holding that 'proliferation is either an unavoidable minor problem in a rapidly transforming international system or even a rather positive demonstration of the responsiveness of legal imagination to social change'.[13] Indeed, the interplay between fragmentation as positive diversification and fragmentation as negative proliferation is a matter of political interpretation and perspectives. 'Every development of international law is good insofar as it is *teleologically* directed towards the greater fulfilment of mankind. Perceptions of breakdown or fragmentation emerge when this objective is blurred, when international lawyers experience a world that has failed them and has malignantly stopped striving for unity.'[14] Applied to the IHRL space, one could argue that judicial fragmentation should be avoided unless it leads to an increased protection of human rights. Indeed, this book does not depict judicial fragmentation as the ultimate threat and danger for IHRL, as it also recognises its important role in improving and adapting the law to emerging needs. As it comes out throughout the book, although convergence is usually desirable, it is possible to

[9] William Elliott Butler, 'Regional and Sectional Diversities in International Law' in Bin Cheng (ed), *International Law: Teaching and Practice* (Stevens & Sons, 1982), 46.

[10] Mario Prost, *The Concept of Unity in Public International Law*, 1st ed. (Hart, 2012), 202–209.

[11] Yuval Shany, *The Competing Jurisdictions of International Courts and Tribunals* (Oxford University Press, 2003); James Crawford and Penelope Nevill, 'Relations between International Courts and Tribunals: The "Regime Problem"' in Margaret A. Young (ed), *Regime Interaction in International Law: Facing Fragmentation* (Cambridge University Press, 2012), 235.

[12] Buckley, Donald and Leach (eds), *Towards Convergence in International Human Rights Law*, 4; Jo Pasqualucci, 'Interim Measures in International Human Rights Law: Evolution and Harmonization' (2005) 38 *Vanderbilt Journal of Transnational Law* 1.

[13] cf Jonathan I. Charney, 'The Impact on the International Legal System of the Growth of International Courts and Tribunals' (1999) 31 *New York University Journal of International Law and Politics* 697; Tullio Treves, 'Conflicts between the International Tribunal for the Law of the Sea and the International Court of Justice' (1999) 31 *New York University Journal of International Law and Politics* 809; Hugh Thirlway, 'The Proliferation of International Judicial Organs and the Formation of International Law' in W. P. Heere (ed), *International Law and the Hague's 750th Anniversary* (T.M.C. Asser Press, 1999).

[14] Martineau, 'The Rhetoric of Fragmentation', 6.

identify instances of 'negative convergence', where courts show a race to the bottom in terms of human rights standards and a 'positive fragmentation', where the divergent ruling increases the level of protection of human rights.

Whatever value and significance one wants to attribute to judicial convergence and fragmentation in IHRL, one should not stop at the assessment of one or the other phenomenon, but it is crucial to investigate further why and under which circumstances they arise and when they can lead to a decreased protection of human rights. In particular, if judicial fragmentation is not really affecting IHRL as we expected despite the differences in terms of history, culture, religion and legal frameworks of the regional systems, the obvious follow-up question is why. What could be the factors that drive this overall convergence? Are there any elements that are likely to trigger fragmentation while others to maintain convergence? Are any of them likely to change in the future? The second part of this book attempts to provide an answer to all these questions. Only if we gain a better understanding of all this, can we avoid triggering the kind of judicial fragmentation that could ultimately undermine the protection of individuals' human rights and the legitimacy and functioning of the international human rights adjudication system.

In order to answer these questions, this book looks at the classical legal factors traditionally linked to international comparative adjudication, but with a strong focus on both what ensures convergence now and what may trigger fragmentation in the future. The theory of interpretation is certainly important.[15] In particular, the fact that all the regional and international bodies have embraced the principle of evolutive interpretation is a strong safeguard for convergence, even though the different interpretation clauses contained in regional human rights instruments leave the door open to a possible fragmentation. Likewise, the development and application of legal principles, tests and doctrines such as necessity and proportionality or deference and subsidiarity are absolutely key to understanding the approach of each body to human rights adjudication.[16] Despite differences in the text of the provisions, the understanding and application of the principle of necessity have found a convergent, yet vague, application across all systems, supporting the current overall convergence. Similarly, all human rights bodies ultimately resort to the proportionality test, possibly intrigued by its flexibility. The entire international system of human rights protection is based on the principle of subsidiarity, and regional systems have often prided themselves on their deferential approach to member states. Nevertheless, the margin of

[15] See Chapter 3.
[16] See Chapters 5 and 6.

appreciation doctrine developed by the European Court of Human Rights (ECtHR) and the conventionality control doctrine developed by the Inter-American Court of Human Rights could be applied in such a contrasting way to easily trigger fragmentation in the future.[17]

In addition, the current judicial convergence is also helped by an increasing judicial dialogue between human rights bodies. As broadly discussed by scholars, the meaningful use of external references is one of the best tools to maintain convergence or, at least, a reasoned and thought-upon fragmentation. However, one of the features of the current judicial dialogue in IHRL is the activism of the African and Inter-American bodies in methodically looking at the case-law of their European counterpart and at the UN system. In the very recent years, both the African and the Inter-American courts have started to significantly reduce the number and importance of external references in their judgments, suggesting that a change in the trend, and therefore in the outcome, is very much possible.

All of the above factors are certainly important and could be pivotal in the explanation of judicial convergence and fragmentation, yet they could be seen as quite narrow, since they do not look outside of the judgments. The law is a social construct,[18] and the case-law of a body is the outcome of the interpretation of a group of individuals. As such, when looking at the reasons why a judicial or quasi-judicial body behaves in a certain way, one should investigate the composition of that body and the people who are called to interpret and apply the law.[19] Through the analysis of the identity and background of international and regional judges and commissioners, this book will show how education and work experience could play a role in maintaining convergence in IHRL.[20]

[17] See Chapter 6.

[18] Carlo Focarelli, *International Law as Social Construct: The Struggle for Global Justice* (Oxford University Press, 2012); Dan Priel, 'Law as a Social Construction and Conceptual Legal Theory' (2019) 38 *Law and Philosophy* 3, 267; Frederick Schauer, 'The Social Construction of the Concept of Law: A Reply to Julie Dickson' (2005) 25 *Oxford Journal of Legal Studies* 3, 493–501.

[19] Benjamin N. Cardozo, *The Nature of the Judicial Process* (Yale University Press, 1921), 9–12; Eric A. Posner and Miguel F. P. de Figueiredo, 'Is the International Court of Justice Biased?' (2005) 34 *The Journal of Legal Studies* 2, 599–630; Susan D. Franck, Anne van Aaken, James Freda, Chris Guthrie and Jeffrey J. Rachlinksi, 'Inside the Arbitrator's Mind' (2017) 66 *Emory Law Journal* 1115; Clifford J. Carrubba, Matthew Gable and Charles Hankla, 'Judicial Behaviour under Political Constraints: Evidence from the European Court of Justice' (2008) 102 *American Political Science Review* 4, 435–452.

[20] See Chapter 4.

Equally, as these human rights institutions do not work in a vacuum, there are other actors and dynamics that could affect their adjudication and impact judicial convergence and fragmentation. In addition to member states and the political pressures they exercise on regional courts, the structure and functioning of the institutions' registries and secretariats could also have an influence on the adjudication. Furthermore, non-governmental organisations could also be extremely influential in steering IHRL adjudication, both by intervening directly in a case and by deciding what to prioritise in the courts' agendas.[21]

All these factors contribute somehow and in different ways to the shaping of IHRL adjudication and, as a consequence, on dynamics such as judicial convergence and fragmentation. They do not all operate at the same time, nor they all have the same impact on each body. Yet, they are all extremely important aspects of the IHRL adjudicatory environment that deserve attention and careful consideration. With regional and international institutions constantly changing and evolving, growing in experience and judgments issued, they are also likely to evolve in the future, possibly changing from being the cause of convergence to being that of fragmentation.

METHODOLOGY

The book addresses the two main questions of whether there is judicial convergence or fragmentation in IHRL and what could be the contributing factors, mainly adopting a doctrinal and comparative methodological approach, complemented by other interdisciplinary methods for the second part.

In line with the current literature, as further explained in Chapter 1, judicial fragmentation is defined as the phenomenon that arises when two courts, or quasi-judicial bodies, seized of the same or similar matter, issue contrasting judgments.[22] On the contrary, judicial convergence is the phenomenon that arises when two courts, or quasi-judicial bodies, seized of the same or similar matter, issue convergent judgments. This implies that if there are no two similar cases brought before two bodies, then it is not possible to assess judicial fragmentation or convergence.

Following these definitions, the book engages with a doctrinal and comparative analysis of primary sources of international human rights law, both at the regional and international level. After an initial perusal of the international

[21] See Chapter 7.

[22] Philippa Webb, *International Judicial Integration and Fragmentation* (Oxford University Press, 2013).

human rights law framework, the book mainly focuses on civil and political rights. In particular, it examines the Universal Declaration and the International Covenant on Civil and Political Rights together with the core human rights instruments of the regional bodies, namely the African Charter on Human and Peoples' Rights, the American Convention on Human Rights, the Arab Charter on Human Rights, the ASEAN Human Rights Declaration and the European Convention on Human Rights. This choice is motivated by the necessity of finding a compromise between ensuring the comprehensiveness of the analysis in terms of both regional scope and human rights issues addressed. Civil and political rights are preferred over social, economic and cultural rights because they are the common denominator between all the systems under analysis and allow a broader evaluation, given the higher number of cases decided by the adjudicatory bodies.

Differently, for the assessment of judicial fragmentation and convergence, the doctrinal and comparative analysis of the case-law takes into consideration only five bodies: the UN Human Rights Committee, the African Commission on Human and Peoples' Rights, the African Court on Human and Peoples' Rights, the European Court of Human Rights and the Inter-American Court of Human Rights. The Arab League and the ASEAN are excluded as they have not produced relevant human rights case-law. As for the three regional human rights systems, this book focuses on bodies that have similar features and issue binding judgments for their member states, as this element may have particular relevance when fragmentation is triggered. Nevertheless, it includes the African Commission on Human and Peoples' Rights due to the limited case-law available from the African Court, especially at the time this research started. Due to the extensive case-law of these five bodies, it was necessary to adopt a selection method to carry out a detailed examination.

As explained in Chapter 2, a first-level analysis has been conducted on all the leading judgments of these bodies concerning all civil and political rights with the only criterion that all four jurisdictions had to have dealt with these rights (see Appendix 2). After this initial screening that revealed substantial convergence, some specific rights and freedoms have been selected on the basis of specific features that may lead to fragmentation and analysed in detail, even including specific topics on which only two bodies ruled. Doctrinal and comparative legal methods were then used to analyse the content of these judgments and views, highlighting situations of convergence and fragmentation. This book considers the case-law of the five bodies up to 30 June 2021.

I perfectly recognise the limit imposed by the methodological choice made. Conducting a quantitative or qualitative study on all judgments through keywords, using for example text analysis, has the merit of including all the judgments issued and may have produced different results. However, it would not have allowed a detailed analysis of the text of the judgments, thus preventing the understanding of hidden or not evident cases of convergence or fragmentation. The methodology chosen ultimately appeared as the most appropriate, considering that the aim of this book is not merely to assess the extent of judicial fragmentation and convergence but, most importantly, to identify the possible causes.

The book adopts the same doctrinal and comparative methods also for identifying the legal factors explaining convergence and fragmentation. However, especially for what concerns the non-legal factors presented in Part II, it was necessary to resort to some empirical analyses. Drawing inspiration from the increasing literature on the importance of including behavioural analysis into legal research,[23] an empirical study has been conducted on the background of the judges, commissioners and committee members of the five bodies under analysis, collecting data from the official websites of these bodies and other internet sources. In addition, this book also benefits from interviews conducted with judges, commissioners and committee members as well as with members of the registries and secretariats of the five bodies and with NGOs involved in litigation before them. The outcome of these exchanges informs and supports arguments and findings based on primary and secondary sources.

STRUCTURE

The book is divided into two parts. Part I focuses on answering the first question, whether judicial fragmentation is actually affecting IHRL and to what extent. To this end, Chapter 1 introduces the issue of fragmentation in public international law, defining the meaning and features of fragmentation and convergence. Drawing inspiration from the ILC Report on fragmentation in public international law, the chapter assesses the likelihood of fragmentation to arise in international human rights law, setting the ground for the following study. Differently, Chapter 2 conducts a screening of the case-law of the five bodies under analysis in order to assess the extent of judicial fragmentation within IHRL. After a general perusal, it focuses on some specific topics, both exploring the prevalent dynamics towards convergence and providing a detailed analysis of the few encountered instances of judicial fragmentation.

[23] See, among others, Franck et al., 'Inside the Arbitrator's Mind', 1115.

Against this background, Part II attempts to identify some explanatory factors of judicial convergence and fragmentation in IHRL. More in detail, Chapter 3 focuses on the approach of treaty interpretation and the resort to judicial dialogue as a key path to judicial convergence. Chapter 4 explores the impact that the composition of the adjudicatory bodies may have on their interpretation and ultimately on convergence and fragmentation and the role played by their secretariats and registries. Chapter 5 reflects on the use and interpretation of two fundamental elements of human rights adjudication, the notions of necessity and that of proportionality. Similarly, Chapter 6 addresses the adoption by the bodies under analysis of the doctrine of deference and subsidiarity and the margin of appreciation. Finally, Chapter 7 discusses other factors that may influence fragmentation and convergence, such as the role of NGOs and civil society actors and the several elements that may prevent a specific case from reaching the merit stage.

PART I

Introducing and Assessing Fragmentation and Convergence in International Human Rights Law

1

Fragmentation and Convergence

Context and Definitions

INTRODUCTION

Fragmentation is a seemingly clear word: 'the process or the state of breaking or being broken into fragments'.[1] As such, it may concern any matter, and its meaning appears quite obvious. However, defining fragmentation in the context of international human rights law (IHRL) requires more in-depth reflection.

The International Law Commission (ILC) published a report in 2006, concluding that fragmentation affects international law (IL) and warned that sub-regimes, such as IHRL, could be similarly affected.[2] To make such an assessment, the first step is to clearly define what fragmentation means and assess whether the features and the causal factors that determined fragmentation in IL can be equally found also in IHRL.

The word 'fragmentation' commonly suggests that a legal system should be united and coherent enough to be affected by a 'diversification' and 'disintegration' process. Despite the fact that the ILC did not consider this something to focus its attention on,[3] a certain degree of unity appears to be a requirement for a fragmentation process to take place or, at least, to determine noteworthy consequences.[4] Looking at the wide range of definitions of 'legal system' proposed by scholars through time, one could question whether IHRL is a

1 Oxford Dictionary of English, 3rd ed. (Oxford University Press, 2010).

2 ILC, 'Fragmentation of International Law: Difficulties Arising from the Diversification and Expansion of International Law', Report of the Study Group of the International Law Commission, Finalised by Martti Koskenniemi (13 April 2006) UN Doc A/CN.4/L.682 (hereinafter ILC Report).

3 ILC Report, 22–25.

4 See, among others, the conclusions of Philippa Webb, *International Judicial Integration and Fragmentation* (Oxford University Press, 2013).

legal system. Just to name a few,[5] according to Austin, a legal system is a set of 'rules issued by the same person or body of persons'.[6] In the view of Kelsen a legal system includes all the rules that can be linked through a 'chain of validity' to a common 'superior' basic norm.[7] For Hart, a legal system only exists as long as the rules are 'obeyed by the bulk of the population'.[8] However, the lack of a shared definition leaves the possibility of seeing any set of rules as a legal system, depending on the different perspectives adopted. And one could reasonably claim that if IL is a legal system, despite the lack of a clear hierarchy of sources and institutions, so is IHRL.[9]

This chapter introduces the notions of both normative and judicial convergence and fragmentation in IL and IHRL. Through a short perusal of the current international and regional human rights instruments, it shows that normative fragmentation finds little space in IHRL. On the contrary, judicial fragmentation may be more relevant in this space. Drawing from existing literature on the matter, the chapter proposes a new definition of judicial fragmentation in IHRL, which focuses on the outcomes of the judgments, following the tradition of adopting a 'user perspective'.[10] Finally, considering the complexity of the issue at stake, this chapter also engages in a discussion of how convergence and fragmentation relate to the concepts of universality and relativism, key for any comparative discussion on human rights.

1.1 FRAGMENTATION IN INTERNATIONAL LAW

Fragmentation of international law, or fragmentation *in* international law is not per se a new phenomenon. To some extent, it has been present in the

[5] For an extensive presentation of all the different theories of legal systems see Joseph Raz, *The Concept of a Legal System: An Introduction to the Theory of a Legal System*, 2nd ed. (Oxford University Press, 1997); Carlo Focarelli, *International Law as a Social Construct* (Oxford University Press, 2012), 255–257.

[6] Raz, *The Concept of a Legal System*, 5.

[7] ibid, 102–105.

[8] Herbert Lionel Adolphus Hart, *The Concept of Law*, 2nd ed. (Oxford University Press, 1994), 114.

[9] Malcom Evans (ed), *International Law*, 4th ed. (Oxford University Press, 2014); Antonio Cassese, *Diritto Internazionale*, 2nd ed. (Il Mulino, 2006); Focarelli, *International Law as a Social Construct*; Dinah Shelton, 'Normative Hierarchy in International Law' (2006) 100 *American Journal of International Law* 291; Jerzy Sztucki, *Jus Cogens and the Vienna Convention on the Law of Treaties* (Springer, 1974); Pierre-Marie Dupuy, *Droit International Public* (Dalloz, 1995), 14–16.

[10] See, among others, Eva Brems and Saïla Ouald-Chaib, *Fragmentation and Integration in Human Rights Law: Users' Perspectives* (Edgar Elgar, 2018)

international legal order since its inception.[11] The understanding and definition of fragmentation have always been problematic because it has continuously struggled between being welcomed as a demonstration of IL's attention to the changing needs of the 'real world' and accused of being a threat to the same essence of IL.[12]

Since the mid-1990s, many presidents of the International Court of Justice (ICJ) repeatedly expressed their concerns about the potential danger of a diversification through proliferation of international specific normative regimes and institutions without any overall plan, which may ultimately undermine the unity of IL and make it fragmented and unmanageable.[13] Judge Guillaume, president of the ICJ from 2000, illustrated the 'unfortunate consequences' that fragmentation in the law may determine such as the phenomena of forum shopping, overlapping jurisdiction and conflicting judgments that would produce a 'serious inconsistency within the case-law'.[14]

One year later, the International Law Commission of the United Nations decided to include the topic 'Risks ensuing from the fragmentation of international law' into its long-term programme of work,[15] eventually culminating in 2006 with the extensive report titled 'The Fragmentation of International Law', finalised by Martti Koskenniemi.[16]

The study acknowledged the existence of an ongoing fragmentation in IL, defined as its diversification and expansion, and found its roots in the proliferation of specific regulatory regimes and the general specialisation and globalisation of IL.[17] Fragmentation of IL is regarded as a natural consequence of

[11] Especially when defined as specialisation in different 'branches'. Extensive explanation will be provided further in this section.

[12] See, for example, Georges Abi-Saab, 'Fragmentation or Unification: Some Concluding Remarks' (1999) 31 *Journal of International Law and Politics* 919.

[13] Gilbert Guillaume, 'La cour internationale de justice. Quelques propositions concrètes à l'occasion du Cinquantenaire' (1996) 100 *Revue générale de droit international public* 331; Sir Robert Jennings, 'The Role of the International Court of Justice' (1997) 68 *British Yearbook of International Law* 58 and Address to the Plenary Session of the General Assembly of the United Nations by Judge Stephen M. Schwebel, President of the International Court of Justice, 26 October 1999, available online on the Court's website www.icj-cij.org/icjwww/ipresscom/iprstats/htm, last accessed 10 February 2022.

[14] Address to the Plenary Session of the General Assembly of the United Nations by Judge Gilbert Guillaume, President of the International Court of Justice, 26 October 2000, available at www.icj-cij.org/icjwww/ipresscom/iprstats/htm, last accessed 10 February 2022.

[15] Official Records of the General Assembly, Fifty-fifth Session, Supplement no 10 (A/55/10), chap. IX.A.1, para. 729; Gerhard Hafner, 'Pros and Cons Ensuing from Fragmentation of International Law' (2004) 25 *Michigan Journal of International Law* 849.

[16] ILC Report, 8.

[17] ibid, 10–11. Some commentators pointed out that from the 1990s there has not been a real and significant increase in international law normative framework and institutional architecture,

the 'fragmentation of the international social world'[18] since the law is developing according to the needs of the international reality.

The report distinguished between two different types of fragmentation affecting IL: legislative and institutional. Dupuy later defined them as normative and judicial fragmentation.[19] While mostly similar in substance, this book will opt for Dupuy's classification for its clearer and more exhaustive definition.

The normative fragmentation is what the ILC Report called 'differentiation between types of special law'.[20] This produces a splitting of international law into 'highly specialised boxes that claim relative autonomy from each other and the general law'[21] possibly being significantly contrasting. These boxes are often called 'special' or 'sub' regimes to highlight their nature and position in relation to the general framework of IL. While they are parts of and thus subjected to IL, their rules are so specific and organic to claim a certain degree of independence. Examples of such regimes are international trade law, environmental law, human rights law, humanitarian law or economic law. Their existence and proliferation may threaten the coherence of IL, as they often operate without taking into consideration the 'legislative and institutional activities in the adjoining fields and the general principles and practices of international law'.[22] While recognising the absence of a single 'legislative will' behind IL, the report stressed the importance of harmonising the various special regimes to strengthen and not to compromise the entire international legal system. Normative fragmentation, indeed, may take place both in the case of a conflict between a special regime and the general law or in the case of conflict among special regimes, such as in the case of the immunity regimes[23] or the maritime transportation of oil.[24]

but rather a 'heterogeneity of the judicial instruments in the international legal order' and the 'increasing activities of international jurisdictions'. cf Julien Fouret and Mario Prost, 'La multiplication des juridictions internationales: E la nécessité de remettre quelques pendules à l'heure' (2002) 15 *Revue québécoise de droit international* 117, 120 (all translations are by the author).

18 ibid.

19 Pierre-Marie Dupuy, 'The Danger of Fragmentation or Unification of the International Legal System and the International Court of Justice' (1999) 31 *New York University Journal of International Law and Politics* 791.

20 ILC Report, 34.

21 ILC, 'Fragmentation of International Law: Difficulties Arising from the Diversification and Expansion of International Law', Conclusion of the work of the Study Group (1 May–9 June and 3 July–11 August 2006) UN Doc A/CN.4/L.702, 5.

22 ILC Report, 11.

23 See Hafner, 'Pros and Cons Ensuing from Fragmentation', 852.

24 ibid.

The institutional fragmentation is equally complex. Alternatively labelled as 'organic', 'decisional' or 'judicial' fragmentation,[25] it takes place when 'two courts seized of the same issue (legal or factual) render contradictory decisions'.[26] Similar to the case of normative fragmentation, the main reason behind this phenomenon is the multiplication of bodies and procedures that enforce IL.[27] That was the case with the test for the attribution of state responsibility for a breach of IL. The 'overall control test' of the International Criminal Tribunal for the Former Yugoslavia (ICTY) in *Tadić*[28] significantly deviated from the 'effective control' test established by the ICJ in *Nicaragua*[29] and reaffirmed later in *Bosnian Genocide*[30] to the extent that the same conduct, if observed under the two tests, may be differently attributed to the state.[31]

While recognising the relevance of both, the ILC decided to focus on the normative fragmentation, leaving the institutional one aside. The report concluded that IL is a legal system and normative fragmentation is affecting it.[32]

Yet, the report reassured that IL has powerful tools to limit fragmentation, such as the principles of *lex specialis derogat legi generali*, *lex posterior derogat legi priori* or *lex superior*.[33] In addition, the report recalled the value of resorting to Article 31(3)(c) of the Vienna Convention on the Law of Treaties (VCLT)[34] with the purpose of achieving a 'systematic integration'

[25] See, among others, Dupuy, 'The Danger of Fragmentation', 2; Martti Koskenniemi and Paivi Leino, 'Fragmentation of International Law? Postmodern Anxieties' (2002) 15 *Leiden Journal of International Law* 3, 553–579 and Webb, *International Judicial Integration and Fragmentation*.

[26] ibid, 6.

[27] See, for example, Dupuy, 'The Danger of Fragmentation', 2.

[28] *The Prosecutor v. Duško Tadić*, IT-94-1-A (ICTY, 15 July 1999).

[29] *Case Concerning Military and Paramilitary Activities in and against Nicaragua (Nicaragua v. United States of America)* (ICJ, 27 June 1986), 110–112.

[30] *Case Concerning the Application of the Convention on the Prevention and Punishment of the Crime of Genocide (Bosnia and Herzegovina v. Serbia and Montenegro)*, Judgment, 26 February 2007, ICJ Reports (2007), 43.

[31] See, among others, Antonio Cassese, 'The *Nicaragua* and *Tadic* Tests Revisited in Light of the ICJ Judgment on Genocide in Bosnia' (2007) 18(4) *European Journal of International Law* 649. Worth remembering is that *Tadic*, differently from *Nicaragua* and *Bosnian Genocide*, addressed the issue of attribution only instrumentally for the characterisation of a conflict.

[32] The debate over the nature of international law as a proper legal system is highly debated in literature. cf Margaret A. Young (ed), *Regime Interaction in International Law* (Cambridge University Press, 2012), 2.

[33] ILC Report, 36–64, 122–125 and 181–188.

[34] Article 31(3) (c) VCLT, concerning the interpretation of treaties, states as follows: '[. . .] 3. There shall be taken into account, together with the context: [. . .] (c) any relevant rules of

through the careful 'harmonisation oriented' use of such article.[35] However, the application of these principles is difficult and limited in the practice by the complex nature and structure of IL. The lack of a clear hierarchy, the fact that sometimes the conflicting norms belong to treaties with different state parties or to different legal regimes or the question of who is entitled to carry out the authoritative interpretation for the sake of Article 31(3)(c) VCLT are certainly further obstacles for such a systematic integration.[36]

The ILC Report significantly fostered the debate on fragmentation among scholars and practitioners, who expressed increasing concerns about the impact that fragmentation may also have on the sub-systems of IL, including IHRL.

1.2 NORMATIVE FRAGMENTATION AND CONVERGENCE IN IHRL

With the assumption that IHRL is a legal system that can be affected by fragmentation, the next question is to what extent this is actually taking place. This section focuses on the first type of fragmentation (and convergence) identified in the ILC Report: the normative one. It defines it in the context of IHRL and provides an outline of the existing human rights norms both at the regional and international level. The proliferation of these sources certainly increases the likelihood of normative fragmentation, yet it only sporadically occurs, thanks to the determinant role played by the adjudicatory bodies called to interpret the norms.

1.2.1 *Defining Normative Fragmentation and Convergence*

Normative fragmentation takes place when two legal frameworks contain provisions that are different in their content or contrast with each other. The ILC defined it as a 'conflict between rules or rule-systems'.[37] In order to adopt such a definition, one should clarify what 'conflict' means. The ILC Report defined it as the situation where 'it is possible for a party to two treaties to comply with one rule only by thereby failing to comply with another rule'.[38] However, the ILC observed that 'a treaty may sometimes frustrate the goals of another treaty without there being any strict incompatibility between the

international law applicable in the relations between the parties'. Vienna Convention on the Law of Treaties, 1969, UN Doc. A/Conf.39/27/1155UNTS331/8 ILM 679 (1969).

35 ILC Report, 213.

36 cf *Hassan v. United Kingdom*, Application no 29750/09 (ECtHR, 16 September 2014), 100–101.

37 ILC Report, 11 at 8.

38 ILC Report, 19 at 24.

provisions',[39] ultimately concluding that a conflict is 'a situation where two rules or principles suggest different ways of dealing with a problem'.[40]

Such a definition appears very vague and, paradoxically, any two norms may suggest different ways to deal with a problem if one wants to interpret them that way. The margin left to the interpretation is very wide and a definition of normative fragmentation should take that into account. Consequently, this book defines normative fragmentation as the situation where two rules cannot be reasonably interpreted as producing the same outcome. In other words, and getting back to the initial understanding of the ILC, normative fragmentation is considered as a conflict of norms. Some scholars called it 'genuine' fragmentation,[41] or 'genuine norm conflict';[42] this restrictive understanding of normative fragmentation arises when 'one norm constitutes, has led to, or may lead to, a breach of the other'.[43]

Within IHRL, normative fragmentation may happen either at the same level, that is, between two regional or international norms, or at different levels, that is, between a regional and an international norm. The degrees of differentiation between rules may vary significantly and, thus, determine different degrees of fragmentation.

The proliferation of normative instruments protecting human rights increases the chances of fragmentation. As outlined in the following sections, the international human rights framework is particularly rich in both binding and non-binding instruments and this makes it easier for two rules to enter into conflict. For example, the rights of persons with disabilities are regulated by at least six specific instruments in addition to the several general covenants that, in one way or another, tackle the issue.[44] Even more remarkable is the number of instruments dealing with the administration of justice and the protection of persons subject to detention: twenty-six specific treaties,

[39] ibid.

[40] ibid at 25.

[41] Webb, *International Judicial Integration and Fragmentation*, 6.

[42] Joost Pauwelyn, *Conflict of Norms in Public International Law: How WTO Law Relates to Other Rules of International Law* (Cambridge University Press, 2003), 175–176.

[43] ibid. See also Erich Vranes, 'The Definition of "Norm Conflict" in International Law and Legal Theory' (2006) 17 *European Journal of International Law* 395–418.

[44] Convention on the Rights of Persons with Disabilities, Optional Protocol to the Convention on the Rights of Persons with Disabilities, Standard Rules on the Equalization of Opportunities for Persons with Disabilities, Declaration on the Rights of Mentally Retarded Persons, Declaration on the Rights of Disabled Persons, Principles for the Protection of Persons with Mental Illness and the Improvement of Mental Health Care, in addition to the relevant provisions contained in the International Covenant on Civil and Political Rights, the International Covenant on Economic, Social and Cultural Rights and the Universal Declaration of Human Rights.

declarations, principles and guidelines and just as many general instruments addressing the topic.[45] To this picture one should also add the relevant regional human rights instruments, making the normative protection extremely rich yet complicated.[46]

Indeed, this extensive normative framework with overlapping norms regulating the same issue certainly increases the likelihood of divergent and contrasting provisions.

Normative parallelism is not per se a problem, and it is not unique to international law, as it exists in a variety of domestic legal settings too.[47] While often not problematic, it produces different effects in the potentially 'anarchical international legal system, which is characterised by a lack of institutional integration'.[48] The difficulty, at times, to apply the principle of *lex superior*, due to the absence of a clear hierarchy of sources of law, and the growth in lawmaking might lead to 'conflicts between rules or rule-systems, deviating institutional practices and, possibly [to] the loss of an overall perspective on the law'.[49]

However, the same development that may determine fragmentation has also produced a growing amount of normative equivalence. Indeed, many of the overlapping norms in IHRL can be considered, if not equal, at least equivalent and convergent.[50]

In this book, normative convergence is defined as the absence of normative fragmentation. This means that normative convergence does not require two norms to be precisely the same but just not to be in conflict. In the absence of a proper definition in literature of what convergence means for two rules,[51]

45 Such as the Standard Minimum Rules for the Treatment of Prisoners, the Body of Principles for the Protection of All Persons under Any Form of Detention or Imprisonment, the United Nations Rules for the Protection of Juveniles Deprived of their Liberty, the Principles on the Effective Investigation and Documentation of Torture and Other Cruel, Inhuman or Degrading Treatment or Punishment and others. The full list is available at the OHCHR website www.ohchr.org/EN/ProfessionalInterest/Pages/UniversalHumanRightsInstruments.aspx, last accessed 10 February 2022.

46 See the Inter-American Convention on the Elimination of All Forms of Discrimination against Persons with Disabilities or the Inter-American Convention to Prevent and Punish Torture.

47 Tomer Broude and Yuval Shany, 'The International Law and Policy of Multi-Sourced Equivalent Norms' in Tomer Broude and Yuval Shany (eds), *Multi-Sourced Equivalent Norms in International Law* (Hart, 2011).

48 ibid, 3.

49 ILC Report, 11.

50 See the work on multi-sourced equivalent norms (MSENs) as presented by Broude and Shany, *Multi-Sourced Equivalent Norms in International Law*.

51 See discussion on the absence of a definition of convergence later in this chapter, in Section 1.4.1.

such an understanding of normative convergence allows accommodating the plurality in IHRL where provisions that are slightly different in the letter do not amount to fragmentation. Indeed, all the few attempted definitions of convergence are very vague and focus more on the dynamic process of two rules being 'less distant' than before, without providing any further guidance.[52]

The following perusal of international and regional human rights instruments will explore the extent of normative fragmentation and convergence in IHRL.

1.2.2 *The Proliferation of Human Rights Normative Frameworks*

The proliferation of normative frameworks was considered by the ILC as one of the triggering factors of fragmentation in IL. Within IHRL, the growth of rules and norms both at the international and regional level is even more conspicuous. Legal pluralism, essential to the development of IL, is even more critical in IHRL. The fundamental and sensitive nature of the rights at stake, particularly subjected to political and social pressure, requires a continuous update and expansion.[53] Moreover, the prominent role that regional systems play in ensuring the promotion and protection of human rights led to further proliferation.

The following sections will show how the picture of the IHRL legal framework is impressively diversified, both in the subject matter and in the international or regional character of the legal sources.

1.2.2.1 International Instruments

At the international level, forty-five treaties regulating various human rights issues have been signed and ratified by a large number of states.[54] Some of them are general instruments, such as the International Covenant on Civil

[52] John Henry Merryman, 'On the Convergence (and Divergence) of the Civil Law and the Common Law' (1981) 17 *Stanford Journal of International Law* 357; Carla M. Buckley, Alice Donald and Philip Leach (eds), *Towards Convergence in International Human Rights Law: Approaches of Regional and International Systems* (Brill-Nijhoff, 2017), 2–30.

[53] G. Cohen-Jonathan, 'La protection des droits de l'homme et l'évolution du droit international', Actes du Colloque de Strasbourg; Société française de droit international, *La protection des droits de l'homme et l'évolution du droit international* (Pedone, 1998), 321; Eva Brems, *Human Rights: Universality and Diversity* (Martinus-Nijhoff, 2001); Ross Mellick, *Development, Ethnicity and Human Rights in South Asia* (Sage, 1998).

[54] See Appendix 1. The number is given by the sixteen treaties and optional protocols within the Human Rights Chapter (Chapter IV) of the UN Treaty Collection, eleven ILO human rights conventions and eighteen conventions and protocols available on the OHCHR website

and Political Rights (ICCPR)[55] or the International Covenant on Economic, Social and Cultural Rights (ICESCR),[56] while others are very specific, such as the Convention on Consent to Marriage, Minimum Age for Marriage and Registration of Marriages.[57] Moreover, there is a significant number of binding instruments within the International Labour Organization (ILO) framework addressing specific issues related to labour rights.[58]

In addition, non-binding human rights instruments have also significantly expanded. Currently, one can count more than fifty international declarations, principles and guidelines according to the non-exhaustive list provided by the Office of the High Commissioner for Human Rights (OHCHR).[59] These instruments are often very specific, offering detailed definitions of and protection to very particular rights and groups of people. The OHCHR divided them into fourteen categories showing the wide-encompassing reach of these instruments: the world conference on human rights and millennium assembly, the right of self-determination, the prevention of discrimination, the rights of indigenous people and minorities, the rights of women, the rights of older persons, the rights of persons with disabilities, the human rights in the administration of justice, social welfare and development, the promotion and protection of human rights, marriage, the right to health, nationality, statelessness and asylum and refugees and war crimes and crimes against humanity. Although states are not legally obliged to respect the provisions contained therein, their existence adds a further layer to the complexity of IHRL, especially when adjudicatory bodies are called to interpret controversial provisions, since different instruments may provide slightly different understandings of similar principles aiming at protecting specific rights.[60]

www.ohchr.org/EN/ProfessionalInterest/Pages/UniversalHumanRightsInstruments.aspx, last accessed 10 February 2022.

[55] International Covenant on Civil and Political Rights 1966, 999 UNTS 171 and its two Optional Protocols.

[56] International Covenant on Economic, Social and Cultural Rights 1966, 993 UNTS and its Optional Protocol (2008).

[57] Convention on Consent to Marriage, Minimum Age for Marriage and Registration of Marriages 1962, 521 UNTS 231.

[58] See Appendix 1. A full list is available on the ILO website at www.ilo.org/dyn/normlex/en/f?p=1000:12001:::NO, last accessed 10 February 2022.

[59] A full updated list of the documents is available on the OHCHR website, at www.ohchr.org/EN/ProfessionalInterest/Pages/UniversalHumanRightsInstruments.aspx, last accessed 10 February 2022.

[60] See Section 1.4.1.

1.2.2.2 Regional Instruments

The already complex international human rights framework is both enriched and intensified by the regional frameworks, answering to local needs and concerns and additional interests of protection. The Council of Europe (CoE) adopted an extensive range of human rights treaties, covering both civil and political rights and economic, social and cultural rights.[61] Similarly, the African Union (AU)[62] and the Organization of American States (OAS)[63] have their general and specific well-established human rights conventions and protocols. Furthermore, also the Arab League and the Association of Southeast Asian Nations (ASEAN) approved the Arab Charter on Human Rights[64] and the ASEAN Human Rights Declaration, respectively.[65] Other regional and sub-regional human rights instruments, with different legal value and nature, have been also adopted, such as the Cairo Declaration and other human rights documents by the Organisation of Islamic Cooperation, the Charter of Fundamental Rights of the European Union and the Great Lakes Protocol on the protection of internally displaced persons.[66]

1.2.3 *Actual and Potential Normative Fragmentation in IHRL*

Normative fragmentation can assume different degrees, according to how much and in which way two rules are 'in contrast'. Recalling the definition provided at the beginning of the section, normative fragmentation is the conflict between rules, understood as the situation where one party, if theoretically subjected to both rules, cannot comply with one without infringing the other.

[61] See Appendix 1. All the treaties adopted by the Council of Europe are available at the Treaty Office of the Council of Europe website http://conventions.coe.int/Treaty/Commun/ListeTraites.asp?MA=44&CM=7&CL=EN, last accessed 10 February 2022.

[62] See Appendix 1. An updated list is also available at the AU website www.au.int/en/treaties, last accessed 10 February 2022.

[63] See Appendix 1. An updated list is also available at the OAS website www.oas.org/dil/treaties_subject.htm, last accessed 10 February 2022.

[64] League of Arab States, *Arab Charter on Human Rights*, 22 May 2004, reprinted in 12 *International Human Rights Reports* 893 (2005) (entered into force on 15 March 2008) [hereinafter Arab Charter]. For an English translation of the Arab Charter, see the University of Minnesota Human Rights Library, available at www1.umn.edu/humanrts/instree/loas2005.html, last accessed 10 February 2022.

[65] ASEAN, *Human Rights Declaration*, 18 November 2012, available at www.asean.org/news/asean-statement-communiques/item/asean-human-rights-declaration, last accessed 10 February 2022.

[66] See Appendix 1 for a full list and details.

Human rights norms, as enshrined in treaties, are so broad, general and susceptible to interpretation that it is very hard to identify cases where a situation of proper normative fragmentation arises. A perusal of the documents listed earlier shows that probably one of the few cases where this occurs is with the 2004 Arab Charter on Human Rights. The Charter clearly states that some economic, social and cultural rights, such as the right to work (Article 34), the right to health (Article 39(1)) and the right to education (Article 41(2)) are granted only to citizens and not to all the people under the state's jurisdiction, such as stated by the ICESCR or other regional instruments.[67]

However, no other situation of obvious clash between norms has been found, since all the other discrepancies or differences in the letter of the norms could be more or less easily overcome at the interpretation stage. This is the case of what can be called 'potential fragmentation' or 'apparent fragmentation or conflict of norms'.[68] Even if two texts appear *prima facie* contrasting, they can easily be harmonised by interpretative means and the conflict can be thus avoided.[69] In these instances, two rules are slightly different in the letter, sometimes with an omission or an added specification, but they do not automatically conflict with each other unless they are interpreted in a certain way. According to the interpretative tools that one wants to use, they can be equally seen as contrasting, and thus leading to fragmentation, or as converging in the same direction.

This is the case for many normative provisions in regional and international instruments. For instance, Article 3(3) of the Arab Charter conditions the principle of equality between men and women to the religious law, stating that '[m]en and women are equal in respect of human dignity, rights and obligation within the framework of the positive discrimination established in favour of women by the Islamic Shari'a, other divine laws and by applicable laws and legal instruments'. The latter may appear in contrast with the principle of non-discrimination set out in Article 2 of Universal Declaration

67 For a deeper analysis of the content of the Arab Charter on Human Rights, see Mervat Rishmawi, 'The Revised Arab Charter on Human Rights: A Step Forward?' (2005) 5 *Human Rights Law Review* 361.

68 Koskenniemi and Leino, 'Fragmentation of International Law?'; William Burke-White, 'International Legal Pluralism' (2004) 25 *Michigan Journal of International Law* 963; Marko Milanovic, 'Norm Conflict in International Law: Whither Human Rights?' (2009) 20 *Duke Journal of Comparative & International Law* 69.

69 ibid, 131; Webb, *International Judicial Integration and Fragmentation*.

of Human Rights (UDHR)[70] and Article 2 of ICCPR[71] as well as of the entire Committee on the Elimination of Discrimination Against Women (CEDAW), but it all depends on the interpretation given in the specific case.

Similarly, the American Convention on Human Rights (ACHR) provides, in Article 4, that the right to life 'shall be protected [. . .] from the moment of conception'[72] differently from what is established in the UDHR or in the ICCPR, where such specification does not appear, leaving the matter undefined.[73] Someone could call this normative fragmentation, but, as proved by the extensive case-law of the Inter-American Commission and Court, the interpretation of the norm in a given case may bring perfect convergence.[74]

On the same line, the African Charter on Human and Peoples' Rights (ACHPR) lacks a limitation clause for what concerns the freedom to manifest religion, freedom of expression and freedom of association, differently from the ICCPR, the European Convention on Human Rights (ECHR) and ACHR. However, as it will be discussed later in the book, the African Commission and the African Court managed to fill this gap through their interpretation, ultimately ensuring convergence.[75]

The previous examples and the few existing studies on normative fragmentation within IHRL show that such a phenomenon is not as extensive and alarming as in general international law.[76] Indeed, the actual or genuine normative fragmentation is significantly limited. On the contrary, the potential one is more conspicuous, but it can be easily solved through a careful and harmonious interpretation.

In conclusion, if normative fragmentation was a predominant issue in IL, to the extent that the ILC decided to focus all its report on it, when it comes to IHRL it seems a minor concern. One of the reasons for the scarcity of conflicting norms may be found in the general nature and letter that often these norms have. This vagueness, which is a feature of both international and regional instruments, allows the adjudicatory bodies to interpret the content of the norms in very different and contrasting ways, keeping the door open to a possible different kind of fragmentation. Interpretation plays a key role in

70 Article 2, UDHR.
71 Article 2, ICCPR.
72 Article 4, ACHR.
73 cf Article 2, ECHR, Article 6, ICCPR and Article 4, ACHPR.
74 See *Baby Boy v. United States* (IACommHR, 6 March 1981).
75 See Chapters 3 and 5.
76 See, among others, Buckley, Donald and Leach (eds), *Towards Convergence in International Human Rights Law*; Marjan Ajevski, 'Fragmentation in International Human Rights Law – Beyond Conflict of Laws' (2014) 32 *Nordic Journal of Human Rights* 87, 90.

determining whether the same normative framework triggers fragmentation or convergence. As the cases of potential normative fragmentation show, sometimes the line between conflicting or harmonious rules is blurred and the role of the body entitled to the application and interpretation of the norm is crucial. As the following section explains, the judicial and quasi-judicial bodies became fundamental in either enhancing the coherence among international and regional rules or in highlighting the differences and determining conflicts.

1.3 JUDICIAL FRAGMENTATION AND CONVERGENCE IN IHRL

The more general the norm, the more important is the role of the interpreter. In the last half-century, there has been a considerable development of international and regional human rights enforcement institutions, with the improvement of the existing bodies and the creation of new ones. As of today, the majority of states in the world fall under the jurisdiction of, at least, a regional and an international human rights judicial or quasi-judicial body.

The reasons behind the spread of human rights adjudicatory bodies are various. One can borrow the reasoning of Shany in explaining the proliferation of judicial institutions in IL and apply it to IHRL.[77] First, the increased density, volume and complexity of international human rights norms, as observed earlier, required correspondingly dispute-settlement institutions to guarantee the smooth operation of the new legal arrangements and the continued clarification and development of their norms. Second, a greater commitment to human rights issues found space in international relations. Third, the positive experience with some international courts and tribunals inspired the creation of similar bodies. Finally, the unsuitability of the existing courts and tribunals to address many types of disputes, especially those involving complicated issues that require great specialisation or are perceived to be addressed on a regional level.[78]

The proliferation of these bodies and their overlapping competencies and jurisdiction increases the likelihood of fragmentation. The international human rights normative framework is particularly suitable for very diverse interpretations, and the arising of fragmentation or convergence mostly depends on the adjudicatory body.

[77] Yuval Shany, *The Competing Jurisdictions of International Courts and Tribunals* (Oxford University Press, 2003).
[78] ibid, 3–4.

This section defines the notions of judicial fragmentation and convergence and presents a perusal of the existing institutional human rights framework, both at the international and regional level, in order to understand the context in which judicial fragmentation and convergence take place.

1.3.1 *Defining Judicial Fragmentation and Convergence*

The expression 'institutional fragmentation' has been largely used and defined in social sciences from different perspectives. In politics, sociology and economics institutional fragmentation refers to a 'patchwork of international institutions that are different in their character (organisations, regimes, and implicit norms), their constituencies (public and private), their spatial scope (from bilateral to global), and their [predominant] subject matter'.[79]

However, the meaning of institutional fragmentation in the context of an analysis on legal outcomes is different since the attention is not on the existence of different institutions but instead on their work of interpretation and application of legal provisions.

The literature on the matter is very confused when it comes to the definition of institutional or judicial fragmentation and convergence. For instance, the ILC Report and some scholars adopted the politics-inspired understanding without providing further explanation or adapting it to the legal context.[80] Others prefer to use the expression 'judicial fragmentation' to underlie the fact that the differentiation lies in the judicial reasoning and outcome that leads to fragmentation.[81]

This book prefers the latter option for its focus and attention to the legal sphere, adopting the definition provided by Webb as a starting point but departing from it in the specification of its features.[82]

As for convergence, there is no definition of judicial convergence, and all the authors rely on the well-established meaning of this term without feeling the need to define it properly in the specific context of case-law analysis. Even articles and books specifically focused on convergence of case-law did not

[79] For instance, Frank Biermann et al., 'The Fragmentation of Global Governance Architectures: A Framework for Analysis' (2009) 9 *Global Environmental Politics* 14, 16.

[80] ILC Report, 12; Pierre-Marie Dupuy, 'Un débat doctrinal à l'ére de la globalisation: Sur la fragmentation du droit international' (2007) 1 *European Journal of Legal Studies* 1.

[81] Webb, *International Judicial Integration and Fragmentation.*

[82] ibid, 6.

engage in any discussion about the definition of convergence, sometimes just limiting the definition to its opposite, fragmentation.[83]

Judicial fragmentation is then here defined as the situation where two judicial or quasi-judicial bodies, seized of the same or similar matter, issue contrasting judgments. On the contrary, judicial convergence is understood as the situation where two judicial or quasi-judicial bodies, seized of the same or similar matter, issue convergent judgments. Two elements are particularly important in this definition. First, the element of similarity between the matters presented before the two bodies. In order to be able to adequately operate a comparison and assess the arising of fragmentation (or that of convergence), it is fundamental for the two cases to be very similar, if not identical, both in the subject matter, the features of the applicants and the underlying domestic legislation.[84] Second, it is important to understand what characterises two contrasting or convergent judgments. Two elements compose a judgment: the reasoning and the outcome. Both for the sake of practicality of the analysis and for the attention to the user's perspective and impact of the judgment, in this book, the main marking element for a judgment will be its outcome. Therefore, two contrasting judgments will be identified as judgments featuring different and contrasting outcomes and two convergent judgments will be those leading to the same, or convergent, outcome. There may be situations where the reasoning and the outcome are not in line, such as instances where the reasoning of two judgments differs but their outcome converges or, vice versa, where the reasoning is similar but the outcome ultimately conflicts. In these instances, it will be the outcome that will determine convergence or fragmentation, but the discordant element of the reasoning will be considered as a signal for a possible shift in the future towards fragmentation/convergence. In light of this, two contrasting reasoning with convergent outcomes will constitute convergence with potential fragmentation while two convergent reasoning with contrasting outcomes will trigger fragmentation but with elements for potential convergence.

83 See Buckley, Donald and Leach (eds), *Towards Convergence in International Human Rights Law*; Mads Andenas and Eirik Bjorge (eds), *A Farewell to Fragmentation. Reassertion and Convergence in International Law* (Cambridge University Press, 2015); Mads Andenas, 'Reassertion and Transformation: From Fragmentation to Convergence in International Law' (2015) 46 *Georgetown Journal of International Law* 685; Nina-Louisa Arold, 'The European Court of Human Rights as an Example of Convergence' (2007) 76 *Nordic Journal of International Law* 305, 305–322.

84 The challenges arising from comparing cases with excessive differences will be discussed in Chapter 2.

Within this picture, there is a third scenario, that of no two bodies ruling on similar issues. In this case, it is not possible to claim convergence, since judicial convergence is not simply the absence of judicial fragmentation. Differently from the normative field, it would be a mistake to consider that two bodies that never rule on the same or similar issue are convergent on that matter since it is challenging to foresee a judicial body's behaviour with enough confidence. On the contrary, in the situation of normative fragmentation or convergence, the absence of contrasting norms can be automatically labelled as convergence, even with different degrees, since, as described earlier, there is no extra element of uncertainty, such as the interpretation, in the mere normative framework.

Institutional or judicial fragmentation may arise between bodies of different levels, such as a regional and an international body, or between bodies at the same level, such as two regional or two international bodies. As Ajevski pointed out, '[T]he fear of fragmentation is no less mitigated when there are no visible points of conflict or interaction between the institutions.'[85] Two bodies such as the European Court of Human Rights (ECtHR) and the Inter-American Court of Human Rights (IACtHR) will never share jurisdiction over the same countries, but fragmentation between them may threaten the coherence of IHRL and determine other negative consequences, such as undermining the legitimacy of the courts and limiting states' compliance. However, when judicial fragmentation is taking place between two bodies that share jurisdiction (either *ratione materiae* or *ratione personae*), the phenomenon can be even more relevant since it can have practical consequences like encouraging the phenomenon of forum shopping.[86]

1.3.2 *The Proliferation of Human Rights Institutions*

The proliferation of normative frameworks led to a proliferation of human rights institutions as well. Human rights instruments often come with their own institutions, tasked with the enforcement of the rights contained therein. The abundance of such mechanisms could undoubtedly strengthen and benefit the international and regional protection of human rights. However, these bodies often operate without reference to, and in coordination with, similar bodies, thus risking transforming the advantage into a problem of fragmentation. In addition, regional systems established more than one

[85] Ajevski, 'Fragmentation in International Human Rights Law', 90.

[86] cf Lorna McGregor, 'The Relationship of the UN Treaty Bodies and Regional Systems' in Scott Sheeran and Sir Nigel Rodley, *Routledge Handbook of International Human Rights Law* (Routledge, 2013), 505–520.

institution for the monitoring and enforcement of their human rights conventions. Together with sub-regional bodies and institutions with human rights-related functions, this plethora of monitoring and adjudication bodies requires close scrutiny for the assessment of fragmentation.

At the international and regional level, there are many such institutions, with different composition and functions. Looking at the composition of the bodies, one can distinguish political bodies and expert bodies. Political or governmental bodies are those institutions composed of representatives of member states, often ambassadors or high-level functionaries, who act on behalf of their respective governments. On the contrary, expert bodies are those institutions composed of independent experts who serve in their personal capacity and should be, therefore, more impartial in their role. Looking at their functions, one could identify two categories: those bodies having monitoring and policy-making functions and those having judicial or quasi-judicial enforcement ones. The former are entitled to monitor the implementation of the respective human rights treaties as well as to promote human rights through policies and campaigns. The latter have the responsibility of ensuring the enforcement of human rights provisions through judicial application of the rules. They can be proper courts, judicial bodies or other institutions having, among others, functions akin to courts, quasi-judicial bodies.

1.3.2.1 International Human Rights Institutions

MONITORING BODIES Within the UN system, there is an extensive number of human rights bodies, with different roles and functions. Created in 1993, the Office of the High Commissioner for Human Rights has quickly become the primary reference for the human rights promotion and protection policy of the UN.[87] With its mostly clerical and diplomatic support, different human rights institutions operate, each with a specific function and role. There are two categories of UN human rights bodies, the Charter-based bodies and the treaty-based bodies.

The Charter-based bodies include the UN Human Rights Council (established in 2006 replacing the Commission on Human Rights) and its monitoring mechanisms. The council is an intergovernmental body, entitled to strengthen the promotion and protection of human rights and has assumed

[87] Daniel Moeckli, Sangeeta Shah and Sandesh Sivakumaran (eds), *International Human Rights Law* (Oxford University Press, 2010), 388–391; Ilias Bantekas and Lutz Oette, *International Human Rights Law and Practice* (Cambridge University Press, 2013), 149.

a leading role in bringing forward the UN human rights agenda. To carry out its functions, the council benefits from two different monitoring mechanisms, established by the UN General Assembly. First, the Universal Period Review (UPR), a state-driven process to periodically assess the status of human rights in every state.[88] Second, the so-called Special Procedures: independent experts with the task of monitoring the application of certain rights in the world or the status of human rights in certain countries.[89] In addition, the Human Rights Council established its own complaint procedures, allowing individuals and groups to submit complaints on human rights violations.[90]

Furthermore, a number of other political bodies within the UN system bear human rights functions. This is the case for the Third Committee of the General Assembly, responsible for social, humanitarian and cultural issues, or the UN Economic and Social Council (ECOSOC), established by Article 62 of the UN Charter, which regularly addresses human rights issues and designs public policies to promote them. Within ECOSOC, worth mentioning is also the Commission on the Status of Women. Moreover, the General Assembly or the Security Council also often discuss human rights issues and adopt important human rights-related declarations or resolutions.[91]

Some expert bodies, such as the UN Treaty Bodies (UNTBs), also undertake monitoring functions. However, they will be presented in the following section since they also carry out quasi-judicial functions.

JUDICIAL AND QUASI-JUDICIAL BODIES Among the treaty-based quasi-judicial bodies, ten treaty bodies are currently in force. These committees, established by the 'core' human rights treaties,[92] are composed of independent experts acting in their personal capacity and monitor and enforce in a quasi-judicial manner their respective treaties.[93] Among them, eight are

88 ibid, 150–160; Moeckli, Shah and Sivakumaran, *International Human Rights Law*, 360–366.

89 ibid, 367–375; Bantekas and Oette, *International Human Rights Law and Practice*, 160–168.

90 See Maja Bova, *Il consiglio diritti umani nel sistema onusiano di promozione e protezione dei diritti umani: Profili giuridici e istituziionali* (Giappichelli, 2011), 214–224 and the webpage dedicated to the Complaint Procedures mechanism, www.ohchr.org/EN/HRBodies/HRC/ComplaintProcedure/Pages/HRCComplaintProcedureIndex.aspx, last accessed on 10 February 2022.

91 Moeckli, Shah and Sivakumaran, *International Human Rights Law*, 392.

92 This is the label used by the same OHCHR; see www.ohchr.org/EN/ProfessionalInterest/Pages/CoreInstruments.aspx, last accessed 10 February 2022.

93 The treaty bodies, aimed at the monitoring and enforcement of the core UN human rights treaties, are the Human Rights Committee (HRC) for the ICCPR; the Committee on Economic, Social and Cultural Rights (CESCR) for the ICESCR; the Committee on the Elimination of Racial Discrimination (CERD) for the Convention on the Elimination of All Forms of Racial Discrimination, the Committee on the Elimination of Discrimination against

entitled to receive individual complaints against states who accepted their jurisdiction.[94] The Human Rights Committee (HRC) is the most developed and with the richest case-law, but other bodies, such as the CEDAW, the Committee on the Rights of the Child (CRC) and the Committee on the Elimination of Racial Discrimination (CERD) are equally very active. However, the acceptance of jurisdiction from states is crucial for carrying out their functions. At the time of writing, 116 states ratified the Optional Protocol to the ICCPR, accepting the jurisdiction of the HRC, 109 the Optional Protocol to CEDAW, but only 37 accepted the jurisdiction of the CRC and 23 that of the CESCR.[95] This is certainly one of the reasons why the HRC plays a privileged role, in addition of having a very wide competence *ratione materiae*, considering that the ICCPR deals with all civil and political rights for everyone and not only with a specific group of people, such as in the case of CEDAW or CRC. All these TBs benefit from the assistance and support of the OHCHR, whose branch on TBs serves as their secretariat.

To complete the picture, the International Court of Justice, while not a proper human rights court, has often had the opportunity to deal with human rights-related issues.[96]

1.3.2.2 European Human Rights Institutions

MONITORING BODIES Within the Council of Europe (CoE), several bodies deal with human rights issues. In addition to the Committee of Ministers and

Women (CEDAW) for the Convention on the Elimination of All Forms of Discrimination against Women, the Committee against Torture (CAT) for the Convention against Torture and Other Cruel, Inhuman and Degrading Treatment, the Committee on the Rights of the Child (CRC) for the Convention of the Right of the Child, the Committee on Migrant Workers (CMW) for the International Convention on the Protection of the Rights of all Migrant Workers and Members of Their Families, the Committee on the Rights of Persons with Disabilities (CRPD) for the International Convention on the Rights of Persons with Disabilities, the Committee on Enforced Disappearances (CED) for the International Convention for the Protection of All Persons from Enforced Disappearances and the Subcommittee on Prevention of Torture and other Cruel, Inhuman or Degrading Treatment or Punishment (SPT) for the Optional Protocol of the Convention against Torture (OPCAT).

94 For the HRC, the CEDAW, the CRC, the CRPD and the Committee on Economic Social and Cultural Rights (CESCR), a state accepts their jurisdiction by ratifying a specific Optional Protocol. Differently, for the other TBs, a state should make a declaration as established by Article 22 of CAT, Article 14 of CERD, Article 31 of CED and Article 77 of CMW.

95 Data updated to the 10 February 2022, available on the OHCHR website at http://indicators.ohchr.org.

96 See, among others, John R. Crook, 'The International Court of Justice and Human Rights' (2004) 1 *Northwestern Journal of International Human Rights* 1.

the Parliamentary Assembly, the two political bodies representing the member states, there are four monitoring bodies composed of independent experts. These are the European Committee for the Prevention of Torture (CPT), the Committee of Experts of the European Charter for Regional or Minority Languages, the Steering Committee for Human Rights (CDDH) and the Commissioner for Human Rights.

This adds to the human rights institutions established within the European Union (EU). In particular, worth mentioning are the EU Agency for Fundamental Rights and the Committee on Citizens' Freedoms and Rights, Justice and Home Affairs working within the European Parliament.

JUDICIAL AND QUASI-JUDICIAL ENFORCEMENT BODIES The enforcement of the European normative framework, in particular of the ECHR and the European Social Charter, is carried out by two expert bodies: the European Court of Human Rights and the European Committee of Social Rights (ECSR).[97]

First established in 1959, the ECtHR has repeatedly been strengthened and developed through different protocols. In 1998, Protocol No. 11 replaced the original two-tier structure comprising the Court and the Commission on Human Rights with a single full-time Court. This change put an end to the Commission's filtering function, enabling applicants to bring their cases directly before the Court. The ECtHR has jurisdiction over any allegation of violation of the ECHR committed by any one of the forty-seven state parties. Differently from the UNTBs, the ECtHR issues legally binding judgments for its member states. This factor significantly reinforces the authority of the Court in the view of the applicants, being often a guarantee for efficiency and effectiveness.[98]

Under the aegis of the CoE, the ECSR is required to monitor and enforce the European Social Charter and to consider collective complaints about violations of the Charter by the state parties. However, the conclusions of the ECSR are not binding for the states, unless the Committee of Ministers, a clear political body, decides to give them a binding force on a case-by-case basis.[99]

[97] Paolo Carrozza and Dinah Shelton (eds), *Regional Protection of Human Rights* (Oxford University Press, 2013), 13–48.

[98] ibid, 20.

[99] For a detailed explanation of the functioning of the European Committee of Social Rights see David John Harris and John Darcy, *The European Social Charter*, 2nd ed. (Transnational Publishers, 2001) and Oliver De Schutter (ed), *The European Social Charter: A Social Constitution for Europe* (Bruylant, 2010).

Within the European Union machinery, the only judicial enforcement body is the European Court of Justice (ECJ). While not explicitly dedicated to human rights, it has recently moved more and more to the interpretation and application of human rights provisions, both belonging to the EU's *corpus legi* and the ECHR's one.[100]

1.3.2.3 American Human Rights Institutions

MONITORING BODIES In the Americas, the structure is similar. The Organization of American States is the main regional body on international affairs with competence on human rights as well. Its Secretary General and the General Assembly, both highly political bodies, can play a key role in fostering human rights in the region.[101]

The monitoring functions are mainly delegated to the Inter-American Commission on Human Rights (IACommHR), an expert body that establishes Special Rapporteurs and working groups for monitoring specific issues or countries. Furthermore, under the coordination of the IACommHR, there are specific monitoring bodies such as the Inter-American Commission of Women and the Committee for the Elimination of All Forms of Discrimination against Persons with Disabilities.[102]

JUDICIAL AND QUASI-JUDICIAL ENFORCEMENT BODIES The ACHR established, in its Chapter VII, an Inter-American Commission on Human Rights to 'promote the respect and [to] defen[d] human rights'.[103] Among its functions, it can take actions following petitions and communication received by '*any person, group of persons or any nongovernmental entity* [...] containing denunciations or complaints of violation of [the] Convention by a State Party'.[104] The Commission began functioning in 1960 with quasi-judicial functions, issuing non-binding views. However, Chapter VIII ACHR envisages also the establishment of a Court, the Inter-American Court of Human Rights. Granted full judicial powers and composed by independent judges, the IACtHR can hear any case submitted by a state party or by the Commission

[100] Javaid Rehman, *International Human Rights Law*, 2nd ed. (Pearson, 2010), 248–251.
[101] Par Engstrom and Courtney Hillebrecht (eds), *The Inter-American Human Rights System: The Law and Politics of Institutional Change* (Routledge, 2020).
[102] Carrozza and Shelton, *Regional Human Rights*, 55–64.
[103] ACHR, Article 41.
[104] ibid, Article 44 (emphasis added).

against any state that accepts its jurisdiction.[105] Differently from those of the Commission, the judgments of the Court are legally binding. Moreover, the Protocol of San Salvador on economic, social and cultural rights extended the jurisdiction of the Commission and the Court to the social and economic rights contained therein.[106]

1.3.2.4 African Human Rights Institutions

MONITORING BODIES The African human rights institutional framework very much mirrors that of the Americas. Within the African Union (AU), the Assembly of the Union and the Executive Council are political bodies representing the member states. Worth mentioning is also the Pan-African Parliament, which is democratically elected by the citizens of the member states and may have a boosting and policy-making role for enhancing human rights in the continent.[107]

The African Commission on Human and Peoples' Rights (ACommHPR) has the duty to monitor the African Charter and other regional human rights provisions. Like the IACommHR, the ACommHPR also can establish Special Rapporteurs, Working Groups and Committees. In addition, a specific Committee on the Rights and Welfare of the Child has been established to enforce the respective Charter.[108]

JUDICIAL AND QUASI-JUDICIAL BODIES The ACommHPR also has quasi-judicial functions and until recently was the only enforcement body available.[109] However, in 2004, the African Court on Human and Peoples' Rights (ACtHPR)

[105] The states recognising the jurisdiction of the Court are twenty-two. Data available at www.cidh.org/Basicos/English/Basic4.Amer.Conv.Ratif.htm, last accessed 10 February 2022.

[106] Additional Protocol to the American Convention on Human Rights in the area of Economic, Social and Cultural Rights 'Protocol of San Salvador', San Salvador, 1978, English version available at www.oas.org/juridico/english/treaties/a-52.html, last accessed 10 February 2022. As of today only 16 countries ratified it.

[107] Morris Kiwinda Mbondenyi, *International Human Rights and Their Enforcement in Africa* (LawAfrica Publisher Ltd, 2011), 285; Bonolo Ramadi Dinokopila, 'The Pan-African Parliament and African Union Human Rights Actors, Civil Society and National Human Rights Institutions: The Importance of Collaboration' (2013) 13 *African Human Rights Law Journal* 302.

[108] African Charter on the Rights and Welfare of the Child, adopted on 1 July 1990 and entered into force on 29 November 1999, available at www.au.int/en/treaties, last accessed 10 February 2022.

[109] Frans Viljoen, *International Human Rights Law in Africa* (Oxford University Press, 2012), 288–466.

entered into force. Applications to the Court may be made by the ACommHPR or other African intergovernmental organisations, by states who have lodged (or against whom has been lodged) a complaint before the Commission and by states whose citizen is a victim of a human rights violation. Applications may also be submitted directly by individuals and by NGOs with Observer Status before the African Commission, however only against those states who have made a specific declaration.[110] The Court issues binding judgments for its state parties, significantly strengthening the enforcement procedures in the African system. Moreover, the African Court has a wide jurisdiction. Article 3, Additional Protocol reads, '[T]he jurisdiction of the Court shall extend to all cases and disputes submitted to it concerning the interpretation and application of the Charter, this Protocol and *any other relevant Human Rights instrument* ratified by the States concerned'.[111] It is certainly a *unicum* for a regional human rights body to have such an extended jurisdiction over international instruments, as explored in Chapter 4. However, it should be underlined that only a few states ratified the Protocol so far, thus giving the Court jurisdiction over only twenty-four states.[112]

1.3.2.5 Other Regional and Sub-regional Human Rights Institutions

In addition, even less developed human rights regional systems have their own institutions. For example, the ASEAN established an Intergovernmental Commission on Human Rights, and the Arab League recently approved the statute of an Arab Court for Human Rights.[113]

Furthermore, there are also sub-regional judicial bodies that, even without an explicit human rights mandate, monitor the compliance of their member states with international and regional human rights obligations. An example is the rich sub-regional African system including the East African Court of Justice (EACJ), the Southern African Development Community (SADC) and Tribunal and the ECOWAS Community Court of Justice.[114] The recent

[110] ibid, 426–434.

[111] Article 3, Protocol to the African Charter on Human and Peoples' Rights on the Establishment of the African Court on Human and Peoples' Rights, 9 June 1998, English version available at www.achpr.org/instruments/court-establishment/#3, last accessed 10 February 2022 (emphasis added).

[112] For the status of signature, accession and ratification of the Protocol see www.achpr.org/instruments/court-establishment/#3, last accessed 10 February 2022.

[113] Joe Stork, 'New Arab Human Rights Court Is Doomed from the Start', *International Business Times*, 26 November 2014.

[114] Solomon T. Ebobrah, 'Litigating Human Rights Before Sub-Regional Courts in Africa: Prospects and Challenges' (2009) 17 *African Journal of International and Comparative Law* 79;

development of these bodies brought to the attention the occurring of overlapping jurisdictions,[115] which facilitate the emergence of contrasting interpretations and application of similar or same provisions.

1.4 FRAGMENTATION AND CONVERGENCE VERSUS RELATIVISM AND UNIVERSALITY: A RECONCILING UNDERSTANDING

1.4.1 *The Debate on Universality and Relativism of Human Rights*

One of the defining elements of human rights is their universality. Yet, scholars and practitioners have long debated over the meaning and application of this concept to human rights, without reaching a conclusion. The 1948 Universal Declaration of Human Rights considers, even in the title, universality as a foundation for human rights and the 1993 Vienna Declaration reiterated its importance by affirming that 'all human rights are universal, indivisible, interdependent and interrelated'.[116]

Yet, the understanding of what this universality entails, and, consequently, whether it should be pursued and wished for, has been at the centre of a long-standing debate. While a detailed discussion of the meaning and value of universality goes beyond the scope of this book, I will briefly recall the main elements of the current debate on the matter to understand how it relates to judicial convergence and fragmentation.

The Oxford Dictionary defines universal as 'of or belonging to or done by all persons or things in the world or in the class concerned, applicable to all cases', thus invoking the concept of all-inclusiveness. This would mean that universal human rights are to be applied to everyone (universal application *ratione personae*) and everywhere (universal application *ratione loci*) and are, therefore, linked to the principle of equality and non-discrimination.[117] Other scholars respond with a formal or functional definition. The former considers that human rights are universal if all (or almost all) states in the world have formally accepted human rights obligations through the ratification of

Solomon T Ebobrah, 'Human Rights Developments in African Sub-Regional Economic Communities during 2012' (2013) 13 *African Human Rights Law Journal* 178.

[115] This is the case, for instance, of some African countries that are party of sub-regional, regional and UN conventions as well as under the jurisdiction of the respective enforcement bodies.

[116] Vienna Declaration and Programme of Action Adopted by the World Conference on Human Rights in Vienna on 25 June 1993, Part I, 5.

[117] Jack Donnelly, *Universal Human Rights in Theory and Practice* (Cornell University Press, 1989), 1.

international treaties and conventions.[118] On the contrary, the functional definition considers that human rights need to be universal to be recognised and respected by states. Therefore, universality in this case is the needed attribute to human rights for them to be effective and, in the words of Donnelly, to provide 'attractive remedies for some of the most pressing systemic threats to human dignity'.[119]

These definitions are not forcibly in contrast with each other, but they could lead to different conclusions when challenged by opposite claims. Indeed, in addition to the challenges of its definition, the concept of universality of human rights has received significant backlash from critical theories, claiming that its origin and foundations were biased and a representation of a limited vision and approach. One of the main critiques moved to the principle of universality of human rights is that of cultural relativism. This focuses on the fact that human rights are historically a Western conception and have been codified as such in a Western-dominated and imperialistic world. Therefore, they do not really reflect a 'universal' understanding of which rights should be granted to human beings across the globe. Cultural relativism relies on the assumption that there is an infinite cultural variability and it is impossible to use absolute paradigms to judge behaviours, as they are only valid within a specific culture.[120] According to cultural relativists, the universality of human rights is a way to impose a specific set of values (in particular western values) to other peoples.[121] As such, universality should be set aside in favour of a pluralistic conception of different culture-based human rights understandings.

Similar concerns about the non-inclusiveness of human rights as historically developed and codified, and perpetrated through the idea of universality,

[118] Clarence Dias, 'The Universality of Human Rights: A Critique' (1993) 103 *Lokayan Bulletin* 44; Catherine Powell, 'Symposium in Celebration of the Fiftieth Anniversary of the Universal Declaration of Human Rights, Introduction: Locating Culture, Identity and Human Rights' (1990) *Columbia Human Rights Law Review* 206; Louis Henkin, 'The Universality of the Concept of Human Rights' (1989) *The Annals of the American Academy of Political and Social Science* 506, 10–16.

[119] Jack Donnelly, 'The Relative Universality of Human Rights'(2007) 29 *Human Rights Quarterly* 2, 281–306, 288.

[120] Abdullahi Ahmed An-Na'im, 'Islam and Human Rights: Beyond the Universality Debate' (2000) 94 *American Society of International Law Proceedings* 95; Arati Rao, 'The Politics of Gender and Culture in International Human Rights Discourse' in Julie Peters and Andrea Wolper (eds), *Women's Rights, Human Rights: International Feminist Perspectives* (Routledge, 1995), 167–175; Paul W. Kahn, *The Cultural Study of Law: Reconstructing Legal Scholarship* (Chicago University Press, 1999).

[121] See, among others, Ferdinand Teson, 'International Human Rights Law and Cultural Relativity' (1985) 25 *Vanderbilt Journal of International Law* 869, 893.

has also been raised by feminist, queer and LGBTQI scholars.[122] In particular, as Otto points out, the affirmation of an unquestionable universality has resulted in a dominance of the rights of first generation and an acceptance of lower standards for the further generation rights. This has slowed the affirmation of the rights of non-dominant groups (women, indigenous people, LGBTQI communities, etc.) and has erased the critiques from those scholars 'on the margins of modernity'.[123]

The two concepts of universality and relativism seem to be impossible to reconcile. However, some scholars have attempted to understand how they can be conceptualised not in conflict with each other. For instance, Nathan used the language of tempered universalism[124] or Brems that of inclusive universality,[125] to accommodate the instances of both sides and show that a reconciliation is possible. Henkin argues that the idea of human rights is undoubtedly universally accepted, politically and legally, while the single human rights (e.g. freedom of expression or prohibition of discrimination) are not. Yet, he does not consider that the latter affects the former.[126] Likewise, Donnelly introduced the concept of 'relative universality'.[127] This describes a scenario where human rights are universal at the concept level, but they are more 'particular' at the level of conception and inevitably more relative and diversified at the level of implementation. Such an understanding could support a harmonised view of the two concepts where universality and relativism are two sides of the same coin and, instead of threatening each other, they complement and strengthen each other. However, not everyone is convinced by this reconciliation attempt. Goodhart, for instance, has suggested abandoning the terminology of universality and relativism altogether to improve the human rights debate.[128] Similar critical voices, such as the one of Otto, point out that the traditional debate between universality and cultural relativism has been 'fuelled by competing versions of capitalism rather than by a desire to

[122] Po-Han Lee, 'LGBT Rights versus Asian Values: De/re-constructing the Universality of Human Rights' (2016) 20 *The International Journal of Human Rights* 7, 978–992; Anne Orford (ed), *International Law and Its Others* (Cambridge University Press, 2006).

[123] Diane Otto, 'Rethinking the Universality of Human Rights Law' (1997) 29 *Columbia Human Rights Law Review* 1, 3.

[124] Andrew J. Nathan, 'Universalism: A Particularistic Account' in Lynda S. Bell, Andrew J. Nathan and Ilan Peleg (eds), *Negotiating Culture and Human Rights* (Columbia University Press, 2001), chapter 13.

[125] Eva Brems, *Human Rights: Universality and Diversity* (Kluwer Law International, 2001).

[126] Henkin, 'The Universality of the Concept of Human Rights'.

[127] Donnelly, 'The Relative Universality of Human Rights'.

[128] Michael Goodhart, 'Neither Relative nor Universal: A Response to Donnelly' (2008) 30 *Human Rights Quarterly* 1, 189–193.

address issues of cultural diversity' and had the only merit of reproducing 'a masculinist narrative of legitimation' to the detriment of women and marginalised groups.[129] Yet, she argues in favour of a transformative universality, based on the acknowledgement of the post-structuralist nature of human rights and their conception and understanding as a continuous dialogue.[130]

1.4.2 *What Is the Relationship between Convergence and Fragmentation and Universalisms and Relativism?*

In light of this debate on universality versus relativism, the next question to answer is what is their relationship with convergence and fragmentation. Simply stating that convergence equals universality and fragmentation relativism would be an excessive simplification.

Whatever the definition and understanding of universality, it is undoubted that the more convergence we have within IHRL, the more the claim for universality is confirmed and supported, showing that human rights are applied and interpreted uniformly across the globe. Likewise, judicial fragmentation could be seen as the result of different local understanding of human rights, influenced by social, religious, cultural and historical factors, thus fostering the idea of relative human rights in time and space. That said, one should reflect on the level and scope of these two sets of concepts. Universality and relativism operate at a theoretical and conceptual level, as a sort of regulatory principles. On the contrary, convergence and fragmentation are rather operational and practical descriptions of judicial phenomena, that is, convergent or contrasting judgments between two or more bodies. Nevertheless, they may suggest some changes in what we consider universal due to the dynamic and continuing evolving nature of what it means. If we have convergence of case-law on a specific interpretation of IHRL that diverges from its 'universal' understanding, this may suggest that we need to change what we believe is universal. Therefore, I believe that the simple equivalence between the two set of terms and the attempt to use the study of convergence and fragmentation to bolster universality or relativism's view is not accurate but, even more importantly, is counterproductive and pointless. Indeed, the approach suggested by Donnelly of reconciling universality and relativism through an understanding of both being fundamental pieces in the IHRL deployment in practice is much more convincing and fitting to the debate on convergence and fragmentation. Universality, hence convergence,

[129] Otto, 'Rethinking the Universality of Human Rights Law', 6–15.
[130] ibid.

understood in a transformative and dynamic way as suggested by Otto, should remain a general regulatory concept to guide IHRL interpretation but relativism and fragmentation could, and should, well arise when needed to respond to specific local needs and to ensure that IHRL delivers on its goal to protect and promote human rights.

CONCLUSION

The extensive scholarly debate on fragmentation in IL suggests that fragmentation could equally spread to IHRL. The previous analysis shows that the IHRL framework offers a fertile ground for fragmentation to arise due to the significant proliferation of human rights norms and institutions both at the international and at the regional level. Despite this proliferation of normative frameworks, normative fragmentation does not appear to be as alarming as one could have expected. This is mainly due to the vagueness and broadness of the text of most human rights provisions that may equally bring convergence or fragmentation depending on the interpretation given to them. It follows that the role of adjudicatory bodies becomes key and their proliferation may further increase the likelihood of judicial fragmentation possibly leading to adverse consequences both for the IHRL system and for the individuals' protection. The following chapter will assess whether these concerns about judicial fragmentation in IHRL are actually confirmed or if, instead, the regional and international adjudicatory bodies bring convergence with their interpretations.

2

Assessing and Exploring Judicial Fragmentation in International Human Rights Law

INTRODUCTION

Chapter 1 concluded that the proliferation of adjudicatory bodies increases the likelihood of judicial fragmentation in IHRL but its existence is still to be proven in practice. A perusal of the case-law of regional and international human rights adjudicatory bodies will reveal that the concerns and worries about fragmentation in IHRL are widely exaggerated and that judicial fragmentation is only marginally affecting IHRL.

This chapter attempts to assess the current trend of judicial fragmentation and convergence in IHRL, identifying the cases where convergence prevails and those where fragmentation arises instead. In order to make such an assessment, Section 2.1 sums up the underlying case-law analysis carried out (available in Appendix 2) and presents some representative cases of situations where fragmentation was to be expected, but convergence ultimately prevailed. Subsequently, Section 2.2 explores in depth the cases where judicial fragmentation has taken place, pointing out causes and features.

2.1 ASSESSING JUDICIAL FRAGMENTATION IN IHRL

There are several ways to assess the extent of judicial fragmentation currently affecting IHRL, each bearing its own merits and limits. Studies so far have been focusing on the UN treaty bodies, the International Court of Justice (ICJ), regional human rights bodies and national courts.[1] To reflect the

[1] Mads Andenas and Eirik Bjorge, *A Farewell to Fragmentation: Reassertion and Convergence in International Law* (Cambridge University Press, 2015) and in particular the chapters by Sir Nigel Rodely, 'The International Court of Justice and Human Rights Treaty Bodies', 87–108; Vera Gowlland-Debbas, 'The ICJ and the Challenges of Human Rights Law', 109–145; Dean Spielmann, 'Fragmentation or Partnership? The Reception of ICJ Case-Law by the European

complexity of IHRL, the key role played by regional bodies and the tension between a possible relative/regional understanding of human rights and a universal/international one, this book examines the judgments and views of the three regional human rights systems' courts and the United Nations Human Rights Committee (HRC). In particular, this study focuses on the European Court of Human Rights (ECtHR), the Inter-American Court of Human Rights (IACtHR) and both the African Court on Human and Peoples' Rights (ACtHPR) and the African Commission on Human and Peoples' Rights (ACommHPR). The decision to include the ACommHPR is motivated by the lower number and variety of judgments issued by the ACtHPR to date, compared to the European and Inter-American counterparts.[2]

Assuming that judicial fragmentation was a widespread phenomenon affecting IHRL, the initial aim of this study was to identify the cases of judicial fragmentation arising between all four jurisdictions and pick a few of them to analyse in detail. Bearing this in mind, the first methodological choice was to focus only on those rights that had been addressed by at least one of the two African bodies. As the African bodies were the institutions that had produced the most limited case-law, this was the most logical decision to coherently restrict the scope of analysis, thus maintaining the possibility of a full comparison between all four jurisdictions. Following this methodological approach, this research focused on a wide-ranging list of twelve rights. It includes the rights to life, to fair trial, to property, to liberty and security, to family, to equality; the prohibition of torture and discrimination; the freedom of expression, thought and religion, association and movement; and the rights and duties of state parties.

As shown in Appendix 2, each right has been individually scrutinised, comparing the four jurisdictions, first in relation to the text of the articles (confirming the substantial normative convergence established in Chapter 1) and then taking into consideration the leading and most important judgments and views that set the reference standards for the judicial interpretation by

Court of Human Rights', 173–190; Mehrdad Payandeh, 'Fragmentation within International Human Rights Law', 297–319. See also Marjan Ajevski (ed), *Fragmentation in International Human Rights Law: Beyond Conflict of Laws* (Routledge, 2017); Carla M. Buckley, Alice Donald and Philip Leach (eds), *Towards Convergence in International Human Rights Law: Approaches of Regional and International Systems* (Brill-Nijhoff, 2017); Eva Brems and Saïla Ouald-Chaib (eds) *Fragmentation and Integration in Human Rights Law* (Edward Elgar, 2018).

2 Especially at the beginning of this research in 2014.

each of the five bodies under analysis.[3] More than 200 cases have been examined together with an extensive literature review on the matter with the help of case-law collections and handbooks on regional and international human rights law.

The hypothesis was that, especially for the most sensitive and controversial rights such as those involving cultural and religious concerns or the need to balance rights and interests, different human rights bodies were adopting contrasting interpretations in their adjudicatory functions, mirroring their international or regional specificities. However, this initial study refuted this assumption. The table of rights produced after this first stage of research revealed a general similarity and a substantial convergence between the judicial interpretation of human rights in the four jurisdictions,[4] and suggested the need to deepen the analysis to find some cases of fragmentation.

This led to the identification of some specific issues within the twelve general rights where the initial analysis showed that the substantial similarity and convergence were less stable and uncontroversial. However, in these cases, it was not possible to maintain the criterion of a comparison between all four jurisdictions, and it was necessary to also include situations where only two bodies expressed their opinion on the matter. Among these specific matters, some confirmed the convergence of case-law regardless of a few

[3] Although the four jurisdictions are not all bound by the principle of judicial precedent, it is still possible to identify the leading judgments of each body for single issues of law. They are identified as the most important judgments that set the law upon some specific points and have been repeatedly cited and referred to in subsequent similar judgments by the same and other bodies. This approach is the same adopted by well-established handbooks and collections of case law such as David Harris, Michael O'Boyle, Edward Bates and Carla Buckley, *Harris, O'Boyle and Warbrick: Law of the European Convention on Human Rights* (Oxford University Press, 2009); Yogesh Tyagi, *The UN Human Rights Committee: Practice and Procedure* (Cambridge University Press, 2011) and Laurence Bourgorgue-Larsen (ed), *The Inter-American Court of Human Rights: Case-Law and Commentary* (Oxford University Press, 2011). However, for the lack of a binding precedent rule, proper of common law systems, there could be additional different judgments and views that differ from those considered 'leading' and taken into consideration here. While all efforts have been made in order to include in the analysis any possible relevant interpretation, it is still possible that some discordant outcomes are missing in the current analysis.

[4] Substantial convergence has been found, for example, on the application of the right to fair trial. Together with a very similar text of the relevant articles, the interpretation by the judicial and quasi-judicial bodies confirmed the equal understanding of the common guarantees for a fair trial. cf Y.L. *v. Canada*, Communication no 112/1981 (HRC, 8 April 1986); *Weiss v. Austria*, Communication no 1086/2002 (HRC, 2002); *Golder v. UK*, Application no 4451/70 (ECtHR, 21 February 1975); *Airey v. Ireland*, Application no 6289/73 (ECtHR, 9 October 1979); *Dacosta Cadogan v. Barbados* (IACtHR, 24 September 2009). The same is true for the right to equality, political participation and education.

elements that may suggest the contrary, while others revealed a clear situation of fragmentation. The following sections explore both these examples, assessing the complexity of convergence and fragmentation. These matters include the beginning of the right to life linked to the so-called reproductive rights, the use of lethal force by public officials, the definition of what constitutes torture or inhuman and degrading treatment and punishments, the definition of arbitrary detention, the limitation of freedom of expression based on hate speech and on defamation, the freedom of assembly, the prohibition of discrimination based on sexual orientation, the freedom to manifest religion, the right to property for indigenous people and the right to marry for same-sex couples. As the aim of this chapter is to give a general overview of the current convergence and fragmentation scenario in IHRL, the details in the analysis of each issue and right will be reasonably limited to offer a wider range of examples. This section only presents a general overview of the seven convergent issues, while Section 2.2 will contain a detailed analysis of the three issues where judicial fragmentation arose, in order to better understand its features and triggering factors.

In light of the above considerations, the following overview does not aim at being exhaustive and covering all possible cases of fragmentation within IHRL. I acknowledge that adopting a different approach to case selection would possibly lead to the identification of other cases of fragmentation. Nevertheless, the examination of the identified cases of fragmentation allows further exploration of the factors that can explain convergence and fragmentation, as discussed in Part II.

2.1.1 *The Right to Life*

At first glance, the right to life seems to have all the features that can trigger judicial fragmentation. There are several controversial issues in the interpretation of this right, such as when life begins or the use of lethal force by public officials. Within the so-called reproductive rights lies the unresolved question of when life begins and, thus, from which exact moment it should be protected as such. This fundamental determination is highly debated and, as in the case of abortion, influenced by cultural, religious and political beliefs.[5]

[5] Christina Zampas and Jaome M. Gher, 'Abortion as a Human Right: International and Regional Standards' (2008) 8(2) *Human Rights Law Review* 249–294; Michael J. Perry, *Toward a Theory of Human Rights: Religion, Law, Courts* (Cambridge University Press, 2006), 52–64; Joanna N. Erdman, 'Theorizing Time in Abortion Law and Human Rights' (2017) 19(1) *Health and Human Rights Journal* 29–40; Rachel Rebouchè, 'Abortion Rights as Human Rights' (2016) 25(6) *Social & Legal Studies* 765–782; Carole J. Petersen, 'Reproductive Justice, Public

Therefore, one may expect that regional and international human rights bodies adopt contrasting positions on the matter. Yet, this is not the case. While keeping their own approach, the HRC, the IACtHR and the ECtHR all recognise that there is no absolute right to life before birth, since such a right must be balanced with the rights of the mother.[6] In cases where the mother has been a victim of rape or violence or where her health and well-being are at stake, all the bodies mentioned above held that abortion does not constitute a violation of the right to life.[7] Regarding all the other circumstances where the right to life of an unborn child could be claimed, none of the regional or international bodies has proposed a definitive and final interpretation. The IACtHR acknowledged the lack of evidence to support the thesis that the embryo should be considered 'a person' and the absence of an agreed definition on when life begins.[8] As such, it found it impossible to adopt one single definition without imposing a 'specific type of belief on others who do not share them'.[9] This conclusion allows the IACtHR to adapt its approach on a case-by-case basis. Similarly, the ECtHR ruled that 'it is neither desirable nor even possible as matters stand, to answer in the abstract the question whether the unborn child is a person for the purposes of Article 2 of the Convention'.[10] Therefore, in cases of abortion 'on demand' states should be granted a wide margin of appreciation in determining when the right to life begins.[11] Looking at these two cases, one could conclude that the two bodies adopt different approaches in addressing the matter, one opting for a case-by-case analysis and

Policy, and Abortion on the Basis of Fetal Impairment: Lessons from International Human Rights Law and the Potential Impact of the Convention on the Rights of Persons with Disabilities' (2015) 28 *Journal of Law and Health* 121–163.

6 *K.L. v Peru*, Communication no 1153/03 (HRC, 24 October 2005); *LMR v Argentina*, Communication no 1608/07 (HRC, 28 April 2011); *Baby Boy*, Case no 2141 (IACommHR, 6 March 1981); *Artavia Murillo et al. ("in vitro fertilization") v Costa Rica* (IACtHR, 28 November 2012); *Paton v. UK*, Application no 8416/79 (ECommHR, 1980); *VO v. France*, Application no 53924/00 (ECtHR, 8 July 2004).

7 The European Court of Human Rights consistently held that legal abortion should be allowed and provided in these cases. On the health of the mother see *Tysiaç v. Poland*, Application no 5410/03 (ECtHR, 20 March 2007); on the health of the foetus, see *R.R. v. Poland*, Application no 27617/04 (ECtHR, 26 May 2011); on pregnancy caused by rape or violence see *P. and S. v. Poland*, Application no 57375/08 (ECtHR, 30 October 2012). Similarly, see the HRC in *LMR v. Argentina*, Communication no 1608/07 (HRC, 28 April 2011) or in *Mellet v. Ireland*, Communication no 2324/13 (HRC, 31 March 2016).

8 *Artavia Murillo*, IACtHR, 224–244.

9 ibid, 185.

10 *VO*, ECtHR, 85.

11 Grégor Puppinck, 'Abortion and the European Convention on Human Rights' (2013) 3 *Irish Journal of Legal Studies* 142, 150. See Chapter 6 on the impact of the use of the margin of appreciation on convergence and fragmentation.

the other relying on the margin of appreciation doctrine.[12] Nonetheless, they both abstain from elaborating a strict interpretative attitude or providing an ultimate definition of 'person' for the sake of application of the right to life. Such an approach leaves a wide margin of interpretation on a case-by-case basis and avoids, for the moment, judicial fragmentation.

The same overall common approach among regional and international bodies can be found on the issue of the use of lethal force by public authorities. Here, the ECtHR, the IACtHR and the HRC developed their own practical tests to assess whether the killing of a person, as a consequence of an action undertaken by public police authority, constitutes a breach of the right to life. A superficial reading of the judgments may trick one into thinking that each body is addressing the issue in their own specific way, due to a different use of the language and a focus on some terms rather than others.[13] Yet, a more in-depth analysis reveals the opposite. For instance, they all identify the principles of legality, precaution, proportionality, necessity and accountability as the key factors in assessing a violation of the right to life. It is generally recognised that, in order not to constitute a violation of the right to life, any action carried out by a public official should be necessary and proportionate to the pursuit of a legitimate aim, such as self-defence or defence of the life of others. The notion of necessity and proportionality is then crucial in assessing the occurrence of a violation of the right to life, and it would not be a surprise to see different interpretations by each judicial body.[14] However, this is just a different use of language and terminology.

In the landmark case of the HRC on the matter, *Guerrero v. Colombia*, the Committee limited its analysis to the acknowledgement that

> the deprivation of life by authorities of the State is a matter of the utmost gravity. . . . The requirements that the right shall be protected by law and that no one shall be arbitrarily deprived of his life mean that the law must strictly control and limit the circumstances in which a person may be deprived of his life by the authorities of a State.[15]

In applying this principle to the facts of the case concerning the killing of seven people during a hostage rescuing operation, the HRC simply noted that

[12] See Chapter 6.

[13] cf *Guerrero v. Colombia*, Communication no 45/1979 (HRC, 31 March 1982); *McCann and Others v. United Kingdom*, Application no 18984/91 (ECtHR, 27 September 1995); *Nachova and Others v. Bulgaria*, Application no 43577/98 and 43579/98 (ECtHR, 6 July 2005); *Montero Aranguren et al. (Detention Center of Catia) v. Venezuela* (IACtHR, 5 July 2006).

[14] See Chapter 5.

[15] *Guerrero*, HRC, 13.1.

'the police action was apparently taken without any warning to the victims and without giving them any opportunity to surrender to the police patrol or to offer any explanation of their presence or intentions [and] [t]here is no evidence that the action of the police was necessary'.[16]

In *McCann and Others v. United Kingdom*, and in following similar cases like *Nachova and Others v. Bulgaria*, the ECtHR went deeper in its analysis of the interpretation of Article 2, but it ultimately adopted the same approach of the HRC. It held that an exception to the right to life should be 'absolutely necessary', to be interpreted in 'a stricter and more compelling' way than when applying the requirement of 'necessary in a democratic society'.[17] In light of the above, 'the circumstances in which deprivation of life may be justified must be strictly construed'.[18] In applying these considerations to the facts of the cases, the ECtHR also stressed the duty of the state to 'minimise the risk of loss of life'[19] by providing clear legal rules and adequate training to the law enforcement officers. Moreover, the Court clarified the high standard of the 'absolute necessity' criterion by observing, in *McCann*, that the justification of the use of lethal force in the case was only '"reasonably justifiable" as opposed to "absolutely necessary" in paragraph 2 of Article 2'.[20]

The IACtHR, in similar cases such as the *Detention Centre of Catia* case, also invoked the same principle of 'absolute necessity'.[21] Here, the IACtHR confirmed that the use of force by state agents may be allowed only in 'exceptional circumstances and should be planned and proportionally limited by the government authorities [...] [and] can only be used once all other methods of control have been exhausted and failed'. Moreover, the 'intentional use of firearms may only be made when strictly unavoidable in order to protect life'[22] and should always be 'reasonable, restricted and controlled'.[23]

On the same page, the African Commission in *Acutan and Amnesty International v. Malawi* found a violation of the right to life because the shooting of peaceful protesters on strike by the police forces was 'arbitrary'.[24]

[16] ibid, 13.2.
[17] *McCann and Others*, ECtHR, 149.
[18] *Nachova and Others*, ECtHR, 94.
[19] ibid, 103.
[20] *McCann and Others*, ECtHR, 154. See Chapter 5, Section 5.1.2.2.
[21] *Detention Center of Catia*, IACtHR, 123.
[22] ibid, 69.
[23] *Zembrano-Velez et al. v. Ecuador* (IACtHR, 4 July 2007), 76. Also worth mentioning is the extensive use by the IACtHR of references to the ECtHR to support the main reasoning of this judgment. Judicial dialogue will be analysed in detail in Chapter 3.
[24] *Acutan and Amnesty International v. Malawi*, Communication no 64/92 (ACommHPR, 1995), 6.

In conclusion, although one could have expected different standards in assessing when the deadly use of force by state officials constitutes a violation of the right to life, all the human rights bodies converged on the understanding that such a force should be used only in extreme circumstances and when no other option is available. Whether labelled 'absolutely necessary', 'not arbitrarily' or 'strictly motivated', the application in the case-law shows that regional and international human rights bodies share a common approach towards this issue, thereby preventing fragmentation.

2.1.2 *The Prohibition of Torture, Cruel, Inhuman and Degrading Treatments*

Another situation where one may expect the presence of judicial fragmentation due to the controversial definition of the terms is the distinction between what constitutes an act of torture, or degrading, cruel and inhuman treatments and punishments.[25]

However, all the bodies agree on the key elements of torture, and the only difference could be spotted in the fact that the ECtHR went further and distinguished between 'cruel', 'inhuman' and 'degrading' treatments or punishments, while the other bodies refrain from operating such a granular distinction. For instance, in *Kudla v. Poland*, the ECtHR 'considered [a] treatment to be "inhuman" because, inter alia, it was premeditated, was applied for hours at a stretch and caused either actual bodily injury or intense physical or mental suffering'.[26] In the same judgment, the ECtHR defined a treatment as degrading when it is 'such as to arouse in the victims feeling of fear, anguish and inferiority capable of humiliating and debasing them'.[27]

Conversely, the IACtHR, despite often making reference to the case-law of the European counterpart and adopting its reasoning, never operated such distinction.[28] The same approach can be found in the case-law of the HRC, which did not consider it necessary to establish sharp distinctions between the different kinds of punishments or treatments.[29] Likewise, the African

[25] See *Soering v. UK*, Application no 14038/88 (ECtHR, 7 July 1989); *Aksoy v. Turkey*, Application no 21987/93 (ECtHR, 18 December 1996); *Selmouni v. France*, Application no 25803/94 (ECtHR, 28 July 1999); *Curtis Francis Doebbler v. Sudan*, Communication no 236/2000 (ACommHPR, 2003); HRC, General Comment No. 20, 10/03/92 CCPR.

[26] *Kudla v. Poland*, Application no 30210/96 (ECtHR, 26 October 2000), 92.

[27] ibid.

[28] *Loyaza-Tamayo v. Peru* (IACtHR, 17 September 1997).

[29] cf HRC, General Comment No. 20/44 (2 April 1992), cited by Malcolm D. Evans and Rod Morgan, *Preventing Torture: A Study of the European Convention for the Prevention of Torture and Inhuman or Degrading Treatment or Punishment* (Diane, 1998), 76.

Commission preferred to invoke all the Acts prohibited by Article 5 ACHPR without distinction between cruel, inhuman and degrading treatments.[30] However, distinguishing between the different categories or considering all of them as equivalent proved to have no impact on the outcome of the judgment, remaining just a label distinction. Moreover, all these human rights bodies, including the ECtHR, decided to abstain from providing an ultimate and rigid definition of the different categories, adopting a very flexible approach towards categorisation.

Nevertheless, they all have been extremely careful in drawing a line between cruel, inhuman and degrading treatments/punishments and torture, with the latter characterised by a higher degree of intensity, gravity and intent.[31] In *Ireland v. United Kingdom*, the ECtHR defined torture as a 'deliberate inhuman treatment causing very serious and cruel suffering', stressing the importance of the intensity of the act and interpreting 'deliberate' as 'intentional'.[32] The IACtHR followed the reasoning of the ECtHR and in *Loyaza Tamayo* held that torture could be differentiated from the other acts on the basis of severity.[33] On the same page, the HRC labelled as torture those acts that had a higher level of intensity or severity, yet without providing a final definition,[34] an approach that was mirrored by the African Commission.[35]

These blurred definitions leave a wide margin of discretion to each body to make distinctions based on any criteria they deem relevant for their determination. Such flexibility in defining one or the other act could generate confusion and inconsistency among different bodies and even within the case-law of a single institution. For instance, the IACtHR in *Velasquez Rodriguez v. Honduras* found that prolonged isolations, an inherent part of an enforced disappearance, constitute cruel and inhuman treatments. On the contrary, in *Castillo Paez v. Peru*, the same Court concluded that these acts were *only* disrespectful to human dignity and did not amount to cruel, inhuman and

30 *Malawi African Association, Amnesty International, Ms Sarr Diop, Union interafricaine des droits de l'homme and RADDHO, Collectif des veuves et ayants-droit, Association mauritanienne des droits de l'homme v. Mauritania*, Communications No. 54/91-61/91-96/93-98/93-164/97-196/97-210/98 (ACommHPR, 11 May 2000), 115–118.

31 ibid; *Loyaza-Tamayo*, IACtHR and *Aksoy*, ECtHR.

32 *Ireland v. United Kingdom*, Application no 5310/71, 18 January 1978, 167.

33 *Loyaza-Tamayo*, IACtHR, 57.

34 See *Rodríguez v. Uruguay*, Communication no 322/1988 (HRC, 9 August 1994) or *Massera v. Uruguay*, Communication no 5/1977 (HRC, 15 August 1979).

35 See, among others, *Sudan Human Rights Organization and Center for Housing Rights and Evictions v. Sudan*, Communications nos 279/03–296/05 (ACommHPR, 27 May 2009), 156, 255.

degrading treatments,[36] thus preventing the establishment of a final approach to the matter. However, this capability of adaptation to the circumstances of the case and the case-by-case analysis are fundamental parts of the essence of human rights conventions, 'living instruments' as the human rights bodies have repeatedly stated.[37] This flexibility, for example, allows the ECtHR and the HRC to interpret their personal integrity provisions to include protection also against moral and psychological suffering, in line with what is envisaged by Article 5 of the ACHR,[38] thus ensuring convergence of case-law.

2.1.3 *The Right to Liberty and Security*

Similarly to what was previously observed, none of the bodies under analysis provided an exhaustive, detailed definition of 'arbitrary' to qualify the detentions that violate the right to liberty and security. This is probably because the term acquired a general and agreed understanding within IHRL and they all considered it not necessary to further explore the matter. This silent assumption of agreement could hide different applications to the specific cases, thus easily triggering fragmentation. However, the application of such a notion in contentious cases does not differ significantly or, at least, not enough to be considered a case of judicial fragmentation.[39]

All the five bodies share the basic understanding that the notion of arbitrariness is not limited to unlawfulness or illegality as it 'extends beyond lack of conformity with national law so that a deprivation of liberty may be lawful in terms of domestic law but still arbitrary'.[40] Nonetheless, they all fail in shedding more clarity on the actual meaning of this, keeping the definition blurry and vague, with the ultimate effect of a convergent case-law. According to the IACtHR, the deprivation of liberty will be nonetheless arbitrary if its

36 The same alternative approach has been adopted also in *Panigua Morales v. Guatemala* (IACtHR, 8 March 1998). cf *Vélasquez Rodriguez v. Honduras* (IACtHR, 29 July 1988) and *Castillo Paez v. Peru* (IACtHR, 3 November 1997).

37 See, for example, *Tyrer v. UK*, Application no 5856/72 (ECtHR, 25 April 1978), 31 and chapter 3.1.

38 cf *Ireland v. UK*, ECtHR and HRC, *General Comment no 20* (n 22).

39 cf *Aquilina v. Malta*, Application no 25642/94 (ECtHR, 29 April 1999); *Niedbata v. Poland* Application no 27915/95 (ECtHR, 4 July 2000); *Gangaram-Panday v. Suriname* (IACtHR, 21 January 1994); *Benavides-Cevallos v. Ecuador* (IACtHR, 19 June 1998); *Van Alphen v. The Netherlands*, Communication no 305/88 (HRC, 23 July 1990); *Taright v. Algeria*, Communication no 1085/02 (HRC, 15 March 2006); *Lloyd Reece v. Jamaica*, Communication no 796/98 (HRC, 14 July 2003).

40 *A and Others v. UK*, Application no 3455/05 (ECtHR, 19 February 2009), 164. See also *Gangaram-Panday*, IACtHR; *Albert Womah Mukong v. Cameroon*, Communication no 458/1991 (HRC, 21 July 1994), 9.8.

reasons or procedures are 'unreasonable, unforeseeable or lacking in proportionality'.[41] Relying extensively on the case-law of the ECtHR and the HRC and fully endorsing their reasoning, the IACtHR added that any restriction of the right to liberty should also be exceptional and strictly proportionate. Failure to comply with this will make it arbitrary and, thus, a violation of the Convention.[42]

Similarly, the ECtHR established that arbitrariness might arise (i) where there have been elements of bad faith or deception from the authorities, (ii) where the order to detain and the execution of the detention did not genuinely conform to the purpose of the restrictions permitted, (iii) where there was no connection between the ground of permitted deprivation of liberty relied on and the place and conditions of detention and (iv) where there was no relationship of proportionality between the ground of detention relied on and the detention.[43] Moreover, the ECtHR, considering the high number of cases received on these issues, further developed these requirements also in the specific context of civil and common law countries. For instance, in *O'Hara v. United Kingdom*, it established that the requirement of promptly bringing an individual deprived of his liberty before a judge should be met within four days.[44] However, a case-by-case approach should always be adopted as shown in *Epple v. Germany*, where a detention of 19 hours before being brought in front of a judge was considered not enough prompt due to the low level of the offences by the applicant.[45] Indeed, the key element to make any assessment is the ascertaining of the proportionality of the restriction in the specific circumstance of the case.[46]

Likewise, the HRC in *Taright v. Algeria* and *Alphen v. Netherlands* held that 'arbitrariness is not to be equated with "against the law", but must be interpreted more broadly to include elements of inappropriateness, injustice and lack of predictability'.[47] Also, in the view of the Committee, the assessment needs to be done on a case-by-case basis as confirmed in *Shafiq v. Australia*, where the HRC found a violation of Article 9 ICCPR because

[41] *Chaparro Alvarez and Lapo Iniguez v. Ecuador* (IACtHR, 21 November 2007), 90–94.
[42] ibid, 93.
[43] cf *James, Wells and Lee v. the UK*, Application nos 25119/09, 57715/09 (ECtHR, 18 September 2012), 191–195; and *Saadi v. the UK*, Application no 13229/03 (ECtHR, 29 January 2008), 68–74.
[44] *O'Hara v. the UK*, Application no 37555/97 (ECtHR, 16 October 2001).
[45] *Epple v. Germany*, Application no 77909/01 (ECtHR, 24 March 2005).
[46] On proportionality see Section 5.2.
[47] *Alphen v. The Netherlands*, Communication no 305/1988 (HRC, 23 July 1990), 5.6; *Taright v. Algeria*, Communication no 1085/02 (HRC, 15 March 2006).

the applicant was lawfully detained for over seven years and the detention had caused him mental illness.[48]

Finally, the African bodies also keep this broad understanding of the notion of arbitrariness, fully relying on the definition established by the other human rights bodies. In particular, in *Article 19 v. Eritrea*, the ACommHPR limited its analysis to the acknowledgement that 'the concept of arbitrary detention is one which both the [African] Commission and other international human rights bodies have previously expounded upon', explicitly citing the HRC's case-law,[49] and ruled on this basis.

This overview of the approaches of the five bodies to the application of the right to liberty in contentious cases and particularly to the understanding of the concept of arbitrariness shows that there is a substantial convergence of case-law. Despite the expectation of possible fragmentation due to the vagueness and generality of the term's definition, all the five bodies proved to have turned this vagueness into a safeguard for convergence, by establishing some key cornerstones and then leaving most of the specific application to a case-by-case assessment.

2.1.4 *The Freedom of Expression*

The right to freedom of expression is a cornerstone of a democratic society and one of those rights whose interpretation and understanding can be deeply influenced by several concerns of different nature, such as religious beliefs, moral concerns, cultural understanding and historical sensibility. It follows that the balance of such right with other fundamental rights and principles may be controversial. However, a perusal of the case-law confirmed that judicial convergence is overall dominating the adjudication of this right, in line with the perception of the interviewed litigators and NGOs involved in this field.[50]

The key to striking a balance between conflicting rights and interests is the application of the principles of necessity and proportionality. As profusely explored in Chapter 5, all the human rights bodies under analysis developed a common understanding of what these two elements entail and how they

48 *Shafiq v. Australia*, Communication no 1324/2004 (HRC, 3 November 2016).

49 *Article 19 v. Eritrea*, Communication no 275/03 (ACommHPR, 27 May 2003), 93.

50 Interviews conducted by the author with legal officers of several NGOs involved in litigation before the ECtHR, IACtHR and HRC held between July and December 2017; cf also Eduardo Andres Bertoni, 'The Inter-American Court of Human Rights and the European Court of Human Rights: A Dialogue on Freedom of Expression Standards' (2009) 332 *European Human Rights Law Review*.

should be applied to the specific cases.[51] This agreement ensured a substantial convergence, with very isolated exceptions.[52] Considering the width and scope of this right, it is impossible to give account to all the issues and only few examples will be presented.

First, it is worth underlying how the African bodies managed, through their interpretation and judicial application, to fill the gap left by the text of Article 9 ACHR, which lacks any provision on the limitation to freedom of expression, to bring it in line with the other regional and international instruments.[53] For instance, in *Konaté v. Burkina Faso*, the ACtHPR explicitly recognised the right of Burkina Faso to restrict the freedom of expression of Mr Konaté as far as such restriction is precisely prescribed by law, serves a legitimate purpose and is necessary, mirroring the letter of the ICCPR, ECHR and ACHR.[54]

Second, human rights bodies achieved, despite the absence of an internationally agreed definition, an overall convergence on hate speech, that is, the restriction to freedom of expression for the control of advocacy of violence, hatred and discrimination. Radio, journalistic or editorial expression equally lose its protection when they incite ethnic, racial or religious hostility and also historical negationist expression is legitimately restricted when pursuing, even indirectly, one of the above aims.[55]

Third, the need to balance the freedom of expression with the right to honour and reputation offers another example of judicial convergence despite the debated nature of the matter. All the four jurisdictions under analysis agree on the fact that, if the defamatory statement concerns a matter of public interest, a significantly wider margin of tolerance should be allowed.[56] However, the controversy lies in how to define public interest. The ECtHR widely defined it as 'any matter of general interest'[57] and the IACtHR and

[51] cf Chapter 5.

[52] See the discussion on prior censorship to an alleged blasphemous movie in Chapter 6, Section 6.6.2.2.

[53] *Lohé Issa Konaté v. Burkina Faso*, Application no 004/2013 (ACtHPR, 5 December 2014). cf Art.9 ACHPR with Art.10 ECHR, Art.19 ICCPR and Art.13 ACHR.

[54] ibid, 126–153.

[55] cf *Mark Anthony Norwood v. United Kingdom*, Application no 23131/03 (ECtHR, 16 November 2004); *Faurisson v. France*, Communication no 550/93 (HRC, 8 November 1996); *Ross v. Canada*, Communication no 736/97 (HRC, 18 October 2000).

[56] *Herrera Uloa v. Costa Rica* (IACtHR, 2004), 131; *Ligens v. Austria*, Application no 9851/82 (ECtHR, 8 July 1986), 42, and *Marquez de Morais v. Angola*, Communication no 1128/02 (HRC, 29 March 2005).

[57] cf *Chauvy and Others v. France*, Application no 64915/01 (ECtHR, 28 September 2000), 67–68 or *Ligens*, ECtHR, 42.

ACtHR followed this broad approach.[58] However, in the application to specific factual cases, some differences emerge. The case-law of the ECtHR and the IACtHR are particularly interesting in this regard, since they may appear divergent, but they actually share the core bulk of requirements for something to be considered of public interest. In *Canese v. Paraguay*, the IACtHR ruled over the complaint of Mr Canese, a journalist tried and charged with slander for questioning the suitability and integrity of a presidential candidate. In examining the legitimacy and necessity of a restriction to freedom of expression, the IACtHR held that 'statements concerning public officials and other individuals who exercise functions of a public nature should be accorded [. . .] a certain latitude in the broad debate on matters of public interest that is essential for the functioning of a truly democratic system'.[59] Differently, the ECtHR, in *Castells v. Spain*, seems to prioritise the concerns on public security over the protection of freedom of expression in political debates.[60] The case concerned the conviction of a member of the Parliament who published a journal article complaining about the inactivity of the authorities. The Court recalled the importance of 'freedom of expression [. . .] especially for an elected representative of the people'[61] and the fact that 'the limits of permissible criticism are wider with the regards to the Government than in relation to a private citizen'.[62] However, it stressed the fact that 'Mr. Castells did not express his opinion from the Senate floor [. . .] but chose to do so in a periodical',[63] and recognised the equally important role of the state to adopt, in his 'capacity of guarantor of public order, measures even of a criminal law nature, intended to react appropriately'.[64] That said, the ECtHR still concluded finding a violation of Article 10, since the applicant was not allowed to properly defend himself and prove the truth of his statements before domestic courts. Although the two reasonings show some divergent stances, the cases do not reach the threshold of fragmentation since, as previously observed, the outcome converged and the facts and the features of the single cases do not allow a proper comparison.

58 *Herrera Uloa*, IACtHR, 131. See also *Zeljko Bodrožić v. Serbia and Montenegro*, Communication no 1180/2003 (HRC, 31 October 2005), 7.2 and *Marquez de Morais*, HRC; *Konaté*, ACtHPR.
59 *Ricardo Canese v. Paraguay* (IACtHR, 31 August 2004), 98.
60 *Castells v. Spain*, Application no 11798/85 (ECtHR, 23 April 1992).
61 ibid, 42.
62 ibid, 46.
63 ibid, 43.
64 ibid, 46.

The other key concept in ruling on defamation cases is the necessity and proportionality of the sanctions imposed for the protection of the right to honour and reputation. Once again, the problem lies in the identification of which sanctions are necessary and proportionate. In the last decades, the international human rights system managed to promote a new understanding of criminal sanctions for defamation charges as not consistent with human rights law. The IACtHR and the ECtHR played a key role in this, by issuing landmark judgments where the practice of criminal convictions in defamation cases was heavily condemned.[65] However, some more recent cases of the IACtHR and the ECtHR represented a step backwards since they both ruled that the imprisonment of individuals accused of defamation did not violate their freedom of expression.[66] Still, there is no conflicting approach among the two bodies, since both Courts issued judgments in contrast with their own precedent case-law.[67] As a matter of fact, the only fragmentation in defamation cases is taking place within the same systems rather than between them.

Finally, the definition of controversial concepts such as that of 'public moral' remains one of the less settled aspects in the case-law on freedom of expression. Regional and international bodies all share the concern about the impossibility of providing an ultimate understanding of public moral that can be applied to all circumstances and all member states, thus opting for keeping these definitions as vague as possible to allow the adaptation to different factual cases and the adoption of varying approaches on a case-by-case basis.[68]

The above analysis shows that convergence dominates the judicial application of the freedom of expression in the practice of the five bodies under analysis. When called to assess restrictions to this right, despite the presence of controversial elements such as national security and public morals, all the bodies under analysis managed to maintain convergence of interpretation by wisely adopting broad definitions and flexibly applying the principles of judicial review, such as necessity and proportionality, or deferential tools. However, in some cases, this has not been fully possible and fragmentation arose.

[65] cf *Herrera Uloa*, IACtHR and *Morice v. France*, Application no 29369/10 (ECtHR, 23 April 2015).

[66] *Memoli v. Argentina* (IACtHR, 22 August 2013) and *Peruzzi v. Italy*, Application no 39294/09 (ECtHR, 30 June 2015).

[67] cf *Morice*, ECtHR; *Peruzzi*, ECtHR and *Memoli*, IACtHR.

[68] cf *Hertzberg and Others v. Finland*, Communication no 61/1979 (HRC, 2 April 1982); *Handyside v. UK*, Application no 5493/72 (ECtHR, 7 December 1976); *Müller and Others v. Switzerland*, Application no 10737/84 (ECtHR, 24 May 1988) and *Otto-Preminger-Institut v. Austria*, Application no 13470/87 (ECtHR, 20 September 1994); cf with *Olmedo-Bustos et al. v. Chile (The Last Temptation of Christ case)* (IACtHR, 5 February 2001).

2.1.5 *The Freedom of Assembly*

The comparison of the case-law of the ECtHR and the HRC on freedom of assembly reveals another interesting situation of slight divergence that may be wrongly confused with fragmentation. Unfortunately, the African bodies ruled only on a few cases on the matter, without addressing the issue in detail, and the IACtHR never decided a case specifically on freedom of assembly, thus keeping it out from this consideration.[69] Both the ECtHR and the HRC have interpreted and applied the freedom of assembly in very similar ways, agreeing on the same definition of peacefulness of an assembly and the circumstances under which an assembly loses its peaceful nature and, thus, its legal protection.[70] However, they diverted in a very doctrinal but important element: the nature and value of prior notice. In *Oya Ataman v. Turkey*, the state prohibited a public assembly because the organisers failed to inform the authorities beforehand. The ECtHR did not consider it a restriction but a 'tool to realise the state's positive obligation to secure freedom of assembly'.[71] On the contrary, the HRC, in *Kivenmaa v. Finland*, appears to have an opposite position. It considered the prior notice as a restriction when wondering whether 'a requirement to notify the police of an intended demonstration in a public place six hours before its commencement may be compatible with the permitted limitations laid down before article 21 of the Covenant'.[72] Such a difference is very technical, and it would be a mistake to consider it an example of fragmentation since it does not affect either the reasoning or the outcome. Indeed, the ECtHR, although not considering prior notice per se as a restriction to the freedom of assembly, ruled that it constituted a violation when the rules on prior consent are so strict to impair the enjoyment of the right.[73] For example, in *Bukta v. Hungary*, the Court was not prevented by its attitude to prior consent from recognising the right to spontaneous or 'urgent' demonstrations, at least as an immediate response to a political event.[74] This ruling shows that the ECtHR adopts a flexible approach towards the issue,

69 cf *Jawara v. The Gambia*, Communication no 147/95–149/96 (ACommHPR, 11 May 2000) and *Lawyers of Human Rights v. Swaziland*, Communication no 251/02 (ACommHPR, 2 July 2005).

70 cf *Ezelin v. France*, Application no 11800/85 (ECtHR, 26 April 1991) and the concluding observation of the HRC on Canada (CCPR/C/CAN/CO.5, 28 October 2005), 20.

71 *Oya Ataman v. Turkey*, Application no 74552/01 (ECtHR, 5 December 2006), 16.

72 *Kivenmaa v. Finland*, Communication no 412/1990 (HRC, 31 March 1994), 9.1.

73 *Éva Molnár v. Hungary*, Application no 10346/05 (ECtHR, 7 January 2009), 37.

74 *Bukta v. Hungary*, Application no 25691/04 (ECtHR, 17 July 2007).

avoiding taking an ultimate stance and keeping open any possibility to review its position on a case-by-case basis.

2.1.6 *Discrimination Based on Sexual Orientation*

Highly subject to cultural and religious influences is also the issue of sexual orientation and LGBTQI rights. Due to the topical and sensitive nature of this matter, one could expect to find fragmented interpretations by the regional courts and the HRC. However, for a series of reasons that will be considered later in this book,[75] such fragmentation has only partially and recently arisen.[76]

The case-law on this matter is too limited to conduct a proper study on convergence and fragmentation and the different facets of such issues are many and very specific. However, at least for what concerns the prohibition of discrimination based on sexual orientation, which is the starting point for any claim of violations of rights in the context of sexual orientation, it is possible to acknowledge a substantial convergence among human rights bodies.[77] The IACtHR delivered two judgments on the matter, strongly defending the rights, respectively, of a lesbian mother to keep the custody of her daughters and of a gay man to receive the survival's pension of his same-sex deceased partner.[78] In both these occasions, the IACtHR considered that Article 1 ACHR should also include sexual orientation as one of the grounds for prohibited discrimination and that 'any regulation, act, or practice considered discriminatory based on a person's sexual orientation is prohibited'.[79]

The HRC case-law on LGBTQI rights is more significant. After having held, in the 1982 case *Hertzberg and Others v. Finland*, that the ban on a radio programme on homosexuality did not constitute a violation of human rights, the Committee was the first UN body, in 1994, to rule that 'the reference to sex in Article 2 and 26 is to be taken as including sexual orientation',[80] departing significantly from its more conservative position of the previous decade. In

[75] See Part II of this book.
[76] See Section 2.2.3.
[77] Dominic McGoldrick, 'The Development and Status of Sexual Orientation Discrimination under International Human Rights Law' (2016) 16(4) *Human Rights Law Review* 613 and Elena Abrusci, 'A Tale of Convergence? Discrimination based on Sexual Orientation in Regional Human Rights Bodies and the Human Rights Committee' (2017) 35(3) *Nordic Journal of Human Rights* 240.
[78] *Atala Riffo and Daughters v. Chile* (IACtHR, 24 February 2012) and *Angel Alberto Duque v. Colombia* (IACtHR, 26 February 2016).
[79] *Atala Riffo*, IACtHR, 91.
[80] *Toonen v. Australia*, Communication no 488/1992 (HRC, 1994), 8.7.

later cases, it confirmed this stance and continued to strengthen LGBT rights,[81] ruling that the refusal to grant a pension for not fulfilling the requirement of 'being in a couple with a member of a different sex' is a violation of the principle of non-discrimination[82] or that invoking the protection of morals to restrict a protest in favour of homosexuality is a restriction of the freedom of expression.[83]

The ECtHR is certainly the body that has had more occasions to address LGBTQI rights and sexual orientation issues, in a variety of cases. It was the first international body to rule that criminal sexual orientation laws constituted a violation of human rights and that the prohibition of discrimination does include 'sexual orientation' as one of the forbidden grounds.[84] However, when facing more sensitive subjects such as adoption, marriage and the legal recognition of the change of gender, the ECtHR opted for a very cautious approach. Although it should be praised for its paramount role in setting new standards of protection, the Strasbourg Court left a significant margin of appreciation to member states, thus issuing sometimes conflicting judgments.[85]

Finally, it is worth mentioning that neither the African Commission nor the African Court had the chance to address the issue in detail; the only exception was a case brought against Zimbabwe, where the manifestation of homosexual identity is prohibited by law.[86] In this case, the applicant decided to withdraw his complaint, after the Commissioner acting as rapporteur stated that 'homosexuality offends the African sense of dignity and morality and is inconsistent with the positive African values'.[87] This episode may be considered as a way to avoid judicial fragmentation, though showing a conflicting approach towards

81 cf *Young v. Australia*, Communication no 941/2000 (HRC, 2004); *X v. Colombia*, Communication no 1361/2005 (HRC, 2007); *Fedotova v. Russian Federation*, Communication no 1932/2010 (HRC, 2012).

82 *Young*, HRC, 10.3–10.4.

83 *Fedotova*, HRC, 10.6–10.8.

84 *Dudgeon v. United Kingdom*, Application no 7525/76 (ECtHR, 22 October 1981); *Salgueiro da Silva Mouta v. Portugal*, Application no 33290/96 (ECtHR, 21 March 2000); *Karner v. Austria*, Application no 40016/98 (24 July 2013).

85 See *Rees v. United Kingdom*, Application no 9532/81 (ECtHR, 17 October 1986); *Christine Goodwin v. United Kingdom*, Application no 28957/95 (ECtHR, 11 July 2002) and *L. v. Lithuania*, Application no 27527/03 (ECtHR, 11 September 2007). See also *Fretté v. France*, Application no 3615/97 (ECtHR, 26 February 2002), *E.B. v. France*, Application no 43546/02 (ECtHR, 22 January 2008), *Gas and Dubois v. France*, Application no 25951/07 (ECtHR, 15 March 2012) and *X and Others v. Austria*, Application no 19010/07 (ECtHR, 19 February 2013).

86 *William A. Courson v. Zimbabwe*, Communication no 136/94 (ACommHPR, withdrawn 22 March 1994).

87 As quoted in Annika Rudman, 'The Protection against Discrimination Based on Sexual Orientation under the African Human Rights System' (2015) 15 *African Human Rights Law Journal* 1, 7–8.

homosexual rights by the African bodies compared to the other regional and international ones. However, since no judgment or conclusion has been issued so far, it is technically not possible to assert that judicial fragmentation is taking place in this area.

In conclusion, while it can be easily asserted that the issue of LGBTQI rights is a sensitive and controversial matter where different judges and committee members' personal opinions may strongly influence their interpretation and adjudication, it is not possible to establish that fragmentation is taking place, at least in the basic understanding of the prohibition of discrimination based on sexual orientation. The IACtHR, HRC and ECtHR all filled the gap in their non-discrimination provisions, interpreting them as including also sexual orientation as a prohibited ground for discrimination. As for other specific issues, the situation is one of weak convergence, mainly due to the impossibility to operate a comparison with other systems given the lack of cases brought before regional bodies other than the ECtHR rather than due to a substantive agreement on standards. Moreover, the evolution of the approach of the ECtHR and HRC towards the topic, in line with the development of the general international attention towards LGBTQI rights and the careful use of the margin of appreciation by the European Court are some of the causes that explain this substantial convergence. However, there is still an open door to fragmentation left by the African bodies and the IACtHR. As shown in Section 2.2.3, when new LGBTQI cases are brought before other institutions, judicial fragmentation with the ECtHR and HRC is more likely to arise.

2.1.7 *The Absence of Fragmentation Explained by the Difference in the Cases*

When assessing the extent of judicial fragmentation in IHRL, one should not forget a basic but extremely important methodological consideration: cases brought before different systems often have different facts and cannot be trivially compared. Indeed, when two cases differ too much in their facts, it is not possible to compare them to assess a situation of fragmentation or convergence on a certain issue. The same violation of a right can take place in so many ways and in so many contexts that often it may not be possible, and sometimes even wrong, to compare the two cases and draw ultimate conclusions. When cases from different regional systems deal with the same rights violation, but the underlying facts significantly diverge, the only evaluation one can do relates to some elements of the reasoning and the conclusions can be only hypothetical and based on the possible application of such an approach in other contexts.

An example of this can be the regional and HRC case-law on survival pensions for same-sex couples. The ECtHR, the IACtHR and the HRC all addressed the issue in several cases, but, so far, it is only possible to conclude that there is a convergence between the HRC and the IACtHR, and nothing else can be said on the situation between these two and the ECtHR.

The HRC in X. *v. Colombia*[88] *and Young v. Australia*[89] and the IACtHR in *Duque v. Colombia*[90] found that denying the right to receive the survival pension after the death of the same-sex partner in the case of an unmarried couple amounted to a violation of the prohibition of non-discrimination contained in Article 26 ICCPR and Article 24 ACHR. On the contrary, the ECtHR in *Mata Estevez v. Spain*[91] and *Aldeguer Tomás v. Spain*[92] held that the denial of the survival pension to an unmarried same-sex couple did not constitute a discriminatory treatment. While on the surface it may resemble a clear case of judicial fragmentation, if one looks at the facts of the cases the assessment changes. In the cases before the HRC and the IACtHR, the Colombian and Australian national legislations allowed individuals in unmarried heterosexual relationships to receive a survival pension in the case of the partner's death. On the contrary, in Spain, the survival pension was reserved to married people and same-sex couples were excluded considering the impossibility for them to enter into marriage. Indeed, it is exactly on this basis that the ECtHR found no discrimination, arguing that Spain was treating equally all unmarried couples, both heterosexual and homosexual. Speculations can be certainly made on how the ECtHR would have addressed a case with similar facts to the ones considered by the HRC and IACtHR. One could argue that the Court would have ruled in favour of the applicants considering the different facts, thus being in line with the HRC and IACtHR. On the other hand, someone else could argue that the decision of the ECtHR not to consider the inner discriminatory situation of homosexual couples not able to marry and thus, differently from heterosexual couples, not able in any way to be eligible for a survival pension shows a contrasting approach that with different facts will possibly lead to fragmentation. In any case, domestic laws are an important factor, determinant for the assessment of an alleged violation, and cannot be ignored when comparing cases from different systems.

[88] *X. v. Colombia*, HRC.
[89] *Young*, HRC.
[90] *Angel Alberto Duque*, IACtHR.
[91] *Mata Estevez v. Spain*, Application no 56501/00 (ECtHR, 10 May 2001).
[92] *Aldeguer Tomas v. Spain*, Application no 35214/09 (ECtHR, 14 June 2016).

In addition to the national legislation, the features and the situation of the applicants at the moment of the violation should be carefully considered when comparing cases for the assessment of convergence or fragmentation. The case-law on the prohibition of extradition when facing imprisonment in death row offers a good example of this. The positions of the HRC and the ECtHR on the matter up to 2003 are generally considered to be contrasting, and this is often invoked as a clear example of judicial fragmentation solved by the HRC with subsequent case-law.[93] However, a careful analysis of the case-law of the two bodies revealed that judicial fragmentation never took place between them. The cases in questions are the ECtHR's *Soering v. United Kingdom*[94] and the HRC's *Kindler v. Canada*,[95] both concerning the extradition of the applicant to the United States where he would have faced the death penalty and, prior to that, a period of detention in death row. In *Soering*, the ECtHR held that even if 'some element of delay between imposition and execution' is inevitable, 'the very long period of time spent on death row in such extreme conditions, with the ever present and mounting anguish of awaiting execution of the death penalty *together with the personal circumstances of the applicant, especially his age and mental state at the time of the offence*, [...] would expose him to a real risk of treatment going beyond the threshold set by Article 3',[96] thus amounting to a violation of the prohibition of torture. The HRC, in *Earl Pratt & Ivan Morgan v. Jamaica* held that the reclusion in death row, while undoubtedly causing mental strain for the convicted prisoner, 'do not per se constitute cruel, inhuman or degrading treatment'.[97] The same reasoning was applied in *Kindler v. Canada*, where the Committee held that Canada did not violate the prohibition of torture and the case was different from *Soering* 'as to the age and mental state of the offender, and the conditions on death row in the respective prison systems'.[98] Many scholars claim a difference between the two bodies on the basis that the HRC, differently from the ECtHR, did not consider the extradition to a country where the applicant would face death penalty and be subject to death row as a violation per se of the prohibition of torture.[99] However, the

93 Manfred Nowak, *UN Covenant on Civil and Political Rights: CCPR Commentary* (N.P. Engel, 2005), 155–160.

94 *Soering*, ECtHR.

95 *Kindler v. Canada*, Communication no 470/1991 (HRC, 30 July 1993).

96 *Soering*, ECtHR, 111 (emphasis added).

97 *Earl Pratt and Ivan Morgan v. Jamaica*, Communication no 210/1986 (HRC, 24 March 1990), 13.6.

98 *Kindler*, HRC, 10.2.

99 Susanne Zühlke and Jens-Christian Pastille, 'Extradition and the European Convention – Soering Revisited' (1999)1 *ZaöRV* 749; Nowak, *UN Covenant on Civil and Political Rights*; Maarten den Heijer, 'Whose Rights and Which Rights? The Continuing Story of Non-

ECtHR in *Soering* did rule that this was not a violation per se but only due to the specific circumstances of the case (namely the age and the mental health of Mr Soering). Therefore, there was no judicial fragmentation between these cases, since the different outcomes are justified by different facts, that is, the different circumstances and position of the applicants.

As it is easy to imagine, it is very unlikely that cases brought before different human rights bodies worldwide have identical facts, context and domestic law. Different societies, different political, cultural and religious contexts highly influence the circumstances and the nature of any human rights violations. However, while identical cases certainly make the comparison easier, as in *Ranjit Singh v. France*[100] before the HRC and *Mann Singh v. France*[101] before the ECtHR, a margin of tolerance should sometimes be accepted when the differences do not affect the position of the applicant and the characterisation of the violation. Nevertheless, such assessment should be made carefully taking into consideration all the factors at stake, domestic law, facts of the violation, features of the victims and socio-political context, like in the cases of *Handölsdalen Sami Village and Others v. Sweden*[102] before the ECtHR and *Yake Axa Indigenous Community v. Paraguay*[103] before the IACtHR.

To conclude, the factual, legal and contextual differences in the cases before regional and international bodies sometimes prevent the assessment of convergence or fragmentation. While in some circumstances it is still possible to speculate on the possible approach that a certain body would adopt in a given case on the basis of its jurisprudence, in the majority of the situations one should only conclude that no fragmentation is taking place, but this is not equal to convergence. Indeed, as repeatedly recalled,[104] the absence of fragmentation does not automatically mean that the systems are converging, especially when there is no case-law from one of the jurisdictions to conduct a comparative analysis.

Refoulement under the European Convention on Human Rights' (2008) 10(3) *European Journal of Migration and Law* 277, 277–314; Daniela Mendez Royo, 'Sistemas de protección internacional de los derechos fundamentales: ¿Son los sistemas regionales más efectivos que los órganos de Naciones Unidas?' (2012) 7 *Revista de Derechos Fundamentales – Universidad Viña del Mar* 29, 29–57.

[100] *Ranjit Singh v. France*, Communication no 1876/2000 (HRC, 11–29 July 2011). See Section 2.2.1.

[101] *Mann Singh v. France*, Application no 24479/07 (ECtHR, 11 June 2007). See Section 2.2.1.

[102] *Handölsdalen Sami Village and Others v. Sweden*, Application no 39013/04 (ECtHR, 30 March 2010). See Section 2.2.2.

[103] *Yake Axa Indigenous Community v. Paraguay* (IACtHR, 17 June 2005). See Section 2.2.2.

[104] See also Chapter 1.

2.1.8 *Concluding Observations*

In conclusion, the phenomenon of judicial fragmentation cannot be considered as a major concern for international human rights law, at least presently. Many are the cases of slight discordance and difference between the interpretative lines of human rights judicial and quasi-judicial bodies, but they rarely reach the threshold of actual fragmentation.

Sometimes the approach of the single bodies has evolved with time in order to adapt to each other and an international common standard, thereby overcoming a previous situation of fragmentation, enhancing judicial convergence. In other instances, some elements in the reasoning may induce one to think that they hold slightly different approaches to similar issues. However, their ultimate approach and outcome were not diverging enough to be considered an example of fragmentation. Nonetheless, those minor differences and conflicts should be carefully monitored since they may increase and produce cases of judicial fragmentation in the future.

To this extent, the following section is of utmost importance for analysing in depth some of the few existing cases of judicial fragmentation, in order to identify the causes and triggering factors for avoiding, if needed, similar situations going forward.

2.2 ANALYSING JUDICIAL FRAGMENTATION IN IHRL

Although the previous section showed that judicial convergence is predominant in IHRL, there are some instances where regional and international human rights bodies triggered fragmentation with their interpretation and adjudication.

This section explores three extremely important situations of judicial fragmentation in IHRL. First, the case of freedom to manifest religion as it is interpreted by the HRC and the ECtHR. Second, the right to property of indigenous people between the IACtHR and the ACommHPR on the one hand and the ECtHR on the other. Finally, the most recent case of judicial fragmentation, namely the right to marry of same-sex couples and gender reassignment between the HRC and ECtHR on one side and the IACtHR on the other.

Three other instances of judicial fragmentation have been observed. One field where one can appreciate different judicial approaches between regional human rights bodies is the protection of the rights of migrants. Differently from the previously analysed cases, this affects both procedural matters and rights interpretation. As Dembour extensively shows and discusses, the IACtHR and the ECtHR have a fundamental contrasting approach towards migrants rights that significantly affect their adjudication on a wide range of rights, triggering judicial fragmentation.[105] This stems from the different assumptions of the two courts in relation to migrants. As Dembour pointed out, 'in the Inter-American system, the migrant is first of all conceived as a human being in need of protection; in the European system he's an alien subject to the control of the sovereign state'.[106] In turn, this could lead the IACtHR to favour the applicant and the ECtHR to favour the state.[107]

In addition to this, judicial fragmentation also affects the restriction to freedom of expression for the protection of public morals and enforced disappearances both between the IACtHR and the ECtHR. However, these situations will not be considered here since the former is very similar in its features to fragmentation on freedom of religion and the latter mainly concerns procedural aspects rather than the merit of the interpretation of the substantial rights.[108] Nevertheless, these cases will be discussed later in this book.[109]

2.2.1 *Freedom to Manifest Religion*

Clear examples of judicial fragmentation can be found in the case-law of the HRC and ECtHR on the freedom to manifest religion, in particular on the wearing of religious attire. Regardless of the context, being that a photograph for an official document, the admission to educational premises or the simple wearing of religious attire in public, the two bodies consistently held different positions. This section presents these three sets of cases, illustrating the features of this judicial fragmentation.

[105] Marie-Bénédicte Dembour, *When Humans Become Migrants* (Oxford University Press, 2015).
[106] ibid, 8.
[107] See also Bas Schotel, *On the Right of Exclusion: Law, Ethics and Immigration Policy* (Routledge, 2012).
[108] On this topic see Ophelia Claude, 'A Comparative Approach to Enforced Disappearances in the Inter-American Court of Human Rights and the European Court of Human Rights Jurisprudence' (2010) 5 *Intercultural Human Rights Law Review* 407; Nikolas Kyriakou, 'An Affront to the Conscience of Humanity: Enforced Disappearance in International Human Rights Law' (PhD thesis, European University Institute, 2012); Gabriella Citroni, 'The Contribution of the Inter-American Court of Human Rights and Other International Human Rights Bodies to the Struggle Against Enforced Disappearance' in Y. Haeck, O. Ruiz-Chiriboga and C. Burbano-Herrera, *The Inter-American Court of Human Rights: Theory and Practice, Present and Future* (Intersentia, 2015).
[109] See the discussion of judicial dialogue and enforced disappearances in Chapter 4, Section 4.2.4.1 and of the role of MoA in freedom of expression in Chapter 6, Section 6.6.2.2.

The first example of judicial fragmentation is between the HRC views in *Ranjit Singh v. France*[110] and the ECtHR admissibility decision in *Mann Singh v. France.*[111]

The cases are based on very similar facts, but the two bodies reached completely different conclusions, with the ECtHR considering the case inadmissible as manifestly ill-founded while the HRC found a violation of the freedom to manifest religion.

The ECtHR's case concerned the claim by Mr Shingara Mann Singh on the requirement for a driving licence photograph. According to the French legislation, this should show the subject 'bareheaded and facing forward', and such a requirement allegedly discriminated against practising Sikhs. Mr Mann Singh argued that the refusal of the French authority to let him wear his turban in the photograph for his licence violated his rights under Article 8 (private and family life), Article 9 (thought, conscience and religion) and Article 14 (discrimination) of the ECHR. Similarly, in *Ranjit Singh v. France*, the HRC considered the refusal of the French authority to renew the residence permit of Mr Ranjit Singh, an Indian refugee with a permanent French residence, on the basis that in the photographs provided for the document he was wearing his Sikh turban and, therefore, he did not 'appear full face and bareheaded'. Moreover, without a residence card, Mr Ranjit Singh was considered an illegal resident in France and, therefore, he could not leave the country nor have access to the free public healthcare system. Therefore, the applicant claimed a violation of Article 18 (freedom of religion), Article 12 (freedom of movement), Article 26 (discrimination) and Article 27 (protection of minorities) of the ICCPR.

The two cases are an excellent example of judicial fragmentation because, in addition to being based on almost identical facts, they both concern the same country and, therefore, the national law regulating the matter is identical. Both the ECtHR and the HRC recognised that the imposition to remove the Sikh turban for identity photographs constituted a restriction on the freedom to manifest religion (Article 9 ECHR and Article 18 ICCPR).[112] The ECtHR endorsed the claim of the applicant that wearing the Sikh turban always and in any circumstance is a core part of a Sikh's religion and identity.[113] Similarly, the HRC recalled its general comment No. 22, where it considered 'that freedom to manifest religion encompasses the wearing of

[110] *Ranjit Singh v. France*, Communication no 1876/2000 (HRC, 11–29 July 2011).

[111] *Mann Singh v. France*, Application no 24479/07 (ECtHR, 11 June 2007).

[112] *Ranjit Singh*, HRC, 8.2; *Mann Singh*, ECtHR, 6.

[113] ibid.

distinctive clothes or head coverings'.[114] Moreover, both the European and the UN body acknowledged that the restriction imposed by the French law was provided by law and was legitimate on the basis of the protection of public safety and order.[115]

The reasoning of the ECtHR and the HRC, similar until this stage, differs when it comes to the assessment of whether that limitation was necessary and proportionate in a democratic society.

The HRC recognised the need of the state 'to ensure and verify, for the purpose of public safety and order, that the person appearing in the photograph [. . .] is, in fact, the rightful holder of the document'.[116] However, it was not convinced by the fact that according to the respondent state wearing 'a Sikh turban covering the top of the head and a portion of the forehead but leaving the rest of the face clearly visible would make it more difficult to identify the author than if he was to appear bareheaded, since he wears his turban all times'.[117] France argued that the requirement of appearing bareheaded for the identity photographs was aimed at reducing the risk of fraud or falsification of residence permit. Yet, in the Committee's view, it was not clear how this could be true.[118] Furthermore, while France described it as a 'one-time requirement, [the HRC noted that] it would interfere with the author's freedom of religion on a continuing basis because he would always appear without his religious head covering in the identity photograph and could, therefore, be compelled to remove his turban during identity check'.[119] In light of the above, the HRC concluded that Mr Ranjit Singh was a victim of a violation of Article 18 ICCPR.[120]

On the contrary, the ECtHR, while stressing the importance of freedom of religion in a democratic society, recalled that it is not an absolute right and it 'did not confer the right to disregard rules that had proved to be justified'.[121] Evoking its previous rulings, the Court compared the present case to other situations where a restriction to the freedom to manifest religion was allowed for national security reasons.[122] Completely in contrast with the position of the

[114] *Ranjit Singh*, HRC, 8.3.
[115] ibid, 8.4; *Mann Singh*, HRC, 6.
[116] *Ranjit Singh*, HRC, 8.4.
[117] ibid.
[118] ibid.
[119] ibid.
[120] ibid, 9.
[121] *Mann Singh*, HRC, 7.
[122] The ECtHR referred to *X v. United Kingdom*, Application no 7992/77 (ECtHR, 12 July 1978); *Karaduman v. Turkey*, Application no 16278/90 (ECtHR, 3 May 1993) and *Phull v. France*, Application no 35753/03 (ECtHR, 11 January 2005) where no violation of Article 9 was found.

HRC, the ECtHR noted that the requirement imposed on the photographs was *needed* by the authorities in charge of public safety for the identification of the driver. The Court seemed not to be concerned about the fact that most probably Mr Mann Singh would have always worn the turban while driving, making identification by the public authority harder if the photograph in the driving licence showed him bareheaded.[123] Finally, the ECtHR considered that the detailed arrangements for implementing such security requirements fell within the state's margin of appreciation[124] and, therefore, that the impugned interference was justified in principle and was proportionate to the aim pursued.[125]

In conclusion, the ECtHR did not find any appearance of a violation of the provisions of the ECHR and declared the case inadmissible.[126]

This overt difference in the approach to the issue and in the final outcome is a clear example of judicial fragmentation. The two applicants, while having experienced very similar circumstances, did not see their freedom of religion equally protected before the two bodies. Indeed, the different interpretations provided by the ECtHR and the HRC are not just a manifestation of two diverse points of view on the matter; they actually have a real impact on the applicants who claimed to be victims of human rights violations.

Moreover, the case-law of the HRC and the ECtHR confirmed such a contrasting approach towards freedom to manifest religion. Another emblematic example of judicial fragmentation between the ECtHR and the HRC is represented by two cases concerning the prohibition of wearing a Muslim headscarf in education.

In *Raihon Hudoyberganova v. Uzbekistan*,[127] concerning the expulsion of a female student from the university because of her refusal to comply with a prohibition to wear an Islamic headscarf, the HRC found a violation under Article 18 ICCPR of her freedom of religion. In a similar case, *Leyla Şahin v. Turkey*,[128] the ECtHR reached a completely different conclusion finding no violation of Article 9 ECHR.

The case concerned, respectively, the obligation to remove the Sikh turban for wearing a motorcycle helmet, the obligation for a Muslim student to submit a bareheaded photograph for his school diploma and the requirement to remove a turban or headscarf for the purposes of an airport security check. cf *Mann Singh*, HRC, 7.

[123] ibid.

[124] ibid, 8.

[125] ibid.

[126] ibid.

[127] *Raihon Hudoyberganova v. Uzbekistan*, Communication no 931/2000 (HRC, 8 December 2004).

[128] *Leyla Şahin v. Turkey*, Application no 44774/98 (ECtHR, 10 November 2005).

In *Hudoyberganova* the Committee expressed and reasoned its position in one single paragraph, reaching the conclusion that a violation of Article 18 had occurred.

> The Committee considers that the freedom to manifest one's religion encompasses the right to wear clothes or attire in public which is in conformity with the individual's faith or religion. Furthermore, it considers that to *prevent a person from wearing religious clothing in public or private may constitute a violation of article 18, paragraph 2, which prohibits any coercion that would impair the individual's freedom to have or adopt a religion*. As reflected in the Committee's General Comment No. 22 (para.5), policies or practices that have the same intention or effect as direct coercion, such as those restricting access to education, are inconsistent with article 18, paragraph 2. It recalls, however, that the freedom to manifest one's religion or beliefs is not absolute and may be subject to limitations, which are prescribed by law and are necessary to protect public safety, order, health, or morals, or the fundamental rights and freedoms of others. [...] The Committee notes that the State party has not invoked any specific ground for which the restriction imposed on the author would in its view be necessary in the meaning of article 18, paragraph 3. Instead, the State party has sought to justify the expulsion of the author from University because of her refusal to comply with the ban. [...] In the particular circumstances of the present case, [...] the Committee is led to conclude, *in the absence of any justification provided by the State party*, that there *has been a violation of article 18*, paragraph 2.[129]

On the contrary, the ECtHR in *Leyla Şahin* considered that the prohibition to Miss Sahin from attending lectures and taking part in examinations due to the wearing of a headscarf and the subsequent suspension from studies did not constitute a violation of her freedom of religion. The Grand Chamber of the ECtHR endorsed the chamber's findings that 'the regulations [...] which placed restrictions of place and manner on the right to wear the Islamic headscarf in universities constituted an interference with the applicant's right to manifest her religion'.[130]

However, the ECtHR confirmed that the restriction was 'prescribed by law'[131] and was pursuing 'the legitimate aims of protecting the rights and freedoms of others and of protecting public order'.[132] To assess whether the limitation imposed was necessary in a democratic society and proportionate to

[129] *Hudoyberganova*, HRC, 6.2.
[130] *Leyla Şahin*, ECtHR, 78.
[131] ibid, 88.
[132] ibid, 99.

the aim, the ECtHR put the principle of secularism at the core of its reasoning. After recalling the need, in a democratic society, to put some restrictions on the freedom to manifest one's religion in order to ensure the respect of everyone's beliefs[133] and the fundamental role that the state plays as neutral and impartial organiser of various religions,[134] the Court recognised that states should enjoy a wide margin of appreciation in these matters.[135] However, such 'margin of appreciation goes hand in hand with a European supervision'.[136] Recalling its previous findings in *Karaduman v. Turkey* and *Dahlab v. Switzerland*, the Court endorsed Turkey's justification for the restriction noting that 'when examining the question of the Islamic headscarf in the Turkish context, it must be borne in mind the impact which wearing such a symbol,[...] may have on those who choose not to wear it'.[137] Indeed, the measure aimed at preventing 'certain fundamentalist religious movements from exerting pressure on students who did not practice their religion or who belonged to another religion'.[138] 'Imposing limitation on freedom in this sphere may, therefore, be regarded as meeting a pressing social need by seeking to achieve those two legitimate aims [protecting the rights and freedoms of the others and maintaining public order]'.[139] In light of the above, and recalling the margin of appreciation given to the state, the ECtHR concluded that no violation of Article 9 had occurred.[140]

On the basis of the same reasoning, the ECtHR equally concluded that no violation of the applicant's right to education (Article 2, Protocol 1 ECHR) had occurred.[141]

The most evident difference between the submissions in the two cases is that, unlike the Turkish government in *Leyla Şahin*, the Uzbek government did not invoke any legitimate aim as the basis for the prohibition of wearing the headscarf. Although it may be argued that, in *Hudoyberganova*, the HRC did not have any other choice than finding a violation of Article 18 and that its view leaves open the possibility of a different conclusion in similar case,[142] a

[133] ibid, 106.
[134] ibid, 107.
[135] ibid, 108–109.
[136] ibid, 110.
[137] ibid, 115.
[138] ibid, 111.
[139] ibid, 115.
[140] ibid, 122–123.
[141] ibid, 157–160.
[142] Marti Scheinin, 'International Human Rights Law and the Islamic Headscarf: A Short Note on the Positions of the European Court of Human Rights and the Human Rights Committee' in W. Cole Durham Jr, Rik Torfs, David M. Kirkham and Christine Scoot (eds), *Islam, Europe and Emerging Legal Issues* (Ashgate, 2012), 84.

careful reading supports the opposite view. Indeed, some elements in the HRC's reasoning suggest that the difference between the two outcomes was not only due to the failure of Uzbekistan to invoke legitimate grounds of limitation. The HRC, for instance, decided to qualify the violation of Article 18 as a breach of the prohibition against *coercion* prejudicing the applicant's freedom to have or to adopt the religion or belief of her choice. By doing so, the Committee considered the fact of the exclusion of a student from her school for being non-compliant with the headscarf ban as something significantly more serious than the mere restriction of freedom to manifest religion. Indeed, while the freedom of manifestation of religion is a qualified right that can be restricted on the grounds set out in Article 18(2), '[t]he freedom from coercion to have or to adopt a religion or belief [. . .] cannot be restricted'.[143] Therefore, it can be presumed that even if the Uzbek government had invoked a legitimate aim for the restriction, as Turkey did in *Leyla Şahin*, the HRC would have ruled in the same way, finding a violation of Article 18.

The same straightforward approach of the HRC for the protection of freedom of religion can be found in another case, *Bikramjit Singh v. France*.[144] Here, again, the facts concern the expulsion of an eighteen-year-old boy from a school because of his refusal to remove his *keski*, a small Sikh turban. The HRC recognised the importance of the principle of *laicité* of the state and the aim of the new French legislation to protect the rights and freedoms of the others avoiding interference with everyone's freedom of religion.[145] However, the Committee observed very firmly that 'the state party has not furnished compelling evidence that, by wearing his *keski*, the author would have posed a threat to the rights and freedoms of other pupils or to order at the school'.[146] Moreover, the HRC held that the expulsion of the boy from the school was a disproportionate measure and the 'State party has not shown how the sacrifice of those persons' rights is either necessary or proportionate to the benefits achieved'.[147] As a consequence, the HRC concluded that France violated Article 18 ICCPR.[148]

By contrast, in *Dogru v. France*[149] and *Kervanci v. France*,[150] cases also concerning the expulsion of pupils from a school for wearing religious attire,

143 HRC, General Comment no 22, CCPR/C/21/Rev.1/Add.4, 8.
144 *Bikramjit Singh v. France*, Communication no 1852/2008 (HRC, 4 February 2013).
145 ibid, 8.6.
146 ibid, 8.7.
147 ibid.
148 ibid, 9.
149 *Dogru v. France*, Application no 27058/05(ECtHR, 4 December 2008).
150 *Kervanci v. France*, Application no 31645/04 (ECtHR, 4 December 2008).

the ECtHR did not ask France to justify why wearing an Islamic headscarf was a threat to 'the rights and freedoms of others, public order and public safety'.[151] Nor did it question how the expulsion of the two girls from the school was contributing to pursuing the invoked legitimate aims. The ECtHR limited itself to the reaffirmation of the importance of the principle of secularism and observed that it falls upon the national authorities 'to take great care to ensure that, in keeping with the principle of respect for pluralism and the freedom of others, the manifestation by pupils of their religious beliefs on school premises did not take on the nature of an ostentatious act that would constitute a source of pressure and exclusion'.[152]

The same reasoning has also been used by the European Court in other similar cases, such as *Jasvir Singh v. France, Aktas v. France, Bayrak v. France, Ghazal v. France and Gamaleddyn v. France*,[153] which have been all declared inadmissible as manifestly ill-founded. This confirms, once again, the consolidation of the ECtHR's approach to the matter and the deep difference with the HRC.

To conclude this analysis, it is worth mentioning the judicial fragmentation arising between the ECtHR and the HRC on the ban of full face veils, as coming out from *S.A.S. v. France*,[154] on the ECtHR's side, and *Yaker v. France* and *Hebbadj v. France*,[155] on the HRC's side.[156]

The cases concerned the ban imposed by the French law on the wearing of any religious attire covering the face in public, the so-called *burqa* ban. The applicants claimed that, by preventing them from wearing the *burqa* or the *niqab*, the ban violated their freedom of religion in addition to other rights (Article 3, 8, 10 and 14 ECHR and Article 18 and 26 ICCPR). In line with its previous case-law on the matter, in *S.A.S. v. France*, the ECtHR did not find any violation of the ECHR. However, in the assessment of whether the ban

[151] *Dogru*, ECtHR, 64.

[152] ibid, 71.

[153] *Jasvir Singh v. France*, Application no 25463/08 (ECtHR, 30 June 2009); *Aktas v. France*, Application no 43563/08 (ECtHR, 30 June 2009); *Bayrak v. France*, Application no 14308/08 (ECtHR, 30 June 2009); *Ghazal v. France*, Application no 29134/08 (ECtHR, 30 June 2009) and *Gamaleddyn v. France*, Application no 18527/08 (ECtHR, 30 June 2009).

[154] *S.A.S. v. France*, Application no 43835/11 (ECtHR, 1 July 2014).

[155] *Yaker v. France*, Communication no 2747/2016 (HRC, 17 July 2018); *Hebbadj v. France*, Communication no 2807/2016 (HRC, 17 July 2018). Considering that the facts and finding of the two cases are identical, this book will mainly refer to the *Yaker* case, considering the more detailed reasoning by the Committee.

[156] See also Sarah Cleveland, 'Banning the Full-Face Veil: Freedom of Religion and Non-Discrimination in the Human Rights Committee and the European Court of Human Rights' (2021) 34 *Harvard Human Rights Journal* 217.

was pursuing a legitimate aim, the ECtHR adopted a different position from the one held in *Leyla Şahin*. Here, the Court rejected the French argument that the law was aiming at ensuring 'gender equality and human dignity'.[157] Specifically, the ECtHR stated that 'a State party cannot invoke gender equality in order to ban a practice that is defended by women -such as the applicant- in the context of the exercise of the rights enshrined in those provisions'.[158] This is a very different stance from the one held in the *hijab* cases like *Leyla Şahin and Dahlab*, where the Court openly considered wearing the *hijab* as hardly complying with the principle of gender equality.[159] However, this position seems to be in line with the dissenting opinion of Judge Tulkens in *Leyla Şahin* where she stated that 'it is not the Court's role to [...] determine in a general and abstract way the signification of wearing the headscarf or impose its viewpoint on the applicant'.[160] While it is highly contradictory that the ECtHR defined the *hijab* contrary to gender equality but not the *burqa*, this evolution and change in the approach of the Court is to be very much welcomed. Likewise, the ECtHR rejected the claim of France that the ban was legitimate for protecting public safety, departing from its previous case-law. However, the Strasbourg Court considered the ban legitimate for the protection of the 'living together' and, thus, no violation of Article 9 was found.[161]

On the contrary, the HRC in *Yaker* and *Hebbadj* rejected France's claim of 'living together' as legitimate aim and considered that the respondent state failed to prove why the wearing of the *niqab* was infringing on the enjoyment of the rights of others.[162] Therefore, it held that the ban was not necessary and proportionate and, as a consequence, found a violation of Article 18. In addition, the Committee also considered the indirect discriminatory treatment that this ban had on Muslim women, finding an additional violation of Article 26 for discrimination on grounds of both gender and religion.[163]

Worth mentioning is the partly dissenting opinion in *S.A.S. v. France* by Judge Nussberger and Jäderblom, criticising the ECtHR position on the acceptance of the 'living together' rationale for justifying the ban.[164] Their reasoning appears very similar to that of the HRC, showing some elements of dissent within the Strasbourg Court and convergence with the UN Committee.

[157] ibid, 119–120.
[158] ibid, 119.
[159] *Dahlab v. Switzerland*, Application no 42393/98 (ECtHR, 15 February 2001).
[160] Dissenting opinión of Judge Tulkens, *Leyla Şahin*, ECtHR, 12.
[161] S.A.S., ECtHR, 121–122.
[162] See *Yake*, HRC, 8.3–8.10.
[163] ibid, 8.13–8.16.
[164] Partly dissenting opinion by Judge Nussberger and Jäderblom in S.A.S., ECtHR, 5.

2.2.1.1 Concluding Observations

The previous analysis confirmed that a judicial fragmentation on the manifestation of freedom of religion is actually taking place between the ECtHR and the HRC.

The phenomenon cannot be considered as a sporadic conflicting decision of the two bodies, but it is more a systematic divergent interpretation of the almost identical letter of Article 9 ECHR and Article18 ICCPR.[165] Indeed, the text of the two articles could certainly not be invoked as a justification for such a conflicting application.[166]

The reasoning of the HRC and of the ECtHR suggests the identification of some elements that can be the factors behind such different understanding and application. Although they will be addressed in detail in Part II, it is still worth mentioning them in relation to the specific cases and topic here analysed.

First, the main explanation of the European approach to the matter is the large use of the margin of appreciation, one of the features of the ECtHR adjudication. As the Court often recalled, when it comes to the national regulation of the manifestation of freedom of religion and the necessary measures to protect public order and national security, a wide margin of appreciation should be granted to states in order to implement the most suitable actions in the specific national context.[167] On the other hand, the HRC has always refused to openly leave a margin of appreciation to the states, thus making its outcomes more direct and straightforward. According to the European Court and to some scholars, the margin of appreciation in the cases concerning freedom of religion is 'an essential constitutional device designed to preserve the fundamental prerequisite and virtue of a liberal democratic society, the value of pluralism',[168] and also a 'necessary tool for the accommodation of individual rights and collective goals'.[169] In the absence of a European consensus on the matter, the ECtHR did wisely use the margin of

[165] For an extensive discussion of the ECtHR's approach to freedom of religion see Thiago Alves Pinto, 'An Empirical Investigation of the Use and Limitations to Freedom of Religion or Belief at the European Court of Human Rights' (2020) 15 *Religion and Human Rights* 96–133.
[166] Article 9 ECHR and Article 18 ICCPR.
[167] cf *Kokkinakis v. Greece*, Application no 14307/88 (ECtHR, 25 May 1993), 47 and, for a comprehensive analysis of headscarf cases in Europe see Dominick McGoldrick, *Human Rights and Religion: The Islamic Headscarf Debate in Europe* (Hart, 2006).
[168] Yutaka Arai-Takahashi, *The Margin of Appreciation Doctrine and the Principle of Proportionality in the Jurisprudence of the ECHR* (Intersentia, 2002), 249.
[169] Monica Lugato, 'The Margin of Appreciation and Freedom of Religion: Between Treaty Interpretation and Subsidiarity' (2017) 52 *Journal of Catholic Legal Studies* 49, 53.

appreciation to endorse its subsidiary role, but by doing so it 'ignored the individual right to manifest bona fide religious convictions and did not attempt to show how a total prohibition of such manifestation was necessary to protect a democratic society'.[170]

Second, it is impossible to ignore the great attention that the ECtHR pays to the principle of secularism of the state. In the cases mentioned earlier, the Court always justified the restriction to the freedom of manifestation of religion on the basis of the protection of the *laicité* of the state, legitimising a strong domestic intervention. Indeed, the Court considered as a fundamental step in its reasoning the political and historical context of the member state, in particular for the determination of the margin of appreciation. By doing so, it certainly respected the principle of subsidiarity but failed to protect the rights of the religious minorities in states with a strong secularist policy or with a majority religion. On the contrary, the HRC, while recognising the importance of secularism as a safeguard for the enjoyment of the freedom of religion, preferred to stand by the side of the individuals belonging to religious minorities. These two different attitudes towards the principle of secularism mirror the two notions of 'liberal' or 'pluralistic' opposed to a 'fundamentalist' secularism, often invoked by scholars.[171] The former understands religions as pertaining only to personal conscience and identity, thus being neither a public responsibility nor the right to enforce a religious (on non-religious) doctrine or practice on citizens. The latter, on the contrary, presumes that religious manifestations should be kept within the private domain and that 'an individual's belief or conviction does not have any place in the public domain' and, therefore, the freedom to manifest religion in public should be highly restricted.[172] The analysed ECtHR's case-law on the freedom to manifest religion shows the shift of the Court from a liberal to a fundamentalist approach on secularism. However, the ECtHR Grand Chamber's position in *Lautsi v. Italy*[173] and in S.A.S. seems to go in the opposite direction, suggesting a more case-by-case and 'country-by-country' approach.

Third, among the factors that may have an influence on the ECtHR's case-law on the subject, there may be the complicated relationship that Europe has with Islam. Without engaging in a detailed discussion on the role and status of

[170] Claudia Morini, 'Secularism and Freedom of Religion: The Approach of the European Court of Human Rights' (2010) 43 *Israel Law Review* 611, 629.

[171] ibid; Zachary R. Calo, 'Pluralism, Secularism and the European Court of Human Rights' (2009) 26 *Journal of Law and Religion* 101; Sylvie Langlaude, 'Indoctrination, Secularism, Religious Liberty and the ECHR' (2006) 55 *International and Comparative Law Quarterly* 929.

[172] Morini, 'Secularism and Freedom of Religion'.

[173] *Lautsi v. Italy*, Application no 30814/06 (ECtHR, 18 March 2011).

Islam in Europe, it is important to take into consideration the impact that 9/11 and fundamentalist Islamic terrorism has had on European countries in the last twenty years. Indeed, in some cases, the ECtHR appeared to stereotype Islam, without conducting a serious and case-by-case analysis of the different facts and circumstances.[174] The often broad and vague approach of the ECtHR seems to give credit to a stereotyped Western view that Islam is oppressive to women by imposing on them the use of the veil and that Muslim groups of faithful believers may easily turn into a threat to public order and security. In her dissenting opinion in *Leyla Şahin*, Judge Tulkens criticised the paternalistic approach of the majority of the judges who accepted the ban of the headscarf as a way to promote gender equality, thus showing a deep ignorance of Islam and a simplicistic understanding of the use of the veil.[175] A similar reluctant approach towards religions that are different from the well-established Christian ones can be observed in the cases related to the use of the Sikh turban. However, a change in the Court's reasoning in S.A.S. should be welcomed in this regard as a positive evolution of the ECtHR's approach to Islam. On the other hand, the HRC's approach confirms its religious neutrality. As a universal body monitoring compliance with a universal human rights treaty, with a composition that mirrors both cultural and religious diversity, the HRC is less likely than any regional body to show preference to any religion or belief in interpreting which practices are more in conformity with human rights provisions.

Indeed, the composition and the nature of the two different bodies can partially explain their conflicting outcomes, as shown in Chapter 4. The ECtHR is a judicial body, mostly composed of former domestic judges, issuing binding judgments for its state parties. Politically speaking, since the state's compliance with the Court's judgments is one of the most important strengths of the European system, the Court avoids holding strong positions against a state on very sensitive matters where no European consensus is available. Conversely, the HRC, composed of experts and academics, acts more as a watchdog of the application of the ICCPR and as a promoter of human rights, in a way that reminds the approach of human rights advocacy. Moreover,

[174] Hilal Elver, *The Headscarf Controversy: Secularism and Freedom of Religion* (Oxford University Press, 2012).

[175] 'However, what, in fact, is the connection between the ban and sexual equality? The judgment does not say. Indeed, what is the signification of wearing the headscarf? [. . .] wearing the headscarf had no single meaning; it is a practise that is engaged in for a variety of reasons. It does not necessarily symbolise the submission of women to men and there are those who maintain that, in certain cases, it can even be a means of emancipating women'. *Leyla Sahin*, ECtHR, dissenting opinion Judge Tulkens.

following the dissenting opinion of Judge Tulkens in *Leyla*, Evans developed a feminist critique of the ECtHR's approach to the headscarf issue. A male-dominated Court, like the one in *Leyla Şahin* with twelve male judges and five female judges, would certainly be more willing to accept 'the assertions of gender inequality by a male-dominated Government' and paid 'little attention to the views of women'.[176] However, looking at the composition of the HRC in *Hudoyberganova*, the feminist theory cannot be invoked as a justification of such a different approach. Indeed, the HRC seems to be even more male-dominated in its composition, with eighteen male members and two female members,[177] but it did not prevent the Committee from taking into consideration the women's perspective on the issue.

In conclusion, many factors may explain the judicial fragmentation between the HRC and the ECtHR on the matter of freedom to manifest religion and the following chapters will attempt to understand them more in detail.

2.2.2 *Indigenous Property Rights*

Judicial fragmentation is affecting another debated issue within IHRL: indigenous land rights.[178]

The complex matter of the communal and ancestral right to property for indigenous people has been widely discussed by scholars and practitioners,[179] and is still in the process of being adequately protected by international rules. Indeed, the UN Declaration on the Rights of Indigenous Peoples (UNDRIP) was adopted only in 2007 and the ILO Convention No. 169 on Indigenous

[176] Carolyn Evans, 'The Islamic Scarf in the European Court of Human Rights' (2006) 7(4) *Melbourne Journal of International Law* 52, 67.

[177] Information gathered on the website of the OHCHR, available at www.ohchr.org/Documents/HRBodies/CCPR/Membership/Membership19772014.pdf, last accessed 10 February 2022.

[178] Part of this section has been previously published by the author. See Elena Abrusci, 'Judicial Fragmentation on Indigenous Property Rights: Causes, Consequences and Solutions' (2017) 21 (5) *The International Journal of Human Rights* 550.

[179] cf Alexandra Xanthaki, *Indigenous Rights and United Nations Standards: Self-determination, Culture and Land* (Cambridge University Press, 2007); Ann Curthoys, Ann Genovese and Alexander Reilly, *Rights and Redemption: History, Law and Indigenous People* (University of New South Wales Press, 2008); Stan Stevens, *Indigenous Peoples, National Parks and Protected Areas: A New Paradigm Linking Conservation, Culture and Rights* (University of Arizona Press, 2014); Roger Plant, *Land Rights and Minorities* (London Minority Group, 1994) and Jo M. Pasqualucci, 'International Indigenous Land Rights: A Critique of the Jurisprudence of the Inter-American Court of Human Rights in Light of the United Nations Declaration on the Rights of Indigenous Peoples' (2010) 27 *Wisconsin International Law Journal* 51.

and Tribal peoples' rights has been ratified so far only by twenty countries.[180] Cultural and historical variables play a key role in recognising the right to communal property to indigenous communities. Indeed, while indigenous communities and minority groups are a reality everywhere, the fact that these communities have had a fundamental role in the history of Latin America and Africa, compared to the history of Europe, significantly affected the protection of their rights especially in the judicial interpretation of regional human rights bodies.

The right to property is similarly articulated in regional human rights instruments; Article 14 of the African Charter, Article 21 of the American Convention and Article 1 of the First Protocol to the ECHR, slightly differing in the text, all establish the principle that everyone should have the right to use and enjoy their property, albeit within the limits that the state may impose on certain legitimate grounds.

However, the application of such provisions in the specific case of land claims by indigenous groups reveals a noteworthy difference in the approach towards the right to collective property of ancestral lands as well as a different understanding of the meaning of 'property' for indigenous people.

This analysis considers the case-law on indigenous land rights of the ECtHR, IACtHR and of the ACommHPR, revealing how the European Court is still too much attached to a private conception of the property and still too reluctant to adapt its jurisprudence to the one of the other regional systems.

The ECtHR has made significant progress from the position of its predecessor, the European Commission, that in 1983 in *G. and E. v. Norway* stated that the 'Convention does not guarantee specific rights to minorities'.[181] However, the two cases *Hingitaq 53 and Others v. Denmark*[182] and *Handölsdalen Sami Village and Others v. Sweden*[183] show that the protection granted to indigenous people claiming their right to property on the ancestral lands in Europe is still insufficient compared to the protection ensured in Africa or America, thus producing a situation of judicial fragmentation.[184]

[180] ILO no 169, 1989. Text of the Convention and updated list of the state parties available at www.ilo.org/dyn/normlex/en/f?p=NORMLEXPUB:12100:0::NO:12100:P12100_ ILO_CODE:C169, last accessed 10 February 2022.

[181] *G. and E. v. Norway*, Application nos 9278/81, 9415/81 (ECommHR, 1983), 30.

[182] *Hingitaq 53 and Others v. Denmark*, Application no 18584/04 (ECtHR, 12 January 2006).

[183] *Handölsdalen Sami Village and Others v. Sweden*, Application no 39013/04 (ECtHR, 30 March 2010).

[184] cf Timo Koivurova, 'Jurisprudence of the European Court of Human Rights Regarding Indigenous Peoples: Retrospect and Prospects' (2011) 18 *International Journal on Minority and Group Rights* 1.

The *Hingitaq 53* case concerned the claims of the Thule tribe (a group of Inughuit) who claimed that the dispossession of their aboriginal lands by Denmark violated their right to a peaceful enjoyment of possessions under Article 1, Protocol 1 ECHR. In 1951, Denmark decided to grant access to the United States to establish an air base in Thule District and in 1953 allowed the United States to expand the base across the entire district, thus forcing the Inughuit to leave their homes and settle in different areas where they could not perform any of their traditional activities. The ECtHR recognised that the Thule tribe had an existing possession prior to the establishment of the air base but it concluded that the expropriation was not an arbitrary measure since it was meant to satisfy a public interest that, at that time, was 'legal and valid'.[185] Moreover, the court acknowledged that the circumstances of the Cold War had justified the decision taken by Denmark and assessed that the applicants had received proper compensation for all the damages and losses, thus striking a fair balance between the interests at stake.[186] In light of the above, the ECtHR rejected the application as being manifestly ill-founded. Furthermore, while the ECtHR recognised, in theory, the specific communal rights of indigenous communities, it ended up not applying them in the present case on the basis of the status of the Thule tribe, arguing that it did not retain 'some or all of its own social, economic, cultural and political institutions' needed for qualifying as a distinct community from the overall indigenous community inhabiting Greenland under Article 1(1)(b) of ILO Convention 169.[187]

The only other relevant case of the ECtHR on the matter is *Handölsdalen Sami Village and Others v. Sweden*. It concerned domestic proceedings about a disputed right of the Sami to use their ancestral land for winter grazing of their reindeer. Many landowners brought proceedings against Sami villages, including the applicants, seeking a judgment forbidding them from using lands without a valid contract with the respective owners. The issue was brought in front of national courts that found a case against the Sami, imposing them with significant fines. The ECtHR, whilst recognising that 'possessions' for the application of Article 1, Protocol 1 include tangible as well

[185] *Hingitaq 53*, ECtHR, The Fact, A.

[186] ibid, The Law, A.

[187] The complainant brought four claims as follows: (1) that they had the right to live in and use their native settlement in Ummannaq/Dundas in the Thule District; (2) that they had the right to move, stay and hunt in the entire Thule District; (3) that the Thule Tribe was entitled to compensation in the amount of DKK 25,000,000 and (4) that each individual was entitled to compensation in the amount of DKK 250,000.

as intangible goods,[188] assessed that the Sami's claim for winter grazing rights in private property could not be regarded as an asset but rather a possession. The ECtHR required the Sami to prove such existing possession over the claimed rights since a possession must be existing in order to receive legal protection.[189] However, the Court held that the Sami were not able to provide such proof and, therefore, rejected the claims as being incompatible *ratione materiae* with the provisions of the ECHR.[190] The only contrasting voice was that of Judge Ziemele who, in her dissenting opinion, pointed out that the reasoning of the ECtHR did not take into consideration the specific features and rights of indigenous people.[191] Recalling the development in the international framework on indigenous rights, Judge Ziemele observed that the burden of proof imposed on the Sami villages was too high and not adequate for the nature of their claim, thus discriminating the Sami villages.[192] Furthermore, it concluded that the ECtHR should have recognised 'the right of indigenous peoples to own the land which such groups have traditionally used and to engage in traditional economic activities'[193] and that the legal technicalities that prevented the latter amount to a violation of the right to fair trial and access to justice.[194]

The ECtHR's position presented in these two cases is completely in contrast with the approach adopted by the IACtHR and the ACommHPR in similar cases. Of particular relevance for the current analysis are four cases decided by the IACtHR (*Mayagna (Sumo) Awas Tingni Community v. Nicaragua*,[195] *Yake Axa Indigenous Community v. Paraguay*,[196] *Sawhoyamaxa Indigenous Community v. Paraguay*[197] and *Saramaka v. Suriname*[198]) and the *Endorois* case (*Centre for Minority Rights Development (Kenya) and Minority Rights Group (on behalf of Endorois Welfare Council) v. Kenya*)[199] brought in front of the ACommHPR in 2003.

188 See, e.g., *Bramelid and Malmström v. Sweden*, Application nos 8588/79 and 8589/79 (ECtHR, 1982), THE LAW, 1 b; *Smith Kline and French Laboratories v. the Netherlands*, Application no 12633/87 (ECtHR, 1990), THE LAW and *Stran Greek Refineries and Stratis Andreadis v. Greece* (Merits), App. No 13427/87 (ECtHR, 1994), 61–62.

189 *Marckx v. Belgium*, Application no 6833/74 (ECtHR, 13 June 1979), 50 and *X v. Federal Republic of Germany*, Application no 8410/78 (ECtHR, 1979), 2.

190 *Handölsdalen*, ECtHR, 56.

191 ibid, dissenting opinion Judge Ziemele, 5.

192 ibid, 2–7.

193 ibid, 2.

194 ibid, 8–10.

195 *Mayagna (Sumo) Awas Tingni Community v. Nicaragua* (IACtHR, 31 August 2001).

196 *Yake Axa Indigenous Community v. Paraguay* (IACtHR, 17 June 2005).

197 *Sawhoyamaxa Indigenous Community v. Paraguay* (IACtHR, 29 March 2006).

198 *Saramaka People v. Suriname* (IACtHR, 28 November 2007).

199 *Centre for Minority Rights Development (Kenya) and Minority Rights Group International on behalf of Endorois Welfare Council v. Kenya* (ACommHPR, 25 November 2009).

The *Mayagna* case, in 2001, was a seminal case for the Inter-American human rights system and the rights of indigenous people, since the IACtHR recognised for the first time that indigenous people have a collective right to property on their ancestral land even if not officially recognised by the state. The facts were similar to the *Hingitaq* 53 case. They concerned the complaints filed by the Mayagna (Sumo) Awas Tingni community against the Government of Nicaragua for having forced them to leave their ancestral lands after granting logging concessions to private owners. However, in contrast with the ECtHR, the IACtHR decided to clearly support the indigenous claims by stating that 'indigenous people, by the fact of their very existence, have the right to live freely in their own territory; the close ties of indigenous people with the land must be recognized and understood as the fundamental basis of their cultures, their spiritual life, their integrity, and their economic survival'.[200] The Court also stressed that the protection of communal lands was afforded 'through an *evolutionary interpretation* of international instruments [...] which precludes a restrictive interpretation of the rights'[201] and held that 'possession of the land should suffice for indigenous communities lacking real title to property of the land to obtain official recognition' of ownership.[202] Furthermore, the IACtHR clarified that the right to property as contained in international human rights treaties has an autonomous meaning and 'cannot be made equivalent to the meaning given [...] in domestic law'.[203] This is significantly different from the understanding of property within the case-law of the ECtHR that relies heavily on the decisions of domestic courts for the determination of the meaning of possession.[204]

Yake Axa Indigenous Community v. Paraguay is another key judgment for the development and strengthening of indigenous property rights. Here the IACtHR dealt with a dispute between private landowners and the Yakye Axa indigenous community, in a way similar to *Handölsdalen*, with the only difference being that the private landowner in Yakye Axa was a farming company rather than private individuals. In supporting the position of the applicant, the IACtHR linked the right to access to traditional lands with the surrounding habitat, holding that 'States must take into account that indigenous territorial rights encompass a broader and different concept that relates to

[200] *Mayagna*, IACtHR, 149.
[201] ibid, 148.
[202] ibid, 151.
[203] ibid, 146.
[204] Giovanna Gismondi, 'Denial of Justice: The Latest Indigenous Land Disputes Before the European Court of Human Rights and the Need for an Expansive Interpretation of Protocol 1' (2016) 15 *Yale Human Rights and Development Law Journal* 42.

the collective right to survival as an organized people, with control over their habitat as a necessary condition for reproduction of their culture, for their development and to carry out their life aspirations'.[205] States have a duty to 'take positive, concrete measures geared toward the fulfilment of the right to a decent life, especially in the case of persons who are vulnerable and at risk' such as indigenous people; a failure to do so would constitute a violation of the right to *vida digna* and therefore Article 4 ACHR. In addition, the IACtHR held that, when returning to ancestral lands is not possible, the selection of alternative lands and/or compensation should be the result of a 'consensus with the indigenous people in accordance with their own mechanism of consultation, values, customs and customary law'.[206] This is an alternative stance from that of the ECtHR in *Hingitaq* 53, where nothing was said about the imposed choice of alternative lands and the quantum of compensation granted by Denmark.[207]

In *Sawhoyamaxa*, the IACtHR adopted a diametrically opposed position compared to the ECtHR in *Hingitaq* 53. Here the IACtHR asserted that 'communities who have unwillingly left their traditional lands, or lost possession thereof, maintain property rights thereto, even though they lack legal title; [...] and who have unwillingly lost possession of their lands, when those lands have been lawfully transferred to innocent third parties, are entitled to restitution thereof or to obtain other lands of equal extension and quality'.[208] Moreover, while dealing with a claim arising out of a dispute between private parties and indigenous communities, the Court said that it must 'assess in each case the legality, necessity, proportionality and fulfilment of a lawful purpose in a democratic society to impose restriction on the right to property, on the one hand, or the right to traditional lands, on the other'.[209] As some scholars pointed out,[210] in *Handölsdalen*, the ECtHR should have also considered the right of the Sami people to their cultural integrity in striking a fair balance with the right to property of the landowners.

[205] *Yake Axa*, IACtHR, 146.

[206] ibid, 149–151.

[207] Ghislain Otis and Aurélie Laurent, 'Indigenous Land Claims in Europe: The European Court of Human Rights and the Decolonization of Property' (2013) 4 *Arctic Review on Law and Politics* 156; Birgitte Feiring, *Indigenous Peoples' Rights to Lands, Territories and Resources* (2013).

[208] ibid, 128.

[209] ibid.

[210] Otis and Laurent, 'Indigenous Land Claims in Europe'; Koivurova, 'Jurisprudence of the European Court of Human Rights'.

Saramaka v. Suriname reinforced all the previous concepts and reaffirmed the strong position of the IACtHR in recognising full ancestral land rights to indigenous communities. Here the Court deeply linked the right to property with the right to use and enjoy natural resources in a way that, if endorsed by the ECtHR, would have produced a different outcome in the *Handölsdalen* case. Indeed, the IACtHR stated that the protection of the communal lands was 'necessary to guarantee their [Saramaka people] survival' and, more importantly, that 'the right to the land itself would be "meaningless" without rights to the natural resources therein'.[211] Therefore, the IACtHR interpreted the right to property as also protecting those 'resources traditionally used and necessary for the very survival, development and continuation of such people's way of life'.[212] Moreover, in the same case, concerning the granting of logging and mining concessions to private companies in a traditional territory without prior consultation with the indigenous people, the IACtHR established that the state is required to implement some 'safeguards' in order to protect the rights and interests of the affected indigenous populations.[213] Compared to both *Hingitaq 53* and *Handölsdalen*, it is evident how the ECtHR did not engage in any of these discussions and did not feel the need to set any safeguards for the protection of indigenous peoples' rights even when ruling against them.

The same approach could also be found in the more recent *Kichwa Indigenous People of Sarayaku v. Ecuador*,[214] issued in 2012. In addition to the above, in this case, the IACtHR held, for the first time, that it was the Sarayaku people as an indigenous community, rather than just the sum of individuals, who suffered a collective violation.[215] Moreover, the court stressed the importance of the 'right to consultation' and effective participation of the indigenous community whose traditional lands are put at risk,[216]

[211] *Saramaka*, IACtHR, 122.

[212] ibid.

[213] 'First, the State must ensure the effective participation of the members of the Saramaka people, in conformity with their customs and traditions, regarding any development, investment, exploration or extraction plan (hereinafter "development or investment plan"), 127 within Saramaka territory. Second, the State must guarantee that the Saramakas will receive a reasonable benefit from any such plan within their territory. Thirdly, the State must ensure that no concession will be issued within Saramaka territory unless and until independent and technically capable entities, with the State's supervision, perform a prior environmental and social impact assessment. These safeguards are intended to preserve, protect and guarantee the special relationship that the members of the Saramaka community have with their territory, which in turn ensures their survival as a tribal people'. ibid, 129.

[214] *Kichwa Indigenous People of Sarayaku v. Ecuador* (IACtHR, 27 June 2012).

[215] ibid, 341 (2).

[216] ibid, E.2.a.

considering it was not only provided by the ACHR but a 'general principle of international law'.[217]

The ACommHPR followed the progressive line of interpretation of the IACtHR, thus diverging considerably from the ECtHR. The *Endorois* case concerned the displacement of the indigenous community Endorois from their ancestral lands following the decision of the Government of Kenya to convert the area into a national reserve for conservation purposes.[218] The ACommHPR took a clear stance in favour of the Endorois community. It openly recognised that 'the encroachment on Endorois land was not proportional to any public need and not in accordance with national and international law'[219] and ordered Kenya to return the lands to the community. By frequently referring to the case-law of the IACtHR, the ACommHPR established that the right to property should be guaranteed to the indigenous community even if the domestic legislation does not recognise collective rights.

2.2.2.1 Concluding Observations

In light of the above, it is possible to conclude that the protection of property rights for indigenous people is fragmented among regional human rights bodies. From the previous analysis, it seems quite clear that the key difference between the regional courts' approaches is that the ECtHR continues addressing indigenous land rights claims as any other private property rights case, without taking into serious consideration the features of the applicant. In *Hingitaq 53*, when rejecting the case and considering the compensation and the alternative land received as proportionate for the Inughuit community, the ECtHR seemed to ignore the needs of the indigenous community and treated it as any group of people being forced to leave their home. In contrast, both the IACtHR and the ACommHPR focused on the specific nature of an indigenous community and reflected on the importance of the land as part of their own culture, history and life. Not surprisingly, the IACtHR often linked the protection of indigenous ancestral land to the concept of *vida digna*, stating that the use and enjoyment of their ancestral land are fundamental to live a life with dignity.[220] The same consideration can be made for

[217] Thomas Antkowiak, 'Rights, Resources, and Rhetoric: Indigenous Peoples and the Inter-American Court' (2013) 35 *University of Pennsylvania Journal of International Law* 113, 157.

[218] *Minority Rights Group International on behalf of Endorois Welfare Council v. Kenya* (ACommHPR, 25 November 2009), 3.

[219] ibid, 238.

[220] See *Xákmok Kásek v. Paraguay* (IACtHR, 24 August 2010), 107.

the *Handölsdalen* case. Here, the ECtHR, when rejecting the case because the applicant was not able to demonstrate the existing possession, did not consider the specificity of indigenous ancestral land rights. First, the court did not recognise the right to collective property over an ancestral land in the absence of a legal title. Second, it completely ignored the fact that for an indigenous community the use of the land for traditional activities is part of its own existence. In contrast, both the IACtHR and the ACommHPR reached the opposite conclusion when dealing with similar situations of a property right claim over land that could not be legally justified and demonstrated. Indeed, they both concluded that the requirement of a legal title should be widely interpreted and that traditional activities connected to the land are fundamental for the survival of the indigenous community.

The cause of the current situation of judicial fragmentation on indigenous property rights is certainly the different approach, on the one hand, of the progressive IACtHR and ACommHPR and, on the other hand, of the conservative ECtHR. Still, the reasons behind the rigid and individualistic attitude of the ECtHR are not fully clear.

The letter of the articles protecting the right to property cannot be considered as the sole cause of such a divergent interpretation. Indeed, as previously recalled, Article 1, Protocol 1 ECHR is actually the most advanced and comprehensive right to property, especially in comparison to the African and American instruments, for its explicit reference to the enjoyment of the property and any 'natural or legal person' as a rights holder. However, the different regional frameworks on minority and indigenous rights should be taken into consideration. The little attention given within the European system to indigenous rights is demonstrated by the lack of any explicit reference to indigenous people in the Framework Convention for the Protection of National Minorities. Although some indigenous groups can fit within the very broad definition of national minority, the absence of a clear mention of the rights of indigenous people in a specific instrument is an evident signal of the lack of interest towards this issue within the European system. Nonetheless, one should not forget that even within the Inter-American and African systems there is no specific reference to or convention on indigenous rights. Therefore, the argument of the different legal framework can only partially explain the phenomenon of fragmentation.

The margin of appreciation, often invoked in cases of fragmentation as a possible explanation, here finds little application. The ECtHR granted a wide margin of appreciation to the states in defining the criteria for attributing the property and negotiating the reparations and the alternative lands, but it did not justify its outcome on this basis. Indeed, this element appears to be marginal for the current issue because, rather than deferring the decision to the national authorities through the tool of the margin of appreciation, the ECtHR seems to have taken a quite clear stance on the matter of indigenous land rights.

The impression from the reading of the two judgments is that the ECtHR was not familiar with indigenous rights and did not know how to properly deal with collective and communal property claims and, opting for a cautious solution, decided to apply its well-established reasoning and understanding of private property rights. The ECtHR relied on the principle of 'eminent domain', also applied to the territories claimed by indigenous communities. On the basis that the indigenous community could not provide any legal title of ownership over the land, the state should be considered as the lawful owner of that land and could dispose of it freely, granting or allocating it to third parties.[221]

On this point, it should also be highlighted that there is a difference in the interests of the parties in the cases brought before, respectively, the Inter-American or African bodies and the ECtHR. On the one hand, the IACtHR and the ACommHPR dealt with contentious cases of indigenous communities against states or private companies and enterprises willing to exploit their lands for mining, forestry or other profit activities. On the other hand, the ECtHR had to deal, in *Handölsdalen*, with individual private landowners who were claiming the property with a legitimate title over the land. The main difference lies in the fact that, in the latter case, there is a conflict of similar interests at stake with the indigenous communities. While states and private companies in the former cases claimed only a right to property over the land linked to the new interest to get economic benefits out of it, private individual landowners in the latter case claimed a right to property together with an already existing attachment to the land and a need to live and use the land in a very similar way to indigenous people. Even though non-indigenous individual landowners do not have the specific 'indigenous' rights, they still invoke their right to live on their land not simply on the basis of a legitimate property acquisition but also because of the paramount importance that the land has for their life and existence. In light of this, striking a fair balance between the two parties' rights seems very difficult and the approach of the ECtHR may be better understood as a way to protect the interests and rights of the

[221] cf Otis and Laurent, 'Indigenous Land Claims in Europe', 158; Economic and Social Council, Commission on Human Rights, Sub-Commission on the Promotion and Protection of Human Rights, 53rd Session, Indigenous Peoples and their Relationship to Land – Final Working Paper Prepared by the Special Rapporteur Mrs. Erica-Irene A. Daes, E/CN.4/Sub.2/ 2001/21.57.

non-indigenous landowners in such a controversial situation. However, what the ECtHR failed to do is to recognise in the first place the right to property of the indigenous community, thus ignoring the conflicts of rights at stake and automatically taking the side of the private landowners, confirming the reluctant approach held in *Hingitaq 53*.

The different general sensibility and attention towards indigenous rights between the regional bodies are easily explained by the history and politics of the countries involved. American and African countries have dealt with indigenous issues for a long time and, currently, these are still at the forefront of the political and social agenda of national and regional institutions. Indigenous communities in Africa and the Americas have played a significant role in the history and politics of the two continents, and they still play a fundamental role in society. The African and the Inter-American human rights systems have amongst their priorities the protection of the indigenous communities,[222] and they actively contributed to the debate within the ILO and the UN bodies for the development of relevant international instruments. Therefore, it is not surprising that, in their judicial interpretation, the rights of the indigenous groups are applied and defended at the maximum level, setting a very high standard of protection.

However, since such a standard is not higher than that contained in the UNDRIP or in the ILO Convention No. 169, that some European countries have ratified too, one could hopefully expect the ECtHR to align itself to the case-law of the IACtHR, contributing to the enhancement of the uniformity of IHRL.

2.2.3 *The Right to Marry for Same-Sex Couples and the Recognition of the Change of Gender Identity*

The last example of judicial fragmentation is the right to marry for same-sex couples and the recognition of the change of gender identity triggered by the IACtHR Advisory Opinion No. 24.[223] In this opinion, issued on 9 January 2018, the IACtHR addressed both the requirements for the recognition of the change of gender identity and the right to marry for same-sex couples, landing on completely different conclusions than the ECtHR or the HRC in their

[222] A proof of this engagement is, for example, the establishment, by the IACommHR, of the Special Rapporteur on the Rights of Indigenous People (www.oas.org/en/iachr/indigenous/mandate/Functions.asp) and, by the ACommHPR, of the Working Group on Indigenous Populations/Communities in Africa (www.achpr.org/mechanisms/indigenous-populations).

[223] *Identidad de género, e igualdad y no discriminación a parejas del mismo sexo*, Opinión consultiva OC-24/17 (IACtHR, 9 January 2018).

ruling on the matter. Although being an Advisory Opinion rather than a contentious case could have encouraged the Court to take a more progressive approach, the contrasting reasoning of the IACtHR triggered judicial fragmentation.

Back in 2016, the government of Costa Rica presented a request for an Advisory Opinion from the IACtHR, seeking answers to the following five questions:

> 1) Considering that gender identity is a protected category within the American Convention, does the state have an obligation to recognise and facilitate the change of name of individuals in accordance with their own gender identity? 2) If so, is the judicial procedure for the change of name, instead of an administrative one, contrary to the American Convention? 3) According to the American Convention, is the current Costa Rican judicial procedure for the change of name not applicable to individuals who wish to change their name based on their gender identity? Should they rather be given the possibility of resorting to a free, fast and accessible administrative procedure? 4) Considering the duty not to discriminate on the basis of sexual orientation, should the State recognise all patrimonial rights deriving from a same-sex relationship? 5) If so, is it necessary for the State to establish a legal institution regulating the legal status of same-sex couples, and to recognise all patrimonial rights stemming from such relationships?[224]

In response to the first three questions, the IACtHR strongly confirmed that sexual orientation and gender identity are protected categories under the American Convention,[225] in line with what the ECtHR had said in *Salgueiro da Silva Mouta v. Portugal*[226] and the HRC in *Toonen v. Australia*.[227] However, the IACtHR decided to take a step forward and held that gender identity is an integral and essential element of a person's identity and its recognition by the state is a requirement for the enjoyment of other fundamental rights, such as human dignity, self-determination, freedom from torture and freedom of expression.[228] On this account, the IACtHR established that Costa Rica had a duty to recognise and facilitate the change of name according to gender identity in order to fully ensure that everyone, regardless of their sexual orientation or gender identity, enjoys the same dignified life (*vida digna*), a concept already extensively used in the above-mentioned

[224] ibid, 3.
[225] ibid, 68–84.
[226] *Salgueiro*, ECtHR, 36.
[227] *Toonen*, HRC.
[228] *Opinion Consultiva no 24*, IACtHR, 98.

indigenous cases.[229] Following this assumption, the IACtHR established that the state has a duty to develop specific procedures for modifying registry entries of gender or sex, name and images, respecting a list of principles that safeguard the rights of transgender people. In particular, these procedures should be: (i) based on a self-perceived gender identity; (ii) based on free and informed consent of the interested person without requiring medical or psychological certificates or other documents; (iii) confidential, and amended documents should not report changes of gender identity; (iv) expedient and, as far as possible, free of charge; (v) not requiring the performance of surgical and/or hormonal treatments.[230]

This is clearly divergent from the ECtHR's position on recognition of gender identity. The ECtHR has repeatedly established the right for a transgender individual to have their new gender recognised. Moreover, it imposes a duty on the state to ensure the possibility for the individual to have a free of charge gender reassignment surgery.[231] However, in *A.P. v. France*,[232] the Strasbourg Court held that France was not in breach of the ECHR when ordering forced medical examination or mental health diagnosis as a requirement for the recognition of the change of gender. This is obviously in contrast with the third requirement set by the IACtHR 'being based on the free and informed consent of the interested person without requiring medical or psychological certificates or other documents'.[233] In reaching this conclusion, the ECtHR invoked the existence of a wide margin of appreciation that France had in deciding whether to require a medical certification in the absence of gender reassignment surgery.[234] It is worth noting that in the same case the ECtHR took anyway a big step forward in establishing that it was against the Convention to make the recognition of the gender identity of a transgender individual conditional on undergoing an operation or sterilising treatment. Furthermore, the ECtHR held that the margin of appreciation granted to member states should be very narrow in this case on the basis of a growing regional consensus on the matter.[235] This shows that the fragmentation between the European and the Inter-American system is most likely due

[229] ibid, 100, 116.
[230] ibid, 171.
[231] *Goodwin*, ECtHR and *Schlumpf v. Switzerland*, Application no 29002/06 (ECtHR, 8 January 2009).
[232] *A.P., Garçon and Nicot v. France*, Application no 79885/12 (ECtHR, 6 April 2017).
[233] *Opinion Consultiva no 24*, IACtHR, 171.
[234] *A.P.*, ECtHR, 143.
[235] ibid, 121–125.

to a different standard of deference to member states and the lack of use of a margin of appreciation theory by the IACtHR.[236]

In addition, also the final part of the opinion, addressing the need of a formal legal recognition of same-sex marriage, triggered fragmentation, this time in relation to the right to marry for same-sex couples. The question was formulated in very general terms, asking the IACtHR whether it was necessary to establish some legal institutions to recognise same-sex relationships and the deriving rights and duties. The IACtHR acknowledged the vagueness of the question and decided to take advantage of this to expand and advance LGBTIQI's rights in the Americas. Recalling the case-law of the ECtHR and the domestic legislation of some countries in the region (with no reference to a regional consensus though), the IACtHR argued that member states have a duty to provide some legal recognition to homosexual relationships. As established by the ECtHR in *Karner v. Austria*, the options are different and include, for example, civil unions and other partnerships. However, in the case of Costa Rica, the Court observed that it would not be necessary to establish a new legal institution, since civil marriage is already in place. Therefore, according to the IACtHR, Costa Rica simply needed to extend the existing institution of marriage to same-sex couples.[237] In supporting this landmark statement, the IACtHR held that any argument in favour of the exclusivity of a heterosexual marriage (because of religious or philosophical beliefs or based on the alleged natural link between marriage and procreation) is not acceptable to justify different treatments between heterosexual and homosexual couples and that 'there is no legitimate aim that could make this distinction necessary and proportionate under the Convention'.[238] Moreover, 'the Court observes that often the opposition to same-sex marriage is based on religious or philosophical beliefs. While recognising the importance of these beliefs [. . .], they cannot be used as parameters of conventionality and cannot guide the Court's interpretation of human rights'.[239] And, even more strongly, the Court opined that 'establishing a legal institution that produces the same effects and grants the same rights as marriage but under a different name carries no purpose, except to socially mark and stigmatise same-sex couples, or at least convey that they are undervalued',[240] thus constituting discrimination.

[236] See Chapter 6.

[237] *Opinion Consultiva no 24*, IACtHR, 218.

[238] ibid, 220. Personal free translation from the official Spanish text.

[239] ibid, 223.

[240] ibid, 224.

This is in open contrast with the position held by the ECtHR in many cases related to the right to marry for same-sex couples such as *Schalk and Kopf v. Austria*[241] and by the HRC in *Joslin v. New Zealand*.[242] In both cases the two bodies held that, while it was a duty of the state to ensure the enjoyment of the right to a family life for homosexual couples in the same way as heterosexual couples, there was no right to enter into marriage for same-sex couples and member states could find the most suitable and convenient arrangement for ensuring the enjoyment of the right to a family life. Indeed, both the ECtHR and the HRC observed that the letter of Article 12 ECHR and Article 23 ICCPR establishes the right to marry between 'a man and a woman' and does not provide such right for 'everyone' or 'all human beings'.[243] Furthermore, the ECtHR argued that marriage is an institution deeply rooted in local societies and its regulation should be left to the single member states. Indeed, the ECtHR noticed that there was no European consensus on gay marriage, being only six out of forty-seven the member states that at the time had adopted domestic legislation allowing gay marriage. In light of this, while recognising the possibility of interpreting Article 12 as allowing same-sex marriage, the ECtHR concluded that there was no violation of the right to marry, since Article 12 does not impose any obligation upon member states to provide the right to marry for same-sex couples.

On the contrary, the IACtHR in this Advisory Opinion acknowledged the lack of a regional consensus (only Argentina, Brazil, Colombia, Uruguay and some Mexican states recognised homosexual marriages at the time) but strongly stated that this should not constitute an obstacle to the advancement of human rights.[244] Even more, in virtue of the conventionality control,[245] all member states are now required to align their domestic legislation with the current interpretation of the ACHR provided by the court, thus establishing a further layer of control over its member states. In conclusion, the above analysis shows that the recent Advisory Opinion of the IACtHR triggered judicial fragmentation on sexual orientation rights and gender identity between the IACtHR, on the one side, and the ECtHR and the HRC on the other. The reasons are several but the doctrine of the margin of appreciation, the regional consensus and the interpretation of norms certainly play a key role, as explored in the following chapter.

[241] *Schalk and Kopf v. Austria*, Application no 30141/04 (ECtHR, 22 November 2010).
[242] *Joslin v. New Zealand*, Communication no 902/1999 (HRC, 2003).
[243] ibid and *Schalk and Kopf*, ECtHR, 57–60.
[244] *Opinion Consultiva no 24*, IACtHR, 219.
[245] See Chapter 3, Section 3.3.4.

CONCLUSION

The analysis presented in this chapter showed that judicial fragmentation is only a limited phenomenon in IHRL, arising only in specific circumstances in the case-law of the three main regional systems and the UN HRC. Even though many of the triggering factors of fragmentation in IL could be equally found in IHRL, a perusal of the case-law of these bodies reveals that there is a substantial convergence of interpretation and judicial application of human rights norms. There are some instances where each body uses a slightly different language or seems to go in a different direction, but, usually, this is not enough to trigger fragmentation, being simply an equivalent way of expressing the same standard or approach. Most of the time there is a substantial convergence on the general application of a right, such as the prohibition of discrimination, and then the eventual fragmentation may arise on a particular application in a very specific context, such as on the granting of the right to marry for same-sex couples.

Likewise, in other situations, the absence of fragmentation can also be explained by the fact that the cases brought before two bodies are often not similar enough to be compared. In particular, the analysis underlined the key role played by the domestic laws and situations that may prevent a comparison on the basis of differences in the facts or in the law. In these instances, far from claiming convergence, the assessment should be suspended waiting for further developments. Nevertheless, this stand-by situation may be misleading as it looks like convergence from the outside because of the absence of fragmentation.

With a limited case-law for some bodies, this bias in numbers and variety of cases prevents the arising of fragmentation in several circumstances, but leaves the door open to the possibility of this fragmentation to arise in any moment when a new case is brought before a body that never ruled on that matter before. Indeed, the absence of fragmentation on a certain topic does not necessarily mean convergence. Especially when some divergent elements in the reasoning can be spotted, special attention should be paid to the development of the case-law on that issue because new cases with different facts may eventually trigger fragmentation.

Moreover, as shown in Section 2.2, some clear cases of judicial fragmentation can be identified, and they all concern specific issues within certain rights where the general approach to the right is convergent, but the particular issue has triggered contrasting interpretations and outcomes. The analysis of the cases allowed the identification of many triggering factors that contributed to judicial fragmentation, such as a different deferential approach to member states and varying importance given to the regional consensus, lack of judicial dialogue, historical and cultural variables and institutional challenges. All these elements, which on their own only partially explain such a complex phenomenon, will be further explored and scrutinised in the following chapters, in order to understand their dual role of triggering fragmentation and ensuring convergence.

PART II

Factors Explaining Judicial Convergence and Fragmentation

3

The Theory of Treaty Interpretation and Judicial Dialogue

INTRODUCTION

As observed in the previous chapter, judicial fragmentation is limited because regional human rights systems and the HRC decided to interpret general and broad provisions in a convergent way. As recalled in Chapter 1, human rights norms are often subject to various interpretations and could be stirred in one direction or the other, possibly leading to convergence or fragmentation.

In light of this, this chapter explores the role of treaty interpretation for judicial convergence and fragmentation and the contribution of judicial dialogue for the maintenance of convergence. The first section introduces the theory of treaty interpretation, and provides a brief overview of the approach adopted by each of the human rights bodies under analysis, linking it with the interpretation clauses contained in their constitutive treaties. The second section focuses on judicial dialogue. After defining it and identifying some of the reasons why a body decides to engage with it, it presents the practice of each human rights body in relation to judicial dialogue, highlighting trends and features and how the latter helps maintaining convergence. Finally, it brings back some cases of fragmentation already identified in Chapter 2 to understand which role judicial dialogue (or its absence) played in maintaining convergence or triggering fragmentation, discovering that the causal-effect link is not always straightforward.

3.1 THE THEORY OF TREATY INTERPRETATION: SUBSTANTIAL CONVERGENCE OF INTERPRETATION METHODS

Human rights treaties, like any treaty under international law, are to be interpreted in a way that is consistent with the Vienna Convention on the

Law of Treaties (VCLT).[1] Even if scholars and judges have often pointed out the peculiarity of IHRL, which requires particular attention in interpreting treaty provisions, the VCLT should always be the point of reference for interpretation.[2] In particular, Article 31 VCLT provides that 'a treaty shall be interpreted in good faith in accordance with the ordinary meaning to be given to the terms of the treaty in their context and in light of its object and purpose'.[3] Sub-paragraphs two and three further provide that when considering the context special attention should be paid to other relevant international law instruments between the parties. Furthermore, Article 32 provides additional means of interpretation.[4]

All four jurisdictions under analysis recognise that the VCLT provisions should regulate their interpretation, but the practical way they interpret such vague guidelines varies.[5] The content of the two articles is, in fact, quite elusive, leaving an extensive space of manoeuvre to the single bodies on how to utilise them. Yet, what can be observed among these bodies is a substantial convergence of interpretation methods, based on the VCLT. For instance, they all agree on the importance of the context for the interpretation of their conventions and charter. In *Soering v. United Kingdom*, the ECtHR held that the 'Convention is to be read as a whole'[6] and in *Legal Resources Foundation v. Zambia* the ACommHPR similarly held that the 'African Charter must be interpreted holistically'.[7] However, as will be later observed, different positions may arise as to what elements are to be taken into consideration when the context is invoked and to which extent external material should be called into the discussion.

As for the 'object and purpose' of the treaty that should always inspire the interpretation of the text, human rights bodies are very much convergent in

1 Vienna Convention on the Law of Treaties (VCLT), Vienna 23 May 1969 (in force 27 January 1980), 1155 UNTS 331.

2 Frédéric Vanneste, *General International Law before Human Rights Courts* (Intersentia, 2010), 227; Jonas Christoffersen, *Fair Balance: Proportionality, Subsidiarity and Primarity in the European Convention on Human Rights* (Martinus-Nijhoff, 2009), 61; Malgosia Fitzmaurice, 'Interpretation of Human Rights Treaties' in Dina Shelton (ed), *The Oxford Handbook of Human Rights Law* (Oxford University Press, 2013), 739–740.

3 Article 31 VCLT.

4 ibid, Article 32.

5 See, for example, the ECtHR in *Golder v. UK*, Application no 4451/70 (ECtHR, 21 February 1975), 30 and the IACtHR in *Mapiripan Massacre v. Colombia* (IACtHR, 15 September 2005), 106.

6 *Soering v. UK*, Application no 14038/88 (ECtHR, 7 July 1989), 103.

7 *Legal Resources Foundation v. Zambia*, Communication no 211/98 (ACommHPR, 7 May 2001), 70.

linking it to the concept of 'effectiveness' of the human rights instruments and applying the *pro homine* principle.[8]

The importance of treaty interpretation in the occurrence or avoidance of judicial fragmentation is further confirmed by the recommendations of the ILC Report, which urged international law courts and tribunals to stick to the systemic integration principle set forth in Article 31(3)(c) in order to avoid fragmentation.[9]

The following paragraphs will dig into specific aspects of treaty interpretation that may have an impact on judicial convergence and fragmentation among human rights bodies.

Amidst efforts to adapt the VCLT principles of interpretation to the peculiarity of human rights treaties, human rights bodies seem to have also agreed on the adoption of an 'evolutive method of interpretation'.[10] This doctrine aims at interpreting human rights treaties as 'living instruments', understanding the development of the society and the law. This is certainly not an innovative methodology in treaty interpretation and stems from the requirement set by Article 31 VCLT to consider the context. As the IACtHR explained in its 1989 Advisory Opinion on *The Interpretation of the American Convention*, 'to determine the legal status of the American Declaration it is appropriate to look to the Inter-American system of today in light of the evolution it has undergone since the adoption of the Declaration'.[11] In a subsequent Advisory Opinion on *The Right to Information on Consular Assistance*, the IACtHR confirmed this approach stating that 'international human rights law [. . .] has made great headway thanks to an evolutive interpretation of international instruments of protection'.[12] In supporting its methodological choice, the IACtHR refers to its European counterpart and the interpretation approach adopted by the ECtHR. Indeed, in *Tyrer v. United Kingdom*, the ECtHR held that 'the Convention is a living instrument, which [. . .] must be interpreted in

8 See later Section 3.1.1.

9 ILC, 'Fragmentation of International Law: Difficulties Arising from the Diversification and Expansion of International Law'. Report of the Study Group of the International Law Commission – Finalised by Martti Koskenniemi (13 April 2006), UN Doc A/CN.4/L.682, 213.

10 Fitzmaurice, 'Interpretation of Human Rights Treaties', 737.

11 *The Interpretation of the American Declaration of the Rights and Duties of Man within the Framework of Article 64 of the American Convention on Human Rights*, Advisory Opinion (IACtHR, 14 July 1989), 37–43.

12 *The Right to Information on Consular Assistance in the Framework of the Guarantees of the due Process of Law*, Advisory Opinion OC-16/99 (IACtHR, 1 October 1999), 112.

the light of present-day conditions'[13] and in *Mapiripan Massacre v. Colombia*, the IACtHR citing the ECtHR in *Tyrer* held that the interpretation of human rights treaties 'must go hand in hand with evolving times and current living conditions'.[14] The African bodies also share the evolutive interpretation of the African Charter even if they never explicitly refer to the latter as a living instrument.[15] Nevertheless, their case-law based on Articles 60 and 61 of the Charter, which will be discussed later in this chapter, is a clear proof of such evolutive interpretation.[16]

Likewise, the HRC has interpreted the ICCPR in a very evolutive way. In *Judge v. Canada*, the HRC openly held that 'the International Covenant on Civil and Political Rights should be interpreted as a living instrument' and that the rights protected therein 'should be applied in context and in the light of present-day conditions'.[17] The General Comments that the HRC periodically issues are inherently inspired by the notion of the ICCPR as a living instrument that needs to be constantly updated in its interpretation taking into consideration the evolution of the law and society.[18]

Considering the evolutive approach towards human rights treaty interpretation, all the human rights bodies under analysis appear to agree upon the need to interpret human rights treaties in light of their object and purpose: the protection of fundamental rights and freedoms. This understanding culminates in the application of the *pro homine* principle to their adjudication, which requires that the most favourable norm to the individual must prevail. This teleological approach has been mainly put forward by the IACtHR that, relying on Article 33 ACHR, emphasised its role of protecting human rights and, hence, applying a natural bias in favour of the applicant.[19] In the European system, the *pro homine* principle is embedded in the 'effectiveness' principle. The latter is essentially the aspiration to meet the objective and purpose of the ECHR when applying it to the given case. As established in *Papamichalopolous and Others v. Greece*, the ECHR should aim to effectively

[13] *Tyrer v. United Kingdom*, Application no 5856/72 (ECtHR, 25 April 1978), 31. For a more detailed analysis of the ECtHR interpretation approach see Eva Brems and Janneke Gerards (eds), *Shaping Rights in the ECHR* (Cambridge University Press, 2013).

[14] *Mapiripan Massacre*, IACtHR, 106.

[15] Magnus Killander, 'Interpreting Regional Human Rights Treaties' (2010) 7 *SYR-International Journal on Human Rights*, 151–152.

[16] ibid and Section 3.2.2.2.

[17] *Judge v. Canada*, Communication no 829/1998 (HRC, 8 August 2003), 10.3.

[18] Cecilia Medina, 'The Role of International Tribunals: Law-Making or Creative Interpretation?' in Dina Shelton (ed), *The Oxford Handbook of International Human Rights Law* (Oxford University Press, 2013), 657–661.

[19] ibid.

protect the fundamental rights and freedoms of the individuals and should always be interpreted in this perspective.[20] The same understanding of effectiveness could be then found again in the IACtHR[21] and the African Commission,[22] bringing the regional bodies on the same line when it comes to the ultimate objective and purpose of their adjudication.

This substantial convergence of interpretation methods, despite some shades of variation, is probably not enough to explain the predominant convergence of case-law among human rights bodies but certainly contributes to it. Although it is difficult to claim that judicial convergence is a direct consequence of convergent interpretation methods, it is still possible to speculate on how different the situation would be if the human rights bodies under analysis decided to adopt completely divergent approaches to interpretation. For example, it could be argued that the current convergence on including sexual orientation as a prohibited ground for discrimination could not have been reached if one of the human rights bodies had decided not to adopt an evolutive interpretative approach. None of the human rights texts, the ECHR, ACHR or ICCPR, mentions 'sexual orientation' as one of the grounds for prohibited discrimination but all of the bodies, the ECtHR, the IACtHR and the HRC, interpreted the provisions in the same way, going beyond the letter of the article.[23] If any of them had opted for a literal interpretation of their treaty provisions, they would have not been able to include sexual orientation as a prohibited ground of discrimination and fragmentation would have arisen.

3.1.1 *Interpretation Clauses*

In addition to the general rules of treaty interpretation of the VCLT, each treaty may have specific interpretation clauses, establishing additional guidelines and directions for interpretation. This is the case of the ACHR, ACHPR and ECHR. The interpretation clauses of the African and American instruments differ quite significantly from the European Convention, potentially leading to a different attitude to interpretation, and, ultimately, to fragmentation.

[20] *Papamichalopolous and Others v. Greece*, Application no 14556/89 (ECtHR, 24 June 1993), 42.
[21] *Ricardo Canese v. Paraguay* (IACtHR, 31 August 2004), 178.
[22] *Scanlen and Holderness v. Zimbabwe*, Communication no 297/05 (ACommHPR, 3 April 2009), 115.
[23] cf *Salgueiro da Silva Mouta v. Portugal*, Application no 33290/96 (ECtHR, 21 March 2000); *Toonen v. Australia*, Communication no 488/1992 (HRC, 1994) and *Atala Riffo and Daughters v. Chile* (IACtHR, 24 February 2012).

Article 29 ACHR provides additional rules of interpretation of the American Convention and states that

> [n]o provision of this Convention shall be interpreted as: [...] b. restricting the enjoyment or exercise of any right or freedom recognized by virtue of the laws of any State Party or by virtue of another convention to which one of the said states is a party; [...] d. excluding or limiting the effect that the American Declaration of the Rights and Duties of Man and other international acts of the same nature may have.[24]

In light of this, the IACtHR has almost always referred to the jurisprudence of other human rights bodies in its reasoning, as will be discussed in the following section, and it has creatively applied the American Convention, successfully harmonising its case-law with other human rights adjudicatory bodies and mostly maintaining convergence.[25] As Cecilia Medina, former judge of the IACtHR, has stated, the IACtHR's judges 'have consistently felt the need to apply the ACHR as creatively as possible', thus interpreting Article 29 as a gateway for the inclusion and harmonisation of external material into the American tradition with the final purpose of ensuring the protection of human rights.[26]

The African Charter on Human and Peoples' Rights contains an explicit provision that does not simply allow the Commission and Court to take into consideration other existing obligations of the parties but goes much further. Article 60 requires the African Commission to

> draw inspiration from international law on human and peoples' rights, particularly from [...] the Charter of the United Nations, [...] the Universal Declaration of Human Rights, other instruments adopted by the United Nations and by African countries in the field of Human and Peoples' Rights, as well as from the provisions of various instruments adopted within the Specialised Agencies of the United Nations.[27]

Such an explicit obligation has been enthusiastically endorsed by the Commission under the more general objective of fostering universalism. Indeed, in *Purohit and Another v. The Gambia*, the ACommHPR stated that it is

[24] Article 29, ACHR.

[25] See, among others, *Bámaca Velásquez v. Guatemala* (IACtHR, 25 November 2000) and *Las Palmeras v. Colombia* (IACtHR, 6 December 2001).

[26] Medina, 'The Role of International Tribunals', 662.

[27] Article 60, ACHPR.

> more than willing to accept legal arguments with the support of appropriate and relevant international and regional human rights instruments, principles, norms and standards taking into account the well-recognised principle of universality which was established by the Vienna Declaration and Programme of Action of 1993 and which declares that 'all human rights are universal, indivisible and interdependent and interrelated'.[28]

Also, the protocol establishing the ACtHPR states, in Article 3, that the Court's jurisdiction should be extended 'to all cases and disputes submitted to it concerning the interpretation and application of the Charter, this Protocol and any other relevant Human Rights instrument ratified by the States concerned'. Such a 'universal' jurisdiction encouraged the ACtHPR, even more than the ACommHPR, to always take into consideration the relevant normative and jurisprudential framework of its member states, other regional systems and international bodies when adjudicating its cases.

On the contrary, there is no similar provision in the ECHR requiring, inviting or suggesting to the ECtHR to draw inspiration from other sources of law when interpreting the Convention. This is probably because, at the moment of the ECHR's drafting, none of the other human rights bodies existed and a judicial dialogue between regional and international bodies was not even imaginable. Nevertheless, the lack of such a provision in the European system may partially explain the different extent of judicial borrowing from and dialogue with the other regional human rights systems. As Fitzmaurice observed, the interpretation clauses of the African and Inter-American systems made it easier for the African bodies and the IACtHR to broaden the scope of their adjudication and look outside their jurisdiction when interpreting their treaties.[29] This framework significantly fostered dialogue and awareness of international and regional human rights standards thus easing the maintenance of convergence. Nevertheless, there are also other elements that can contribute to the current convergence as it will be shown in this and following chapters.

3.2 JUDICIAL DIALOGUE

The previous section left some open questions on the use of external material when interpreting human rights instruments. Article 31 VCLT does not say anything specific about the use of external references and Courts have

[28] *Purohit and Another v. The Gambia*, Communication no 241/01 (ACommHPR, 29 May 2003), 48.

[29] Fitzmaurice, 'Interpretation of Human Rights Treaties', 756–757.

adopted different positions about what sources should be taken into consideration when analysing the 'context' and the extent to which they should use these materials. Moreover, the Inter-American and African systems have different interpretation clauses encouraging or requiring their adjudication bodies to look outside their regional systems when interpreting a given right.[30] These interactions with other case-law and normative frameworks can be included under the big umbrella of judicial dialogue and can significantly affect judicial convergence and fragmentation.

This section explores the role of judicial dialogue in the debate on convergence and fragmentation. First, it defines judicial dialogue and investigates some of the reasons why judicial and quasi-judicial bodies do or do not engage in it. Second, it analyses the approach of the different bodies towards judicial dialogue, highlighting trends and features and providing a closer look at some concrete examples.

3.2.1 *Definition, Features and Challenges*

Judicial dialogue is generally understood as the use of external materials, such as decisions by courts, as an element of influence, even if limited, in the interpretation and application of the law.[31] Sometimes referred to as 'cross-referencing' or 'judicial borrowing', depending on the features of this dialogue, this phenomenon has been the focus of increasing scholarly attention in the last decade.[32] As Slaughter explained, judicial dialogue can also assume different forms and go beyond the reference to each other's case-law.[33] Indeed, if one way to engage in such dialogue is through the citation of another body's case-law or reasoning, another way is directly and informally through meeting with judges.[34] While the latter will be discussed in the next chapter, the

[30] See previous section, Chapter 4, Section 4.1.1.

[31] Amrei Muller and Hege Elisabeth Kjos (eds), *Judicial Dialogue and Human Rights* (Cambridge University Press, 2017), 9.

[32] Laurence Burgorgue-Larsen and Nicolas Montoya Cespedes, 'El diálogo judicial entre la Corte Interamericana de Derechos Humanos y la Corte Europea de Derechos Humanos', *Protección multinivel de derechos humanos. Manual* (Red de Derechos Humanos y Educación Superior, 2013); Eduardo Andres Bertoni, 'The Inter-American Court of Human Rights and the European Court of Human Rights: A Dialogue on Freedom of Expression Standards' (2009) 334 *European Human Rights Law Review* 1; Cristopher McCrudden, 'Common Law of Human Rights?: Transnational Judicial Conversations on Constitutional Rights' (2000) 20 *Oxford Journal of Legal Studies* 499.

[33] Anne-Marie Slaughter, 'A Typology of Transjudicial Communication' (1994) 29 *University of Richmond Law Review* 99.

[34] ibid.

former is the focus of the current section. In the following discussion, the expression 'judicial dialogue' will refer only to the citation or cross-citation of human rights bodies' case-law.

Judicial dialogue is then used here as a general term, including situations of one-sided dialogue, dialogue limited to the citation of a case and dialogue that determines the adoption of the same or similar reasoning based on a borrowed approach.

3.2.1.1 Why Engage in Judicial Dialogue?

Judicial dialogue between human rights bodies has increased in recent decades, facilitated by the development of comprehensive and easy to access case-law databases, which make human rights jurisprudence available to everyone.

The question that arises is why these bodies engage with the use of external references and the answers are many and complex, being often impossible to identify the specific causes in each situation.

The first and most logical reason is that an external citation may be helpful for supporting the argument the body is making. A judgment or a view from another court or quasi-judicial body is often referenced to buttress some passages of the reasoning or the conclusions and to show that other institutions share the same view on the topic.[35] This is the strongest kind of reference as it shows the influence of the external jurisprudence and it ensures convergence.

Second, acknowledging the existence of external case-law on similar facts contributes to strengthening the coherence and legitimacy of IHRL as an organic *corpus juris* and, consequently, it increases the legitimacy of all the bodies involved, both those who make the reference and those who are cited.[36] As it will be later observed, this could be particularly helpful for the youngest and less established bodies or those struggling with state compliance and with member states reluctant to recognise their authority. In addition, quasi-judicial bodies issuing non-binding views may significantly benefit from

[35] cf Sandesh Sivakumaran, 'The Influence of Teachings of Publicists on the Development of International Law' (2017) 66 *International & Comparative Law Quarterly* 1, 1–37.

[36] Reem Bahdi, 'Globalization of Judgment: Transjudicialism and the Five Faces of International Law in Domestic Courts' (2002) 34 *George Washington International Law Review* 555; Laurence R. Helfer and Anne-Marie Slaughter, 'Toward a Theory of Effective Supranatonal Adjudication' (1997) 107 *Yale Law Journal* 273–392; Claire L'Heureux-Dube, 'The Importance of Dialogue: Globalization and the International Impact of the Rehnquist Court' (2013) 34 *Tulsa Law Review* 15, 21.

referring to human rights courts whose judgments are binding, to give strength to their conclusions and encourage member states' compliance.

Third, the increasing workload of the human rights bodies required judges, commissioners and committee members to find ways to efficiently and quickly address and adjudicate the subject-diverse applications brought to their attention. Looking at the case-law of different human rights bodies on the same matter could be a practical help, allowing busy and overcharged bodies to save time.[37]

Fourth, by aligning its case-law with internationally recognised standards, a given body may avoid political accusation from its member states. Referring to the case-law of other bodies could help to adopt a progressive interpretation of the human rights instruments in line with their evolutive interpretation.[38] As Flanagan and Ahern underlined, judicial dialogue is a strategic technique to achieve a set purpose and 'critical opportunism and the aspiration to membership of an emerging international guild appear to be equally important strands in judicial attitudes toward foreign law'.[39] Likewise, authors observed that courts engage with selective dialogue only with those bodies they deem prestigious enough to be worth borrowing.[40]

Fifth, a body can resort to judicial dialogue to improve the quality of its reasoning. As Viljoen pointed out, for young bodies such as the African Commission, the use of external referencing could be linked to their increasing reasoned and well-researched findings as part of the development of their reasoning.[41] Similarly, also for well-established bodies, engaging in judicial dialogue could be beneficial since, as Helfer and Slaughter observed in the

[37] For example, in 2020 the ACtHPR received forty-eight applications and rendered twenty-seven judgments; the IACtHR received twenty-three cases and rendered twenty-three judgments, twenty-five provisional measures and one advisory opinion and the ECtHR received 41,700 applications and rendered 1,901 judgments. Data available at IACtHR, Annual Report 2020; ECtHR, Analysis of statistics 2020; and ACtHPR, Statistics, available at www.african-court.org/cpmt/statistic, last accessed 10 February 2022.

[38] See, for example, Frans Viljoen, *International Human Rights Law in Africa* (Oxford University Press, 2012), 327.

[39] Brian Flanagan and Sinead Ahern, 'Judicial Decision-Making and Transnational Law: A Survey of Common law Supreme Court Judges' (2011) 60 *International and Comparative Law Quarterly* 1, 28.

[40] Muller and Kjos (eds), Judicial Dialogue and Human Rights, 9; Magdalena Forowicz, *The Reception of International Law in the European Court of Human Rights* (Oxford University Press, 2010), 355; Erik Voeten, 'Borrowing and Nonborrowing among International Courts' (2010) 39 *The Journal of Legal Studies* 547, 573.

[41] Viljoen, *International Human Rights Law in Africa*, 325.

case of the HRC, there is a visibly positive impact on the quality of reasoning when relevant external jurisprudence is considered.[42]

Sixth, a body can use the external material as a counter-argument, especially when the cited reasoning is flawed and easy to rebut. In this case, an external reference will not influence convergence but rather leads to fragmentation, although a reasoned and thought upon one. However, strategically, this will not be a common occurrence for newer and less established bodies that will avoid presenting themselves in clear contrast with more established institutions. Likewise, considering the increasing caseload of some bodies, there is often not enough time to conduct thorough research and include and discuss the contrasting positions from other bodies. In these cases, the reference to an external source is often included only when there is a very important case whose reasoning a given body wants to reject.

Finally, judicial dialogue may significantly increase the convergence and the harmonisation of IHRL and ensure a uniform interpretation of human rights standards. Many scholars have conducted analyses to prove the convergent effect of judicial dialogue, highlighting the determinant role of the political context of the adjudication in ensuring full harmonisation.[43]

3.2.1.2 Why Not Engage in Judicial Dialogue?

Despite previous observations, an excessive use of this form of interaction between human rights bodies may also bring adverse consequences and there are many reasons why judicial and quasi-judicial bodies may be reluctant to engage in judicial dialogue.[44]

First, the use of external references could be perceived as an excessive delegation of authority and, thus, as an admission of lack of competence on the given matter with the ultimate consequence of diminishing the legitimacy

[42] Helfer and Slaughter, 'Toward a Theory of Effective Supranational Adjudication'.

[43] See Killander, 'Interpreting Regional Human Rights Treaties', 163; Lucas Lixinski, 'Treaty Interpretation by the Inter-American Court of Human Rights: Expansionism at the Service of the Unity of International Law' (2010) 21(3) *European Journal of International Law* 585, 601–602; Jo M. Pasqualucci, 'Criminal Defamation and the Evolution of the Doctrine of Freedom of Expression in International Law: Comparative Jurisprudence of the Inter-American Court of Human Rights' (2006) 39 *Vanderbilt Journal of Transnational Law* 379; Bertoni, 'The Inter-American Court of Human Rights and the European Court of Human Rights'.

[44] David S. Law and Wen-Chen Chang, 'The Limits of Global Judicial Dialogue' (2011) 86 *Washington Law Review* 523, 530–535.

of that body.[45] Furthermore, in contrast with the assumption made in the previous section, some scholars have argued that an excessive reference to external material for supporting the main reasoning of the judgment might in some cases lead to less state compliance.[46]

Second, the lack of external references may be caused by ignorance of other bodies' case-law. The increasing workload and the need to speed up the adjudication process may put some bodies in the situation of not having enough time to undertake a comprehensive survey of the relevant case-law from other systems and include them in their judgments. This may be particularly true in the absence of an equipped secretariat/registry or if the secretariat/registry is not charged with this duty, as discussed in the previous chapter.[47]

Third, judges, commissioners and committee members may be aware of the relevant case-law from other bodies but decided not to include any reference both for reasons of length and time and for not explicitly showing the influence that a specific body has on their adjudication. This may be particularly true for an international body such as the HRC that may prefer avoiding the risk of being accused of relying too much on the jurisprudence of one particular regional system. Considering this, the lack of external references does not always mean that there is no hidden external influence behind the adjudication.

Finally, in some cases, a body may be called to adjudicate a specific topic for the first time and may not have any other relevant jurisprudence to cite on the same issue. This is clearly the case for the ECtHR that, due to the high number and wide range of applications received, is often the first human rights body to adjudicate on some very specific circumstances without the possibility of drawing inspiration from its counterparts.

3.2.1.3 Concluding Observations

Before this section ends, two further points that could affect the analysis of judicial dialogue need to be discussed.

[45] Gerald L. Neuman, 'The External Reception of Inter-American Human Rights Law' (2011) *Quebec Journal of International Law* 99, 114; Helfer and Slaughter, 'Toward a Theory of Effective Supranational Adjudication', 377; Voeten, 'Borrowing and Nonborrowing among International Courts', 566.

[46] Forowicz, *The Reception of International Law*; Neuman, 'The External Reception of Inter-American Human Rights Law', 115.

[47] See Chapter 4.

First, the role played by the submission of parties and amicus curiae for a given case can be determinant for the likelihood of the body to engage with judicial dialogue. It is generally acknowledged that the more external references are included in parties' submissions and those of the amicus curiae, the higher is the likelihood that the final judgment will contain these references.[48] Such an assumption has been confirmed through interviews with judges and committee members: they all explained it as a natural consequence of the lack of time of the registries and secretariats to conduct thorough comparative law research and the willingness of these bodies to engage in judicial dialogue when presented with the possibility.[49]

Second, one should pay attention to the so-called false citations, that is, those citations that are often added by law clerks and assistants after the main reasoning is developed and that have no real influence on the judgment itself. Indeed, as it comes out from the above overview, the relation between the use of external references and their influence is not always clear. As scholars highlighted, quantitative studies on the number of references used are not enough to assess the influence of a specific body or framework over another body.[50] The importance given to an external source varies significantly according to the habits of a certain body and to the place in the judgment where such references are employed. As Neuman and Voeten warned, there is a risk of overestimating the influence of citations that are sometimes just 'decorative and rhetorical'.[51] To this extent, one should carefully detect where and how the external citation is used and whether it is relevant for adjudicating the case. Nevertheless, there are objective limits to this study since it is not possible to assess with certainty the actual role and purpose of a citation and, in the following sections, an approximation based on the extent and location of the citation will be forcibly made.

On the merit of this dialogue, convergence could be preferred for the protection of universality of human rights and the prevention of potentially dangerous effects of fragmentation on IHRL. Yet, an excessive judicial borrowing, with entire reasoning quoted from other bodies, may annul the

48 Laura van der Eynde, 'Encouraging Judicial Dialogue. The Contribution of Human Rights NGOs' Briefs to the European Court of Human Rights' in Muller and Kjos (eds), *Judicial Dialogue and Human Rights*, 339–400.

49 Interview conducted with senior legal officers from the ECtHR and IACtHR's registry and from the OHCHR's secretariats and with judges of the ECtHR and IACtHR and HRC's committee members between July and September 2017.

50 McCrudden, 'Common Law of Human Rights'.

51 Voeten, 'Borrowing and Nonborrowing among International Courts', 555; Neuman, 'The External Reception of Inter-American Human Rights Law', 125.

specificity and additional value of regional bodies and UNTBs. Ultimately, this would prevent a genuine dialogue that is based on the acknowledgement of the existence of other positions but also on the development of an own approach. Finding a balance between blindly mirroring another body's case-law and ignoring the existence of external material is the real challenge for human rights bodies. This balance is a judicial dialogue that mostly ensures convergence and consistency in line with a cosmopolitan view of international human rights adjudication, but can also allow pluralism and a well-reasoned fragmentation.[52]

3.2.2 *Judicial Dialogue in the Practice of Human Rights Bodies: Fostering Convergence*

Once agreed on the definition and features of judicial dialogue, it is time to look at the practice of the five bodies under analysis in relation to judicial dialogue, highlighting how and to what extent their referencing each other has helped maintain convergence and avoid judicial fragmentation.

3.2.2.1 The Inter-American Court of Human Rights

A perusal of the judgments issued by the IACtHR clearly shows an evident pattern of external referencing to international and regional human rights case-law and international legal instruments. The significant resort to external sources has been considered by some scholars as the natural requirement and consequence of the evolutive[53] and expansionist[54] interpretation of the ACHR provided by the Court.

Since the beginning of its functioning, the IACtHR has regularly supported its interpretation of the ACHR provisions with references to the *corpus juris* of IHRL and explicitly stated such practice and its rationale in an Advisory Opinion in 1999.[55] Citing the ICJ, the IACtHR held that the interpretation

[52] This is in line with what Slaughter argued in 'Judicial Globalization', 1108. See also Clara Marsan-Raventós, 'From Judicial Dialogue to Cosmpolitan Norms' and Luca Pasquet, 'Dialogue or Interaction? A Non-Cosmpolitan Reading of Transjudicial Communication' in Muller and Kjos (eds), *Judicial Dialogue and Human Rights.*

[53] Marijke de Pauw, 'The Inter-American Court of Human Rights and the Interpretative Method of External Referencing' in Yves Haeck, Oswaldo Ruiz-Chiriboga and Clara Burbano-Herrera (eds), *The Inter-American Court of Human Rights: Theory and Practice, Present and Future* (Intersentia, 2015), 4.

[54] Lixinski, 'Treaty Interpretation by the Inter-American Court of Human Rights', 585.

[55] Advisory Opinion No. 16, IACtHR.

of the convention rights should always be informed by and contextualised within the broader international human rights framework, carefully taking into consideration its development and evolution.[56]

Several quantitative studies on citations confirmed such a trend. In a study conducted on 102 judgments of the IACtHR, Miller found that the Court referenced the ICJ, ECtHR and ECJ 45 times.[57] Voeten discovered that in the 126 judgments issued in the period between 2000 and 2006, the IACtHR referred to the ECtHR in 60 per cent of them, with this possibly being an underestimation due to the 'irregular citation standard' often adopted by the Inter-American Court. Moreover, Voeten pointed out that the high number of citations came together with the high importance of these references for the IACtHR's rulings.[58]

These external citations cover a wide range of subject-rights and are very recent, suggesting close attention to the development of the ECtHR's case-law given by the members of the registry and judges of the Court.[59] The same findings have been confirmed by another study that covered all the IACtHR's judgments until March 2014. Domínguez observed that the IACtHR referred to the case-law of the ECtHR in 131 judgments out of the 275 issued, which is in 47.63 per cent of the cases. The number is particularly striking if compared to the ECtHR that, according to Dominguez, cited the IACtHR only in 37 out of 16,500 judgments, which is merely 0.22 per cent of the cases.[60] Domínguez confirmed that the references to Strasbourg had been used in relation to many different rights, even on matters where the IACtHR's case-law is very well developed such as torture and inhuman and degrading treatment and fair trial provisions.[61] As Mac-Gregor concludes, 'the references to the European precedents have been fundamental in the construction of the *Inter-American Corpus Juris*'.[62]

Similarly, the IACtHR referred to the African system, in particular to the Commission, in some important rulings with the clear intent of surveying the

56 ibid, 113–115.

57 Nathan Miller, 'An International Jurisprudence? The Operation of "Precedent" Across International Tribunals' (2002) 15 *Leiden Journal of International Law* 483, 489.

58 Voeten, 'Borrowing and Nonborrowing among International Courts'.

59 ibid, 557.

60 Cristiana Domínguez, 'Inter-American Court of Human Rights and European Court of Human Rights: From Observation to Interaction on Human Rights' in Haeck, Ruiz-Chiriboga and Burbano-Herrera (eds), *The Inter-American Court of Human Rights*.

61 ibid, 741–742.

62 Eduardo Ferrer Mac-Gregor, 'What Do We Mean When We Talk about Judicial Dialogue?' (2017) 30 *Harvard Human Rights Law Journal* 88–127, 101.

international human rights framework in order to confirm its convergence with the IHRL adjudication.[63]

Looking at the citation pattern, it strikes that the UN framework also occupies an important place in the external sources for the IACtHR. The HRC is by far the most cited of the TBs, both for its jurisprudence and for General Comments and Concluding Observations on country reports.[64] In particular, General Comment No. 18 on the definition of discrimination and General Comment No. 27 on freedom of movement have been particularly invoked by the Court.[65] The reference to UN soft law also extended to the UN Guiding Principles on Internal Displacement and, as suggested by Neuman, the IACtHR in the *Moiwana Village* case converted 'global soft law into regional hard law'.[66]

This constant effort by the IACtHR to support its judgments with external sources has had a varying reception from scholars and commentators. While some criticised the IACtHR for insufficient consideration of the regional consensus and the local perspective,[67] the majority saluted this practice, underlying the 'unifying impact' that it may have on international human rights law.[68] Indeed, it is unquestionable that the IACtHR, by continuously mapping the international human rights framework and making reference and aligning its jurisprudence to it, has significantly fostered convergence in IHRL and limited the instances of judicial fragmentation. Some examples can be presented to better understand how judicial dialogue has influenced convergence.

In 2005, the IACtHR delivered a judgment in *Caesar v. Trinidad and Tobago*, where it had to assess whether a twenty-year imprisonment with hard

[63] See *Maya Indigenous Communities of the Toledo District v. Belize* (IACommHR, 12 October 2004), 149; *Ecuador v. Colombia* (IACommHR, 21 October 2011), 117 and *Herrera Uloa v. Costa Rica* (IACtHR, 2004), 113–116.

[64] Neuman, 'The External Reception of Inter-American Human Rights Law', 109.

[65] See *Gelman v. Uruguay* (IACtHR, 24 February 2011), 205 and *Miguel Castro-Castro Prison v. Peru* (IACtHR, 25 November 2006), 331.

[66] Neuman, 'The External Reception of Inter-American Human Rights Law', 210. Moreover, the IACtHR has repeatedly cited the work of the UN Working Group on Enforced or Involuntary Disappearances, the UN Committee on Economic, Social and Cultural Rights, the Committee on the Rights of the Child, the Committee against Torture, the Committee on the Elimination of Discrimination against Women and the Human Rights Council and UN Special Rapporteurs.

[67] ibid.

[68] Lixinski, 'Treaty Interpretation by the Inter-American Court of Human Rights'; de Pauw, 'The Inter-American Court of Human Rights and the Interpretative Method of External Referencing'; Ludovic Hennebel, 'The Inter-American Court of Human Rights: The Ambassador of Universalism' (2011) *Quebec Journal of International Law* 57.

labour and fifteen strokes constituted a cruel, inhuman and degrading punishment.[69] To draw the line of what constitutes a violation of Article 5 ACHR, the IACtHR made extensive use of materials from international and regional bodies. In addition to the UN Special Rapporteur on Torture,[70] the IACtHR quoted the HRC's General Comment No. 20 and its concluding observations on Trinidad and Tobago together with its views in *Sooklal v. Trinidad and Tobago*.[71] Moreover, it also looked at the European system and borrowed the ECtHR's reasoning in *Tyrer v. United Kingdom* and *Ireland v. United Kingdom*.[72] This case-law perusal led the IACtHR to conclude that there is an international agreement on the fact that corporal punishments have an inherently cruel, inhuman and degrading nature.[73] In light of this, the Court ruled in favour of the applicant, finding a violation of Article 5 ACHR.

Freedom of expression is another area where frequent judicial dialogue has ensured convergence, particularly in relation to journalists. The case-law on defamation offers a good example of the convergent effects that judicial dialogue can have on regional and international human rights bodies.[74] Specifically, *Herrera Uloa v. Costa Rica* concerned the criminal conviction of Mr Herrera Uloa for having published defamatory articles against the representative of Costa Rica to the International Atomic Energy Agency. The IACtHR made extensive references to the ECtHR in deciding this case. It cited the Strasbourg Court to define the proportionality test to be used on these types of cases,[75] and the IACtHR also mirrored the ECtHR in its recognition of the key role that freedom of expression, media and journalism play in a democratic society.[76] Moreover, following its European counterpart, the IACtHR recognised the special position of politicians and public figures saying that

> statements concerning public officials and other individuals who exercise functions of a public nature should be accorded [...] a certain latitude in the broad debate on matters of public interest that is essential for the functioning of a truly democratic system. [...] Those individuals who have an influence on matters of public interest have laid themselves open voluntarily to a more intense public scrutiny and, consequently, in this domain, they are subject to

69 *Caesar v. Trinidad and Tobago* (IACtHR, 11 March 2005).
70 ibid, 61.
71 ibid, 62–63.
72 ibid, 64.
73 ibid, 70.
74 See, for example, Chapter 6, Section 6.6.1.2.
75 *Herrera Uloa*, IACtHR, 123.
76 ibid, 120–124.

a higher risk of being criticized, because their activities go beyond the private sphere and belong to the realm of public debate.[77]

In light of the previous considerations, exactly in line with the ECtHR, the IACtHR concluded that Costa Rica violated the applicant's freedom of expression by restricting his freedom in a disproportionate way.

As pointed out by some commentators, the reason for this extensive referencing is twofold. On the one hand, the IACtHR uses external references as means of persuasion, authority and legitimacy.[78] On the other hand, this is another way for the Court to reaffirm 'its universalist conception of international human rights law', borrowing concepts and interpretations from other jurisdictions to increase the protection of human rights in the Americas and strengthening the convergence of the whole human rights system.[79] In fact, the external referencing operated by the IACtHR is not simply a nominal citation of other court's rulings, but it is sometimes a proper 'borrowing' of tests, standards and reasoning that are then embedded in the Inter-American jurisprudence. This has been the case, for example, of the test to adopt in defamation cases. In the *Herrera Uloa* case presented above, and confirmed later in *Ricardo Canese v. Paraguay*, the Court summarised the ECtHR's case-law and the existing position of the ACommHPR on the matter before concluding that it was '*logical* and *appropriate* that statements concerning public officials [...] should be accorded [...] a certain latitude' so that their honour would be protected, but only 'in accordance with the principles of democratic pluralism'.[80] Similarly, the IACtHR used the CRC, the HRC and the ECtHR's case-law and other soft-law instruments like the Beijing Rules and the Riyadh Guidelines to interpret and apply to the factual cases the very broadly framed Article 19 ACHR.[81]

3.2.2.2 The African Bodies

The ACommHPR and ACtHPR can be rightly considered as champions of judicial dialogue, even more so than the IACtHR if one looks at the number and frequency of citations to regional and international human rights bodies.

77 ibid, 131.

78 Slaughter, 'A Typology of Transjudicial Communication', 99.

79 Hennebel, 'The Inter-American Court of Human Rights: The Ambassador of Universalism', 57.

80 *Herrera Uloa*, IACtHR, 128.

81 *See* Juridical Condition and Human Rights of the Child, Advisory Opinion OC-17/02 (IACtHR, 2002) and "*Juvenile Re-education Institute*" *v. Paraguay* (IACtHR, 2 September 2004), 211.

As discussed in the previous section, such an external opening of the African bodies is justified by the content of Articles 60 and 61 of the African Charter that provides for the Commission and Court to draw inspiration from a wide range of international human rights sources. Moreover, resorting to judicial dialogue could be seen as a necessity for the African bodies, looking for legitimacy and influence on their member states. However, this trend has been slightly changing in the last few years, showing a more Africa-centred reasoning and case-law in line with the development and growth of the African human rights bodies.

THE AFRICAN COMMISSION ON HUMAN AND PEOPLES' RIGHTS The attitude of the African Commission towards judicial dialogue and the use of external references has been the focus of studies by a few scholars.[82]

As highlighted by Viljoen, the ACommHPR has not always been inclined to refer to external sources.[83] Indeed, only since the 2000s has it started to regularly look outside the African region and engage in a dialogue with regional and international human rights bodies. As Viljoen explained, this initial reluctance 'may in part have been a deliberate attempt not to alienate states and to establish the Commission as an African institution, but in part also reflected the initial absence of reasoned and well-researched findings'.[84] However, this attitude changed since the publication of the 14th Annual Activity Report on the period 2000–2001, where, for the first time, the Commission showed the use of several references to UN documents and the case-law of the ECtHR, IACtHR and IACommHR.[85]

In contrast with this initial period of cautious use of external sources and limited application of Articles 60 and 61 ACHPR, the Commission extraordinarily evolved in its practice of external citations.[86] As Neuman reported, between 2000 and 2008, the ACommHPR cited the case-law of the IACtHR and the IACommHR in eight cases out of seventy-one. More frequent is the citation of the ECtHR's case-law but not as much as one may expect

[82] Hélène Tigroudja, 'The African System of Protection of Human Rights: A Laboratory for Universal Human Rights? Analysis of the External References in the Case-Law of the African Commission on Human and Peoples' Rights' (1 July 2011). Available at SSRN: https://ssrn.com/abstract=1968128; Killander, 'Interpreting Regional Human Rights Treaties', 144; Viljoen, *International Human Rights Law in Africa*; Neuman, 'The External Reception of Inter-American Human Rights Law'.

[83] Viljoen, *International Human Rights Law in Africa*, 345.

[84] ibid.

[85] ACommHPR, 14th Annual Activity Report on the period 2000–2001, AHG/229, 12 July 2001.

[86] Neuman, 'The External Reception of Inter-American Human Rights Law', 104.

considering the considerably larger body of decisions of the European system or the educational background of its members as analysed in the following chapter.[87] Significantly more prevalent in the views of the ACommHPR is the HRC that, either through its case-law or its General Comments and Concluding Observations, is almost always mentioned by the ACommHPR.[88] The engagement in judicial dialogue with other human rights bodies is very wide and not strictly related to specific rights or topics. In almost all its cases, the African Commission has used at least the HRC to support its reasoning and very often it goes beyond the simple referencing, borrowing the entire reasoning and interpretation from other regional and international institutions.[89] By doing so, it openly encourages convergence among human rights bodies and puts itself in line with the case-law of the other regional and international systems. Some examples could clarify this behaviour, especially on debated issues such as the definition of what constitutes cruel, inhuman and degrading punishments, the limitation of freedom of expression for journalists and the freedom of religion.

In 2003, the African Commission ruled in the case *Doebbler v. Sudan*, concerning the complaints by female students who had been arrested for immorality and sentenced to lashes carried out in public on their bare backs, which left permanent scars.[90] The applicants argued that such a punishment was grossly disproportionate and constituted cruel, inhuman and degrading punishment. Ruling in favour of the applicants, the Commission supported its reasoning by quoting the ECtHR in *Tyrer*, and held that lashings are always to be considered cruel, inhuman and degrading punishments.[91] The Commission justified the resort to the ECtHR's case-law on the basis that the letter of Article 3 ECHR was 'substantially similar' to Article 5 ACHPR.[92] This may imply that, in the mind of the ACommHPR, once the normative framework is 'substantially similar', then the interpretation should be equally convergent and the interpretation provided by other regional or international bodies could or should be taken into consideration.

The ACommHPR held a similar position in *Scanlen & Holderness v. Zimbabwe*,[93] a 2009 case on journalists' freedom of expression. The applicants claimed that the compulsory licensing imposed on journalists was an

87 ibid, 105.
88 ibid.
89 Tigroudja, 'The African System of Protection of Human Rights', 12.
90 *Doebbler v. Sudan*, Communication no 236/00 (ACommHPR, 4 May 2003).
91 ibid, 38 quoting *Tyrer*, ECtHR.
92 ibid, 38.
93 *Scanlen and Holderness*, ACommHPR.

infringement of their freedom of expression. The African Commission had to resort to external sources due to the very limited formulation of Article 9 ACHPR. In this case, the Commission decided to look at the Inter-American system and dedicated six paragraphs to unpack the IACtHR's position on compulsory licensing of journalists.[94] Invoking the IACtHR's Advisory Opinion No. 5/85, the ACommHPR borrowed the entire reasoning of the IACtHR and held that such an imposition was aimed at controlling journalists and unlawfully limiting their freedom of expression, thus amounting to a violation of Article 9.[95] The Commission explained its decision to embed the position of the IACtHR in its view on the basis that it found 'a great deal of persuasion in the reasoning and approach adopted by the Inter-American Court'[96] and recalled Articles 60 and 61 ACHPR that 'enjoin the Commission to seek inspiration from other international human rights instruments, precedent and doctrine'.[97]

A final example of judicial borrowing that ensured convergence relates to freedom of religion as elaborated in *Garreth Anver Prince v. South Africa*.[98] The case concerned the complaints by the Rastafari community that the prohibition of the use of cannabis, employed in sacramental rituals by the Rastafari, constituted a violation of their freedom of religion. The Commission decided to rely on the case-law of the HRC, and in particular on *Singh Bhinder v. Canada*, to hold that, even if the law did restrict the freedom of religion of the Rastafari community, such a restriction was reasonable and directed towards objective purposes compatible with the ACHPR and ICCPR.[99] It is worth noting that, in this case, the ACommHPR did not bring any justification for the use of the HRC's case-law for adjudicating the case, suggesting that no explanation is needed when a UNTB, and in particular the monitoring body of the ICCPR, is involved.

The consistent universalistic approach of the ACommHPR in a very wide range of rights and freedoms seems a strong safeguard against fragmentation from the African region and there are no hints that may suggest a change in the Commission's approach towards judicial dialogue.

The reasons behind such an attitude, which will be also discussed for the African Court, may be various. As scholars have repeatedly highlighted, one

94 ibid, 93–98.
95 ibid, 98.
96 ibid, 97.
97 ibid.
98 *Garreth Anver Prince v. South Africa*, Communication no 255/02 (ACommHPR, 7 December 2004).
99 ibid, 42–43.

important element is the need of the African bodies to gain legitimacy before its member states and push for compliance, and the consistent use of references to well-established human rights bodies may support the Commission in strengthening its views.[100] In this picture, the effect of ensuring convergence of case-law seems to be mostly a side effect of the need to gain respect and legitimacy from its member states. However, this does not explain the pre-2000 behaviour of the Commission.

This continuous borrowing from other regional systems, sometimes preferring external case-law over its own or African jurisprudence, may determine situations of internal fragmentation or incoherence, while maintaining international convergence. Although internal fragmentation is not the focus of this book, acknowledging its existence is important because it shows how fragile the current convergence can be. This is the case, for example, of the 2009 *Darfur* case, concerning the eviction of the indigenous Black African tribes from the Darfur region that allegedly constituted a violation of their rights under the African Charter.[101] The applicants argued that the forced eviction constituted a violation of their right to housing, in line with the case-law of the Commission on the matter. Indeed, in a previous ruling in 2001, the *Ogoniland* case,[102] the ACommHPR held that, even if the African Charter did not contain a specific provision on the right to housing, forced eviction should be considered as a violation of the right to housing implicitly guaranteed by Article 14, 16 and 18(1). Nevertheless, the ACommHPR surprisingly decided to change its approach to the case. Making extensive reference to the ECtHR, especially to the *Selçuk and Asker v. Turkey* case concerning forced eviction from their houses,[103] the ACommHPR ruled that forced eviction constituted cruel and inhuman treatment, borrowing exactly the same reasoning of the ECtHR.[104] Considering the higher political and social impact of finding a violation of the prohibition of torture rather than a violation of the right to housing, it could be argued that the choice of the Commission may be justified by the desire of giving additional strength to its views. Yet, it is still unclear why the Commission decided to do so without mentioning its precedents or even just distinguishing the two cases.

[100] Viljoen, *International Human Rights Law in Africa*; Killander, 'Interpreting Regional Human Rights Treaties', 144.

[101] *Sudan Human Rights Organisation & Centre on Housing Rights and Evictions (COHRE) v. Sudan*, Communication nos 279/03–296/05 (ACommHPR, 27 May 2009).

[102] *Social and Economic Rights Action Centre (SERAC) and Another v. Nigeria*, Communication no 155/96 (ACommHPR, 27 October 2001).

[103] *Selçuk and Asker v. Turkey*, Application nos 12/1997/796/998–999 (ECtHR, 24 April 1998).

[104] *SERAC*, ACommHPR, outcome.

THE AFRICAN COURT ON HUMAN AND PEOPLES' RIGHTS The ACtHPR has a similar universalistic approach when interpreting the ACHPR, which represents a strong insurance for convergence of IHRL. Yet, in the last few years this trend has been slightly changing.

An analysis conducted on all the judgments on the merit rendered so far shows an evolving trend. Out of the fifty-three judgments on the merit, thirty-nine contained references to UN instruments and particularly to the ICCPR.[105] In thirty-five judgments there are references to the ECtHR's case-law and in nineteen to the IACtHR and to the HRC. This means that in more than two judgments out of three there is at least one reference to an external source, demonstrating a solid commitment to engage in judicial dialogue outside the African continent.

However, the trend is slightly changing as the most recent cases show fewer references to external materials, preferring the UN system to the European or Inter-American ones, avoiding quotations from external judgments when possible and moving most of the references from the main text to the footnotes. For instance, in one of its first judgments, *Konaté Issa v. Burkina Faso*, dealing with freedom of expression, the ACtHPR dedicated more than three pages recalling the relevant case-law of the ECtHR, IACtHR and HRC, extensively quoting salient extracts.[106] In the recent *Kennedy Owino Onyachi and Others v. Tanzania*, concerning allegations of torture and a violation of the right to liberty, the ACtHPR again took the relevant case-law of the ECtHR, IACtHR and HRC into consideration. However, this time, the Court limited this contribution to the footnotes, leaving the main part of the text to its own considerations, showing a more experienced and reasoned approach.[107] Indeed, while perfectly aligning to the position held by the ECtHR, IACtHR and HRC on the matter, here the African Court mirrored what the European Court does when resorting to external sources; it takes inspiration from other bodies' jurisprudence, but it says it with its own words, inserting it into the regional context and linking it to its own previous jurisprudence. Likewise, also the recent case-law on fair trial, and, in particular, *Yahaya Zumo Makame and 3 Others v. Tanzania*[108] and *Hongue Eric*

[105] Study personally conducted on all the judgments on the merit available on the ACtHPR website up to 30 June 2021.

[106] *Lohé Issa Konaté v. Burkina Faso*, Application no 004/2013 (ACtHPR, 5 December 2014).

[107] *Kennedy Owino Onyachi and Others v. Tanzania*, Application no 003/2015 (ACtHPR, 28 September 2017).

[108] *Yahaya Zumo Makame and 3 Others v. Tanzania*, Application no 023/2016 (ACtHPR, 25 June 2021).

Noudehouenou v. Benin,[109] show a slow but steady departure from the habits of referencing the ECtHR. Very few are the cases on the matter that contain explicit references to the ECtHR or the IACtHR and most of these are only in the footnotes, without explicit mention in the judgment's main text. This is also due to the fact that the ACtHPR has now a more extensive case-law to refer to and the external references are, therefore, being slowly replaced by internal ones.

A wide spectrum of rights is covered by the judgments, ranging from freedom of expression to the right to life, the prohibition of torture and right to a fair trial. The topic or issue of the case is not determinant in choosing whether to include an external reference, but it influences which regional fora are called into dialogue. For example, in *African Commission on Human and Peoples' Rights v. Kenya*, concerning the rights of the Ogiek indigenous community, the ACtHPR decided to refer to the case-law of the IACtHR and HRC only, leaving the ECtHR out of the picture.[110] The choice is probably motivated by scarcity of European case-law on the matter and the fact that the IACtHR's approach to indigenous rights is by far the most developed among regional bodies. On the contrary, in *Abubakari v. Tanzania*, concerning conditions of detention and the right to a fair trial, the ACtHPR chose to mention only the ECtHR, regardless of the extensive Inter-American case-law on the matter.[111]

As the African Court is choosing to decrease its references to the European and Inter-American counterparts, one can see that this is less evident in cases concerning rights that the ACtHPR has not yet addressed extensively. For instance, in *Sebastien Germain Marie Aikoue Ajavon v. Benin*, a case concerning a wide range of rights as a result of biased elections, the ACtHPR extensively quoted the ECtHR, IACtHR and HRC as well as the ICJ.[112] Likewise, in *Fidele Mulindahabi v. Rwanda* and *Boubacar Sissoko and 74 Others v. Mali*, concerning the right to equality and non-discrimination linked to the right to work, the Court heavily referenced external sources.[113]

[109] *Hongue Eric Noudehouenou v. Benin*, Application no 003/2020 (ACtHPR, 4 December 2020).

[110] *African Commission on Human and Peoples' Rights v. Kenya*, Application no 006/2012 (ACtHPR, 26 May 2017).

[111] *Abubakari v. Tanzania*, Application no 007/2013 (ACtHPR, 3 June 2016).

[112] *Sebastien Germain Marie Aikoue Ajavon v. Benin*, Application no 013/2017 (ACtHPR, 28 November 2019).

[113] *Fidele Mulindahabi v. Rwanda*, Application no 004/2017 (ACtHPR, 26 June 2020) and *Boubacar Sissoko and 74 Others v. Mali*, Application no 037/2017 (ACtHPR, 25 September 2020).

There are no hints to suggest whether this endless effort to engage in a dialogue with the other human rights bodies and consequently to maintain convergence is moved by a desire to strengthen the universality of human rights and the coherence of IHRL or simply by reasons of political convenience for enhancing the state's compliance with its judgments. It is worth noting that, as distinct from the ACommHPR, the ACtHPR did not feel the need to justify why and on which legal basis it borrowed the reasoning of other human rights bodies, suggesting a more embedded attitude towards judicial dialogue probably flowing from Article 3 of the Additional Protocol to the ACHPR.

In conclusion, the ACtHPR is fully engaging in judicial dialogue with both regional and international human rights bodies, and by doing so, it contributes to convergence. The interpretation clauses contained in the ACHPR and the extended jurisdiction granted by Article 3 of the Protocol establishing the Court, encouraged such an approach, which is also hopefully helping the Court to increase legitimacy and state-compliance. However, recent judgments show that the Court is adopting a more mature approach towards external references moving from using them as a core substitution to its reasoning to using them as a source of inspiration. This may lead to a fair balance between maintaining convergence and preserving regional features.

3.2.2.3 The European Court of Human Rights

The ECtHR has always appeared quite reluctant to engage in a real judicial dialogue with other regional and international human rights bodies, considering its own and its member states' case-law enough for adjudicating its cases. As Judge Angelika Nussberger observed, the task of the ECtHR, like any other human rights court or quasi-judicial body, is 'to adjudicate and not to academically develop the law' and, therefore, it uses external references only when such external material is relevant for deciding the case.[114] The judicial dialogue within the ECtHR resembles more a 'judicial monologue' and if one looks at the number of cases where the ECtHR referred to the African bodies, the IACtHR and the HRC this impression is confirmed.

The ECtHR referred to the African Commission or Court in only 25 cases out of the 20,071 issued, amounting to a mere 0.1 per cent. Slightly higher is the number of judgments where the IACtHR is cited, 91 out of 20,071, being 0.45 per cent. Significantly more recurrent are the references to the HRC,

[114] Angelika Nussberger, 'The ECtHR's Use of Decisions of International Courts and Quasi-Judicial Bodies' in Muller and Kjos (eds), *Judicial Dialogue and Human Rights*.

both to its views and its General Comments, which can be found in 258 cases (1.3%).[115] However, there are two considerations to make. First, in the early years of the ECtHR, none of the other human rights bodies were in operation, and the ECtHR did not even have the possibility to reference them. Second, the trend is positive, with almost the totality of the external reference being made in judgments issued after 2000 and with an increasing rate of judicial dialogue over the years. This may suggest that the ECtHR is slowly engaging more and more in judicial dialogue and is opening its adjudication to external influence or, at least, it is acknowledging the existence of external views and material. This is in line with the changing background of the new judges appointed at the Court, as shown in the next chapter.

Moreover, as scholars and ECtHR's judges have highlighted, the low number of references to external sources in the European system could be partially explained by how cases are adjudicated in the ECtHR. Approximately 95 per cent of the ECtHR's cases are decided by a single judge or by a committee without giving extensive reasoning and, therefore, with very little space for judicial dialogue.[116] Looking at the citations by the ECtHR, it is evident that most of the references can be found in the Grand Chamber's judgments,[117] whose cases are subject to a major scrutiny and for which the registry conducts a more comprehensive comparative law research.[118]

The amount of judicial dialogue of the ECtHR varies significantly according to the articles involved and, as scholars have observed, it is more evident in cases under Article 8, the right to a private and family life. This is probably due to the broad scope of the article and to the sensitive issues related to the political, social, cultural and religious concerns that may affect the enjoyment of such a wide provision.

Worth stressing is that a similarly positive trend of references to other human rights bodies' case-law can be found in cases under Article 14, the prohibition of discrimination,[119] confirming that the Court resorts more

[115] All these data are a personal elaboration made on the basis of the HUDOC database of the ECtHR, updated to 30 June 2021.

[116] See Nussberger, 'The ECtHR's Use of Decisions' and Erik Mose as cited by Nussberger, ibid, 420.

[117] See the data reported by Domínguez, 'Inter-American Court of Human Rights and European Court of Human Rights', 745.

[118] Information collected during an interview with members of the registry of the ECtHR conducted in Strasbourg in July 2017.

[119] Data from the HUDOC database show that almost a third of the cases where the ECtHR made references to external material involved a complaint also under Article 14 ECHR.

frequently to comparative law and judicial dialogue when dealing with rights entailing sensitive and debated issues.

Nonetheless, judicial dialogue is not confined to Article 8 and 14 and, even if limited, has helped to avoid judicial fragmentation in many other situations. An example is the ECtHR's case *Gafgen v. Germany*, where the applicants claimed that a threat of torture can constitute inhumane treatment under Article 3 ECHR.[120] The ECtHR made large use of the case-law of the IACtHR and extensively quoted the reasoning in *Maritza Urrutia v. Guatemala* to support its argument in favour of the applicant and conclude that Germany did violate Article 3 by threatening that the applicant be subjected to torture-like treatments.[121] This dialogue between the two courts, which culminated in a full convergence on this matter, was probably caused by several factors that are impossible to identify clearly. However, it should be acknowledged that the amicus curiae submitted by the NGO Redress played a key role in *Gafgen* to boost judicial dialogue, as explicitly recognised by the ECtHR.[122]

Similarly, a positive trend of increasing judicial dialogue can be found in the case-law on the right to political participation. In *Sitaropoulos v. Greece*, concerning the right to vote of expatriates, the ECtHR decided to draw inspiration from the interpretation of Article 13 ACHPR rendered by the ACommHPR in *Purohit v. Gambia* and from the HRC's General Comment on Article 25 ICCPR.[123]

Finally, a clear example of how the ECtHR is increasingly committed to engaging in judicial dialogue is the comparison of two cases, *Cruz Varas and Others v. Sweden* from 1991 and *Mamatkulov and Askarov v. Turkey* from 2005. In both situations, the ECtHR had to rule on whether interim decisions should be considered as binding for the member states. In the former, the ECtHR ruled that the interim measures of the European Commission were not binding and in doing so, it did not refer to any external material.[124] On the contrary, in the 2005 case, the ECtHR recalled Article 31(3)(c) VCLT and considered it necessary to interpret the ECHR in a way that would be consistent with other principles of international law. It observed that

> the ICJ, the Inter-American Court of Human Rights, the Human Rights Committee and the Committee against Torture of the United Nations,

[120] *Gafgen v. Germany*, Application no 22978/05 (ECtHR, 1 June 2010).
[121] ibid, 66, 108.
[122] ibid, 108. The role of *amicus curiae* in fostering convergence will be discussed in the Chapter 7.
[123] *Sitaropoulos and Giakoumopolous v. Greece*, Application no 42202/07 (ECtHR, 15 March 2012), 30–31.
[124] *Cruz Varas and Others v. Sweden*, Application no 15576/89 (ECtHR, 20 February 1991).

> although operating under different treaty provisions to those of the Court, have confirmed in their reasoning in recent decisions that the preservation of the asserted rights of the parties in the face of the risk of irreparable damage represents an essential objective of interim measures in international law. Indeed, it can be said that, whatever the legal system in question, the proper administration requires that no irreparable action be taken while proceedings are pending.[125]

This shows increasing attention of the ECtHR to external material and how the Strasbourg court is particularly keen in drawing inspiration from international and other regional sources when it needs to depart from its established approach. This flexibility and willingness to adapt its case-law to the development of law and society is in line with the theory of the evolutive interpretation of the ECHR as a living instrument and could facilitate the reaching of convergence between human rights bodies.

On a last note, it should be acknowledged that, in most of the cases, the ECtHR did not have the chance to reference other bodies' jurisprudence because the subject matter of the cases brought before its attention was completely new and no other body had ruled on it before.[126] Considering the high number of diversified applications the Strasbourg Court receives, it is often the case for the ECtHR to be the first one to be called to adjudicate on a new issue and set new standards of interpretation without the possibility of referencing to other bodies.

3.2.2.4 The Human Rights Committee

The HRC has adopted a peculiar approach towards judicial dialogue, moving between silently taking inspiration from other human rights bodies and explicitly sticking to its own jurisprudence and interpretation. Indeed, as scholars have pointed out, the number of external references contained in the HRC's views is very low and would suggest that the HRC is not at all open to a judicial dialogue with regional human rights bodies, thus potentially increasing the risk of fragmentation.[127]

[125] *Mamatkulov and Askarov v. Turkey*, Application no 46827/99 and 46951/99 (ECtHR, 4 February 2005), 124.

[126] See also the reflection by Mac-Gregor, 'What Do We Mean When We Talk about Judicial Dialogue', 105.

[127] Neuman, 'The External Reception of Inter-American Human Rights Law', 99, 111; Scott Davidson, 'Introduction' in Alex Conte (ed), *Defining Civil and Political Rights: The Jurisprudence of the United Nations Human Rights Committee* (Ashgate, 2009), 11.

An analysis conducted through the official OHCHR database for the HRC case-law[128] shows that out of 902 cases references to the IACtHR appear only in 22 cases, while to the ACommHPR in 3 cases and 1 to the ACtHPR. Slightly higher is the number of references to the ECtHR, sixty-one, but it is still low compared to the total number of views adopted by the HRC.

An interesting data point is that the references to the case-law of regional systems are extremely common in the parties' submissions (126 cases reference the ECtHR, 20 the IACtHR and 1 the ACommHPR) while they are very rare in the merit section of the views, showing a limited engagement of the Committee with external material. Moreover, several times the reference to the three regional bodies appears in the separate opinions rather than in the merit section of the view (for example, in twenty-four cases out of sixty-one mentioning the ECtHR) because the case was also brought before the regional body and the HRC had to rule on the admissibility to its forum. Hence, the cases where the HRC drew explicit inspiration from the regional human rights courts to interpret the ICCPR are extremely few.

In addition, the analysis reveals that there is no consistent pattern of citation of a regional body when a particular right or topic is concerned, thus precluding any further speculation.

Nonetheless, the HRC actually looks outside its case-law and is aligning silently to the jurisprudence of the regional bodies, significantly reducing the likelihood of fragmentation. An example is the case-law on death penalty and, in particular, the reasoning of the HRC in *Thompson v. St. Vincent and the Grenadines*, whose links with the case-law of the IACtHR are evident.[129] The case dealt with mandatory death penalty for certain crimes and the HRC argued that this violated the right to life because it failed to take into consideration the circumstances of each case.[130] As observed by Cheesman,[131] the HRC's reasoning was mirroring the IACtHR's ruling in *Hilaire v. Trinidad and Tobago*.[132] However, the HRC did not make any explicit reference to the

[128] The database is available at http://juris.ohchr.org/, last accessed 1 September 2021. The database in its research function for keywords is limited in time and shows only results from 2000 onwards (with few random exceptions).

[129] *Thompson v. St. Vincent and the Grenadines*, Communication no 806/1998 (HRC, 18 October 2000)

[130] ibid, 8.2.

[131] Chloe Cheesman, 'The Death Penalty as Addressed by Regional and International Human Rights Bodies: Exploring Jurisprudential Cross-fertilisation and Harmonisation' in Carla M. Buckley, Alice Donald and Philip Leach (eds), *Towards Convergence in International Human Rights Law: Approaches of Regional and International Systems* (Brill Nijhoff, 2016), 85.

[132] *Hilaire, Constantine and Benjamin et al. v. Trinidad and Tobago* (IACtHR, 21 June 2002), 153–170, 200.

IACtHR even if the *Hilaire* case was repeatedly mentioned in the applicant's submission.

The above discussion suggests that even if, on the surface, the HRC appears reluctant to engage in judicial dialogue with regional bodies, in actual practice it sometimes draws inspiration from them and, by doing so, it increases the chances of maintaining convergence. As briefly recalled in the first section, a reason for the lack of references to regional bodies might be the fact that the HRC, as an international body, does not want to selectively choose one or another regional system to be mentioned in its adjudication to avoid accusations of being biased. Therefore, the HRC may silently draw inspiration from the regional systems without explicitly citing them, thus explaining both its mostly convergent case-law and the low rate of external citations.

3.2.3 *The Lack of Judicial Dialogue between Human Rights Bodies: Triggering Fragmentation*

If judicial dialogue can increase the likelihood of convergence of case-law, the lack of this dialogue does not always determine fragmentation but surely increases its probability. The following sections present two examples where the lack of dialogue between courts could be considered one of the reasons for judicial fragmentation.

3.2.3.1 Indigenous Peoples' Rights

As presented in detail in Chapter 2, the issue of indigenous property rights triggered a situation of judicial fragmentation between the ECtHR, IACtHR and ACommHPR.[133] The lack of a proper judicial dialogue between these bodies should be definitely considered one of the reasons behind the divergent approach of the IACtHR and ACommHPR on one side and the ECtHR on the other. Indeed, in both *Handolsdalen Sami Village and Others v. Sweden* and *Hingitaq 53 v. Denmark* the ECtHR did not make any reference to the IACtHR, despite its well-developed jurisprudence on the matter.

The *Handolsdalen* case was similar in facts to the *Yakye Axa Indigenous Community v. Paraguay* case from the IACtHR and the ECtHR could have taken inspiration from the latter in adjudicating on such a novel matter for the European system. On the contrary, the ECtHR decided to completely ignore

[133] See Chapter 2, Section 2.2.2.

the case-law of the IACtHR and the existence of any international instruments on indigenous rights. Even in the section of the judgment dedicated to the relevant applicable law, the ECtHR included only domestic law, with no mention at all to international instruments as it usually does.[134]

The ECtHR took a similar approach in *Hingitaq* 53, triggering fragmentation with the IACtHR. Here the ECtHR showed a slightly more open attitude towards external references, but failed to include the relevant case-law in its investigation. Indeed, the judgment acknowledged the existence and the content of the ILO Convention No. 169 on indigenous people and allegedly drew inspiration from that to assess whether the applicants were to be considered an indigenous community.[135] The relevant articles of the ILO Convention were reported in full, giving the impression that the ECtHR was recognising the need to refer to a specific international framework for the protection of indigenous people. However, such a long presentation in the section dedicated to the relevant domestic and international law was not accompanied by a similar consideration in the main section of the admissibility decision, and the ECtHR ultimately failed to properly interpret the content of the ILO Convention No. 169.[136]

In particular, it looks like the ECtHR missed the mark on what constitutes an indigenous community and in this regard the lack of dialogue with the IACtHR is even more evident. The ECtHR made no mention at all to the extensive case-law of the IACtHR on indigenous peoples' rights anywhere in the text. However, the jurisprudence of the IACtHR would have been extremely useful for the ECtHR in interpreting the ILO Convention and to better understand the definition of indigenous community. Such reluctance of the ECtHR to look at the objectively more developed case-law of its American counterpart could be considered one of the elements that led to fragmentation or at least as one missed opportunity that could have avoided fragmentation.

The African Commission did not make the same mistake as the ECtHR in its *Endorois* case. The ACommHPR recognised the lack of a specific definition in the African Charter of what constitutes an indigenous 'people' and what specific protections should be provided to indigenous communities.[137] In order to fill this gap, the African Commission made a detailed perusal of the

[134] *Handölsdalen Sami Village and Others v. Sweden*, Application no 39013/04 (ECtHR, 30 March 2010).

[135] *Hingitaq 53 and Others v. Denmark*, Application no 18584/04 (ECtHR, 12 January 2006), 14.

[136] ibid, 15–19.

[137] *Centre for Minority Rights Development (Kenya) and Minority Rights Group International on behalf of Endorois Welfare Council v. Kenya* (ACommHPR, 25 November 2009), 147–148.

relevant African instruments first,[138] and then moved on to the results of the UN Working Group on Indigenous Populations, the UN Special Rapporteur on the rights of indigenous peoples and to the ILO Convention No. 169.[139] Still, the main contribution that helped the Commission to adjudicate this case came from the case-law of the IACtHR, which was repeatedly cited and quoted throughout the judgment.[140] However, it should be mentioned that the ACommHPR did not only reference the UN and Inter-American systems, but also extensively cited the ECtHR when considering alleged violations of freedom of religion linked to the right to property.[141] The ACommHPR understood the peculiarity of the case-law of the two bodies and used the ECtHR's jurisprudence to define the meaning and scope of application of the provisions in general and the IACtHR's jurisprudence for its application to the case of indigenous populations. By doing this, it developed a comprehensive judicial dialogue and harmonisation of the different regional systems' case-law under a universalistic perspective.

3.2.3.2 Freedom of Religion

Another case of judicial fragmentation partially attributable to a lack of judicial dialogue is the divergent case-law between the ECtHR and HRC on freedom of expression of religion. As analysed in detail in Chapter 2, this situation of fragmentation became evident in two sets of cases: *Mann Singh v. France*[142] of the ECtHR compared with *Ranjit Singh v. France*[143] of the HRC and *Leyla Şahin v. Turkey*[144] of the ECtHR compared with *Raihon Hudoyberganova v. Uzbekistan*[145] of the HRC.

To briefly recall the facts of the cases, the first two applications dealt with the requirement of being 'bareheaded' in the driving licence's photograph. According to the applicants, such an obligation discriminated against practising Sikhs, who would not be allowed to wear their traditional turban in the photo.[146] The ECtHR's judgment was the first to be delivered, and it did not

[138] ibid, 149–151.
[139] ibid, 149–157.
[140] ibid, 158–161, 171, 185, 194–195, 197–198, 205–208, 216–217, 227, 233–234.
[141] ibid, 188, 201–202, 217.
[142] *Mann Singh v. France*, Application no 24479/07 (ECtHR, 11 June 2007).
[143] *Ranjit Singh v. France*, Communication no 1876/2000 (HRC, 11–29 July 2011).
[144] *Leyla Şahin v. Turkey*, Application no 44774/98 (ECtHR, 10 November 2005).
[145] *Raihon Hudoyberganova v. Uzbekistan*, Communication no 931/2000 (HRC, 8 December 2004).
[146] For a more detailed analysis of the facts see Chapter 2, Section 2.2.1.

contain any reference outside the European space. Although it could not have contained any reference to the HRC's case-law, which had not ruled on the matter before, it could have included a perusal of relevant international and comparative law and, specifically, a reference to the HRC General Comment No. 22 on Freedom of Religion that discussed at length the freedom to wear religious attire.[147]

Similarly, in the following *Ranjit Singh v. France* by the HRC there is no reference at all to external material. Quite surprisingly due to the similarities in facts, there is no mention of the previous ruling of the ECtHR in *Mann Singh*, not even an acknowledgement of the existence of the ECtHR judgment. Yet, this is understandable considering that the HRC's position is significantly different from the ECtHR and mentioning such a contrasting ruling would have hindered its reasoning. Acknowledging the ECtHR's position would have obliged the HRC to, at least, reflect upon it and more firmly ground its conclusion. Although it can be argued that fragmentation would have been triggered anyway, the lack of any dialogue between the two bodies facilitated the arising of fragmentation at least because it did not encourage any consideration of different possible approaches. Nonetheless, one cannot exclude that an internal debate within the HRC took place even without evidence in the judgment.

A similar lack of dialogue between the ECtHR and the HRC could be found in the 'headscarf' cases. This time both bodies could have referred to each other considering that the ECtHR's chamber judgment was issued in June 2004, the HRC's views in December 2004 and then the ECtHR's Grand Chamber judgment came the year after in November 2005.

Yet, no mention of the ECtHR could be found in the HRC's *Raihon Hudoyberganova v. Uzbekistan*, even though the Chamber delivered its judgment in *Leyla Sahin* before the HRC's view. Of particular interest in this regard is the dissenting opinion of Ruth Wedgwood in the HRC's case, who argued that the vague facts of the case would more logically suggest that the prohibition of wearing a *hijab* did not constitute a violation of the freedom to manifest religion.[148] Referring to the chamber's judgment in *Leyla Sahin*, Wedgwood observed that the reasoning of the ECtHR would have helped in considering the issue from a different perspective and concluded that states should be allowed to restrict forms of dress that interfere with effective pedagogy and pose a threat to public order or which restrict others' rights. If

[147] CCPR General Comment No. 22: Article 18 (Freedom of Thought, Conscience or Religion), 30 July 1993, CCPR/C/21/Rev.1/Add.4.

[148] *Hudoyberganova*, HRC, separate opinion of Ruth Wedgwood.

the HRC had adopted such an approach, it would have ruled in line with the ECtHR and avoided fragmentation.

In line with the HRC, the ECtHR's Grand Chamber in *Leyla Şahin* left the relevant comparative and international case-law out of the picture and developed its reasoning without even acknowledging the HRC's views in *Hudoyberganova*. This complete lack of dialogue or even acknowledgement between the two bodies could certainly be considered as contributing to fragmentation.

3.2.4 *When Judicial Dialogue Is Not Enough for Ensuring Convergence*

The previous analysis showed that judicial dialogue may contribute to convergence and that a lack of it may increase the likelihood of fragmentation. However, judicial dialogue and convergence/fragmentation do not always benefit from a causal relationship and there are also cases where human rights bodies engage in judicial dialogue but still trigger fragmentation. Two examples of this are the case-law on enforced disappearances and on the right to marry for same-sex couples.

3.2.4.1 Enforced Disappearances

Judicial fragmentation is currently taking place between the ECtHR and IACtHR on enforced disappearances, especially on the questions of who can submit a case before the courts, and which substantive rights are linked to enforced disappearances. In brief, on the victim standing for enforced disappearances cases, the IACtHR developed a very victim-friendly two-stage test. First, it examines whether the individual is a relative of the disappeared person, that is, a parent, sibling, child, spouse or domestic partner and second, if the person fails to meet the first requirement, it takes into consideration the 'proximity of the ties, the degree of involvement in the search and the degree of suffering'.[149] In contrast, the ECtHR prefers a different approach, called by some scholars 'functional',[150] that focuses on the degree of involvement of the individual in the search for the disappeared person, refusing the automatic acknowledgement of the status of victim to a very close relative of the disappeared person merely on the basis of family ties.[151] By requiring a high degree

[149] Nikolas Kyriakou, 'An Affront to the Conscience of Humanity: Enforced Disappearance in International Human Rights Law' (PhD thesis, European University Institute, 2012), 116.

[150] ibid.

[151] See, among others, *Akdenix and Others v. Turkey*, Application no 2395/94 (ECtHR, 31 May 2001), 101 and *Cakici v. Turkey*, Application no 23657/94 (ECtHR, 8 July 1999), 98.

of involvement of the relative into the investigation of the alleged disappearances, the ECtHR manages to limit the caseload but poses huge obstacles to the relatives who are of young or old age or to all those who are not able to actively engage in the investigations.[152]

The history and reality of the two courts could certainly explain, at least in part, such a different approach. Due to the high number of applications, the ECtHR had to come up with some gate-keeping mechanisms to limit this overwhelming amount of complaints. In the specific case of enforced disappearances, the chosen path has been to establish stricter requirements for qualifying as a *victim*. On the contrary, the IACtHR, benefitting also from the filter role of the Inter-American Commission, does not have such a problem and could adopt a more victim-friendly and open-gate approach. Nevertheless, this different attitude towards the identification of the victim has enormous consequences in the practice of who can actually bring a claim before these bodies and, subsequently, on which rights the violation can be invoked.

The second aspect of fragmentation concerns the link between enforced disappearances and the prohibition of torture. Since *Velazquez Rodriguez*, the IACtHR held that 'isolation and deprivation of communication are in themselves cruel and inhuman treatment, harmful to the psychological and moral integrity of the person'[153] amounting to an automatic violation of the prohibition of torture for all the direct victims of enforced disappearances, without the need for the victim to provide further evidence and maintaining the burden of proof on the state.[154] On the contrary, the ECtHR usually does not find a violation of Article 3 (prohibition of torture) in enforced disappearances cases for the direct victim, requiring the applicant to prove 'beyond reasonable doubt' that torture or an inhuman and degrading treatment was imposed on the victim.[155] As Citroni pointed out, even in cases where the ECtHR found that the victim was deprived of his or her liberty by state agents and that he or she would be presumably dead with clear state responsibility, the European Court 'failed to extend the presumption to the violation of the prohibition of torture and declared that "in the absence of any relevant information or evidence, the Court is unable to establish, to the necessary degree of proof, the exact way in which the direct victim dies and whether it was

[152] *Musikhanova and Others v. Russia*, Application no 27243/03, 81 (ECtHR, 4 December 2008) and *Dzhambekova and Others v. Russia*, Application nos 27283/03 and 35078/04 (ECtHR, 11 May 2009), 307.

[153] *Velazquez Rodriguez*, IACtHR, 156.

[154] ibid.

[155] *Zaurbekova and Zauberkova v. Russia*, Application no 27183/03 (ECtHR, 22 January 2009).

subjected to ill-treatment"'.[156] It goes without saying that such an open difference between the two courts' approaches is a genuine case of judicial fragmentation.

Differently from what has been observed in the previous sections, judicial fragmentation is arising regardless of the quite copious dialogue between the two courts. Indeed, the ECtHR repeatedly cited the IACtHR case-law on the matter and in particular *Velasquez Rodriguez v. Honduras* and followed the IACtHR's lead on many key aspects in adjudicating enforced disappearances' cases. For instance, in *Kurt v. Turkey* the ECtHR adopted the IACtHR's approach on exhaustion of domestic remedies citing *Velazquez Rodriguez*, *Godínez Cruz v. Honduras* and *Cabellero-Delgado and Santana v. Colombia*. Similarly, in *Ertak v. Turkey*, the Strasbourg Court cited the IACtHR in the same three cases to identify the features of enforced disappearances cases.

Nevertheless, judicial fragmentation still arose between the two bodies as they could not find a point of convergence in relation to victim's standing and the link between enforced disappearances and torture. In the same above-cited cases, where the ECtHR cited and followed the IACtHR in relation to several aspects, the two courts completely diverted on other aspects, thus proving that judicial dialogue is not always enough to ensure convergence between two bodies. It would be certainly wrong to assert that fragmentation here was due to ignorance of other courts' case-law since the ECtHR did cite the IACtHR extensively; the decision of the ECtHR was very much a conscious choice of adopting a different approach for answering to its own needs and challenges of adjudication. The ECtHR engaged in a selective dialogue only on elements that it found convenient and appropriate to support its own judicial agenda.

3.2.4.2 Right to Marry for Same-Sex Couples

Another issue where an extensive judicial dialogue did not ensure a safeguard against fragmentation is the right to marry for same-sex couples. As already presented in Chapter 2, the IACtHR Advisory Opinion No. 24 on gender identity, equality and non-discrimination for same-sex couples triggered judicial fragmentation with the ECtHR and the HRC.[157]

[156] ibid; Gabriella Citroni, 'The Contribution of the Inter-American Court of Human Rights and Other International Human Rights Bodies to the Struggle Against Enforced Disappearance' in Y. Haeck, O. Ruiz-Chiriboga and C. Burbano-Herrera, *The Inter-American Court of Human Rights: Theory and Practice, Present and Future* (Intersentia, 2015), 395.

[157] See Chapter 2, Section 2.2.3.

In its Advisory Opinion, the IACtHR established that preventing same-sex couples from entering into marriage while the institution of marriage is allowed for heterosexual couples constitutes discrimination based on sexual orientation and 'there is no legitimate aim that could make this distinction necessary and proportionate under the Convention'.[158]

This stands in clear contrast with the positions of the ECtHR in *Schalk and Kopf v. Austria* or of the HRC in *Joslin v. New Zealand*, where the two bodies held that limiting the right to marry to heterosexual couples did not amount to discrimination based on sexual orientation, where a civil partnership or other similar instrument was enough to guarantee the enjoyment of the right to private and family life. Moreover, according to the ECtHR, the absence of a regional consensus on the matter prevented the court from establishing a further obligation on the member states.[159]

However, similarly to the previous case on enforced disappearances, this situation of judicial fragmentation came together with a high degree of judicial dialogue. In line with its tradition of extensively mentioning external materials, the IACtHR cited the ECtHR and the HRC throughout the whole opinion, even in support of its key principles.[160] For example, the IACtHR openly declared to align itself to the ECtHR in *Schalk and Kopf v. Austria* when asserting that same-sex couples do have a right to a private and family life to the same extent of heterosexual couples.[161] On the same line, it cited the HRC in *Young v. Australia* to hold that providing different services on the basis of sexual orientation constitutes discrimination. Nonetheless, the final paragraphs bringing the conclusion that triggered fragmentation did not contain any external reference, and the IACtHR relied only on the selected jurisprudence and legislation from its member states. Also in this case, one can observe how the IACtHR engaged in a selective judicial dialogue only to the extent it was convenient to make its case but ready to move back to the regional framework when this was more appropriate to support its argument.

These two examples show that judicial dialogue is not always enough to ensure convergence of case-law, since the actual influence of a citation in the judgment may be limited and only superficial. In light of this, the increasing number of external citations by regional human rights courts are certainly to be seen as a signal of enhanced network of human rights bodies but cannot be

158 *Identidad de género, e igualdad y no discriminación a parejas del mismo sexo, Opinión consultiva* OC-24/17 (IACtHR, 9 January 2018), 220.
159 For a more detailed discussion see Chapter 2, Section 2.2.3.
160 *Advisory Opinion No. 24*, 204–205.
161 ibid, 192.

considered per se as the ultimate safeguard against fragmentation, which can be triggered anyway.

CONCLUSION

The difference in the interpretation clauses contained in the regional instruments might offer a chance for contrasting interpretation, thus triggering fragmentation. However, all five bodies chose to follow the VCLT and, harmoniously, somehow departed from it to adopt a more evolutive interpretative approach focused on the *pro homine* principle. They could have taken different paths and adopted divergent approaches, but they did not, thus contributing to maintaining convergence.

This chapter showed the increasing role of judicial dialogue in the practice of regional and international human rights bodies. Differently embraced by each institution and for different reasons, judicial dialogue may represent an important tool in ensuring reciprocal acknowledgement of case-law and standards of interpretation and, ultimately, in bringing convergence. However, judicial dialogue and judicial convergence do not have a cause-effect relation, as one can exist without the other. Furthermore, the link between a reference included in a judgment and the actual influence it had on the adjudication is not easy to ascertain and the practice of resorting to judicial dialogue is continuously evolving, thus preventing an ultimate optimistic conclusion. Nevertheless, increasing awareness of other bodies' interpretations can only have beneficial effects on the quality of the adjudication even if it ultimately leads to contrasting judgments.

In conclusion, although judicial dialogue as a phenomenon is important in the debate on convergence and fragmentation, what matters is the ultimate adoption of the same tests and standards and interpreting rights in a convergent way. The following chapters will investigate whether this is happening but not before gaining a better understanding of what could be the structural and institutional reasons for the different attitudes towards human rights interpretation and judicial dialogue.

4

The Composition of the Courts and Other Adjudicative Bodies and the Role of Their Secretariats

INTRODUCTION

Courts, commissions and committees are composed of human beings, comprising judges, commissioners, committee members or staff from their secretariats. They are constantly called upon to make decisions on which cases to consider, how to address a certain issue and, ultimately, how to rule in a given case. All these degrees of possibilities and choices make these individuals extremely pivotal in the maintenance of convergence or for the triggering of fragmentation. Although we often have the illusion that the law applies in an objective way, and that the judges are only the '*bouche de la loi*',[1] intermediaries between the law and its application in a specific case, this is often not true. Back in the 1920s, Cardozo pointed out that subconscious elements ('inherited instincts, traditional beliefs, acquired convictions') influence judges' behaviour.[2] Recent studies have confirmed the importance of looking at the individuals who make, interpret or teach the law in order to fully understand their roles in influencing how the law is interpreted and applied. For instance, Roberts has concluded that international law is not really international because of the identity, background and practice of international lawyers,[3] Carruba and others have demonstrated that the behaviour of the judges of the European Court of Justice reflects that of their member states,[4] Posner and Figueiredo found a correlation between the ICJ's judges voting

[1] Charles de Secondat Baron de Montesquieu, *The Spirit of the Laws*, Cambridge Texts in the History of Political Thought (Cambridge University Press, 1989)

[2] Benjamin N. Cardozo, *The Nature of the Judicial Process* (Yale University Press, 1921), 9–12.

[3] Anthea Roberts, *Is International Law International?* (Oxford University Press, 2017)

[4] Clifford J. Carrubba, Matthew Gable and Charles Hankla, 'Judicial Behaviour under Political Constraints: Evidence from the European Court of Justice' (2008) 102 *American Political Science Review* 4, 435–452.

behaviour and the political, cultural and wealth traditions of their member states[5] and Frank and Van Aaken proved that the profile of arbitrators has an impact on their approach to adjudication.[6]

Following this logic, if one has to identify the factors that could possibly explain the current situation of convergence and fragmentation in IHRL, one should not forget to look at who decides the cases. The composition of the bodies and the identity, background, personal history and attitude of judges, commissioners and committee members could significantly influence their adjudication[7] and, therefore, convergence and fragmentation. However, this examination should also extend to the personnel working in these institutions and preparing the cases, such as the staff of the secretariats.

This chapter investigates these two elements, exploring how they contribute to convergence and fragmentation. First, it reviews the composition of each of the five bodies under analysis, with special attention to the educational and professional background of the members who sit on the bench. Second, it explores the organisation and activities of the registries and secretariats of the human rights bodies, highlighting the role played by the meetings between judges, commissioners and committee members.

4.1 THE COMPOSITION OF THE BODIES

The composition of human rights bodies can heavily influence their interpretation and reasoning. As suggested by some scholars,[8] an investigation on the merits of who sits and takes decisions within these institutions is key for understanding how and why rights are interpreted and applied in a certain way. To really understand how these bodies work and if there is something in

5 Eric A. Posner and Miguel F. P. de Figueiredo, 'Is the International Court of Justice Biased?' (2005) 34 *The Journal of Legal Studies* 2, 599–630.

6 Susan D. Franck, Anne van Aaken, James Freda, Chris Guthrie and Jeffrey J. Rachlinksi, 'Inside the Arbitrator's Mind' (2017) 66 *Emory Law Journal* 1115.

7 Cardozo, *The Nature of the Judicial Process*; Roberts, *Is International Law International*; Posner and de Figueiredo, 'Is the International Court of Justice Biased'; Franck et al., 'Inside the Arbitrator's Mind'; Debra Chopp, 'Addressing Cultural Bias in the Legal Profession' (2017) 41 *New York University Review of Law and Societal Change* 3, 367–406; Richard A. Posner, 'Judicial Behavior and Performance: An Economic Approach' (2005) 32 *Florida State University Law Review* 1259, 1259–1279; Christoph K. Winter, 'The Value of Behavioral Economics for EU Judicial Decision-Making' (2020) 21 *German Law Journal* 240, 240–364; Masua Sagiv, 'Cultural Bias in Judicial Decision Making' (2015) 35 *Boston College Journal of Law & Social Justice* 2, 229–256.

8 ibid; Paolo Carrozza and Dinah Shelton (eds), *Regional Protection of Human Rights* (Oxford University Press, 2013) and Philippa Webb, *International Judicial Integration and Fragmentation* (Oxford University Press, 2013).

their structure and composition that can justify fragmentation or convergence, the first thing to do is to examine the rules of procedure on the composition of the bodies and to look for similarities and differences.

Following this preliminary assessment, this chapter delves into the investigation of the identity of judges, commissioners and committee members sitting on these bodies, gathering and analysing information about their education and previous experiences that might be useful for explaining some patterns in their interpretation towards convergence or fragmentation. However, considering the challenges of establishing a cause-effect link, the findings of this empirical analysis need to be checked against the judicial behaviour of judges in their separate opinions, in order to understand whether we can conclude that their identity actually had an impact on their adjudication.

4.1.1 *Rules and Procedures on the Composition of the Bodies*

The ECtHR is a permanent court composed of forty-seven judges elected by the Parliamentary Assembly of the Council of Europe (CoE) 'from a list of three candidates nominated by the High Contracting Party' and who are nominated in their personal capacity for a period of nine years without possibility of being re-elected.[9] The judges should be independent from their national government and, to this aim, they are prevented from engaging in any activity that may undermine their impartiality and independence. The judges work on a full-time basis and are remunerated by the CoE accordingly.

The IACtHR is structured similarly, composed of judges elected by the General Assembly of the Organization of American States (OAS) for a six-year term, but with the possibility of being re-elected for a second term.[10] The member states can nominate any individual with the required competencies of any nationality within OAS member states, not limited to the states that actually accepted the jurisdiction of the Court.[11] As in the case of the ECtHR, the judges serve in their personal capacity, and there cannot be two judges who are nationals of the same state.[12] The main difference, though, is in the numbers. While in the ECtHR there is a judge for each member state, in the IACtHR there are only seven judges, from seven different nationalities, out of

9 ECHR, Articles 21–23.

10 James Cavallaro et al., *Doctrine, Practice and Advocacy in the Inter-American Human Rights System* (Oxford University Press, 2019), 43–46 and 65–70.

11 For example, Judge Buergenthal, a US citizen, was the first judge of the IACtHR from a non-member state.

12 ACHR, Article 52.2.

the twenty-five member states. Moreover and differently from the ECtHR, IACtHR judges perform their duties on a part-time basis except for the president who has a full-time commitment. However, the increasing workload of cases is slowly transforming the IACtHR into a permanent court as well. Notwithstanding this silent evolution, the ACHR does not provide any limitation to the activities of the judges outside the court, thus failing to impose such a high safeguard for impartiality and independence as in the case of the ECtHR.

In line with the IACtHR, the African Court is composed of eleven judges (out of the thirty member states) nominated by the member states of the Additional Protocol[13] and elected by the Assembly of the African Union (AU) for six years with the possibility of serving a second term.[14] As in the case of the IACtHR, only the president sits as a full-time judge while the others have part-time appointments. However, Article 18 imposes limitations on the external activities of judges, in a similar fashion to Article 21 ECHR, stating that 'the position of judge of the Court is incompatible with any activity that might interfere with the independence or impartiality of such a judge'.[15]

The African Commission does have a different composition, due to its different role and nature as a quasi-judicial body. Accordingly, it is composed of eleven members, nominated by the state parties to the ACHPR and elected by the AU Assembly for a six-year period with the possibility of re-election.[16] They serve in their personal capacity but, while senior civil servants and ambassadors are now excluded, criticisms have been made about the frequent appointment of individuals who were working closely with or at the dependence of their government.

Completely different is the situation of the HRC. As a UN Treaty Body, the HRC is composed of eighteen independent experts, serving in their personal capacity, who are elected for a renewable term of four years by the state parties to the ICCPR. The HRC members only have a part-time appointment considering that the Committee meets only three times a year for a four-week period.[17]

This brief overview already unveils a difference in the number of judges and members who sit on the bodies that could play a role in leading to

[13] Protocol to the African Charter on the Establishment of the African Court on Human and Peoples' Rights, 10 June 1998 (entered into force 25 January 2004).

[14] ibid, Article 15.

[15] ibid, Article 18.

[16] ACHPR, Articles 31–36.

[17] Rules of Procedure of the Human Rights Committee, CCPR/C/3/Rev.10, 11 January 2012, Rule 2.

convergence or fragmentation, as the structure of the courts can have an impact on the adjudication.[18] The European Court has one judge per member state, while the other bodies have significantly fewer judges than member states. The special attention that the ECtHR gives to the interest and concerns of its member states is also shown by the fact that the ECHR provides that 'there shall sit as an *ex officio* member of the Chamber and the Grand Chamber the judge elected in respect of the High Contracting Party concerned. If, for any reason, that judge is unable to sit, a person chosen by the President of the Court from a list submitted in advance by that Party shall sit in the capacity of judge'.[19] This provision demonstrates the strong interest of the ECtHR to carefully take into consideration the national perspective of the respondent state and allow its national judge to intervene in the adjudication. Such a guarantee, absent in all the other regional systems or the HRC, seems a protective measure to ensure that the state's situation is duly considered. Conversely, both the African and Inter-American Court's rules of procedures clearly state that the judge whose national state is a party to the case should not participate in the hearing and deliberation.[20] This may suggest that the ECtHR is institutionally more inclined to be biased towards its member states' position and, indeed, some scholars have stressed the possible influence of the judges' relationship with their member states and the appointment's procedure on their judicial behaviour.[21] However, as demonstrated by empirical studies, the national judges in the ECtHR have proven to be very impartial, more than other international courts.[22] Nevertheless, as Voeten highlighted, the voting behaviour of national judges changes when they have to examine controversial cases that deal with the national interest and security, where they, indeed, adopt a more protectionist approach towards their national state.[23] In light of this, the composition of the ECtHR, in terms of number and make-up of judges, compared to the other human rights bodies, could be

18 Lee Epstein, 'How Institutions Structure Judicial Behaviour: An Analysis of Alarie and Green's *Commitment and Cooperation on High Courts: A Cross-Country Examination of Institutional Constraints on Judges*' (2019) 69 *University of Toronto Law Journal* 275–293.

19 ECHR, Article 26(5).

20 Rules of Procedure of the African Court on Human and Peoples' Rights, 20 June 2008, Rule 8 and Rules of Procedures of the Inter-American Court of Human Rights, 29 January 2009, Article 19.

21 Richard A. Posner, 'What Do Judges and Justices Maximize? (The Same Things Everyone Else Does)' (1993) 3 *Supreme Court Economic Review* 1, 1–28 and Posner and de Figueiredo, 'Is the International Court of Justice Biased'.

22 Erik Voeten, 'The Impartiality of International Judges: Evidence from the European Court of Human Rights' (2008) 102(4) *American Political Science Review* 417.

23 ibid, 427–428.

considered as an additional explanatory factor of judicial fragmentation when this arises as a consequence of highly 'politicised' and controversial cases, such as the well-known *Bankovic* case.[24]

4.1.2 *Who Are the Judges?*

If the composition of these bodies can have an influence, a more in-depth analysis into the personal profiles of the judges may help comprehend why certain human rights bodies tend towards convergence or fragmentation. Considering the wide margin of interpretation left to the adjudicatory bodies, the profile of who sits on these bodies assumes very high importance. Some scholars suggested that the identity and personal history of judges of international courts could be particularly relevant for understanding their behaviour in interpreting convention rights.[25] Several studies have been conducted looking at specific variables in the judges' background, especially for the ICJ and ECJ.[26] However, very few scholars have attempted a detailed analysis and investigation of this particular aspect of human rights institutions.

Some scholars focused on the influence of political or philosophical opinions, some on the role of sex and race,[27] some on the influence of their member states politics and policies[28] and others on the potential gain for their personal careers.[29] The following empirical analysis looks at two particular variables in the personal profile that may be identified as possible explanatory factors for convergence or fragmentation: education and work experience.[30] The choice of these two variables is motivated by the stronger potential

[24] cf *Bankovic and Others v. Belgium and 16 Other States*, Application no 52207/99 (ECtHR, 12 December 2001).

[25] Voeten, 'The Impartiality of International Judges'; Carrubba, Gabel and Hankla, 'Judicial Behavior under Political Constraints', 45–52; Lawrence Baum, 'What Judges Want: Judges' Goals and Judicial Behavior' (1994) 47(3) *Political Research Quarterly* 749, 749–768.

[26] ibid and Posner and de Figueiredo, 'Is the International Court of Justice Biased?', 599–630.

[27] See, among others, Cassia Spohn, 'The Sentencing Decisions of Black and White Judges: Expected and Unexpected Similarities' (1990) 24 *Law & Society Review* 1198 and Gregory C. Sisk et al., 'Charting the Influences on the Judicial Mind: An Empirical Study of Judicial Reasoning' (1998) 73 *New York University Law Review* 1377, 1385–1421.

[28] See, among others, Voeten, 'The Impartiality of International Judges'; Winter, 'The Value of Behavioral Economics', 240–364.

[29] Baum, 'What Judges Want: Judges', 749–768.

[30] Due to the limits of feasibility of this research, the analysis on the African Commission and the HRC will be restricted to the current members due to the difficulties in getting reliable information about the previous members. The data used in this study have been taken from the official websites of the three regional systems and of the OHCHR and from complementary online research on other relevant websites (e.g. academic institutions linked to the judges/members, personal websites, professional associations websites, etc.).

relationship between them and judicial convergence, but further research on other variables could be also extremely useful and interesting. An examination of the available online data on the current and previous members of the five bodies analysed in this book, coupled with interviews and further research, reveals surprising trends that confirm the need to go beyond the judgments and pay adequate attention also to the 'human environment' around IHRL case-law. The study shows the situation in two different moments in time, 2018 and 2021. Even though only three years have passed between the first and the second analysis, one can observe interesting changes and developments that could anticipate future trends.

4.1.2.1 The Educational Background

The investigation into the educational background of the judges and members of the regional systems could help establish the degree of cross-fertilisation between regional bodies. Education, especially university education, significantly influences the reasoning and understanding of legal provisions. Undertaking university education in a continent different from that of origin may considerably expand the mind of the judge, introducing them to a completely different way to approach legal concepts and adjudication. This may result in an endogenous assimilation of another regional perspective on human rights, and a higher likelihood of convergence with the human rights perspective of the area where studies were pursued. Considering the different attitude of each body towards judicial dialogue and convergence,[31] one may expect that in the Inter-American and African bodies there is a higher percentage of judges and members who attended universities outside their continent compared to the ECtHR. This could further explain the higher attention paid to achieving convergence by the African and Inter-American bodies and their willingness to adopt the reasoning and case-law of other regional systems. Moreover, due to the copious use of references to the ECtHR by the Inter-American and African bodies observed in Chapter 3, the assumption is also that the percentage of members of the IACtHR and African bodies who undertook university studies in Europe is higher than that of European judges who studied outside Europe.[32]

[31] See Chapters 3, 5 and 6.

[32] For the sake of this analysis, university education includes any undergraduate and postgraduate course (Master degrees and PhDs but not short courses diplomas) awarded by a public or private university.

TABLE 1. *Members' education*

Bodv	Members	Education outside the continent		Education in Europe	
		2018	2021	2018	2021
ACommHPR	Current	82% (9/11)	55% (6/11)	73% (8/11)	45% (5/11)
ACtHPR	Current	73% (8/11)	45% (5/11)	63% (7/11)	36% (4/11)
	Total	76% (18/25)	68% (20/29)	66% (15/25)	58% (17/29)
IACtHR	Current	57% (4/7)	57% (4/7)	57% (4/7)	57% (4/7)
	Total	51% (20/39)	50% (20/40)	51% (20/39)	50% (20/40)
ECtHR	Current	15% (7/47)	15% (7/47)	–	
	Total	6%(13/190)	8% (16/205)	–	
HRC	Current	50% (9/18)	44% (8/18)	50% (9/18)	66% (12/18)

Sources: Personal elaboration from official websites of the African Commission on Human and Peoples' Rights, African Court on Human and Peoples' Rights, Inter-American Court of Human Rights, European Court of Human Rights and OHCHR and other online research, updated to June 2021.[33]

Table 1 shows a clear trend, confirming the hypothesis. The European judges are those who, by far, received a less international university education, both in their current composition and in the cumulative analysis over time (15% and 6%/8%). The very low percentage of ECtHR judges who studied outside Europe is in contrast with the very high percentage of the African Commissioners (82% in 2018 and 55% in 2021), African Court's judges (73% and 76% in 2018 and 45% and 68% in 2021) and even Inter-American judges (57% and 51% in 2018 and 2021). Very balanced was the case of the HRC, where around half of the current members studied outside their continent. If one assumes that undertaking university studies outside their continent opens the mind and exposes them to alternative perspectives and approaches, this data confirms the permeation from other legal traditions of the ACommHPR, ACtHPR and IACtHR, which may ultimately help convergence. On the contrary, the ECtHR appears more Euro-centric, thus possibly leading to a more self-centred case-law and, in some cases, to fragmentation with other human rights systems. However, the comparison between 2018 and 2021 data

[33] cf www.echr.coe.int/Pages/home.aspx?p=court/judges; www.corteidh.or.cr/index.php/en/about-us/composicion; http://en.african-court.org/index.php/judges/current-judges; http://en.african-court.org/index.php/judges/former-judges and www.achpr.org/about/, last accessed 10 February 2022.

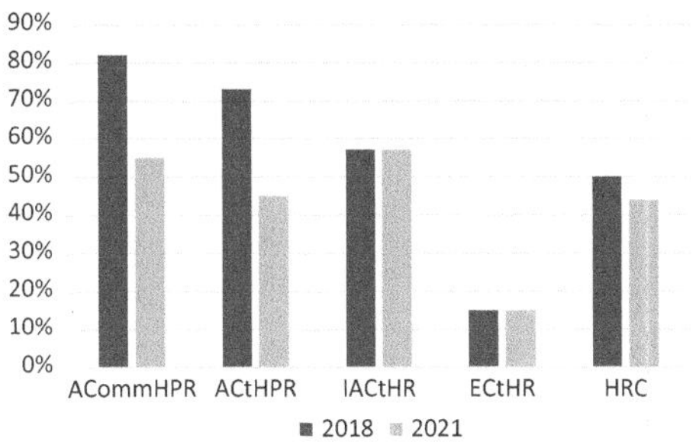

FIGURE 1 Current members who received university education outside their continent (percentage)

shows a significant decrease in the number of African judges and commissioners who received education outside their continent and in Europe (82% vs 55% for the ACommHPR and 73% vs 45% for the ACtHPR).

Moreover, Table 1 reveals another interesting trend. Among those numerous non-European judges, commissioners and committee members who studied outside their continent, the percentage of those who studied in Europe is particularly high. In addition to more than half of the members of the HRC, a high percentage of the judges and commissioners of the IACtHR, ACtHPR and ACommHPR (ranging in the 51–73% in 2018 and 36–57% in 2021) received their higher legal education in Europe. These numbers confirm the perception of the Inter-American and African systems being extremely close to the European system.

As evident from Figure 1, the number of judges and commissioners of the Inter-American and African bodies who attended university studies outside their continent is impressively high, especially when compared to the low number of European judges who got any education from outside Europe, even though with some decrease over time. University education is particularly important because it is the moment when the minds are shaped the most and, especially in the context of legal studies, it sets the reference standards and interpretation paradigms that a judge will be using throughout their career. For an African or an Inter-American judge/commissioner, having studied law in Europe means being very familiar with the European legal culture and heritage and being able to both understand and adopt in their own case-law the European regional concerns.

Moreover, this personal legal fertilisation invalidates most of the 'cultural relativism' arguments for fragmentation, since the African or Inter-American judges could have embedded the European approach to human rights adjudication to the extent of naturally replicating it and applying it to the adjudication of cases before their own regional bodies. African and Inter-American judges have been in a way 'Europeanised', and they are, therefore, applying European values back home. This contributes to the globalisation and, in a way, Europeanisation of human rights and certainly brings more convergence to the entire system. Although it physiologically facilitates convergence, this phenomenon has the downside of determining a one-sided convergence, with the Inter-American and African bodies referencing and adhering to the European standards and very rarely the opposite.[34] However, the 2021 data shows that this Europeanisation of the African bodies is significantly decreasing. If confirmed over time, this could suggest a trend towards a more Africa-centred composition and, as a consequence, probably adjudication. This is a likely natural evolution of a regional human rights system still in the growing stage and it is a signal of a healthy development into a leading one. Yet, the existing strong safeguard against fragmentation offered by the composition of the body could diminish in time and open the door to emerging examples of fragmentation.

4.1.2.2 The Professional Background

The other element worth investigating in this study is the professional background of judges and members of regional bodies. At a glimpse, one can observe that there is a substantial similarity in the general profile of the judges and members of these bodies. Indeed, in all the three courts almost all judges are or have been national judges, except the IACtHR where the number of career academics is slightly higher and the HRC where almost the totality of the members are academics. However, what differs significantly is the international work experience that these judges and members had before being appointed. Voeten has already shown that judges' previous employment could influence their behaviour in court,[35] looking at the case of the ECtHR and to those judges who, before their appointment, were diplomats of their national states. In this research, the analysis is extended to the judges and members of all the five bodies under analysis, with the aim of identifying those who had previous work experience in international organisations (such as the UN) or international tribunals (such as the ICJ, ICTY, ICTR).

A further degree of analysis also identifies those who served as members of the UN Treaty Bodies (TBs) or as mandate holders of UN Special Procedures (SPs). Intuitively, the more these judges and commissioners have been engaging with the UN human rights system, the more they may be ready

[34] cf Chapter 3.
[35] Voeten, 'The Impartiality of International Judges'.

TABLE 2. *Members' work experience (international organisations/courts)*

Body	Members	International organisations and courts		UNTBs members or SPs mandate holders	
		2018	2021	2018	2021
ACommHPR	Current	9% (1/11)	18% (2/11)	9% (1/11)	9% (1/11)
ACtHPR	Current	37% (4/11)	32% (3/11)	18% (2/11)	9% (1/11)
	Total	32% (8/25)	35% (10/29)	16% (4/25)	14% (17/29)
IACtHR	Current	14% (1/7)	14% (1/7)	14% (1/7)	14% (1/7)
	Total	31% (12/39)	30% (12/40)	13% (5/39)	12.5% (5/40)
ECtHR	Current	15% (7/47)	13% (6/47)	4% (2/47)	4% (2/47)
	Total	12% (22/190)	12% (24/205)	1.5% (3/190)	2% (5/205)
HRC	Current	16% (3/18)*	11% (2/18)	–	–

* For the HRC, the work experience variable is 'Regional human rights bodies'.

Sources: Personal elaboration from official websites of the African Commission on Human and Peoples' Rights, African Court on Human and Peoples' Rights, Inter-American Court of Human Rights and European Court of Human Rights and other online research, updated to June 2021.

and willing to reinforce the principle of universality of human rights in their adjudication practices, striving for convergence and making references to UN instruments and case-law. In the case of the HRC, the analysis investigates if its members had previous work experience in regional systems.

As Table 2 shows, there is a great difference between the regional bodies when it comes to members' prior work experience in international organisations and courts but no significant change over time. In general, the percentage is very low (an average of 15%), showing little movement of staff between regional and international human rights bodies. However, the ACtHPR hosts the highest percentage of judges having worked previously for international organisations and courts (over 30%). Similar figure for the IACtHR (30–31%) but only when the total number of current and previous judges is considered, thus showing a decreasing trend of Inter-American judges previously serving in international organisations or judicial bodies. The following graph clarifies this trend.

Figure 2 shows the general low percentage of members with previous experience in international or regional bodies and the trend over time. As observed above, these data show a decreasing trend in the case of the IACtHR, probably due to the historical changes in Latin America and the stabilisation of democratic governments. Moreover, the graph shows a slight decreasing

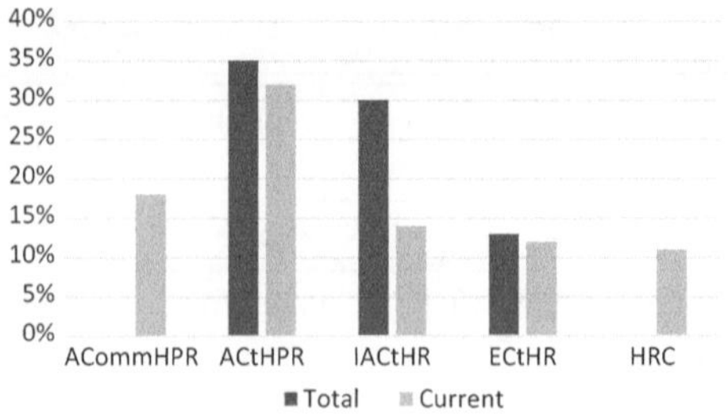

FIGURE 2 Current and total members with previous work experience in international organisations and courts, 2021 data (percentage)

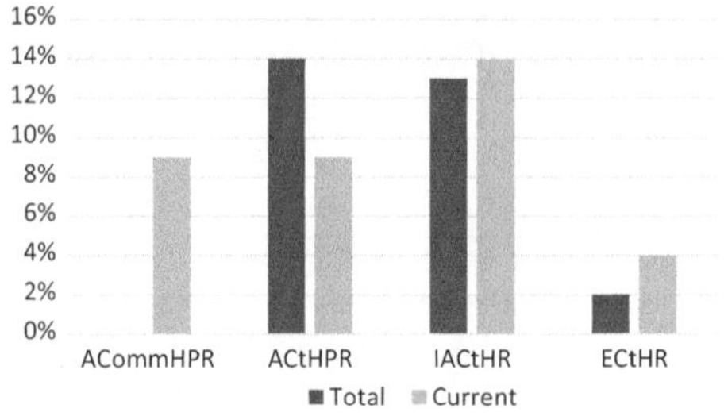

FIGURE 3 Current and total members previously working in UNTBs or SPs, 2021 data (percentage)

trend for the ACtHR and an increasing one for ECtHR, yet these variations are still too small to be considered relevant. The following graph will present the other variable taken into consideration, the percentage of those members who previously served as TBs members or SPs mandate holders.

As evident from Figure 3, the number of regional judges and commissioners who previously served in UNTBs or as SPs mandate holders is generally very low. Yet, a clear trend emerges. The ACtHPR and the IACtHR register a significantly higher percentage (9–14% for the ACtHPR and 14–13% for the IACtHR) especially if compared to the ECtHR (4–2%). The low presence of previous UNTBs members or SP mandate holders within the ECtHR is even more striking if one thinks that 8 per cent of the Inter-American judges were former members of the HRC while in the European case the corresponding percentage is only 0.5 per cent. This situation could be compared to the HRC that has in its current composition only 2 out of 18 members (11%) with previous work experience in regional human rights bodies. This proportion seems in line with those shown by the African and Inter-American bodies and higher than the ECtHR. Nevertheless, considering the role and nature of the HRC, one could expect a more significant cross-fertilisation member-wise with regional human rights systems. The limited presence of former employees of the three regional human rights bodies could indeed be an explanation of the relatively limited acknowledgement by the HRC of the regional bodies' case law.

All this data could contribute to explaining why the African and Inter-American bodies are usually more concerned with referencing international standards and reaching convergence of judicial interpretation. Serving as a member of one of the UNTBs or a SP mandate holder made these judges familiar with both UN case-law, UN instruments in different fields of human rights and with the challenges of the UN system in establishing universal standards of rights. On the contrary, the fact that the overwhelming majority of the ECtHR is composed of former national judges with probably just a limited knowledge of the international systems, especially outside the EU and CoE contexts, contributes to the internal development of the ECtHR jurisprudence without giving much consideration to the international and other regional examples.

Another interesting element to investigate in the work experience of judges and members of human rights bodies is whether they have been working as academics and, in that case, whether they have been engaging with research and teaching in comparative and international law subjects. The hypothesis is that judges and members of human rights adjudicatory bodies that are or used to be academics in those areas tend to be less 'parochial' than those who only served as national judges or diplomats. Academics are, indeed, significantly more exposed to different legal cultures and approaches and they develop, through their job, a more informed and less self-referential way of addressing any specific issue, appreciating the value of supporting their own argument with elements coming from diverse legal environments.

Table 3 highlights quite a distinctive pattern from those previously observed. As anticipated, the IACtHR has the highest number of academics in its current formation (71%) and its total one (52%) compared to the other regional human rights bodies. Similarly high is the number of academics in the HRC (61%). Interesting is the case of the ECtHR and the African bodies. If in 2018 the ECtHR had a significant high percentage (60%) and the African bodies a very low one (18% and 27%), in 2021 the situation changed completely. Both the ECtHR and the ACtHPR landed on 45 per cent and the ACommHPR is slightly lower at 33 per cent, showing a significant increase on the African side and a decrease on the European one.

As shown in Figure 4, the difference lies also in the percentage of judges and members who, as academics, have engaged with international and comparative legal subjects as familiarity with these subjects may further increase

TABLE 3. *Members' work experience (academia)*

Body	Members	Former or current academics		Focus on comparative and international law	
		2018	2021	2018	2021
ACommHPR	Current	18% (2/11)	33% (3/11)	18% (2/11)	18% (2/11)
ACtHPR	Current	27% (3/11)	45% (5/11)	27% (3/11)	36% (4/11)
	Total	16% (4/25)	31% (9/29)	16% (4/25)	28% (8/29)
IACtHR	Current	71% (5/7)	71% (5/7)	57% (4/7)	57% (4/7)
	Total	51% (20/39)	52% (21/40)	41% (16/39)	42% (17/40)
ECtHR	Current	60% (28/47)	45% (21/47)	36% (17/47)	30% (14/47)
	Total	39% (75/190)	36% (73/205)	28% (53/190)	29% (59/205)
HRC	Current	61% (11/18)	61% (11/18)	61% (11/18)	55% (10/18)

Sources: Personal elaboration from official websites of the African Commission on Human and Peoples' Rights, African Court on Human and Peoples' Rights, Inter-American Court of Human Rights, European Court of Human Rights and OHCHR and other online research, updated to June 2021.

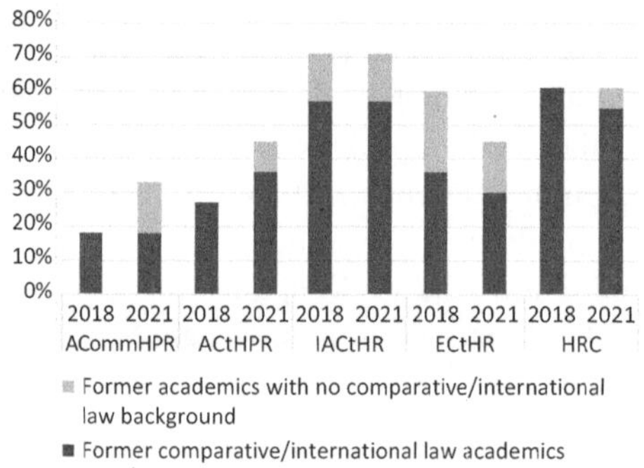

FIGURE 4 Current members currently or previously working in academia with specialisation subjects (percentage)

the awareness of other regional and international bodies' case-law and could potentially foster convergence.

The IACtHR and the HRC have very high numbers of academics with expertise in those subjects and the trend is quite steady across time. The African bodies saw an increase in the number of academics but not all the new academics were experts in international and comparative subjects. On the contrary, the ECtHR saw a decreasing number of former academics, yet the number of experts in international and comparative law remains the same, even if relatively low. Such data, especially compared to the IACtHR, show a picture of the European judges as potentially less cosmopolitan and open to judicial dialogue with other human rights bodies, due to their subject expertise. However, the trend seems to be evolving over time and this could suggest that the situation may drastically change, showing the continuous adjustment of the regional systems.

4.1.2.3 Assessing the Impact of Personal Background on Separate Opinions

Following the above analysis, one doubt remains on whether the educational and working background of judges have an actual impact on the interpretation of convention rights. To answer this complex question, this chapter looks at the separate opinions (concurring and dissenting) of a sample of current and previous regional judges[36] (the members of the African Commission cannot issue separate opinions).[37] The hypothesis is that those judges with a university education outside their continent and/or with a working background in international organisations and courts, and especially within UNTBs or SPs, or in academia, should be more inclined to mention UN or other international and regional instruments and case-law in their separate opinions. As discussed in the previous chapter, the use of external references has merits and drawbacks and should be carefully analysed,[38] but, even recognising the limitations, this element is here considered as the only way to have a confirmation of the individual behaviour of a judge.

THE AFRICAN COURT ON HUMAN AND PEOPLES' RIGHTS The ACtHPR has issued significantly less judgments than their counterparts. However, in the

[36] For reasons of feasibility, the study focuses on all judges from the African and the Inter-American Courts, due to the lower number of judgments issued, and on a selection of the ECtHR's judges. These have been chosen within those who had an educational background outside their continent or those who previously worked for international organisations and courts or had academic positions in international and comparative legal subjects. Nevertheless, to complete the analysis, these separate opinions have been compared with those of judges and members that do not have such a background.

[37] cf Other examples of analysis of separate opinions such as Fred J. Bruinsma and Matthijs de Blois, 'Rules of Law from Westport to Wladiwostok: Separate Opinions in the European Court of Human Rights' (1997) 2 *Netherlands Quarterly of Human Rights* 175. The analysis of the separate opinions presented in this section is updated at June 2021.

[38] Chapter 3.

cases where judges issued separate opinions, it is possible to identify a pattern in support of the hypothesis.[39]

Justice Fatsah Ouguergouz, one of the first members of the Court elected in 2006 and then confirmed for a second term, has been one of the most active judges in writing separate opinions. After receiving a law degree in France, Justice Ouguergouz obtained a PhD in international law from the Graduate Institute of International Studies in Geneva.[40] Before being appointed, he also worked extensively for the UN and in particular for the OHCHR and the ICJ. His wide and rich background is reflected in his separate opinions. Justice Ouguergouz always made extensive reference to the case-law of other regional or UN bodies as well as international documents and treaties. For instance, in *Michelot Yogogombaye v. Republic of Senegal*,[41] he largely quoted the case-law of the HRC and the IACtHR, while in *Efoua Mbozo'o Samuel v. Pan African Parliament*[42] attention was paid to the work of the ICJ. The case-law of the ECtHR often emerges in Justice Ouguergouz's separate opinions since he cited the Strasbourg Court in almost the totality of his cases. Moreover, he proved to be particularly concerned about the risks of judicial fragmentation between human rights bodies as it emerged in *Tanganyika Law Society and Legal and Human Rights Centre v. United Republic of Tanzania*, where he dedicated an entire section of his separate opinion to the need of judicial dialogue between regional and international human rights bodies for avoiding fragmentation.[43]

Likewise, Justice Balise Tchikaya, professor of international law and with an educational background in France, almost always cited the ECtHR, IACtHR and the UN in his separate opinions. For example, in *Kennedy Ivan v. Tanzania*, *Ally Rajabu and Others v. Tanzania* and *Evodius Rutechura v. Tanzania*, Justice Tchikaya referred to all the three systems in his separate opinions.[44] Moreover, in *Jebra Kambole v. Tanzania*, he extensively argued in favour of adopting a margin of appreciation,[45] invoking the importance of

39 Separate opinions available at http://en.african-court.org/index.php/cases/2016-10-17-16-18-21#finalised-cases, last accessed 10 February 2022.

40 Information available at www.africancourtcoalition.org/index.php?option=com_content&view=article&id=32:afr..&Itemid=&lang=en, last accessed 10 February 2022.

41 *Michelot Yogogombaye v. Senegal*, Application no 001/2008 (ACtHPR, 15 December 2009).

42 *Efoua Mbozo'o Samuel v. Pan African Parliament*, Application no 010/2011 (ACtHPR, 30 September 2011).

43 *Tanganyka Law Society v. United Republic of Tanzania*, Applications nos 9 and 11/2011 (ACtHPR, 14 June 2013), 16.

44 cf *Kennedy Ivan v. Tanzania*, Application no 025/2016 (ACtHPR, 28 March 2019); *Ally Rajabu and Others v. Tanzania*, Application no 007/2015 (ACtHPR, 28 November 2019) and *Evodius Rutechura v. Tanzania*, Application no 004/2016 (ACtHPR, 25 June 2021).

45 See Chapter 6.

universality of human rights.[46] As for the other judges of the ACtHPR, only a few of them issued separate opinions. For instance, Justice Elsie Nwanwuri Thompson wrote a separate opinion in *Mohamed Abubakari v. United Republic of Tanzania*[47] where she extensively mentioned the case-law of the ECtHR and the HRC. In line with our hypothesis, this could be explained by her university legal education at Queen Mary University of London.[48]

A comparison with the separate opinions of judges who did not study outside the African continent nor had any previous work experience in international organisations, such as Lady Justice Stella Isibhakhonemn Anukam or Justice Ben Kioko confirms the hypothesis. Indeed, they only mentioned the IACtHR and the UN bodies in two cases, and never referenced the ECtHR.[49] Other judges that fall within this category, such as Justice Ntyam Ondo Mengue, Justice Jean Emile Somda and Justice Hamdi Faraj Fanoush, have never issued any separate opinion so far. The findings, despite the low number of judgments, confirmed the initial hypothesis of a correlation between the education or work background and the disposition to include references to regional and international human rights systems in separate opinions. Moreover, they constitute further validation of the special attention that African judges reserve to the European systems, in line with their educational background and experiences in Europe.

THE INTER-AMERICAN COURT OF HUMAN RIGHTS The IACtHR shows similar features, as the analysis was limited by the relatively low number of separate opinions. Nevertheless, it is still possible to infer something from the behaviour of these six judges and the content of their separate opinions.

Judge Antônio Augusto Cançado Trindade is by far the most prolific judge in the history of the IACtHR. After receiving his LLM and PhD from the University of Cambridge, Judge Cançado Trindade worked for the UN in different capacities.[50] His dissenting and concurring opinions definitely reflect his deep knowledge of the UN and European systems. Since his first years at the Court, Judge Cançado Trindade issued many extensive separate opinions

46 *Jebra Kambole v. Tanzania*, Application no 018/2018 (ACtHPR, 15 July 2020).

47 *Mohamed Abubakari v. Tanzania*, Application no 007/2013 (ACtHPR, 3 June 2016).

48 Information available at http://en.african-court.org/index.php/judges/former-judges, last accessed 10 February 2022.

49 *Minani Evarist v. Tanzania*, Application no 027/2015 (ACtHPR, 21 September 2018) and *Jebra Kambole v. Tanzania*, Application no 018/2018 (ACtHPR, 15 July 2020).

50 Information available at www.icj-cij.org/court/?p1=1&p2=2&p3=1&judge=167, last accessed 10 February 2022.

referring to the ECtHR case-law,[51] such as in *El Amparo v. Venezuela*.[52] Similarly, UN documents and the HRC case-law, together with the others TBs' case-law, found space in Judge Cançado Trindade's separate opinions, as in *Castillo Petruzzi et al. v. Peru*,[53] *'The Last Temptation of Christ' (Olmedo-Bustos et al.) v. Chile*[54] and *Trujillo Oroza v. Bolivia*.[55]

An analogous active approach towards the referencing of the ECtHR and UN bodies could be found in the separate opinions of former Judge Cecilia Medina Quiroga. Before being appointed to the IACtHR, Judge Medina served as a member of the HRC from 1995 to 2002.[56] In her dissenting and concurring opinions, she repeatedly mentions the case-law of the HRC but just as much as the EctHR, although one could have expected more attention to the views of the body where she worked for so many years. Examples of this are 19 *Merchants v. Colombia*[57] and *Gómez Palomino v. Peru*[58] as well as *González et al. ("Cotton Field") v. Mexico*.[59]

Looking at the current judges of the IACtHR, Judges Eduardo Ferrer Mac-Gregor Poisot, Eduardo Renato Vio Grossi and Patricio Pazmino Freire, all with a PhD from European universities and previous work experience in European academic institutions, have issued quite a high number of separate opinions containing several references to the EctHR[60] but also to the UNTBs case-law and general comments, UN SPs documents and UN official treaties.[61] In particular, Judge Ferrer Mac-Gregor Poisot has been issuing very

[51] *Gangaram-Panday v. Suriname* (IACtHR, 21 January 1994); *Castillo Páez v. Peru* (IACtHR, 3 November 1997); *Loyaza-Tamayo v. Peru* (IACtHR, 17 September 1997); *Genie Lacayo v. Nicaragua* (IACtHR, 13 September 1997).

[52] *El Amparo v. Venezuela* (IACtHR, 14 September 1996).

[53] *Castillo Petruzzi et al. v. Peru* (IACtHR, 4 September 1998).

[54] *Olmedo-Bustos et al. v. Chile (The Last Temptation of Christ case)* (IACtHR, 5 February 2001).

[55] *Trujillo Oroza v. Bolivia* (IACtHR, 27 February 2002).

[56] Biographical information available at www.iccnow.org/documents/Medina_CV.pdf, last accessed 10 February 2022.

[57] *The 19 Merchants v. Colombia* (IACtHR, 5 July 2004).

[58] *Gómez-Palomino v. Peru* (IACtHR, 22 November 2005).

[59] *González et al. ("Cotton Field") v. Mexico* (IACtHR, 16 November 2009).

[60] cf Eduardo Ferrer Mac-Gregor Poisot's separate opinions in *Cabrera García and Montiel-Flores v. Mexico* (IACtHR, 26 November 2010); *Supreme Court of Justice (Quintana Coello et al.) v. Ecuador* (IACtHR, 21 August 2014); *Constitutional Tribunal (Camba Campos et al.) v. Ecuador* (IACtHR, 28 August 2013); Eduardo Renato Vio Grossi's in *Barbani Duarte et al. v. Uruguay* (IACtHR, 26 June 2012) or *Casa Nina v. Peru* (IACtHR, 24 November 2020) and Patricio Pazmino Freire's in *Indigenous Communities of the Lhaka Honhat Association (Our Land) v. Argentina* (IACtHR, 6 February 2020).

[61] cf Eduardo Ferrer Mac-Gregor Poisot's separate opinions *Suárez Peralta v. Ecuador* (IACtHR, 21 May 2013); Eduardo Renato Vio Grossi's in *Xákmok Kásek v. Paraguay* (IACtHR, 24 August

detailed and thorough discussion of comparative case-law from the EctHR, ACtHPR, HRC and other UN bodies in his separate opinions.[62]

Likewise, other judges with previous work experience as academics or with education received in Europe, such as Judges Franco, Maculay, Perez Manrique and Sierra Porto have often mentioned the African, European and UN systems in their separate opinions,[63] sometimes also referring to the importance of adopting a 'universalistic understanding of human rights and human dignity'.[64]

To further confirm the hypothesis, it is useful to verify whether judges without such a 'cosmopolitan' background, namely those who have not received university education outside the American continent and have not previously worked as academics or in international courts or organisations, actually refrain from citing the other regional and international human rights bodies.

If one looks at the separate opinions of Judge Manuel E. Ventura Robles, Roberto F. Caldas, Sergio Garcia Ramirez and Judge Eugenio Raul Zaffaroni, such assumption is confirmed. Judge Ventura Robles, in his nine dissenting and concurring opinions, referred to the ECtHR case-law only in one occasion[65] and to the General Assembly resolutions in another one.[66] Likewise, Sergio Garcia Ramirez issued forty-eight separate opinions and mentioned the ECtHR in only two of them[67] and the work of the UN Sub Commission for the Protection of Minorities in the other three.[68] Similarly, Judge Roberto F. Caldas never cited the case-law of the ECtHR in his five separate opinions, except for the acknowledgement, in one case, that his interpretation of the

2010) and *Artavia Murillo et al. ("in vitro fertilization") v. Costa* Rica (IACtHR, 28 November 2012).

62 See, on this, the separate opinions in *Muelle Flores v. Peru* (IACtHR, 6 March 2019); *Employees of the Fireworks Factory of Santo Antônio de Jesus and Their Families v. Brazi* (IACtHR, 15 July 2020) and *Martínez Esquivia v. Colombia* (IACtHR, 6 October 2020).

63 cf, among others, Leonardo A. Franco's partially dissenting opinion in *Salvador-Chiriboga v. Ecuador* (IACtHR, 31 August 2012); Margarette May Maculay's concurring opinion in *Furlan and Family v. Argentina* (IACtHR, 31 August 2012); Antonio Sierra Porto and Ricardo Cesar Perez Manrique's separate opinion in *Employees of the Fireworks Factory of Santo Antônio de Jesus and Their Families v. Brazi* (IACtHR, 15 July 2020).

64 cf, partly dissenting opinion of Judge Antonio Sierra Porto in *Dismissed Employees of Petroperú et al. v. Peru* (IACtHR, 23 November 2017).

65 *Salvador Chiriboga*, IACtHR.

66 *Miguel Castro-Castro Prison v. Peru* (IACtHR, 25 November 2006).

67 *Myrna Mack Chang v. Guatemala, Merits* (IACtHR, 25 November 2003); *Tibi v. Ecuador* (IACtHR, 7 September 2004).

68 *Castillo Páez*, IACtHR; *Bámaca Velásquez v. Guatemala* (IACtHR, 25 November 2000); *Mayagna (Sumo) Awas Tingni Community v. Nicaragua* (IACtHR, 31 August 2001).

Convention was 'in line with the European case-law'.[69] Finally, Judge Zaffaroni never mentioned external material in his five separate opinions.

This validates the initial hypothesis that judges with a foreign educational background and previous work experience within international courts and organisations or academia are more likely to reference the ECtHR and UN bodies' case-law in their separate opinions. On the contrary, those without such a background proved to be more reluctant in mentioning other regional or UN bodies' case-law.

However, it is interesting to note that the amount of references to other international and regional systems is not as high as one may have expected from the background of the judges under analysis. This could be explained by the nature of separate opinions (as optional additions that judges may or may not issue) and to the political backlash they could experience. Finally, it should be noted how the 'Europeanisation' of the IACtHR, already suggested by the educational background of a large number of judges, is confirmed by the constant reference to the ECtHR in its judges' separate opinions, much more than to any UN body.

THE EUROPEAN COURT OF HUMAN RIGHTS The ECtHR shows quite a different pattern. The European judges turned out to be generally reluctant to translate their background in conspicuous references to regional and international systems in their separate opinions with only one exception. Indeed, among the sample of ten judges with foreign education or international work background,[70] only eight issued concurring or dissenting opinions with explicit references to the Inter-American, the African systems or UN documents, bodies and case-law, and just in a small number of cases.

Judge Iulia Motoc, who served as a UN Special Rapporteur and a member of different UNTBs, has included references to the ICJ, ILC or the UN CRPD in only two cases, *Chiragov and Others v. Armenia*[71] and *Kacper Nowakowski v. Poland*,[72] and to the HRC, Human Rights Council, CEDAW and UN CRC in *Correia de Matos v. Portugal*,[73] *Carvalho Pinto de Sousa Morais v. Portugal*[74] and *D.M.D. v. Romania*.[75]

[69] *Garibaldi v. Brazil* (IACtHR, 23 September 2009).

[70] The same includes five current judges (Judge Motoc, Judge Lemmens, Judge Seibert-Fohr, Judge Haruntyunyan and Judge Huseynov) and five former judges (Judge Zupancic, Judge Sicilianos, Judge Keller, Judge Kalaydjeva and Judge Pettiti).

[71] *Chiragov and Others v. Armenia*, Application no 13216/05 (ECtHR, 16 June 2015).

[72] *Kacper Nowakowski v. Poland*, Application no 32407/13 (ECtHR, 10 January 2017).

[73] *Correia de Matos v. Portugal*, Application no 56402/12 (ECtHR, 4 April 2018).

[74] *Carvalho Pinto de Sousa Morais v. Portugal*, Application no 17484/15 (ECtHR, 25 July 2017).

[75] *D.M.D. v. Romania*, Application no 23022/13 (ECtHR, 3 October 2017).

Judge Paul Lemmens, who studied in the USA and served as a member of the UN Human Rights Advisory Panel in Kosovo, mentioned UN GA resolutions in *Asady and Others v. Slovakia*[76] and *Saçilik and Others v. Turkey*,[77] the UN CRPD in *Enver Şahin v. Turkey*[78] and in *Béláné Nagy v. Hungary*[79] and the UN CAT in *Nait-Litman v. Switzerland.*[80]

Judge Bostjan Zupancic, former member of the UN Committee against Torture (CAT), referred to the UN CAT, UNHCR as well as to the UN CRC, ICCPR and ICESCR in *O'Keeffe v. Ireland*,[81] *T.A. v. Sweden*,[82] *K.A.B. v. Sweden*,[83] *D.N.W. v. Sweden*,[84] *M.Y.H v. Sweden*[85] *and N.M.B. v. Sweden.*[86]

Similarly, Judge Linos-Alexandre Sicilianos, former member of the UN Committee on the Elimination of Racial Discrimination (CERD), has issued only three separate opinions mentioning the case-law of the IACtHR, HRC or the ICJ or the work of the UNHCR or the ILC in *Magyar Helsinki Bizottság v. Hungary*,[87] *Baka v. Hungary*[88] and *Antwi and Others v. Norway.*[89]

Slightly more prolific is Judge Helen Keller who, after having served as a member of the HRC, has mentioned the case-law of the Committee in four judgments.[90] In addition, Keller has cited the work of the UN CRPD in *Kocherov and Sergeyeva v. Russia*[91] and *Hiller v. Austria.*[92]

Judge Zdravka Kalaydjieva, former international legal officer for the UN Mission in Bosnia and Herzegovina, brought her previous work experience into some of her separate opinions, like in *Lautsi and Others v. Italy*[93] where

76 *Asady and Others v. Slovakia*, Application no 24917/15 (ECtHR, 24 March 2020).
77 *Saçilik and Others v. Turkey*, Application no 43044/05 (ECtHR, 14 April 2015).
78 *Enver Şahin v. Turkey*, Application no 23065/12 (ECtHR, 30 January 2018).
79 *Béláné Nagy v. Hungary*, Application no 53080/13 (ECtHR, 13 December 2016).
80 *Nait Liman v. Switzerland*, Application no 51357/07 (ECtHR, 21 June 2016).
81 *O'Keeffe v. Ireland*, Application no 35810/09 (ECtHR, 28 January 2014).
82 *T.A. v. Sweden*, Application no 48866/10 (ECtHR, 19 December 2013).
83 *K.A.B. v. Sweden*, Application no 17299/12 (ECtHR, 5 September 2013).
84 *D.N.W. v. Sweden*, Application no 29946/10 (ECtHR, 4 October 2013).
85 *M.Y.H. v. Sweden*, Application no 50859/10 (ECtHR, 27 June 2013).
86 *N.M.B. v. Sweden*, Application no 68335/10 (ECtHR, 27 June 2013).
87 *Magyar Helsinki Bizottság v. Hungary*, Application no 18030/11(ECtHR, 8 November 2016).
88 *Baka v. Hungary*, Application no 20261/12 (ECtHR, 23 June 2016).
89 *Antwi and Others v. Norway*, Application no 26940/10 (ECtHR, 14 February 2012).
90 *Y.Y. v. Turkey*, Application no 14793/08 (ECtHR, 10 March 2015); *Garib v. The Netherlands*, Application no 43494/09 (ECtHR, 23 February 2016); *Fáber v. Hungary*, Application no 40721/08 (ECtHR, 24 July 2012); *El Masri v. "The Former Yugoslav Republic of Macedonia"*, Application no 39630/09 (ECtHR, 13 December 2012).
91 *Kocherov and Sergeyeva v. Russia*, Application no 16899/13 (ECtHR, 3 April 2016).
92 *Hiller v. Austria*, Application no 1967/14 (ECtHR, 22 November 2016).
93 *Lautsi v. Italy*, Application no 30814/06 (ECtHR, 18 March 2011).

she referenced the UN CRC, in *Jones and Others v. United Kingdom*[94] where she cited the case-law of the UN CAT or in *Dvorski v. Croatia*[95] where she substantiated her argument by mentioning the HRC and the IACtHR.

Similarly, Judge Louis Edmond Pettiti, who worked for the UNESCO before joining the ECtHR, has cited the UNHCR in *Chahal v. United Kingdom*[96] and the ICCPR, the ICESCR and the UDHR in *Petrovic v. Austria*[97] and *Kosiek v. Germany*.[98]

Surprisingly, Judge Armen Haruntyunyan, who worked for the United Nations in different capacities, Judge Latif Huseynov, who served in the UN Human Rights Council Advisory Committee and Judge Anja Seibert-Fohr, who has been member and president of the UN Human Rights Committee, never mentioned external sources. Yet, it should be considered that they issued a very limited number of separate opinions and are all relatively new to the ECtHR (Judge Seibert-Fohr joined the Court only in January 2020).

On the contrary, the only judge who constantly referred to international and other regional human rights bodies is Judge Paulo Pinto de Albuquerque, a Portuguese judge without any foreign education or work experience in international courts or organisations. However, Judge Pinto de Albuquerque worked as an adjunct professor of international law and human rights law at the University of Chicago for five years before being appointed a judge in the ECtHR, thus confirming a link between an academic career and the inclination towards cross-referencing. In his various separate opinions, Judge de Albuquerque has constantly supported his argument citing the case-law of the IACtHR or the HRC or invoking international human rights treaties and documents.[99] In an interview, Judge de Albuquerque confirmed his commitment to ensure a stronger dialogue with other human rights bodies and to bring the ECtHR's case-law in line with both regional and international human rights hard and soft law, pursuing the idea of universality of human rights.[100]

94 *Jones and Others v. UK*, Application nos 34356/06, 40528/06 (ECtHR, 14 January 2014).
95 *Dvorski v. Croatia*, Application no 25703/11 (ECtHR, 28 November 2013).
96 *Chahal v. UK*, Application no 22414/93 (ECtHR, 15 November 1996).
97 *Petrovic v. Austria*, Application no 20458/92 (ECtHR, 27 March 1998).
98 *Kosiek v. Germany*, Application no 9704/82 (ECtHR, 28 August 1996).
99 cf, among others, *Maktouf and Damjanovic v. Bosnia and Herzegovina*, Application nos 2312/08, 34179/08 (ECtHR, 18 July 2013); *Abdullahi Elmi v. Malta*, Application no 25794/13 (ECtHR, 22 November 2016); *Baka*, ECtHR; *Al Dulimi and Montana Management Inc. v. Switzerland* Application no 5809/08 (ECtHR, 21 June 2016) and *Valiuliene v. Lithuania* Application no 33234/07 (ECtHR, 26 March 2013).
100 Interview conducted by the author with Judge de Albuquerque in Strasbourg on 6 July 2017.

All the previous findings strongly support the general hypothesis of this study. Indeed, they all confirm the theory that those with international education or work experience tend to refer to other regional or international human rights systems more than colleagues without such an international background. However, the number of these separate opinions is very low, and there are many judges with remarkable profiles who have not issued any separate opinions with references to other bodies.

Moreover, if we adopt a different research method and look directly for separate opinions from ECtHR's judges containing references to the UN, the IACtHR or the African system, an interesting and unexpected element emerges. In some cases, judges without a cosmopolitan background proved to be equally or more likely to cite the case-law of regional human rights bodies or the UN. A good example is Judge Ineta Ziemele, who in several cases supports her separate opinions through references to the IACtHR or to other relevant human rights bodies. She has done so particularly in cases concerning the two subject matters where the IACtHR has a well-known more advanced jurisprudence: indigenous peoples' rights and enforced disappearances. On indigenous rights, Judge Ziemele was the only one who issued a separate opinion, supporting her argument with the case-law of the IACtHR and the reference to the ILO Convention No. 169 and the UNDRIP.[101] In landmark cases on enforced disappearances, such as *El-Masri*,[102] *Kurt*[103] or *Çiçek*,[104] the separate opinions containing references to the Inter-American systems have been various and issued by both judges with international education or work experience and judges without such a background.[105]

In conclusion, the findings confirmed, although partially, the initial assumption. The majority of the analysed judges included references to regional and international human rights frameworks in their separate

[101] *Handölsdalen Sami Village and Others v. Sweden*, Application no 39013/04 (ECtHR, 30 March 2010), dissenting opinion.

[102] *El Masri*, ECtHR.

[103] *Kurt v. Turkey*, Application no 24276/94 (ECtHR, 25 May 1998).

[104] *Çiçek v. Turkey*, Application no 25704/94 (ECtHR, 27 February 2001).

[105] In *El-Masri* a joint concurring opinion of judges Tulkens, Spielmann, Sicilianos and Keller contained many references to the IACtHR and UN bodies and instruments; in *Kurt* a dissenting opinion of Judge Pettiti made reference to South American countries but failed to mention the Inter-American system; in *Çiçek* Judge Maruste (a former academic but not in international subjects) and Gölcüklü (without any 'interesting' background) issued a concurring and a partially dissenting opinion full of references to the UN and Inter-American bodies and instruments. In other cases on enforced disappearances, like *Timurtas v. Turkey*, *Er and Others v. Turkey*, the separate opinions did not contain any reference to sources external to the ECtHR.

opinions, even though to varying degrees. Contrarily to the case of the African and Inter-American courts, the academic background in the ECtHR context proves to be more correlated to the propensity to cross-reference, while the professional background in international organisations seems to have a lower impact. Moreover, in those subject matters where the ECtHR had more to learn from the other regional systems, as in the case of indigenous rights or enforced disappearances, the call for convergence with the existing international case-law of other bodies has been made mainly by judges without the background under analysis.

However, while separate opinions could be a very important tool for identifying the distinctive approaches of some judges, they can also be limited.[106] They are a limited tool since they are not compulsory and left at the discretion of the judge. This voluntary nature makes them highly dependent on the personality of the single judges and their willingness and attitude to express their own separate views. Indeed, the diplomacy inside the Court should not be ignored since for some judges it may be strategically convenient to try and influence the majority decisions rather than openly express their own divergent views. Not surprisingly, this is in line with what Arold observed about the convergence of legal *mentalités* within the ECtHR.[107] She argued that in the ECtHR case, differences between the judges mattered only occasionally and 'unanimity is understood as a sign for higher legitimacy'[108] and, according to the judges she interviewed, it is the commonality and harmony that make the ECtHR different from other courts and keep it ideologically homogeneous. Moreover, in the specific case of the ECtHR, where the forty-seven judges have never considered one case together, there is the additional variable of the facts of the cases that a certain judge happens to deal with. Therefore, the information that separate opinions can provide is certainly important and can help understand some phenomena and explain some outcomes, but it has to be carefully checked against all the limitations and biases these opinions naturally have.

4.1.3 *Concluding Observations*

The hypothesis that the composition of the bodies affects their adjudication proved to be correct. In particular, educational and work backgrounds can

[106] See also Bruinsma and de Blois, 'Rules of Law from Westport to Wladiwostok'; Voeten et al., 'The Politics of International Judicial Appointments', 669–701.

[107] Nina-Louisa Arold, 'The European Court of Human Rights as an Example of Convergence' (2007) 76 *Nordic Journal of International Law* 76.

[108] ibid, 320.

influence the reasoning of international judges and can therefore contribute to fragmentation or convergence. As this chapter demonstrated, there is a correlation between the greater inclination and willingness of the IACtHR and the African bodies to cite other regional and international human rights case-law and the judges' personal background. More specifically, the previous analysis showed that the number of judges or members who undertook university education outside their continent or who previously worked for international organisations or courts is directly related to the attitude of their institution to reach or maintain convergence through cross-referencing and judicial borrowing. This turned out to be particularly true in the case of the ECtHR, which has been more reticent to actively engage in judicial dialogue, an attitude that can be explained by its lower number of judges with international education or work experience.

In addition, education and professional background also has an impact on the behaviour of individual judges. This is evident following an analysis of their separate opinions. In the cases before the IACtHR and ACtHPR, the study confirmed the hypothesis of a correlation between judges' personal background and their attitude to mention other regional and international human rights instruments and case-law. On the other hand, at the ECtHR, the hypothesis was only partially supported, also considering the limited nature of separate opinions in Strasbourg. As highlighted by Bruinsma and de Blois, separate opinions are indispensable for a Court's legitimation, but judges themselves often have reservations towards using them.[109]

Moreover, work experience appears to have a varying impact across the different regional courts. While prior professional experience in the UN or other international courts and organisations seems to be very relevant in the case of the African and Inter-American courts, in the case of the ECtHR an academic background appears much more decisive.

In addition to this empirical analysis on the background of human rights bodies' members, it is worth reflecting on another point. Interviews with judges and HRC members revealed how they all feel to be part of the same community that shares the common project and goal of promoting and protecting human rights worldwide. This feeling of common belonging to an 'international college of judges'[110] encourages the maintenance of convergence and the mutual support of others' work and achievements.

[109] Bruinsma and de Blois, 'Rules of Law from Westport to Wladiwostok', 186.

[110] See, for instance, Eran Sthoeger and Michael Wood, 'The International Bar' in Cesare Romano, Karen J. Alter and Yuval Shany (eds), *The Oxford Handbook of International Adjudication* (Oxford University Press, 2014), 639–654.

In conclusion, the personal identity and history of the members of regional bodies may have an impact on the body's attitude towards convergence or fragmentation, with a particular relevance in the case of the African and Inter-American systems, whose mostly convergent jurisprudence and significant amount of judicial borrowing from the ECtHR could be rooted back to the 'Europeanisation' of African and Inter-American judges (even though we can observe signs of a changing trend for the African system). This is certainly not a discovery in international judicial studies, and it does not take place only in the field of human rights. For instance, Prott showed how the main cultural influence found in the decisions of Asian, South American and African judges is that of the 'European legal system in which they were trained'.[111] This 'Europeanisation' of African and South American judges could be inserted in a more comprehensive framework that, through the application of post-colonial theories, attempts to explain such a phenomenon including also political, historical and economic elements at a more macro level. This international relations–based approach could represent an interesting avenue for further research on the issue.

4.2 THE ROLE OF THE SECRETARIAT

Human rights courts and quasi-judicial bodies are not only composed of judges and commissioners but also of clerical staff, who play a key role in their functioning. It follows that secretariats could have a significant impact on the adjudication as well. The judges, commissioners or committee members cannot deal, alone, with everything related to a case, and they highly rely on the assistance and support of secretariat staff throughout all the stages of the examination of a contentious case.[112]

The structure, functions and size of the secretariats/registries in the three regional systems and the HRC differ significantly. This dissimilarity may contribute to explain the attitude of a certain court to judicial dialogue or the possibility to be fully aware of the existing international jurisprudence on the matter and to bring more convergence than fragmentation.

In particular, the size and the internal organisation and tasks of the secretariat are the two elements that can particularly affect the functioning of the

[111] Lyndell V. Prott, *The Latent Power of Culture and the International Judge* (Abingdon, 1979).

[112] Stephanie Carter and Cristina Hoss, 'The Role of Registries and Legal Secretariats in International Judicial Institutions' in Cesare Romano, Karen J. Alter and Yuval Shany (eds), *The Oxford Handbook of International Adjudication* (Oxford University Press, 2014), 711–732.

human rights bodies under analysis and may possibly explain convergence and fragmentation.

The ECtHR benefits from an impressively large and well-organised registry to deal with the enormous number of individual complaints it receives every year. The registry of the Court is composed of approximately 640 lawyers, translators and administrative and clerical employees coming from different member states of the CoE.[113] The registry has a key role in the reception and preparation of the cases. Divided into thirty-one case-processing divisions, its main task is to provide legal and administrative support to the Court in the exercise of its judicial functions. Each case brought before the Court is assigned to a registry's lawyer who prepares the case for the judge chosen as rapporteur. In this preparatory phase, the lawyer in the registry conducts a perusal of the relevant case-law on the subject matter of the application. The aim is to provide the judge-rapporteur with a comprehensive framework of the relevant internal, national, regional and international jurisprudence and judicial interpretation of the legal issues at stake. However, this careful and constant support from the registry to the judges could be improved for ensuring a more constant judicial dialogue with other human rights bodies. Interviews conducted with both senior lawyers of the registry and ECtHR's judges brought further insights.[114] They confirmed that the work of the registry has a high impact on the external material referred to in the final judgment. For high-profile cases and those reaching the Grand Chamber, the registry always provides a careful study on the relevant case-law from international and regional bodies. Nevertheless, for those cases that do not reach this stage, the international and regional case-law analysis is carried out if the judge-rapporteur specifically requests it. Moreover, lawyers of the registry confirmed that the presence of the case-law of the HRC, IACtHR and African bodies in the preparation material depends very much on the personal expertise and knowledge of the single lawyers or on the requests of the judge. Indeed, the general approach and prominent interest of the ECtHR's registry is rather focused on its member states and the European Court of Justice's (ECJ) case-law. In addition to the case-processing divisions, the registry counts several other sections dealing with different activities.[115] For instance, the research

[113] All the information on the registry of the ECtHR are available on the official website of the court www.echr.coe.int/Pages/home.aspx?p=court/howitworks&c=#newComponent_1346157759256_pointer, last accessed 10 February 2022.

[114] Interviews conducted in Strasbourg with senior legal officers of different branches of the ECtHR's registry on 6th and 7th July 2017.

[115] These are: case-law information and publications, research and the library, just satisfaction, press and public relations, language department and internal administration.

division has been actively working with the registry of the IACtHR with the aim of strengthening the cooperation dialogue between the two regional systems.[116] However, considering the high number of staff and the dedicated offices, one could expect a bigger effort from the ECtHR in ensuring judicial dialogue and including other actors than the IACtHR, such as the African bodies or the UNTBs, in the activities on the agenda. Moreover, interviews with ECtHR's judges revealed that there is a varying perception of the exhaustiveness of the research conducted by the registry. On the one hand, some judges felt that the registry provides them with a sufficiently detailed overview of the relevant case-law from other human rights bodies for each case they are called to adjudicate. On the other hand, an equal number of interviewed judges indicated that the research on comparative law outside the European region is usually not comprehensive enough and they need to integrate it with their own research or with other specific requests.[117]

The IACtHR has a registry with the same functions as that of the ECtHR but significantly smaller in size. The registry of the Court is composed of approximately twenty-four full-time lawyers and around twenty temporary visiting practitioners who work on the cases forwarded by the Commission.[118] This is also due to the relatively low number of cases submitted and the fact that the Commission already provides some basic research to them. The Court's registry and the Commission's secretariat, composed of around seventy people in different roles and capacities,[119] work very much together, especially for what concerns the preliminary research on contentious cases and the international and inter-institutional relationships of the Inter-American system. As for the internal organisation of the secretariat and the registry, the structure is similar to the European counterpart with a litigation, a research and a press and outreach division.[120] However, differently from the latter, the Inter-American system also includes a specific division dealing with institutional development and inter-institutional relations, whose aim is to strengthen the links with national, regional and international human rights

[116] CoE/ECtHR, *References to the Inter-American Court of Human Rights and Inter-American Instruments in the Case-Law of the European Court of Human Rights*, Research Report, December 2016; Council of Europe/European Court of Human Rights & Inter-American Court of Human Rights, Dialogue across the Atlantic: Selected Case-Law of the European and Inter-American Human Rights Courts (Wolf Legal Publishers, 2015).

[117] Interviews conducted in Strasbourg with seven judges of the ECtHR on 6th and 7th July 2017.

[118] Information acquired through interviews with a previous member of the IACtHR's registry in September 2017.

[119] Information available on the official website of the IACommHR, www.oas.org/en/iachr/mandate/staff.asp, last accessed 10 February 2022.

[120] ibid.

bodies.[121] Moreover, notwithstanding the low number of staff, the Commission and Court's secretariat gives high attention to research what other international, regional and national courts have said about similar legal points. As it emerged from the interviews with a senior legal officer of the IACtHR's registry, it is common practice for the registry to particularly highlight those cases where the regional or international human rights case-law is controversial in order for the judges to be fully aware of the possible fragmentation scenario that can be triggered by a certain reasoning and outcome. In addition, thanks to the cooperation established with distinguished universities in Europe, which complement the work of the secretariat with jurisprudential research, the IACtHR managed to engage in a fruitful judicial dialogue for each case under its analysis. Nevertheless, the lack of an adequate number of staff in the registry assisting the Court and the increasing number of cases arriving from the Commission makes the Court unable to be always aware of all the existing international and domestic case-law. In this regard, a key role is played by the amicus curiae received by the Court, as discussed later in the book.[122]

Similarly, the African system benefits from a secretariat at the Commission level and a registry at the Court one. Both are in charge of preparing the cases before their respective bodies, and, in doing so, they pay significant attention to the perusal of the relevant case-law from other regional and international courts. However, both the secretariat and the registry lack an adequate number of staff but they are nevertheless committed to ensuring a fruitful dialogue with other human rights bodies, always including thorough research on the applicable case-law in the preparation of a case. The Court's registry has a total of sixty-seven members of staff and only ten legal officers, in charge of preparing the case for the judge-rapporteur. However, despite the small-size and under-resourced registry, there is a strong attention to the dialogue and relations with the ECtHR, the IACtHR and the UN system. There are dedicated focal points for each of these institutions and the legal officers and the registry's senior staff always participate in information sharing events with other regional counterparts. Interviews with the Registrar, Deputy Registrar and Head of Legal Division revealed that also in the preparation of cases there is a strong attention to the relevant case-law of the ECtHR, IACtHR and UN bodies.[123] Although there is no rigid structure, when

[121] ibid.

[122] See Chapter 7, Section 7.1.1.

[123] Interviews conducted online with the Registrar, Dr Robert Eno, Deputy Registrar, Mr Nouhou Diallo and Head of Legal Division, Ms Grace Wakio Kakai in October 2021.

researching on a new case, the registry always looks first at the African Commission and to the ECOWAS, with the aim of building and strengthening an African human rights jurisprudence. Usually, this stage is followed by a perusal of the relevant case-law from the ECtHR and IACtHR and, possibly, from the relevant UN committees. Worth noting is that the relevant case-law from the member states is rarely considered at this stage, except in the case of controversial issues. Interviews also confirmed the extremely important role of the registry in shaping the ACtHPR's case-law considering that the part-time appointment of the judges and their limited time available makes the registry's preparatory work particularly determinant.

The HRC is in a very different position because it does not have its own secretariat, but it shares it with the other nine TBs. The secretariat of the TBs at the OHCHR is composed of only sixteen lawyers, overloaded with several tasks that go beyond the reception of individual complaints, such as preparing the materials for state reports or the TB's general comments. As reported by a Human Rights Officer of the secretariat, the lack of personnel, due to the limitation of funds and the many competing challenges that the OHCHR has to address every day, makes it very hard for them to conduct a thorough research on each complaint received.[124] Moreover, their priority is usually to maintain a dialogue with the other UN bodies and institutions and in face of time constraints they prefer to include references to other UNTBs and Special Rapporteurs rather than the regional bodies. As a result, the support the secretariat can give to the HRC is important yet limited and, as highlighted by some HRC members,[125] it leaves most of the research on the individual complaints to the single members of the Committee. Consequently, there are some Committee members who decide to undertake their own research, but, in the majority of the cases, the awareness on international and regional case-law is low, and this is reflected in the limited use of external references in the Committee's views.[126]

[124] Interview conducted with a senior human rights officer of the OHCHR, TBs branch, Geneva, July 2017.

[125] Sarah Cleveland, intervention in the plenary on 'Reform of the International and Regional Systems', INTRAlaw Human Rights Colloquium, 'Interaction between Human Rights: Fifty Years of the Covenants', Aarhus, 29–30 September 2016.

[126] As for the internal organisation and structure, the secretariat working with the HRC is a division of the general OHCHR that is articulated in four subdivisions: Civil, Political, Economic, Social and Cultural Rights Section, Groups in Focus Section, Capacity-Building and Harmonization Section and Petition and Inquiries Section. Organisational chart available at www.ohchr.org/Documents/AboutUs/OHCHR_orgchart_2014.pdf, last accessed 10 February 2022.

Recalling the importance of judicial dialogue for maintaining convergence, one could expect that a larger or more organised secretariat leads to a more frequent use of external references by its body. However, what we observed seems to suggest rather the contrary. The IACtHR and the African bodies are the most active in judicial dialogue regardless of their significantly smaller and understaffed secretariat. In light of this, one could infer that, contrary to the initial assumptions, smaller secretariats can actually lead to cross-referencing and convergence even more than larger ones, suggesting that convergence might be more a matter of organisation, priorities and allocation of resources rather than size.

In conclusion, while the secretariat certainly has the potential to play a key role in ensuring better dialogue, and thus convergence between regional bodies and the HRC, in practice this does not tend to happen. The only element that appears relevant is the internal structure and organisation and the priority within the institution on which judicial dialogue should be privileged.

4.3 THE ROLE OF MEETINGS BETWEEN THE MEMBERS OF HUMAN RIGHTS BODIES

Another factor that could foster convergence between human rights bodies is the possibility for judges and commissioners to regularly meet and share their views and perspectives. Every year several meetings are organised by the different bodies, with different agendas, to bring together members of the three regional systems and discuss the development of IHRL and possible ways for enhancing cooperation and dialogue.

These meetings are of two kinds: bilateral and multilateral. Bilateral meetings are very common between the IACtHR and the ECtHR and to a lesser extent between the IACtHR and the African bodies. Since 2011, the IACtHR has established a good practice of yearly visits to its counterpart in Europe as well as hosting representatives from Europe or Africa.[127] The number of meetings and institutional exchange programmes has increased over the years and, for example, in 2015, the IACtHR visited the ACtHPR in Arusha and the ECtHR in Strasbourg and received in San José the representatives of the ACommHPR.[128] This institutional cross-fertilisation extends also to the

[127] Inter-American Court of Human Rights, Annual Report 2011, available at www.corteidh.or.cr/index.php/en/court-today/informes-anuales, last accessed 10 February 2022.

[128] Inter-American Court of Human Rights, Annual Report 2015, available at www.corteidh.or.cr/index.php/en/court-today/informes-anuales, last accessed 10 February 2022.

registry's staff. Indeed, the ECtHR and the IACtHR established in 2013 an exchange programme, which allows one lawyer from each body to make every two years 'a professional visit to conduct research in order to obtain a better knowledge of these two regional systems and to encourage continuing collaboration between the two organs'.[129] The two designated lawyers 'incorporated work teams and proceedings of the respective court, and carried out activities to divulge the main procedural aspects relating to the management and processing of cases, as well as the case law of the two courts. In addition, they identified a series of best procedural practices that could be incorporated into the daily tasks of both organs'.[130]

Recognising the importance of stronger and closer collaboration between regional human rights courts, the ACtHPR, ECtHR and IACtHR signed in 2018 the San José Declaration, establishing a Permanent Forum of Institutional Dialogue among the three courts.[131] The forum committed to organise periodic meetings both between judges and registry's staff with the aim of 'strengthen[ing] their democratic institutions and human rights protection mechanisms, and to overcome the common challenges and threats to the effective validity of human rights by working together'.[132] Following the meeting in San José, the three courts met again in Kampala in 2019 and committed to biannual meetings and the publishing of a common annual report of relevant case-law from the three bodies, stressing the importance of judicial dialogue among them for the strengthening of the whole international human rights law system.[133] This new arrangement for closer cooperation (which saw another meeting in 2021) has been extremely welcomed by the judges and staff of the regional courts. Interviews with members of the ACtHPR registry confirmed how important these opportunities are for sharing best practices and learning from each other how to overcome common obstacles. Even if their aim is not the harmonisation of international human rights law, the idea of universality of human rights and the importance of supporting each other's work is at the basis of these meetings.

[129] ibid, 145.

[130] ibid.

[131] The Inter-American Court of Human Rights, the African Court on Human and Peoples' Rights and the European Court of Human Rights, The San José Declaration, 2018, available at www.echr.coe.int/Documents/San_Jose_Declaration_2018_ENG.pdf, last accessed 10 February 2022.

[132] ibid.

[133] The Inter-American Court of Human Rights, the African Court on Human and Peoples' Rights and the European Court of Human Rights, Kampala Declaration, 2019, available at www.echr.coe.int/Documents/Kampala_Declaration_ENG.pdf, last accessed 10 February 2022.

The other kind of meetings between human rights adjudicatory bodies are those organised under the aegis of the OHCHR. Initiated in 2010, the workshops on 'enhancing cooperation between international and regional mechanisms for the promotion and protection of human rights' have regularly been held every year with representation from the OHCHR and the three main regional systems.[134] The meetings concerned several different areas of intervention for strengthening the relations between the regional and UN actors in the protection and promotion of human rights. Attention was focused on the importance of reaching convergence through judicial dialogue and other measures aimed at ensuring consistency and coherence within international human rights, considering contradictory human rights standards a challenge to cooperation.[135]

All these forms of gatherings are equally important for building a common understanding and approach towards human rights adjudication and represent a strong contribution to convergence. Sharing best practices and lessons learnt, both procedural and substantial, helps the courts and the committees fill in the gaps that they may have and exposes their interpretation to that of the other systems. The interviews conducted with judges of the ECtHR and IACtHR and HRC's committee members confirmed the contribution of all these meetings to increasing the awareness about each other's jurisprudence and offering a great opportunity to solve misunderstandings and discrepancies in the interpretation of certain rights.

CONCLUSION

All regional and international human rights judicial and quasi-judicial bodies are composed of people that eventually decide how to adjudicate any given case. The personal profiles and backgrounds, as well as beliefs and personality of decision makers may significantly influence their approach to adjudication and, ultimately, contribute to convergence or fragmentation with the other bodies. For the maintenance of convergence of case-law, it is of paramount importance to acknowledge that the members of different human rights bodies feel part of the same community of human rights experts and lawyers working towards the same ultimate goal of ensuring the respect for human rights worldwide. This common, shared mission contributes to the systemic convergence of their outcomes, that is, judgments and views.

134 Information on such meetings available on the website of the OHCHR at www.ohchr.org/EN/Countries/NHRI/Pages/Cooperation.aspx, last accessed 10 February 2022.

135 A/HRC/23/18, 53–54.

The endogenous Europeanisation of African and Inter-American judges and commissioners, due to their educational background, can partially explain the constant dialogue of the African and Inter-American bodies with the ECtHR and the predominant convergence regardless of regional relativism. Similarly, the judges' professional background, either as former members of international organisations or as academics, proved to have an influence on their adjudication, encouraging judicial dialogue.

As for the role of the secretariats and registries of the human rights bodies in fostering convergence or easing the triggering of fragmentation, a brief overview of their organisation and functioning showed that they might be able to influence the adjudication. Interviews with senior officers from the different secretariats/registries confirmed that it is not the size but rather the organisation and the internal agenda of these institutions that help the case-law convergence. In particular, they revealed that the IACtHR's registry is specifically required to conduct thorough research of other regional and international human rights bodies' case-law with the intent, among others, of avoiding fragmentation. The ACtHPR's registry as well focuses extensively on the case-law of the other regional courts when preparing the case, even though this is slightly changing due to the increasing availability of African case-law. On the contrary, the ECtHR focuses more on the dialogue with the ECJ or domestic tribunals, leaving the initiative to engage with a cross-regional human rights dialogue to the single judges. Notwithstanding, the recent initiative to set up a permanent forum between the three courts shows a real commitment to foster dialogue and cooperation and strengthens even more the idea of a common project of promotion of international human rights law and the belonging to the same college of international human rights lawyers and judges.

In conclusion, the composition of human rights bodies and their supporting institutions is of fundamental importance to understand the current situation of judicial convergence and fragmentation in IHRL. However, it is now necessary to assess to what extent these structural elements that may encourage convergence through judicial dialogue are applied in the case-law and the judicial behaviours of human rights bodies for the development of common tests and tools. The following chapters will investigate whether this dialogue led to a common understanding of judicial review tests and principles and a common application of deference and subsidiarity doctrines.

5

Calibrating Judicial Scrutiny

The Notions of Necessity and Proportionality

INTRODUCTION

The previous chapters showed that the theory of treaty interpretation, the practice of judicial dialogue between bodies and the composition of the bodies all partially contribute to explaining the current situation of convergence and fragmentation in IHRL. Still, it is yet to be assessed which elements in the actual adjudication could help to understand the prevailing convergence over fragmentation. This chapter focuses on two of them, the notions of necessity and proportionality. Deeply rooted in the case-law of all the five bodies under analysis, necessity and proportionality are fundamental principles for calibrating opposite rights and interests and adjudicating human rights cases.

Necessity and proportionality are addressed and analysed together because of the interconnection between them.[1] When the assessment of necessity is required, a proportionality test is equally involved. Both come particularly into play when a body is called to assess whether a certain restriction imposed by the state on an individual right is justified, that is, whether a fair balance has been struck between competing rights and interests. However, while almost always used together, they do have different origins, evolutions and places in IHRL adjudication.

The definition and judicial application of the notion of necessity and proportionality are presented separately in order to appreciate the many points of convergence among different systems.

[1] Jonas Christoffersen, *Fair Balance: Proportionality, Subsidiarity and Primarity in the European Convention on Human Rights* (Martinus-Nijhoff, 2009); Janneke Gerards, 'How to Improve the Necessity Test of the European Court of Human Rights' (2013) 11 *International Journal of Constitutional Law* 466.

This chapter engages with an assessment of the attitude of the five bodies under analysis towards the notions of necessity and proportionality, showing that, despite apparent differences, they all managed to ensure convergence of case-law and harmonisation of jurisprudence.

The first section introduces the principle of necessity, exploring its meaning, use and judicial application in the practice of the human rights bodies. In particular, it shows how human rights bodies have managed to overcome textual differences such as 'necessary in a democratic society' and 'necessary' or reaching a common understanding of expressions such as 'strictly necessary'. The second section then turns to the related principle of proportionality, highlighting similarities and differences between the five bodies under analysis. On this basis, this chapter discusses how the interpretation and application of these principles could contribute to convergence and fragmentation in IHRL.

5.1 THE PRINCIPLE OF NECESSITY: A TALE OF CONVERGENCE

The principle of 'necessity' can be found in all the regional and international human rights covenants, conventions and charters.[2] Sometimes conjugated into the expression 'necessary in a democratic society' or made more compelling as 'absolutely necessary' or 'strictly necessary', it always relates to a permissible restriction on a given right. In other words, the principle of necessity requires the state not to limit the enjoyment of certain rights unless it is necessary to do so.[3] This caveat concerns almost all rights except those whose enjoyment is of an absolute value, such as the prohibition of torture, cruel, inhuman and degrading treatment and the right to life in most circumstances.

The contexts and rights where the principle of necessity operates can vary. It is most commonly used in relation to the right to private and family life, freedom of religion, freedom of expression and freedom of assembly and association, which are explicitly subject to legitimate restrictions, only where such restrictions are necessary to pursue one of the legitimate aims provided

[2] The principle of necessity finds wide application in other branches of international law. For a thorough discussion see Jens David Ohlin and Larry May, *Necessity in International Law* (Oxford University Press, 2016).

[3] Yutaka Arai-Takahashi, *The Margin of Appreciation Doctrine and the Principle of Proportionality in the Jurisprudence of the ECHR* (Intersentia, 2002), 12. See also Lawrence Hill-Cawthorne, 'The Role of Necessity in International Humanitarian and Human Rights Law' (2014) 47 *Israel Law Review* 225 and Gerards, 'How to Improve the Necessity Test of the European Court of Human Rights'.

therein.[4] However, the same expression could also be found in other provisions, such as in relation to the right to life or fair trial, which will be discussed later.

To fully understand its meaning and role in human rights adjudication, the following analysis focuses on the differences and similarities of the principle of necessity both in international and regional instruments and in its judicial application.

5.1.1 *The Principle of Necessity in International and Regional Instruments: A Fertile Ground for Fragmentation?*

The term 'necessary' or 'necessity' is included in different ways in the provisions of the relevant regional and international instruments. The differences in the text are several and may suggest a deep difference in the understanding and application of this principle.

The ECHR uses the notion of necessity in a very wide range of rights and different formulations.[5] In Article 2, establishing the right to life, it provides that the deadly use of force could be legitimate only when it is 'no more than absolutely necessary'; in Article 5, on the right to liberty and security, it establishes that the lawful arrest or detention of a person is legitimate when it is considered necessary to prevent their committing an offence or fleeing after having done so; in Article 6, on the right to a fair trial, it provides that a judgment should be pronounced publicly unless it is 'strictly necessary in the opinion of the court' or, finally, in Article 1, Protocol 1, it allows the state to restrict the right to property if it deems it necessary in accordance with the general interest. In addition, Articles 8–11 and Article 2 Protocol 4, establishing, respectively, the right to a private and family life, freedom of thought conscience and religion, freedom of expression, freedom of assembly and association and freedom of movement, provide that these rights and freedom could be legitimately restricted when such restrictions are prescribed by law, pursue a legitimate aim and are 'necessary in a democratic society'.

The ACHR employs the term necessary in a similar number of cases, although mostly sticking to the simple formulation 'necessary'.[6] This is the case with Article 8, on fair trial, allowing a criminal proceeding to be private only when 'necessary to protect the interests of justice'; Article 17, establishing

4 See, for example, the ECHR, ACHR, ICCPR and ACHPR as discussed in detail later in this section.

5 European Convention on Human Rights, 1954.

6 American Convention on Human Rights, 1969.

the duty upon state parties in case of dissolution of a family to make provisions 'necessary for the protection of any children' or Article 18, that allows state parties to regulate the use of name 'if necessary'. Similarly to the ECHR, also Articles 15, 16 and 22, establishing, respectively, the right to assembly, freedom of association and freedom of movement, provide that the rights and freedoms contained therein could be restricted if 'necessary in a democratic society'. Contrary to the ECHR, Articles 12 and 13, on freedom of conscience and religion and freedom of thought and expression, use a different formulation omitting the reference to democratic society, stating that the restrictions to these freedoms are legitimate when 'necessary' to ensure or protect one of the listed interests or goals.

The ICCPR mirrors almost perfectly the ACHR as for the right to fair trial (Article 14), right to family (Article 23) and the differentiation between when the restriction is legitimate if 'necessary in a democratic society' (freedom of assembly and association – Article 21 and 22) and when 'necessary' for pursuing one of the legitimate aims (freedom of movement, freedom of religion and freedom of expression – Articles 12, 18 and 19).[7]

At the opposite extreme compared to the ECHR stands the African Charter.[8] Here the notion of necessity is very scarcely employed, limited to Article 11, establishing the freedom of assembly, and providing that any restriction to such a right is legitimate only if necessary, prescribed by law and when pursuing one of the listed legitimate aims.

This overview shows a very diversified picture of the employment of the principle of necessity in the regional and international instruments. With the African Charter as the exception, the three other conventions share the same use of necessity in relation to the right to fair trial and to the addition of 'necessary in a democratic society' for what concerns the freedom of association and assembly. In contrast, they diverge in relation to the right to life that entails the necessity test only in the ECHR and in relation to right to privacy, freedom of expression and freedom of religion, where the restrictions should be 'necessary in a democratic society' in the ECHR and only necessary in the ICCPR and ACHR. The reasons for this convergence and divergence are not clear, probably being linked both with the political situation at the time of the drafting of these instruments and with the desire for diversification from the existing instruments. Since the ECHR was the first of these instruments to be adopted in 1954, followed by the ICCPR in 1966 and the ACHR in 1969, one may assume that the similar provisions are due to the influence of the ECHR

7 International Covenant on Civil and Political Rights, 1966.
8 African Charter on Human and Peoples' Rights, 1986.

on the ICCPR and the ACHR. Still, this does not explain why the other provisions were not drafted following the ECHR example as well. The analysis of the *travaux preparatoires* for the article on freedom of assembly and association of the ICCPR and ACHR could help in understanding the rationale behind such a choice. The *travaux preparatoires* for the ICCPR's article on freedom of assembly reveal that a debate took place on whether the limitations listed in the article should be qualified by the words 'necessary in a democratic society'.[9] The supporters of the amendment that was finally adopted claimed that 'freedom of assembly could not be effectively protected if the states parties did not apply the limitations clause according to the principles recognised in a democratic society'.[10] By the same reasoning, the expression 'necessary in a democratic society' was included in the letter of the freedom of association as well.[11] Apparently, such an argument was not equally convincing in the context of the right to privacy, freedom of religion and freedom of expression. An amendment to insert a uniform limitation clause for Articles 17–21 mirroring the ECHR, thus including the expression 'necessary in a democratic society', was proposed by Denmark and the Netherlands and put to vote. However, in all three cases, the amendment was rejected due to the opposition of the USSR and African, South American and Eastern European countries without further explanation.[12]

Similarly, during the discussion on the drafting of the ICCPR provision on the right to life, the Netherlands proposed to include a limitation clause mirroring Article 2 ECHR but the amendment was also rejected on the basis that the list of possible restrictions would have never been exhaustive and would have just caused more confusion.[13]

The *travaux preparatoires* for the ACHR do not contain any reference to such debates.[14] However, the voting behaviour of the OAS member states in the drafting of the ICCPR, repeatedly opposing the proposals to include provisions mirroring the ECHR, may allow some speculation. One may assume that, at the time, there was no desire of converging with the

9 See UN Document A/2929.

10 ibid, 54.

11 ibid, 56.

12 See the voting records reported in UN General Assembly, Report of the Third Committee, A/5000, 5 December 1961; UN General Assembly, Report of the Third Committee, A/4625, 8 December 1960.

13 See UN General Assembly, Report of the Third Committee, A/3764, 5 December 1957, 35.

14 Documents of the 1969 Inter-American Conference on Human Rights (*Travaux préparatoires*) where the American Convention on Human Rights was adopted, available at www.oas.org/en/iachr/mandate/basic_documents.asp, last accessed 10 February 2022.

Council of Europe on the formulation of these human rights provisions. Probably for political reasons, the OAS member states wanted to maintain their autonomy and distinguish their instrument from the European one, preferring to follow the UN example and, therefore, the ICCPR rather than the ECtHR.

A similar historical motivation could be identified as the reason for the distinctiveness of the African Charter. As pointed out by some scholars,[15] the drafting of the Charter was a manifesto of the African independence from the dominance of the European and white western tradition, with a clear desire to adopt a new human rights instrument different from the Universal Declaration or other UN instruments dominated by states with 'white populations with largely European and Christian traditions'.[16] Proposals to include a limitation clause similar to the ECHR, ACHR or ICCPR in the provision on freedom of religion and freedom of expression had been formulated; however, both of them were rejected on the basis that Article 27(2) already provided a limitation clause to be applied in relation to all the Charter's rights.[17] Indeed, it states that 'the rights and freedoms of each individual shall be exercised with due regard to the rights of others, collective security, morality and common interest'.[18] The expression 'with due regard to' leaves margin of interpretation to the Commission and Court and, even if the immediate meaning would not be 'necessary' as in the ECHR, ACHR and ICCPR, the application of this provision in the actual cases may encourage such interpretation.[19]

In conclusion, the principle of necessity is employed differently in regional and international human rights instruments, possibly due to the historical and political context that surrounded the drafting of these instruments. This divergence could create a fertile ground for judicial fragmentation but, as it will be now discussed, the lack of the inclusion of 'necessity' or the different adoption of the expression 'necessary in a democratic society' could still be considered as natural differences in the text that is easily harmonised at the judicial stage.

[15] Richard Gittleman, 'The African Charter on Human and Peoples' Rights: A Legal Analysis' (1982) 22(4) *Virginia Journal of International Law* 667, 667–670; Frans Viljoen, 'The African Charter on Human and Peoples' Rights: The Travaux Preparatoires in the Light of Subsequent Practice' (2004) 25(9–12) *Human Rights Law Journal* 313, 314–318.

[16] Seminar on the Regional Commissions on Human Rights with Special Reference to Africa, UN Doc. ST/TAO/HR/39 (1969) (held in Cairo, United Arab Republic, 2–15 September 1969), 6.

[17] Viljoen, 'The African Charter on Human and Peoples' Rights', 321.

[18] ACHPR, Article 27(2).

[19] See following Section 5.1.2.2.

5.1.2 *The Principle of 'Necessity' at the Adjudicatory Level: Towards Convergence*

Despite such a diversified picture of the use of necessity in treaty provisions, its judicial application by regional bodies and the HRC has been very similar, filling the gaps to reach a harmonised and convergent case-law.

Looking at the case-law of the four systems under analysis and taking into consideration the textual differences highlighted in the previous section, there are two instances where such a convergent approach can be particularly observed. First, in the definition of the meaning and application of 'necessary in a democratic society' for the adjudication of freedom of religion, expression, assembly and association even when not explicitly provided in the treaty provisions. Second, on the harmonised use of different terms like 'absolutely necessary' or 'strictly necessary' or none of the above in relation to very sensitive rights, such as the right to life.

However, before engaging in a discussion of specific applications of the principle of necessity, it is important to understand its general meaning. The following section explores the meaning of necessity in IHRL as it comes out from the case-law of the five bodies. On this basis, the two further sections investigate the principles of 'necessary in a democratic society' and 'absolutely necessary'.

5.1.2.1 The Meaning of Necessity in IHRL

In logic, the principle of necessity would entail that if one says that X is necessary for Y, then Y could not happen but for X. One could expect that a human rights body, when interpreting the text of a provision containing the word 'necessary', adopted the same rationale. It would follow that, to be acceptable, a restriction to a fundamental right or freedom should be the only possible way to pursue the invoked legitimate aim. On the contrary, in IHRL, when a court says that, for example, the censorship of a book, thus the restriction of freedom of expression of an individual, is necessary to protect public morals, it does not exactly follow the above logic. Without providing an ultimate definition of what necessity means, human rights bodies seem to have converged on the understanding that necessity in IHRL should be interpreted in a slightly more flexible way. It appears that, in IHRL case-law, necessity does not mean that this is the only way through which the legitimate aim can be protected, but that it is one of the several possible ways in which it may be protected.[20]

The first human rights body to address the meaning of necessity was the ECtHR. In *Handyside v. United Kingdom*, it held that 'the adjective "necessary" [. . .] is not synonymous with "indispensable", neither has it the flexibility of such expressions as "admissible", "ordinary", "useful", "reasonable" or "desirable"'.[21] According to the ECtHR, the notion of necessity implies the existence of a 'pressing social need' requiring a restriction of a convention's right, and the initial assessment should be left in the hands of the member state.[22] In *Sunday Times v. United Kingdom* and following judgments, the ECtHR restated the point that 'necessary' should not be interpreted in such a strict way as to suggest indispensability. On the contrary, linking it to the expression 'necessary in a democratic society', the ECtHR confirmed that the assessment of necessity requires to decide 'whether the "interference" complained of corresponded to a "pressing social need", whether it was proportionate to the legitimate aim pursued [and] whether the reasons given by the national authorities to justify it are "relevant and sufficient"'.[23]

This very vague and stretchy definition has been mirrored by all the other human rights bodies.

The IACtHR, in its Advisory Opinion 5/85 on the *Compulsory membership in an association prescribed by law for the practice of journalism*, held that the conclusion reached by the ECtHR in *Sunday Times* on the attributes of necessity (not being synonymous with indispensable, useful, reasonable or desirable and implying the existence of a pressing social need) equally applies to the ACHR.[24] In light of this, the IACtHR ruled that a compelling governmental interest should exist to prove the presence of such a necessity and that, in case there are different alternative measures for achieving the legitimate aim available, the measure that is least restrictive of the applicant's rights should be chosen.[25] This inclusion of the 'least restrictive measure' requirement is the Inter-American answer to the ECtHR's margin of appreciation as explored in the following chapter. Moreover, following the lead of the ECtHR, the IACtHR established that for assessing the necessity of a

[20] See, for instance, Hill-Cawthorne, 'The Role of Necessity in International Humanitarian and Human Rights Law'.

[21] *Handyside v. UK*, Application no 5493/72 (ECtHR, 7 December 1976), 48.

[22] ibid, 50.

[23] *Sunday Times v. UK*, Application no 6538/74 (ECtHR, 16 April 1979), 62.

[24] *Compulsory Membership in an Association Prescribed by Law for the Practice of Journalism*, Advisory Opinion OC-5/85 (IACtHR, 13 November 1985), 46.

[25] ibid.

restriction, a proportionality test should be applied.[26] The same understanding of the notion of necessity has been applied to all freedom of expression cases,[27] as well as those related to the right to private life,[28] thus confirming the fully convergent approach of the IACtHR with the ECtHR even in the absence of a detailed operational definition of necessity.

Likewise, the African bodies followed the example set by the ECtHR and, in the few cases where they dealt with issues involving the principle of necessity, they simply quoted the Strasbourg Court and applied the principle in the same way. In *Konaté v. Burkina Faso*, the African Court embedded the balancing test of the ECtHR and the IACtHR so much that it dedicated an entire section to the assessment of the fulfilment of the necessity requirement, needed to establish whether the restriction to the freedom of expression of the applicant was legitimate under the African Charter.[29] That said, the African bodies have not properly defined necessity, keeping the matter blurred and vague and relied on the proportionality test to reach conclusions.[30]

Finally, the HRC has never actually defined what necessity means in the ICCPR. Moreover, as observed in the previous chapter, the practice of judicial dialogue is less common in the HRC case-law, and it is not possible to find an exhaustive citation of the ECtHR and IACtHR case-law on the matter to support its understanding of necessity. However, the General Comments provide some clarity. In General Comment No. 34 on Article 19 on the freedom of expression, the HRC continued to refrain from defining necessity but offered some examples. 'Restrictions must be "necessary" for a legitimate purpose. Thus, for instance, a prohibition on commercial advertising in one language, with a view to protecting the language of a particular community, violates the test of necessity if the protection could be achieved in other ways that do not restrict freedom of expression. On the other hand, the Committee has considered that a state party complied with the test of necessity when it transferred a teacher who had published materials that expressed hostility towards a religious community to a non-teaching position in order to protect

[26] ibid. See Section 5.2.3.

[27] See *Herrera Uloa v. Costa Rica* (IACtHR, 2004); *Ricardo Canese v. Paraguay* (IACtHR, 31 August 2004); *Tristán Donoso v. Panama* (IACtHR 27 January 2009).

[28] See *Chaparro Álvarez and Lapo Íñiguez v. Ecuador* (IACtHR, 8 September 1998) where the IACtHR held that 'the measures adopted are appropriate to achieve the purpose sought; iii) that they are necessary, in the sense that they are absolutely essential to achieve the purpose sought and that, among all possible measures, there is no less burdensome one in relation to the right involved, that would be as suitable to achieve the proposed objective'.

[29] *Lohé Issa Konaté v. Burkina Faso*, Application no 004/2013 (ACtHPR, 5 December 2014).

[30] *Mtikila v. Tanzania*, Application nos 9/2011 and 11/2011 (ACommHPR, 2013), 107.1 and *Konaté*, ACtHPR, 155, 166.

the rights and freedom of children of that faith in a school district.'[31] Similarly, in General Comment No. 27 on freedom of movement, it held that 'it is not sufficient that the restrictions serve the permissible purposes; they must also be necessary to protect them. Restrictive measures must conform to the principle of proportionality; they must be appropriate to achieve their protective function; they must be the least intrusive instruments amongst those, which might achieve the desired result; and they must be proportionate to the interest to be protected'.[32] This very blurred and vague approach towards necessity is in line with the regional bodies' position, thus helping keeping convergence in the absence of a final definition.

As emerged from this brief overview, the principle of necessity is of paramount importance when balancing rights, but it is hardly a self-sustaining principle, being either the first step of a proportionality test or its outcome. Nonetheless, in the debate on convergence and fragmentation, it is worth underlying that all the human rights bodies decided to interpret this principle in this way, going beyond the traditional meaning of the necessity test, thus contributing to convergence.

5.1.2.2 'Necessary' versus 'Necessary in a Democratic Society'

A specific circumstance where one could observe a particular convergent trend in human rights adjudication is the approach towards the two expressions 'necessary' and 'necessary in a democratic society'. The following perusal will show how, despite textual differences, all the human rights bodies reached full convergence on the understanding of these two expressions and on the circumstances when they should be used and applied.

THE EUROPEAN COURT OF HUMAN RIGHTS The ECtHR has extensively addressed the restrictions to the rights set forth in Articles 8–11, and it was repeatedly called to provide a definition of what constitutes 'necessary in a democratic society' for the sake of the application of these provisions. In *Sunday Times*, the Court elaborated further the concept of necessity and pressing social need mentioned in *Handyside* establishing that, in order to assess whether a pressing social need actually existed, and thus justifying the restriction, 'account must be taken of any public interest aspect of the case'.[33] The ECtHR applied the same understanding to other cases under Articles 8,

[31] HRC, General Comment No. 34, CCPR/C/GC/34, 33.
[32] HRC, General Comment No. 27, CCPR/C/GC/21/Rev.1/Add.9, 11–16.
[33] *Sunday Times*, ECtHR, 62.

9, 10 and 11. For instance, in *United Communist Party of Turkey v. Turkey*, alleging a violation of the freedom of association based on the political orientation of the party, the ECtHR stated that 'the only type of necessity capable of justifying an interference with any of those rights is, therefore, one which may claim to spring from "democratic society"'.[34] Moreover, it held that the Court does not only consider 'whether the respondent State exercised its discretion reasonably, carefully and in good faith; it must look at [...] whether the reasons adduced by the national authorities to justify it are "relevant and sufficient"'.[35] That said, the ECtHR did not actually provide a proper definition of what 'necessary in a democratic society' means in practice. In all the judgments, the ECtHR simply stated that, in order to assess the necessity of the restriction, two elements should be taken into consideration: the proportionality of the restrictive measures to the legitimate aim and the margin of appreciation that member states should enjoy.[36] Both these elements will be the focus of the next section and Chapter 6.

THE INTER-AMERICAN COURT OF HUMAN RIGHTS The IACtHR clarified, since the beginning of its activity, that the lack of the exact wording 'necessary in a democratic society' did not constitute a departure from the ECtHR approach in relation to freedom of religion and expression and right to privacy. In the Advisory Opinion on *Compulsory membership*, the IACtHR provided a very exhaustive discussion of the scope of 'necessary' under Article 13 and how it extends to the rights under Articles 11, 12, 15 and 16.[37] In explaining what necessary means, the IACtHR referred to the formulation in the ECHR stating that

> [i]t is true that the European Convention uses the expression "necessary in a democratic society" while Article 13 of the American Convention omits that phrase. This difference in wording loses its significance, however, once it is recognized that the European Convention contains no clause comparable to Article 29 of the American Convention, which lays down guidelines for the interpretation of the Convention and prohibits the interpretation of any provision of the treaty "precluding other rights and guarantees [...] derived from representative democracy as a form of government".[38]

[34] *United Communist Party of Turkey v. Turkey*, Application no 19392/92 (ECtHR, 30 January 1998), 45.
[35] ibid, 47.
[36] See, among others, *Handyside*, ECtHR, 48 or *Sunday Times*, ECtHR, 62.
[37] Advisory Opinion No 5 IACtHR.
[38] ibid, 44.

Such an authoritative interpretation, repeatedly invoked by all the judgments where the notion of necessary was involved, clears any doubt about whether the difference in the text between 'necessary in a democratic society' and a mere 'necessary' could bring fragmentation in the case-law between the ECtHR and the IACtHR.

THE HUMAN RIGHTS COMMITTEE Like the IACtHR, the HRC ultimately did not make a distinction between the notion of necessity contained in Article 18 or 19 and the 'necessary in a democratic society' contained in Article 20 and 21 or the lack of a reference to necessity in Article 17. An analysis of the case-law of the HRC on Article 17, 18 and 19 shows that there has been a slow development of the approach of the Committee towards the principle of necessity towards a full convergence with the ECtHR's concept of 'necessity in a democratic society'. In its first cases on Articles 17–19, the HRC stuck to the letter of the provisions and to the simple 'necessity' formulation, without giving much explanation of its meaning.[39] From the beginning of the 1990s, in cases concerning the violation of freedom of expression, the HRC linked the principle of necessity to the context of a democratic society, with the freedom of expression and access to information being a cornerstone of a democratic society.[40] In *Kivenmaa v. Finland*, the HRC expanded the requirement under Article 21 of a restriction being necessary for a democratic society to Article 19, since the violation of both articles was claimed by the applicant.[41] Notwithstanding these openings towards the adoption of a 'necessary in a democratic society' wording, the HRC continued sticking to the language used in the Covenant, until the late 2000s where the wordings of the ECHR's limitation clause became more and more used by the Committee. For instance, in *Vitaly Symonik v. Belarus*, the HRC found a violation of the freedom of expression of the applicant because the respondent state had failed to demonstrate, among other things, that the restrictive measures were necessary in a democratic society.[42] The same approach was adopted in *Unn and Ben Leirvag and Others v. Norway*, where the Committee, explicitly referring to a previous ruling of the ECtHR, held that restrictions to freedom of religion

[39] See *Grille Motta v. Uruguay*, Communication no 11/1977 (HRC, 29 July 1980) and *Hertzberg and Others v. Finland*, Communication no 61/1979 (HRC, 2 April 1982).

[40] See, for example, *Park v. Republic of Korea*, Communication no 628/1995 (HRC, 5 July 1996), 10.3; *Gauthier v. Canada*, Communication no 633/1995 (HRC, 5 May 1999), 13.6; *Laptsevich v. Belarus*, Communication no 780/1997 (HRC, 20 March 2000), 8.2.

[41] *Kivenmaa v. Finland*, Communication no 412/1990 (HRC, 31 March 1994).

[42] *Vitaly Symonik v. Belarus*, Communication no 1952/2010 (HRC, 24 October 2014), 7.5.

should meet the requirement of being necessary in a democratic society.[43] Yet, the recent case-law does not show a consistent use of the principle of 'necessity in a democratic society', but rather an interchangeable use of one or the other alternative without providing a sound explanation for such a choice.[44] The limited reasoning of the Committee on this point and the inconsistent use of the two necessity tests does not allow making any hypothesis on why the HRC decided to adopt one or the other. Without having any visible impact on the reasoning or the outcome of the judgment, the Committee sometimes decided to stick to the simple 'necessity' test[45] while other times it linked it to the concept of democratic society.[46] The increasing judicial dialogue with the ECtHR or the background of new members of the HRC could be possibly considered influential elements, but it is not possible to identify any proper causal link. Therefore, it could be argued that the principle of 'necessity' and that of 'necessity in a democratic society' bear the same meaning before the HRC. This is also supported by the fact that the HRC did not provide a proper definition of any of the two principles, relying in both cases on the assessment of the proportionality, or reasonableness, of the restriction to establish whether the latter was necessary for achieving the legitimate aim.[47]

THE AFRICAN BODIES The African bodies have aligned to the other regional and international human rights institutions in recognising the importance of the necessity in assessing the legitimacy of a restriction to the Charter's rights and the relevance of the expression 'necessary in a democratic society'. For instance, despite the absence of any reference in the letter of the freedom of expression's provision, both the African Commission and Court, since the beginning of their adjudication, adopted a necessity test in assessing whether a breach of the Charter had occurred. In *Mtikila v. Tanzania*, the African Commission, referring to the practice of both the ECtHR and the IACtHR, acknowledged that the '[j]urisprudence regarding the restrictions on the exercise of rights had developed the principle that the restrictions must be

43 *Unn and Ben Leirvag and Others v. Norway*, Communication no 1155/2003 (HRC, 23 November 2004). See Chapter 3 for a more detailed discussion of the case.

44 See, among others, *Sister Immaculate Joseph and Others v. Sri Lanka*, Communication no 1249/2004 (HRC, 21 October 2005) and *Nurbek Toktakunov v. Kyrgyzstan*, Communication no 1470/2006 (HRC, 28 March 2011).

45 ibid, 7.5.

46 See, on a case with similar facts concerning freedom of expression, *Zeljko Bodrozic v. Serbia and Montenegro*, Communication No. 1180/2003 (HRC, 31 October 2005), 7.

47 See the aforementioned HRC cases and *Hertzberg*, HRC, individual opinion of Mr Torkel Opsahl that pointed out the lack of a definition of the principle of necessity.

necessary in a democratic society; they must be reasonably proportionate to the legitimate aim pursued'.[48] In light of the failure of Tanzania to prove such a compelling necessity, the Commission found a violation of the freedom of association.[49]

5.1.2.3 The Restriction of the Right to Life When 'Absolutely Necessary'

Another circumstance where fragmentation may arise on the basis of a different notion of necessity is the legitimate use of deadly force in the context of the right to life.

As previously observed, the letter of the provisions in the different instruments is slightly different. The ECtHR allows the use of force when it is absolutely necessary while no mention of possible limitations is provided in the other human rights documents except the prohibition of arbitrary deprivation of life. However, as extensively explained in Chapter 2, what happens is just a different use of terminology, and the case-law of the ECtHR, IACtHR and HRC is very much convergent on the matter. Indeed, in *Guerrero v. Colombia*, the HRC recognised that 'the deprivation of life by authorities of the State is a matter of the utmost gravity. [. . .] The requirements that the right shall be protected by law and that no one shall be arbitrarily deprived of his life mean that the law must strictly control and limit the circumstances in which a person may be deprived of his life by the authorities of a State'.[50] In applying this principle to the case concerning the killing of seven people during a hostage rescuing operation, the HRC simply noted that

> the police action was apparently taken without any warning to the victims and without giving them any opportunity to surrender to the police patrol or to offer any explanation of their presence or intentions [and] [t]here is no evidence that the action of the police was necessary.[51]

In *McCann and Others v. the United Kingdom*,[52] and in following similar cases, the ECtHR held that an exception to the right to life should be 'absolutely necessary', to be interpreted in 'a stricter and more compelling' way than when applying the requirement of 'necessary in a democratic society'.[53] The ECtHR also stressed the duty of the state to 'minimise the risk

[48] *Mtikila*, ACommHPR, 106.
[49] ibid, 126.
[50] *Guerrero v. Colombia*, Communication no 45/1979 (HRC, 31 March 1982), 13.1.
[51] ibid, 13.2.
[52] *McCann and Others v. UK*, Application no 18984/91 (ECtHR, 27 September 1995).
[53] ibid, 149.

of loss of life by providing clear legal rules and adequate training to the law-enforcement officers'.[54] Moreover, the Court clarified the high standard of the 'absolute necessity' by observing that the justification of the use of lethal force in the case was only '"reasonably justifiable" as opposed to "absolutely necessary" prescribed by paragraph 2 of Article 2'.[55] The IACtHR also invoked the same principle of 'absolute necessity', in cases similar to *McCann* like the *Detention Centre of Catia* case.[56] Here the Court confirmed that the use of force by state agents may be allowed only in

> exceptional circumstances and should be planned and proportionally limited by the government authorities [...] [and] can only be used once all other methods of control have been exhausted and failed.[57]

Moreover, the 'intentional use of firearms may only be made when strictly unavoidable in order to protect life' and should always be 'reasonable, restricted and controlled'.[58]

CONCLUDING OBSERVATIONS The previous overview shows that regional and international human rights bodies are very much convergent on the use and meaning of the notion of necessity in human rights adjudication. Despite the differences in the text of their respective treaties, when called to rule on a case involving a balance of rights and interests, all the bodies under analysis similarly resorted to the notion of necessity (or, interchangeably, necessity in a democratic society) with the same understanding.

As for the meaning, none of these bodies actually provided a proper definition, keeping the concept vague and flexible to fit many different situations and contexts, simply relying on the assessment of the proportionality of the restriction. This vagueness may be one of the causes of such a convergent approach that allows every single body to feel and act autonomously while remaining in line with the other institutions. The judicial dialogue between the different bodies and the need of the younger institutions to strengthen their legitimacy through reference to more established ones are factors that encourage such convergence.[59] Still, the lack of a rigid and exhaustive meaning of the principle of necessity is probably the ultimate

54 ibid, 154.
55 ibid, 156.
56 *Montero Aranguren et al. (Detention Center of Catia) v. Venezuela* (IACtHR, 5 July 2006), 123.
57 ibid, 67.
58 ibid, 69.
59 See Chapter 3 on judicial dialogue.

reason why everyone agrees on its use: it allows a wide margin of manoeuvre while keeping convergence and strengthening each body's position.

This successful story of convergence is linked with the principle of proportionality, which has been ultimately chosen by all the five bodies as the way to assess the existence of the necessity of a given restriction. The following section will analyse the use of the proportionality principle in the four jurisdictions, in order to assess whether such a convergence is maintained once a more operational step is undertaken.

5.2 THE PRINCIPLE OF PROPORTIONALITY IN THE CASE-LAW OF REGIONAL COURTS AND THE HRC

In order to assess whether a specific restriction to a right or freedom is necessary to pursue a legitimate aim or 'necessary in a democratic society', courts and quasi-judicial bodies have decided to adopt a proportionality test.[60] Differently from necessity, the principle of proportionality is not present in any of the international human rights instruments, but it has been chosen by their monitoring bodies and increasingly used and applied in the adjudication of human rights cases, in almost all the circumstances where the necessity of a measure was questioned.[61] Indeed, the two notions go hand in hand, and the proportionality test could be considered as one possible operative principle for assessing necessity.

Adopting a proportionality test is not new in legal adjudication. Widely used by domestic courts, especially by the German courts, it soon expanded to regional fora, such as the ECJ and the human rights regional courts.[62] The theory of proportionality, especially as coming from the German tradition, provides three aspects of this notion: (1) the adequacy of the restrictive measures to pursue the legitimate aim, (2) the necessity of such measures for the purpose and (3) the proportionality *strictu sensu* assessing whether there are actually more advantages than disadvantages for the restriction.[63] While

[60] Yutaka Arai-Takahashi, 'Proportionality' in Dina Shelton (ed), *Oxford Handbook of International Human Rights Law* (Oxford University Press, 2013), 450.

[61] Christoffersen, *Fair Balance: Proportionality, Subsidiarity*, 12–20; Peter Hulsroj, *The Principle of Proportionality* (Springer, 2013), 5.

[62] Arai-Takahashi, 'Proportionality', 447–448.

[63] cf Robert Alexy, 'The Construction of Constitutional Rights' (2010) 4 *Law and Ethics of Human Rights* 20, 24–26. See also the extensive debate on the merits and drawbacks of proportionality in Francisco J. Urbina, *A Critique of Proportionality and Balancing* (Oxford University Press, 2017); Grant Huscroft, Bradley Miller and Gregoire Webber (eds), *Proportionality and the Rule of Law: Rights, Justification, Reasoning* (Cambridge University

this three-stage assessment is not always followed homogeneously by human rights bodies, the core understanding of the notion is the same: proportionality is the reasonableness of a given restriction.[64] As mentioned, the principle of proportionality is not found anywhere in the international and regional human rights instruments, but it is a judicial creation elaborated to assess the necessity of a restriction to a protected right. Proportionality is not the only principle for assessing the necessity of a restriction to a convention right, but all the bodies under analysis have chosen it as the main test for balancing contrasting rights and interests.

As highlighted by several scholars, the common understanding of the proportionality test, or the lack of a strict definition and application of such a principle, allowed the regional and international bodies to 'stabilise' their jurisprudence and reach a substantive convergence of case-law on many sensitive issues under freedom of expression, religion, private life and political participation.[65]

The following perusal of the attitude of the five bodies towards proportionality will offer an understanding of why and how these bodies chose to apply this principle, appreciating the similarities between systems.

5.2.1 *The European Court of Human Rights*

The ECtHR is the human rights body that used and developed the principle of proportionality to the greater degree in its case-law. The ECtHR was the first to explicitly use the proportionality test in its very first judgment, *Lawless*, in 1961.[66] From that moment, the Court adopted it so widely that it is now considered as a 'general principle in the Convention system'.[67] Indeed, as Roly Ryssasdal, former president of the ECtHR, said '[t]he theme that runs through the Convention and its case law is the need to strike a balance

Press, 2014); Ermioni Xanthopoulou, *Fundamental Rights and Mutual Trust in the Area of Freedom, Security and Justice: A Role for Proportionality?* (Hart, 2020), 46–61.

[64] Kai Möller, 'Balancing and the Structure of Constitutional Rights' (2007) 5 *ICON* 453, 463.

[65] Marjan Ajevski, 'Freedom of Speech as Related to Journalists in the ECtHR, IACtHR and the Human Rights Committee – A Study of Fragmentation' (2014) 32 *Nordic Journal of Human Rights* 118; Orsolya Salát, 'Comparative Freedom of Assembly and the Fragmentation of International Human Rights Law' (2014) 32 *Nordic Journal of Human Rights* 140; Lucas Lixinski, 'Comparative International Human Rights Law: An Analysis of the Right to Private and Family Life across Human Rights "Jurisdictions"' (2014) 32 *Nordic Journal of Human Rights* 99.

[66] *Lawless v. Ireland*, Application no 332/57 (ECtHR, 1 July 1961).

[67] Arai-Takahashi, 'Proportionality', 453.

between the general interest of the community and the protection of the individual's fundamental rights'.[68]

The proportionality test is used in different respects, but its relevance is of utmost importance in relation to the rights and freedoms containing a limitation clause. In all the situations where there is a restriction to the right to private or family life, freedom of religion, freedom of expression, freedom of assembly and association, right to property, freedom of movement and the procedural rights concerning the expulsion of aliens, the ECtHR adopts a proportionality test. Proportionality, as explained in *Handyside*[69] and in following judgments, is required to assess the presence of a pressing social need demanding the restriction. Simply put, proportionality assesses whether a reasonable balance had been struck between the interfering measure and the legitimate aim. To do so, the ECtHR put the burden of proof on the state, which needs to prove that the restriction was indeed suitable and necessary for achieving the aim.

The context of the violation plays a fundamental role considering that the ECHR is a living instrument and the assessment of what constitutes a 'pressing social need' is heavily contextual, and factors such as the regional consensus are highly relevant.[70] In *Silver v. United Kingdom*, a case alleging a violation of Article 8, the Court summarised its approach towards the balance of rights set out in all the provisions with limitation clauses. It held that

> (a) the adjective "necessary" is not synonymous with "indispensable", neither has it the flexibility of such expressions as "admissible", "ordinary", "useful", "reasonable" or "desirable"...; (b) the Contracting States enjoy a certain but not unlimited margin of appreciation in the matter of the imposition of restrictions, but it is for the Court to give the final ruling on whether they are compatible with the Convention ...; (c) the phrase "necessary in a democratic society" means that to be compatible with the Convention, the interference must, inter alia, correspond to a "pressing social need" and be "proportionate to the legitimate aim pursued"...; (d) those paragraphs of Articles of the Convention which provide for an exception to a right guaranteed are to be narrowly interpreted [...].[71]

68 ibid.

69 *Handyside*, ECtHR.

70 The discussion on the definition and impact of the regional consensus is the object of the following chapter.

71 *Silver and Others v. United Kingdom*, Application nos 5947/72, 205/73, 7107/75, 7113/75 and 7136/75 (ECtHR, 24 September 1982), 97.

The element of the margin of appreciation, which will be discussed in detail in the next chapter, is then invoked when the ECtHR decides to leave to state parties the final assessment on whether a restriction was necessary for a democratic society or, said otherwise, proportionate to the legitimate aim pursued.

The same approach of *Silver* has been used to decide cases under Article 9 on freedom of religion. In *Manoussakis v. Greece*, the Court held that the denial of permission to use a private room for worship and the subsequent imprisonment of the applicant for failure to comply with this decision was a disproportionate restriction to his freedom of religion and 'accordingly, [not] necessary in a democratic society'.[72] The stricter scrutiny adopted here was justified by the Court on the basis of the importance of the right at stake, the freedom to manifest religion. Similarly, in *Tolstoy Miloslavsky v. United Kingdom*, a case concerning restriction of freedom of expression to protect the reputation of others, the Court ruled in favour of the applicant, holding that the national law at the time did not ensure 'a reasonable relationship of proportionality to the legitimate aim pursued'.[73] Moreover, it noticed that the size of the award by the domestic court was disproportionately large, and less intrusive alternatives were both possible and available. In *Garaudy v. France*[74] and *Witzsch v. Germany*,[75] the ECtHR dealt with the conviction of the applicants for having denied the existence of the Holocaust and related Nazi crimes. The ECtHR applied the proportionality test to assess whether these restrictions were necessary in a democratic society and concluded that, due to the high value of the legitimate aim pursued, the restrictive measures adopted were in this case proportionate.

The three-stage test of proportionality in German doctrine (suitability, necessity and proportionality *stricto sensu*) is not consistently applied by the ECtHR, especially for what concerns the second element: the requirement that the less restrictive alternative is always to be chosen. However, as highlighted by some scholars, there is a gradual tendency towards its inclusion in the assessment of proportionality.[76] In *Otto-Preminger-Institut v. Austria*, the ECtHR ruled that no breach of Article 10 occurred because the seizure and confiscation of an allegedly blasphemous movie were proportionate to the legitimate aim of protecting the freedom of religion of others, granting a wide

[72] *Manoussakis v. Greece*, Application no 18748/91 (ECtHR, 26 September 1996), 53.
[73] *Tolstoy Miloslavsky v. United Kingdom*, Application no 18139/91 (ECtHR, 18 February 2008), 55.
[74] *Garaudy v. France*, Application no 65831/01 (ECtHR, 24 June 2003).
[75] *Witzsch v. Germany*, Application no 7485/03 (ECtHR, 30 September 1999).
[76] Arai-Takahashi, 'Proportionality'; Christoffersen, *Fair Balance: Proportionality, Subsidiarity*.

margin of appreciation to the respondent state.[77] However, dissenting opinions of three judges pointed out that the restriction of freedom of expression was not proportionate and, hence, not necessary in a democratic society, since there were less intrusive measures available for protecting the freedom of religion of others without impairing the applicant's freedom of expression so much.[78] In recent cases, the ECtHR has adopted a stricter interpretation of proportionality, embracing the less restrictive alternative, linked to the *chilling effect* doctrine on cases involving political expression.[79]

In general, the approach of the ECtHR towards proportionality is quite flexible, and it adapts to the specific facts and context of the case. Such flexibility is probably the reason for the success of the proportionality test in the ECtHR's case-law that allows the Court to have a structured guideline on how to establish whether a fair balance has been struck while keeping a wide margin of free interpretation to adapt it to the complexities of each specific case.

5.2.2 *The Human Rights Committee*

The attitude of the HRC towards proportionality is a clear example of an evolutionary development that culminated in a full convergence with the ECtHR and the other human rights bodies.

In the first cases where the HRC could have used a proportionality test, namely cases under Articles 17–21 where a limitation clause was provided, the Committee did not opt for the language of proportionality, preferring the principle of reasonableness.[80]

In the 1988 General Comment No. 16 on Article 17 (Right to Privacy), the HRC held that the concept of arbitrariness in Article 17 was to be interpreted as reasonableness. In other words, the committee made clear that restrictions to Article 17 do not constitute a breach of the ICCPR as long as they are in line with the Covenant and are 'reasonable in the particular circumstance'.[81] The principle of reasonableness was then applied in the individual complaints, both in relation to Article 17 and to Articles 18 and 19. For instance, in *Singh*

77 *Otto-Preminger-Institut v. Austria*, Application no 13470/87 (ECtHR, 20 September 1994).

78 ibid.

79 See, among others, *Cumhuriyet Vakfi and Others v. Turkey*, Application no 28255/07 (ECtHR, 8 October 2013) and *Ricci v. Italy*, Application no 30210/06 (ECtHR, 8 October 2013). See also *Piermont v. France*, Application nos 15773/89 and 15774/89 (ECtHR, 27 April 1995)

80 See, for example, *Jarvinen v. Finland*, Communication no 295/1988 (HRC, 15 August 1990) or *Bwalya v. Zambia*, Communication no 314/1988 (HRC, 14 July 1993).

81 HRC, General Comment No. 16, HRI/GEN/1/Rev.9, 8 April 1988, 4.

Bhinder v. Canada, on the restriction to freedom of religion by requiring the applicant to remove his Sikh turban to wear a safety helmet, the Committee found no breach of Article 18 considering the restriction a reasonable measure compatible with the Covenant.[82]

Only in 1994, when the HRC decided the *Toonen* case, the principle of reasonableness was finally linked to proportionality.[83] The case dealt with the Tasmanian national law criminalising homosexuality that allegedly amounted to a violation of Article 17 ICCPR. In ruling in favour of the applicant, the Committee stated that it 'interprets the requirement of reasonableness to imply that any interference with privacy must be proportional to the end sought and be necessary in the circumstances of any given case'.[84] Applying such reasoning to the given case, the HRC concluded that the provisions of the Tasmanian Criminal Code were not meeting 'the "reasonableness" test in the circumstances of the case, and that they arbitrarily interfere[d] with Mr Toonen's right under article 17, paragraph 1'.[85]

From this moment on, the HRC decided to increasingly adopt the proportionality test, both in its views on individual complaints and in its General Comments, without giving any explanation for its different approach. Indeed, it is not clear why the Committee decided to switch from reasonableness to necessity and proportionality. Nothing in the HRC's reasoning suggests that the meaning of reasonableness and necessity and proportionality actually differs. This is confirmed by the way in which the HRC introduced the principle of proportionality in *Toonen*, saying that the principle of reasonableness implies that the restriction should be proportionate. The principle of reasonableness has its origins and finds large use in administrative law, especially in common law countries. According to the UK House of Lords, the principle of reasonableness, or rationality, is a broad standard of review that establishes that a decision should not be 'beyond the range of responses open to a reasonable decision-maker'.[86] However, even domestic courts do not agree on the relationship between the reasonableness and the necessity/proportionality test. For instance, the Irish Supreme Court, in the landmark case *Meadows v. Minister for Justice, Equality and Law Reform*, established that the proportionality test was instrumental for establishing the reasonableness of a limitation to human rights. In this way, the proportionality test appears as

82 *Singh Bhinder v. Canada*, Communication no 208/1986 (HRC, 9 November 1989), 6.2.

83 *Toonen v. Australia*, Communication no 488/1992 (HRC, 1994).

84 ibid, 8.3.

85 ibid, 8.6.

86 Sir Bingham MR in *R v. Ministry of Defence, ex p Smith* (1996) QB 517, 554.

stringent or less stringent than reasonableness and not vice versa, as the UK courts held. This contrast shows the complexity of drawing a line between the two tests and this could help to explain the shift from reasonableness to proportionality in the HRC's case-law.

Yet, the reason why the Committee felt the need to simply change words, keeping the same test, remains unclear. One hypothesis could be the desire to converge with the other human rights systems to establish a harmonious international case-law. Adopting the same language as the regional bodies allows the HRC to engage in a more fruitful judicial dialogue and to get inspiration from the other bodies' jurisprudence. Yet, no evidence of this specific intent could be found.

In its General Comment No. 27 on freedom of movement, recalled later in General Comment No. 34 on freedom of expression, the HRC explained its position on proportionality: 'it is not sufficient that the restrictions serve the permissible purposes; they must also be necessary to protect them. Restrictive measures must conform to the principle of proportionality; they must be appropriate to achieve their protective function; they must be the least intrusive instrument amongst those which might achieve the desired result, and they must be proportionate to the interest to be protected'.[87] This reasoning mirrors what the IACtHR and the ECtHR have in different words stated and it includes all the elements of the three-stage proportionality test.[88]

In individual complaint cases, the principle of proportionality played a fundamental role. For instance, in line with the ECtHR's ruling in *Garaudy* and *Witzsch*, the HRC, in *Faurisson v. France*, found that the Gayssot Act criminalising anti-Semitic comments was proportionate to the legitimate aim of preventing incitement to anti-Semitisms and, therefore, the Committee did not find any violation of freedom of expression.[89] The HRC recognised that the legitimate aim pursued, the right to be free from incitement to racism and anti-Semitism, was so important that 'it could not have been achieved in the circumstances by less drastic means'.[90]

5.2.3 *The Inter-American Court of Human Rights*

The Inter-American Court followed the example of its European counterpart in its approach towards proportionality since the beginning of its adjudication

87 HRC, General Comment No. 27, CCPR/C/21/Rev.1/Add.9, 2 November 1999.
88 See, for the ECtHR *Handyside* and for the IACtHR *Herrera Uloa*.
89 *Faurisson v. France*, Communication no 550/1993 (HRC, 8 November 1996).
90 ibid, 9.

on rights requiring a balancing test. Nevertheless, while the ultimate meaning and understanding are the same, the structure adopted by the IACtHR seems more rigorous and consistent in its case-law. Since the first case on freedom of expression in 2001, *The Last Temptation of Christ*, the IACtHR, heavily referred to the ECtHR's case-law, stating that any restriction to the freedom of expression should be proportionate to the legitimate aim sought.[91]

In *Escher et al. v. Brazil*, concerning the violation of the right to private life by telephone conversation's tapping, the IACtHR stated that, to be compatible with the ACHR, any restriction should meet the requirements of the fivefold test to be 'established by law, [...] have a legitimate purpose and [...] be appropriate, necessary and proportionate'.[92] The same test has been used in cases concerning freedom of expression[93] or other aspects of the right to private life.[94] As to how to practically assess the proportionality of a restriction, the IACtHR is clearer and more consistent in its definitively smaller case-law. The three-stage test of suitability, necessity and proportionality *stricto sensu* is fully embraced by the IACtHR. In its Advisory Opinion on *Juridical Condition and Rights of Undocumented Migrants*, the Court stated that 'limitation must respond to criteria of necessity and proportionality in order to attain a legitimate objective' and in order to 'examine the proportionality and the need [...] we must consider whether there are other measures that are less restrictive of the said right'.[95] The same approach has been adopted in the cases concerning violations of freedom of expression.[96] In *Herrera Uloa*, the IACtHR held that 'the restriction must be proportionate to the legitimate interest that justifies it and must be limited to what is strictly necessary to achieve that objective. It should interfere as little as possible with effective exercise of the right to freedom of expression'.[97] Recalling the case-law of the ECtHR and the importance of freedom of expression in a democratic society, the Court concluded that the conviction of the applicant for defamation was disproportionate and, hence, constituted a violation of his freedom of expression.[98]

91 *Olmedo-Bustos et al. v. Chile (The Last Temptation of Christ case)* (IACtHR, 5 February 2001), 69.

92 *Escher et al. v. Brazil* (IACtHR, 6 July 2009).

93 See *Donoso*, IACtHR, 76.

94 See *Artavia Murillo et al. ("in vitro fertilization") v. Costa* Rica (IACtHR, 28 November 2012), 89.

95 *Juridical Condition and Rights of the Undocumented Migrants*, Advisory Opinion OC-18/03 (IACtHR, 17 September 2003), 57.

96 See *Herrera Uloa*, IACtHR; *The Last Temptation of Christ*, IACtHR; *Canese*, IACtHR; *Donoso*, IACtHR.

97 *Herrera Uloa*, IACtHR, 123.

98 ibid, 135 and 207.

The famous case *Artavia Murillo v. Costa Rica* could provide further clarity on the IACtHR's application of the proportionality test. The case concerned the prohibition of in vitro fertilisation procedures, thus preventing the applicant from enjoying her right to family life. The IACtHR engaged in a detailed proportionality analysis.[99] After acknowledging that the restriction was suitable to pursue a legitimate aim, it went on to survey the existing practice of other Latin American and European countries in order to assess whether such a full ban was the less intrusive way to do so. Once it determined that other less restrictive options were available, the IACommHR concluded that the ban was excessive and found a violation of the ACHR.[100]

In conclusion, the approach of the IACtHR to proportionality is in line with that of the ECtHR, as proved by the continuous references to the case-law of the ECtHR in the assessment of proportionality. The Inter-American bodies appear more rigorous in following a structured proportionality test. However, most of this consistency is probably due to the low number of cases and to a relatively small jurisprudence that began only in 2001 when the HRC and the ECtHR already fully converged on proportionality. Still, the essence and rationale behind the proportionality assessment and the impact on adjudication are the same as the HRC and the ECtHR.

5.2.4 *The African Commission and Court of Human and Peoples' Rights*

As for the African bodies, both the Commission and the Court, since their first pronouncements, have always considered the principle of proportionality as the key element in reviewing the legitimacy of any restriction. In *Constitutional Rights Project and Others v. Nigeria*, dealing with freedom of expression, the Commission pointed out that 'limitations must be strictly proportionate with and absolutely necessary for the advantages which follow'.[101] Similarly, in *Endorois*, addressing an alleged violation of the right to property, the ACommHPR confirmed that 'limitations on rights [. . .] must be reviewed under the principle of proportionality'.[102] Only in *Zimbabwe Lawyers for Human Rights & Associated Newspapers of Zimbabwe v. Zimbabwe*, the Commission clarified its understanding of proportionality.

[99] *Artavia Murillo*, IACtHR.
[100] ibid, 110–111.
[101] *Constitutional Rights Project and Others v. Nigeria*, Communication no 140/94 and 145/95 (ACommHPR, November 1999), 42.
[102] *Centre for Minority Rights Development (Kenya) and Minority Rights Group International on behalf of Endorois Welfare Council v. Kenya* (ACommHPR, 25 November 2009), 213.

It held that 'the principle of proportionality or proportional justice is used to describe the idea that the punishment for a particular offence should be proportionate to the gravity of the offence itself. The principle of proportionality seeks to determine whether, by State action, there has been a balance between protecting the rights and freedoms of the individual and the interests of society as a whole'.[103] In line with other regional and international bodies, such a definition of proportionality remains very vague and, hence, subjected to very different interpretations. In the same current, it is the African Court that, in *Konaté*, engaged with an assessment of the proportionality of the restriction to the applicant's freedom of expression to assess a breach of the Charter. The Court, recalling the case-law of the ECtHR, IACtHR and HRC, stated that 'in order to consider the need for a restriction on freedom of expression, [. . .] this assessment must ascertain whether the restriction is a proportionate measure to achieve the set objective'.[104]

As for how this proportionality should be measured, the Court took into consideration the aligned approaches of the ECtHR, IACtHR and HRC and endorsed the three-stage proportionality test that requires restrictions to be 'appropriate to achieve their protective function, [. . .] be the least disturbing means among those that might help achieve the desired result and [. . .] be proportionate to the interest to be protected'.[105]

The fact that the African Court and Commission followed word by word the example of the other human rights bodies is not a surprise and definitely not limited to the proportionality test. As discussed in the previous chapters, the constant struggle of the African Court in particular to legitimise itself and its jurisprudence has led it to continuously base its judgments on the case-law of other well-established human rights institutions.

CONCLUSION

This chapter showed that, despite textual differences and surface discrepancies in the chosen wording, the four systems under analysis are now fully converging in the interpretation and application of the principles of necessity and proportionality. Considering the key role that the two principles play in the adjudication of balancing rights and interests, the fact that all the bodies agree

[103] *Zimbabwe Lawyers for Human Rights & Associated Newspapers of Zimbabwe v. Zimbabwe*, Communication no 284/03 (ACommHPR, 2009), 176.

[104] *Konaté*, ACtHPR, 145.

[105] ibid, 153 quoting the HRC General Comment No. 34 on Article 19, 33.

on the same understanding of necessity and proportionality is a strong safeguard against fragmentation.

The judicial interpretation of the five bodies filled any gaps left by the textual differences in the Conventions and Charters. Mostly following the example of the ECtHR, whose text employed the principle of necessity the most, and relying on judicial dialogue, the HRC, IACtHR and the African bodies decided to resort to the principle of necessity for assessing any situation where two contrasting rights or interests were to be balanced. Thanks to the flexibility and vagueness of the principle, the apparent difference between 'necessary' and 'necessary in a democratic society' disappeared. Similarly, the lack of a reference to the required 'absolute necessity' in the ACHR and ICCPR for what concerned the use of deadly force restricting the right to life was overcome by case-law, where the HRC, IACtHR and ECtHR employ the same 'necessity' test even if using different words, maintaining convergence among the systems. The necessity test, and any of its degrees such as 'absolute' or 'strict', is not rigidly defined and its evaluation is forcibly subjective and left to the discretion of the adjudicatory bodies on the basis of the facts of the single case. Together with the fact that its assessment relies on the application of the proportionality test, this flexibility is what makes it a very handy tool in adjusting differences between systems and approaches by, in the end, rendering harmonious and convergent conclusions.

The same consideration applies to the principle of proportionality. As one of the possible ways to operationally assess the necessity of a restriction to a fundamental right or freedom, the proportionality test has been chosen by all the bodies under analysis that now apply it as one of the core principles of their adjudication. Regardless of whether they adopt a more or a less structured test or whether they have changed the label from reasonableness to proportionality, like in the case of the HRC, they all converge on the use of proportionality over other balancing techniques. Like for necessity, the principle of proportionality is also extremely flexible in its definition and application, and this is the key to its success among all human rights bodies. There is not a single way to apply the proportionality test, and it allows plenty of space to adjust to the features of the given case. This convergence in the use of the proportionality test, probably boosted by the increasing judicial dialogue between bodies, overall prevents fragmentation.

Indeed, balancing rights and interests is one of the most delicate operations where cultural, social and historical factors can play an important role and influence the judicial outcome. That is why a strong agreement on the balancing method significantly mildens the effects of these factors and ensures an ultimate convergence. Still, the door to a more fragmented case-law remains open. The difference between the reasonableness and the proportionality tests is very blurred and not well established in international jurisprudence; the potential difference in adjudication using one or the other test could be greater and possibly lead to higher chances of fragmentation.[106] This may bring a more arbitrary application of the balancing test and a more deferent approach by the HRC. Alternatively, it could simply leave the matter confused and far from being settled once and for all. Moreover, the harmonisation reached by the proportionality test may be further altered by the large use of the margin of appreciation made by the ECtHR in contrast with the other bodies. This is what the following chapter will discuss.

[106] cf Marko Milanovic, 'Human Rights Treaties and Foreign Surveillance: Privacy in the Digital Age' (2015) 56(1) *Harvard International Law Journal* 81, 81–146; and, for instance, *R v. Ministry of Defence, ex p Smith* (1996) QB 517UK or Lord Steyn in *R (on the application of Daly) v. Secretary of State for the Home Department* (2001) 2 AC 532, 547.

6

Deference, Subsidiarity and Regional Consensus

The Margin of Appreciation Doctrine

INTRODUCTION

The approach to deference and subsidiarity certainly affects the adjudication of human rights cases in a prominent manner and can also contribute to convergence and fragmentation. From the well-known and debated margin of appreciation (MoA) of the European Court of Human Rights (ECtHR) to the newly developed conventionality control (CC) doctrine of the Inter-American Court of Human Rights (IACtHR), different attitudes to deference and subsidiarity have been adopted by the four jurisdictions under analysis. As observed in the previous chapter, the proportionality test in the ECtHR strongly relies on the application of the MoA, thus making it an essential element in the ECtHR's adjudication. Recalling the definition of judicial fragmentation as the situation where two courts, or quasi-judicial bodies, seized with the same or similar matters issue contrasting judgments, it appears evident how a different understanding and application of the principles of deference and subsidiarity can increase the likelihood of fragmentation to arise. On the contrary, relying on the same subsidiarity doctrines could provide the adjudicatory bodies with similar instruments to reach convergent outcomes.

Before delving into how the three regional systems and the UN Human Rights Committee (HRC) deal with the principles of deference and subsidiarity and the related concept of regional consensus, some preliminary definitions are required.

Deference, subsidiarity and MoA are very much interconnected and often used interchangeably. However, a distinction should be drawn between these concepts considering the different approaches adopted by the four systems.

Within IHRL, judicial deference is generally defined as the decision of an international or regional tribunal to yield or submit its judgment to that of national authorities.[1] In other words, an international or regional human rights body has the option to 'defer' a particular matter to the member state concerned, deciding not to exercise its authority to speak over that matter and leave it to the domestic authorities of the member state. Scholars have rarely engaged with the definition of deference, often adopting it as a general term including specific doctrines, such as the MoA.[2] Indeed, judicial deference broadly indicates the possibility for an international human rights court to engage in a certain way with its member states. It can assume different forms, and the MoA is one of them.

Differently, the principle of subsidiarity could be considered as one of the main reasons behind the adoption of judicial deference. Legg argues that the nature of deference in IHRL is 'the practice of assigning weight to reasons for a decision on the basis of external factors'.[3] Among these external factors, there is also the principle of subsidiarity.[4] Subsidiarity has been largely discussed by commentators, which elaborated different definitions and theories.[5] Carrozza consideres subsidiarity as the structural basis of any legitimate regional system of human rights protection.[6] According to Neuman, subsidiarity describes, in general terms, 'a relationship between two institutions or norms, by which one supplements the other in appropriate circumstances'.[7] In contrast with this neutral and descriptive definition, Føllesdal proposes a normative theory of subsidiarity,[8] considering it as a 'rebuttable presumption for the local', claiming that states should have prima facie prioritisation when deciding

[1] Jorge Contesse, 'Contestation and Deference in the Inter-American Human Rights System' (2016) 79 *Law and Contemporary Problems* 123.

[2] Marisa Iglesias Vila, 'Subsidiariedad y tribunals internacionales de derechos humanos: Deferencia hacia los estados o división cooperativa del trabajo?'(2017) 79 *Derecho Pontificia Universidad Católica del Perú* 191; Samantha Besson, 'Subsidiarity in International Human Rights Law – What Is Subsidiary about Human Rights?' (2016) 61 *The American Journal of Jurisprudence* 1, 69–107; Andrew Legg, *The Margin of Appreciation in International Human Rights Law* (Oxford University Press, 2012).

[3] ibid, 17.

[4] Gonzalo Candia, 'Comparing Diverse Approaches to the Margin of Appreciation: The Case of the European and the Inter-American Court of Human Rights' (9 March 2014). Available at SSRN: https://ssrn.com/abstract=2406705.

[5] cf Jonas Christoffersen, *Fair Balance: Proportionality, Subsidiarity and Primarity in the European Convention on Human Rights* (Martinus-Nijhoff, 2009).

[6] Paolo Carrozza, 'Subsidiarity as a Structural Principle of International Human Rights Law' (2003) 97(1) *American Journal of International Law* 37.

[7] Gerald L. Neuman, 'Subsidiarity' in Dina Shelton (ed), *The Oxford Handbook of International Human Rights Law* (Oxford University Press, 2013), 361.

[8] Contesse, 'Contestation and Deference in the Inter-American Human Rights System'.

issues of international law.[9] When applied to international and regional human rights bodies, subsidiarity entails that states are in a better position to enact and adopt laws and policies to protect and enforce their citizens' human rights. Especially when striking a balance between opposed social values is required, the decision should be taken by the democratically elected representatives of the member states.[10] In light of this, state parties should be granted a certain latitude of discretion by supranational bodies.

The third element coming into play is (regional) consensus. Consensus has often been invoked as the basis of deference, and the lack of consensus is one of the primary justifications for granting a wider margin of discretion.[11] A judicial body in search of consensus among its member states looks at the national legislation policies and case-law enacted by its state parties in order to assess whether a certain agreement already exists. This is seen as a necessary step to interpret the Convention or Charter in such a progressive way as to go beyond the letter of the provision without infringing the sovereignty of states.[12]

This chapter explores how the four systems under analysis have been dealing with deference and subsidiarity, highlighting differences and similarities in order to identify to what extent these two elements could contribute to convergence or fragmentation in IHRL. As it may be apparent, the relationship between the human rights body and their member states, and the potential backlash from them, plays a key role in shaping the deferential approach of a body. This element will be discussed later in this chapter.

The way a court, committee or commission engages with deference and subsidiarity defines its approach to adjudication and profoundly affects its case-law. On a scale of deference, on one extreme there is the ECtHR with the MoA doctrine, a strong subsidiarity rationale and a decisive regional consensus. On the opposite end, there is the IACtHR with the conventionality

9 Andreas Føllesdal, 'Subsidiarity and International Human-Rights Courts: Respecting Self-Governance and Protecting Human Rights – Or Neither?' (2016) 79 *Law and Contemporary Problems* 147.

10 Yuval Shany, 'All Roads Lead to Strasbourg?: Application of the Margin of Appreciation Doctrine by the European Court of Human Rights and the UN Human Rights Committee' (2018) 9 *Journal of International Dispute Settlement* 2; Legg, *The Margin of Appreciation*, 7.

11 For a discussion on the nature and role of regional consensus in Europe see Jens T. Theilen, *European Consensus between Strategy and Principle* (Nomos, 2021).

12 Dominic McGoldrick, 'Affording States a Margin of Appreciation: Comparing the European Court of Human Rights and the Inter-American Court of Human Rights' in Buckley, Donald and Leach (eds), *Towards Convergence in International Human Rights Law: Approaches of Regional and International Systems* (Brill-Nijhoff, 2016); Kanstantsin Dzehtsiarou, *European Consensus and the Legitimacy of the European Court of Human Rights* (Cambridge University Press, 2015).

control doctrine that significantly limits the action of its member states even if some hints of deference are still detectable. In the middle of the spectrum we can find both the HRC and the African bodies, struggling between upholding the universality of rights and the independence from the European human rights system on the one hand, and granting deference and margin of discretion to their member states using a MoA-like language, on the other. Such a complex scenario may have a significant impact on the judicial convergence or fragmentation of these bodies' case-law.

6.1 THE MARGIN OF APPRECIATION DOCTRINE BEFORE THE ECTHR

6.1.1 *Origins and Evolution*

The ECtHR developed its own doctrine of judicial deference based on the principle of subsidiarity, the so-called margin of appreciation. The MoA is a judicial invention of the ECtHR, as it cannot be found anywhere in the European Convention or its drafting history. Scholars have extensively debated over the definition, scope and value of this judicial doctrine of deference.[13] Yurow describes it as 'the latitude of deference or error which the Strasbourg organs will allow to national legislative, executive, administrative and judicial bodies before it is prepared to declare a national derogation from the Convention, or restriction or limitation upon a right guaranteed by the Convention, to constitute a violation of one of the Convention's substantive guarantees'.[14] Similarly, Arai-Takahashi defines the MoA as the 'latitude a government enjoys in evaluating factual situations and in applying the provisions enumerated in international human rights treaties'.[15]

[13] Legg, *The Margin of Appreciation*; Howard Charles Yourow, *The Margin of Appreciation Doctrine in the Dynamics of European Human Rights Jurisprudence* (Kluwer Law International, 1996); Yutaka Arai-Takahashi, *The Margin of Appreciation Doctrine and the Principle of Proportionality in the Jurisprudence of the ECHR* (Intersentia, 2002); Marisa Iglesias Vila, 'Subsidiarity, Margin of Appreciation and International Adjudication within a Cooperative Conception of Human Rights' (2017) 15 *International Journal of Constitutional Law* 2, 393–413; Dean Spielmann, 'Allowing the Right Margin: The European Court of Human Rights and the National Margin of Appreciation Doctrine: Waiver or Subsidiarity of European Review?' (2017) 14 *Cambridge Yearbook of European Legal Studies*, 381–418; Steven Greer, 'The Interpretation of the European Convention on Human Rights: Universal Principle or Margin of Appreciation?' (2010) 3 *UCL Human Rights Review* 1–14; Janneke Gerards, 'Margin of Appreciation and Incrementalism in the Case Law of European Court of Human Rights' (2018) 18 *Human Rights Law Review* 3, 495–515.

[14] Yourow, *The Margin of Appreciation Doctrine*, 13.

[15] Arai-Takahashi, *The Margin of Appreciation Doctrine*, 3.

The first appearance of the MoA was in the context of derogations from the ECHR under Article 15. In the 1961 landmark case *Lawless v. Ireland*, the language of a MoA was used for the first time to grant member states a certain discretion in their interpretation and application of the Convention's rights.[16] However, it was only in *Handyside v. United Kingdom* that the ECtHR explicitly defined and applied the MoA doctrine.[17] The case concerned the publication of a children's book considered inappropriate for the controversial encouragement to smoke marijuana and engage in sexual acts. The author of the book was convicted for possessing obscene volumes for gain, and the books were seized and destroyed, since they were considered against public morals and decency. Mr Handyside filed a complaint before the ECtHR claiming that the United Kingdom violated his freedom of expression under Article 10 ECHR. The Strasbourg Court ruled in favour of the respondent state, finding that the conviction of Mr Handyside was an interference with his rights under Article 10, but it did not amount to a violation of the ECHR. After having established, in line with Article 10.2, that the restriction of the applicant's freedom of expression was prescribed by law and was pursuing one of the legitimate aims, namely the protection of morals, the Court needed to assess whether such a restriction was 'necessary in a democratic society'.[18] In doing so, the Court argued that

> State authorities are in principle in a better position than the international judge to give an opinion on the exact content of these requirements as well as on the 'necessity' of a restriction or penalty intended to meet them. [...] The requirement of morals varies from time to time and from place to place, especially in our area which is characterised by a rapid and far-reaching evolution of opinions on the subject. [...] *This margin [of appreciation]* is given both to the domestic legislator and to the bodies, judicial among others, that are called upon to interpret and apply the laws in force. [...] The machinery of protection established by the Convention is subsidiary to the national systems safeguarding human rights.[19]

Since *Handyside*, the ECtHR invoked the MoA in a large number of cases concerning restrictions of rights, especially for Articles 8–11 ECHR, which provide a limitation clause. The doctrine of the MoA, based on the underlying principle of subsidiarity, has been lately included in Protocol 15 to the ECHR,

[16] *Lawless v. Ireland*, Application no 332/57 (ECtHR, 1 July 1961).

[17] *Handyside v. United Kingdom*, Application no 5493/72 (ECtHR, 7 December 1976).

[18] ibid, 47.

[19] ibid, 48–49.

approved in June 2013.[20] Article 1 provides that the preamble of the Convention should be amended as to add the following paragraph:

> Affirming that the High Contracting Parties, in accordance with the principle of subsidiarity, have the primary responsibility to secure the rights and freedoms defined in this Convention and the Protocols thereto, and that in doing so they enjoy a margin of appreciation, subject to the supervisory jurisdiction of the European Court of Human Rights established by this Convention.[21]

This confirmed and reinforced the ECtHR approach towards subsidiarity to the extent that the President of the Court, Robert Spano, defined the current phase of the ECtHR as the 'age of subsidiarity'.[22] Such a stage is, indeed, characterised by the adoption of a robust and coherent subsidiarity approach, allowing for a diversified implementation of human rights guarantees at national level and an ultimately increased diversity in the protection of human rights.[23]

6.1.2 *The Features of the MoA before the ECtHR*

In order for a state party to enjoy a certain level of deference in a given case, all the requirements set by the second paragraph of Articles 8–11 ECHR should be first met. The restriction of a convention right should always be prescribed by law, pursuing a legitimate aim among those listed, and it should be 'necessary in a democratic society'. The deferential attitude of the ECtHR applies mainly to the third element, that is, the assessment of whether the state struck a fair balance between the rights of the applicant and the public interest that the restriction aimed at protecting. Indeed, the MoA is not designed as a *free pass* for member states to avoid complying with obligations set forth by the ECHR but only as a doctrine aimed at respecting the 'better position' rationale of domestic authorities over international ones.

Moreover, the MoA is not a standard and indiscriminate doctrine that fits all cases in the same way. The ECtHR always conducts a careful analysis before granting a MoA to the respondent state. As explicitly stated in *Handyside*, 'the domestic margin of appreciation [...] goes hand in hand with European

[20] Protocol No. 15 amending the Convention on the Protection of Human Rights and Fundamental Freedoms, 24 June 2013.

[21] Protocol 15 ECHR, Article 1.

[22] Robert Spano, 'Universality or Diversity of Human Rights?: Strasbourg in the Age of Subsidiarity' (2014) 14 *Human Rights Law Review* 487, 491.

[23] ibid.

supervision. Such supervision concerns both the aim of the measure challenged and its necessity'.[24] Therefore, it is not a right of the state, and the Court surely has the authority to refuse to grant it or establish that the state had stepped outside its margin of appreciation.[25] The breadth of the MoA is usually decided on the basis of the competing interests at stake in the specific case. As the ECtHR has repeatedly explained, 'where a particularly important facet of an individual's existence or identity is at stake, the margin allowed to the State will be restricted'.[26]

This is why in some cases concerning the sexual orientation of an individual, the Court granted a very narrow margin of appreciation.[27] Similarly, the ECtHR's scrutiny is intensified and the MoA is consequently narrower in cases related to the enjoyment of fundamental rights, such as the right to life, the right to be free from torture and inhuman and degrading treatments or rights and freedoms closely linked with a democratic society, namely the right to political participation, freedom of association or political speech.[28] However, this does not mean that the ECtHR has never granted a MoA to its member states in the limitation of the rights above, considering that the MoA is a 'factually sensitive doctrine',[29] which varies on a case-by-case basis.

On the other hand, the ECtHR has generally allowed a broader margin in cases concerning the restriction of Articles 8–11 ECHR (private life, religion, expression, association) on the basis of the protection of national security or public morals.[30] Relying on the fundamental principle of 'regional consensus', when sensitive issues are at stake (such as same-sex marriage or the ban on the wearing of the Islamic burqa), the ECtHR always looked at the practice of its member states and granted a wider MoA in the absence of consensus.[31] The influential role of regional consensus in the adjudicatory practice of the ECtHR is another confirmation of the importance of subsidiarity in

[24] *Handyside*, ECtHR, 49.
[25] cf *Oliari and Others v. Italy*, Application nos 18766/11 and 36030/11 (ECtHR, 21 July 2015).
[26] *Evans v. United Kingdom*, Application no 6339/05 (ECtHR, 10 April 2007), 77.
[27] See *Oliari*, ECtHR.
[28] Arai-Takahashi, *The Margin of Appreciation Doctrine*; Christoffersen, *Fair Balance: Proportionality, Subsidiarity and Primarity*.
[29] Pablo Contreras, 'National Discretion and International Deference in the Restriction of Human Rights: A Comparison between the Jurisprudence of the European and the Inter-American Court of Human Rights' (2012) 11 *Northwestern Journal of International Human Rights* 28, 43.
[30] See, for example, *Handyside*, ECtHR or *Klass and Others v. Germany*, Application no 5029/71 (ECtHR, 6 September 1978).
[31] See *S.A.S. v. France*, Application no 43835/11 (ECtHR, 1 July 2014) or *Schalk and Kopf v. Austria*, Application no 30141/04 (ECtHR, 22 November 2010). See also Theilen, *European Consensus between Strategy and Principle*.

the reasoning of the Court. As Carrozza pointed out, the comparative exercise carried out by the ECtHR in assessing the extent of regional consensus is key to determining the level of subsidiarity to be accorded to its member states on a given issue.[32]

6.2 THE IACTHR AND THE CONVENTIONALITY CONTROL DOCTRINE: IS THERE ROOM FOR SUBSIDIARITY AND DEFERENCE?

The Inter-American Court seems to have followed a different path regarding deference and subsidiarity. Indeed, the MoA never found an explicit place in its judgments and, on some occasions, the Court openly rejected it together with its constitutive elements, such as the regional consensus. The IACtHR always preferred to apply very close scrutiny, deferring very little to its member states, developing the doctrine of the conventionality control that arguably goes in the opposite direction of the MoA.[33]

As highlighted by some scholars,[34] the main reasons for such an approach are the history of the Court with its member states and the nature of the cases that the Court had to deal with. The first case decided by the Court only dates back to 1988, more than twenty years after the first case before the ECtHR. This entails that the IACtHR, having had a shorter institutional life could still be in the process of developing its own doctrines. Moreover, the historical and political situation of its member states, struggling between dictatorships and fragile democracies, did not offer enough assurances to the Court for a deferential approach in its human rights adjudication.

In addition, the cases that the IACtHR was confronted with significantly influenced its approach. From the first one, *Velazquez Rodriguez v. Honduras*,[35] the almost totality of the cases that the Court examined in the first decades of its life dealt with enforced disappearances, arbitrary detentions, extrajudicial killings or, in general, violations of fundamental rights, such as the right to life, the prohibition of torture and the right to

[32] Paolo G. Carrozza, 'Uses and Misuses of Comparative Law in International Human Rights: Some Reflections on the Jurisprudence of the European Court of Human Rights' (1998) 73 *Notre Dame Law Review* 1230.

[33] See Section 6.2.2.

[34] Contesse, 'Contestation and Deference in the Inter-American Human Rights System'; Contreras, 'National Discretion and International Deference'; McGoldrick, 'Affording States a Margin of Appreciation'; Andreas Follesdal, 'Exporting the Margin of Appreciation: Lessons for the Inter-American Court of Human Rights' (2017) 15 *International Journal of Constitutional Law* 2, 359–371.

[35] *Velazquez Rodriguez v. Honduras* (IACtHR, 29 July 1988).

personal liberty and integrity. Such rights do not allow much margin of deference even in the European system, due to their fundamental role in protecting the individual and the principles of democracy.

However, in the last decades, the Court started receiving applications concerning other rights as well, such as freedom of expression or private life, where states may invoke some margin of appreciation.

The following sections will first explore the relation of the IACtHR with the MoA and then discuss the doctrine that seems to have prevailed in the IACtHR's adjudication, the conventionality control doctrine.

6.2.1 *The IACtHR and the MoA*

Scholars suggest that a change of approach in the Inter-American Court's attitude towards subsidiarity has occurred and highlighted that the IACtHR has, indeed, used some language pertaining to the margin of appreciation.[36] The first occasion was in an Advisory Opinion rendered in 1984, concerning the proposed amendments to the constitutional rules regulating naturalisation in Costa Rica. The Court was asked to rule on whether such amendments were compatible with the rights set forth by the American Convention. The IACtHR observed that

> [o]ne is here dealing with values which take on concrete dimensions in the face of those real situations in which they have to be applied and which permit in each case a certain *margin of appreciation* in giving expression to them. [...] [Therefore] it is for the granting state to determine whether and to what extent applicants for naturalisation have complied with the conditions deemed to ensure an effective link between them and the value system and interests of the society to which they wish to belong.[37]

Even if the Court did not explicitly refer to the ECtHR,[38] the use of the same MoA rationale is clear. Moreover, the IACtHR embraced a strong subsidiarity approach in stating that 'there exists no doubt that it is within the sovereign power of Costa Rica to decide what standards should determine

[36] Contesse, 'Contestation and Deference in the Inter-American Human Rights System'; McGoldrick, 'Affording States a Margin of Appreciation'; Legg, *The Margin of Appreciation*.

[37] *Proposed Amendments to the Naturalization Provisions of the Constitution of Costa Rica*, Advisory Opinion OC-4/84 (IACtHR, 19 January 1984), 58–59.

[38] The IACtHR referred to the ECtHR in the Advisory Opinion in a different paragraph, dealing with the definition of discriminatory treatment.

the granting or denial of nationality to aliens who seek it, and to establish certain reasonable differentiations'.[39]

The other circumstance where the IACtHR used the language of the MoA was in a contentious case delivered in 2004, *Herrera Uloa v. Costa Rica*. The case concerned the conviction of a journalist for defamation, which, according to the applicant, amounted to a violation of his freedom of expression. In ruling in favour of the applicant, the IACtHR repeatedly mentioned the role of a margin of discretion left to its member states. For instance, quoting the ECtHR, the Court argued that 'there should be a reduced margin for any restriction on political debates or debates on matters of public interest'.[40] Moreover, in determining whether the applicant suffered a violation of his right to a fair trial, the IACtHR recognised that '[s]tates have a *margin of discretion* in regulating the exercise of that [judicial] remedy'.[41] Although the MoA was not explicitly adopted, the position of the IACtHR in this case, as well as its reasoning, was very much in line with that of the ECtHR, granting its member states a certain discretion in regulating judicial remedies under a general supervision of the Court.[42]

These two cases could suggest that the IACtHR tested out how to enforce subsidiarity and the Court is going towards convergence with its European counterpart on the application of a MoA doctrine.

However, I rather argue that the IACtHR actually took more steps in the opposite direction, leaving the cases above as mere isolated examples of a deferential approach, while choosing to invest on the very much different 'conventionality control' doctrine.[43]

6.2.2 *The IACtHR and the Conventionality Control Doctrine: The Rejection of the MoA*

The conventionality control (CC) doctrine, the expression that was first used by Judge García Ramírez in his separate opinion in *Myrna Mack Chang v. Guatemala*,[44] establishes that national judges and authorities should abstain

[39] ibid, 59.

[40] *Herrera Uloa v. Costa Rica* (IACtHR, 2004), 127.

[41] ibid, 161.

[42] See Contreras, 'National Discretion and International Deference'.

[43] cf Claudio Nash Rojas, 'La doctrina del margen de apreciación y su nula recepción en la jurisprudencia de la Corte Interamericana de Derechos Humanos' (2017) 11 *Anuario Colombiano de Derecho Internacional* 71, 71–100.

[44] *Myrna Mack Chang v. Guatemala, Merits* (IACtHR, 25 November 2003), Separate Opinion of Judge Sergio García Ramírez.

from applying domestic laws that are not compatible with the ACHR as interpreted by the Court even in contentious cases concerning other state parties. The CC doctrine was explicitly formulated in *Almonacid-Arellano v. Chile*, where the IACtHR stated that

> [t]he Court is aware that domestic judges and courts are bound to respect the rule of law, and therefore, they are bound to apply the provisions in force within the legal system. But when a State has ratified an international treaty such as the American Convention, its judges, as part of the State, are also bound by such Convention. This forces them to see that all the effects of the provisions embodied in the Convention are not adversely affected by the enforcement of laws which are contrary to its purpose and that have not had any legal effects since their inception. In other words, the Judiciary must exercise a sort of 'conventionality control' between the domestic legal provisions which are applied to specific cases and the American Convention on Human Rights. To perform this task, the Judiciary has to take into account not only the treaty, but also the interpretation thereof made by the Inter-American Court, which is the ultimate interpreter of the American Convention.[45]

Such a doctrine of control over domestic legislation and courts has been applied several times in a multitude of cases related to various articles of the Convention.[46] In addition, the 'expansive approach' of the IACtHR towards the protection of human rights led the Court to ruling, in *Gelman v. Uruguay*, that an amnesty law voted by popular referenda constituted a violation of the ACHR and lacked validity because it prevented authorities from investigating and punishing those responsible for gross and massive human rights violations.[47] Here, the Court extended the CC requiring all state authorities, and not only judges, to exercise such a control. Moreover, it explicitly added that all state parties to the Conventions and their organs were legally required to exercise the conventionality control using the Court's interpretation of the treaty even if their State was not a party to the case.[48]

As Cassese stated, commenting on the ruling of the IACtHR in *Barrios Altos v. Peru*, this 'is the first time that an international court determines that national laws are devoid of legal effects within the state system where they

45 *Almonacid-Arellano v. Chile* (IACtHR, 26 September 2006), 124.

46 See *Olmedo-Bustos et al. v. Chile (The Last Temptation of Christ case)* (IACtHR, 5 February 2001) dealing with freedom of expression or *Tibi v. Ecuador* (IACtHR, 7 September 2004), Separate Opinion of Judge Sergio García Ramírez.

47 *Gelman v. Uruguay* (IACtHR, 24 February 2011).

48 ibid, 193, 239. See also *Gelman v. Uruguay*, Monitoring Compliance with Judgment (IACtHR, 20 March 2013), 66–69.

have been adopted and consequently obliges the state to act as if these laws have never been enacted'.[49] In this regard, the CC doctrine goes against the subsidiarity principle stated in the preamble of the Convention, demanding the Convention to operate not only complementarily but rather in a concurrent manner at the highest level of the national legal system, thus risking to make the Court an *absolutist* international body.[50]

In light of this, the CC doctrine could be considered as going in the opposite direction to the MoA, leaving no margin at all to the member states as to how to interpret the Convention and actually imposing on their authorities an additional burden of conformity with any interpretation of the Convention ever rendered by the Court.[51] Furthermore, the extension of the CC doctrine also to laws approved by the people through public consultation (two referenda in this case) has been heavily criticised by scholars as it has been considered the denial of state and popular sovereignty as well.[52]

On a similar note, the IACtHR has adopted a clear stance on the value of regional consensus in its adjudication. In *Atala Riffo v. Chile*, the Court explicitly departed from the European position holding that 'the alleged lack of consensus in some countries regarding full respect for the rights of sexual minorities cannot be considered a valid argument to deny or restrict their [homosexual] human rights or to perpetuate and reproduce the historical and structural discrimination that these minorities have suffered'.[53] The same reasoning was confirmed in *Duque v. Colombia*.[54] However, it should be acknowledged that sometimes the IACtHR has looked at the domestic legislation of its member states while deciding a case, but it has always done so in order to support its position in favour of the applicant and never to grant a

49 Antonio Cassese and Mireille Delmas-Marty, *Crimes internationaux et juridictions internationales* (Presses Universitaires de France, 2002), 13–16.

50 Ariel E. Dulitzky, 'An Inter-American Constitutional Court? The Invention of the Conventionality Control by the Inter-American Court of Human Rights' (2015) 50 *Texas International Law Journal* 45, 53–55; Contesse, 'Contestation and Deference in the Inter-American Human Rights System'. According to Dulitzky, the CC doctrine envisages an integration principle that complements subsidiarity. Indeed, the fundamental of subsidiarity being the state in a better position to implement human rights exists also in the CC but what changes is that the IACtHR, and not the state, is the final interpreter of the ACHR.

51 See, among others, Rojas, 'La doctrina del margen de apreciación', 71–100.

52 Roberto Gargarella, 'Symposium: The Constitutionalization of International Law in Latin America Democracy and Rights in Gelman v. Uruguay' (2015) 109 *AJIL Unbound* 115.

53 *Atala Riffo and Daughters v. Chile* (IACtHR, 24 February 2012), 92.

54 *Angel Alberto Duque v. Colombia* (IACtHR, 26 February 2016), 123.

margin of discretion to the respondent state on the basis of a lack of regional consensus.[55]

In light of the above, it is clear that the IACtHR's approach to deference, subsidiarity and the role of consensus is very different from that of the ECtHR. As previously recalled, the reasons behind this divergence could be identified in the historical and socio-political context of the IACtHR's member states or in the type of cases brought before the Court. As Judge Cançado Trindade clearly explained,

> Fortunately, such doctrine has not been developed within the inter-American human rights system. [. . .] How could we apply [the margin-of-appreciation doctrine] in the context of a regional human rights system where many countries' judges are subject to intimidation and pressure? How could we apply it in a region where the judicial function does not distinguish between military jurisdiction and ordinary jurisdiction? How could we apply it in the context of national legal systems that are heavily questioned for the failure to combat impunity? [. . .] We have no alternative but to strengthen the international mechanisms for protection.[56]

Such a strong position dated back to 2008 and the democratic stability of many countries in the region has been fluctuating since then, but the situation is continuously changing. If the concerns of Judge Cançado Trindade are the only obstacles to the development of a MoA-like doctrine in the Americas, and considering the fact that the Court is receiving more and more variegated cases dealing with almost all the rights protected by the ACHR, one could expect that in the future the IACtHR will likely abandon such a close scrutiny on its member states and move towards a more deferential approach, somehow similar to the ECtHR's MoA. However, considering the recent political developments in the region, the minimum requirements set by Judge Cançado Trindade seem to be still very far away.

6.3 THE HUMAN RIGHTS COMMITTEE: WHAT SPACE FOR THE MOA DOCTRINE?

The HRC has never explicitly adopted a MoA doctrine or any other formal subsidiary or deferential approach. However, a perusal of its case-law shows

[55] cf *Gomes Lund et al. v. Brazil* (IACtHR, 24 November 2010) or *Gelman*, IACtHR (24 February 2011) or *Identidad de género, e igualdad y no discriminación a parejas del mismo sexo*, Opinión consultiva OC-24/17 (IACtHR, 9 January 2018).

[56] Antonio Cançado Trindade, *El derecho internacional de los derechos humanos en el siglo XXI* (Editorial Juridíca de las Americas, 2008), 389–390.

that there is a gap 'between the perceived rejection of the MoA doctrine [. . .] and its actual practice of employing substitute MoA-like approaches'.[57] As Shany highlights, the language of the Committee suggests that the HRC is not hostile to some elements of the MoA doctrine and the alternative approaches developed ultimately produce the same effects. This discrepancy between the perceived and the actual approach of the HRC towards subsidiarity and deference could in part explain why there is more convergence with the ECtHR than one may expect.

The HRC has, in theory, rejected the MoA in its case-law. In *Lansman et al. v. Finland*, concerning Article 27 ICCPR and the rights of minorities, it openly states that 'the scope of its freedom is not to be assessed by reference to a margin of appreciation, but by reference to the obligations it has undertaken in Article 27'.[58] Moreover, in its General Comment No. 34 on freedom of expression, the Committee restated the same concept. 'The Committee reserves to itself an assessment of whether, in a given situation, there may have been circumstances which made a restriction of freedom of expression necessary. In this regard, the Committee recalls that the scope of this freedom is not to be assessed by reference to a margin of appreciation'.[59]

However, a careful analysis of the case-law of the HRC reveals that, in its views, the Committee engaged with the language of the MoA, using terminology like 'margin' and 'discretion' and ending up granting deference to member states in a similar fashion to the ECtHR's MoA. In the words of James Crawford, the Committee has been speaking the language of the MoA doctrine silently.[60] For instance, the HRC showed to be very deferential to states that conducted fact-finding assessments once it had established that the process was not arbitrary or amounted to a denial of justice. This applies to cases dealing with extradition and deportation,[61] or to cases concerning alleged procedural flaws in domestic judicial proceedings.[62] The rationale behind it, like in the case-law of the ECtHR, is the better position of the member states in assessing the facts. Especially due to limited time, capacities

[57] Shany, 'All Roads Lead to Strasbourg?'.
[58] *Lansman et al. v. Finland*, Communication no 511/1992 (HRC, 11 June 1992).
[59] Human Rights Committee, General Comment No. 34 on Article 19: Freedom of opinion and expression, 12 September 2011, CCPR/C/GC/34.
[60] James Crawford, 'Preface' in Arai-Takahashi, *The Margin of Appreciation Doctrine*.
[61] cf *RG v. Denmark*, Communication no 2351/2014 (HRC, 1 April 2015), *X v. Norway*, Communication no 2474/2014 (HRC, 5 November 2015) or *FM v. Canada*, Communication no 2284/2013 (HRC, 5 November 2015).
[62] cf *Van Meurs v. Netherlands*, Communication no 215/1986 (HRC, 13 July 1990), *Arenz v. Germany*, Communication no 1138/2002 (HRC, 24 March 2004).

and resources available to the HRC, such a deferential approach turns out to be more of a necessity than a choice for the Committee.[63] When it comes to norm-balancing, the HRC has officially refrained from adopting a MoA doctrine, probably moved by the concerns on whether it was actually wise to leave the interpretation, definition and balancing of human rights norms to domestic authorities, with the possible outcome of a 'tyranny of the majority' that would limit the protection of vulnerable groups and individuals.[64] Moreover, similarly to the IACtHR, the HRC has to deal with the socio-political context of many member states whose democracy and human rights records are not outstanding and could raise trustworthiness concerns on as to whether they should be afforded a margin of discretion.

That said, in the famous case *Hertzberg v. Finland*, in 1982, the HRC expressly used the MoA doctrine, justifying the restriction on the freedom of expression for the protection of morals arguing that 'public morals differ widely. There is no universally applicable moral standard. Consequently, in this respect, a certain margin of discretion must be accorded to the responsible national authorities'.[65] After this case, the HRC has never mentioned again the application of a MoA doctrine in such an explicit way. However, some forms of MoA language and approach could be found nonetheless in norm-balancing cases. For instance, in *Faurrison v. France* and in other cases,[66] the Committee adopted the approach of the 'minimum scrutiny', imposing a relatively light burden on states for justifying a difference in treatment that does not affect 'suspect categories'.[67]

Moreover, the HRC has also adopted a restrictive interpretation of the ICCPR in the absence of consensus among its member states. This is the

63 See Shany, 'All Roads Lead to Strasbourg?'.

64 ibid; Eyal Benvenisti, 'Margin of Appreciation, Consensus and Universal Standards' (1999) 31 *International Law and Politics* 843.

65 *Hertzberg and others v. Finland*, Communication no 61/1979 (HRC, 2 April 1982), 10.3.

66 *Faurisson v. France*, Communication no 550/1993 (HRC,8 November 1996); *Castañeda v. Mexico*, Communication no 2022/2012 (HRC, 18 July 2013) on the denial to disclose electoral materials to protect democracy; *Singh Bhinder v. Canada*, Communication no 208/1986 (HRC, 9 November 1989) on the prohibition to wear a religious attire for complying with safety requirements; *Prince v. South Africa*, Communication no 1474/2006 (HRC, 31 October 2007) on the prohibition to use cannabis in religious practices and *Paez v. Colombia*, Communication no 195/1985 (HRC, 12 July 1990) on the modality of religious education in public schools.

67 The doctrine of the minimum scrutiny or 'rational basis' has been taken from US constitutional law. cf *US v. Carolene Products Co.*, 304 US 144, 152 (1938) or *Craig v. Boren*, 429 US 190, 210–211 (Powell J., concurring) ('the relatively deferential "rational basis" standard of review normally applied takes on a sharper focus when we address a gender-based classification').

case, for example, for same-sex marriage, where the HRC provided a very literal interpretation of Article 23 ICCPR, leaving the possibility to its member states to extend it to same-sex couples or limit it to heterosexual couples.[68] Such an approach does not diverge much from the regional consensus doctrine applied by the ECtHR. However, a significant difference lies in the fact that the Committee experiences greater difficulties in establishing a consensus at the international level, counting 168 state parties with very diverse socio-political and cultural environments. In conclusion, the HRC is officially not adopting a MoA doctrine or any similar deferential approach. This is probably due to rhetorical or universalistic reasons,[69] or to the need to show independence from the ECtHR. Nonetheless, in practice, many MoA-like approaches found space in the HRC's case-law, granting deference and margin of discretion to the member states with a very similar outcome to that of the MoA in the European context.

Such a similarity in the final result could help explain the predominance of judicial convergence over fragmentation. On a final note, similarly to what happens in the case of the ECtHR, these deferential tools are not always and consistently used. Rather, their usage varies according to the facts of the cases and to the countries involved, thus creating further confusion on the standard of interpretation of the Committee and its jurisprudence.

6.4 THE AFRICAN COMMISSION AND COURT: IN SEARCH OF A MOA?

The ACommHPR and the ACtHPR have a very confused attitude towards deference and subsidiarity. Indeed, in the limited relevant case-law, it is possible to observe a cautious approach towards the MoA and some elements that suggest a willingness to embrace a stronger subsidiarity doctrine, granting more deference to member states.

In 1993, in the Final Declaration of the Regional Meeting for Africa, the African leaders agreed on the fact that 'the universal nature of human rights is beyond question; their protection and promotion are the duty of all states, regardless of their political, economic or cultural systems'.[70] However, they then added that 'no ready-made model can be prescribed at the universal level

[68] *Joslin v. New Zealand*, Communication no 902/1999 (HRC, 2003).

[69] See Dominic McGoldrick, 'A Defence of the Margin of Appreciation and an Argument for Its Application by the Human Rights Committee' (2016) 65 *International and Comparative Law Quarterly* 21.

[70] Final Declaration of the Regional Meeting for Africa of the World Conference on Human Rights in Report of the Regional Meeting for Africa of the World Conference on Human Rights, Tunis, 2–6 November 1992, UN Doc A/CONF.157/AFRM/14 (24 November 1992).

since the historical and cultural realities of each nation and the traditions, standards and values of each people cannot be disregarded'.[71] These two seemingly contrasting statements, the former in favour of a universal approach and the latter suggesting a very strong defence of the subsidiarity principle, reflect the struggle of the African bodies in their adjudication of human rights contentious cases.

In *Constitutional Rights Project and Another v. Nigeria*, the African Commission held that '[t]he African Charter should be interpreted in a culturally sensitive way, taking into full account the different legal traditions of Africa and finding expression through the laws of each country'.[72] However, the Commission never actually followed such an approach, which would be very deferential to its member states. In the more recent *Prince v. South Africa*, the Commission addressed in detail its attitude towards the MoA and subsidiarity.[73] The ACommHPR recognised that the principle of subsidiarity, as well as the MoA doctrine, is inherent to the African Charter. Moreover, as a regional body, the ACommHPR also acknowledged that it cannot 'claim to be better situated than local courts in advancing human and peoples' rights' and, therefore, states should have a certain 'latitude under specific Articles in allowing them to introduce limitations', because only the member states have 'direct and continuous knowledge of [their] society, needs, resources, economic and political situation, legal practice and the fine balance that need to be struck between the competing and sometimes conflicting forces that shape [their] society'.[74] Yet, the Commission pointed out that such a deference is not absolute and it is to be granted under its strict control. Moreover, no mention has ever been made in this or other cases to the role of regional consensus or to the practice of other member states in deciding a given case.

This partial opening to the MoA by the African Commission is not mirrored by the Court that, as to date, has never adopted the MoA doctrine or any MoA-like language. The only references made to it could be found in three cases. In the first one, *Tanganyika Law Society v. United Republic of Tanzania*, the Court summed up the existing international case-law on the assessment of legitimate restrictions to rights based on 'social needs', presenting the MoA doctrine as applied by the ECtHR.[75] However, in the merit stage, the Court

[71] ibid.

[72] *Constitutional Rights Project and Others v. Nigeria*, Communications no 140/94 and 145/95 (ACommHPR, November 1999), 26.

[73] *Prince v. South Africa*, Communication no 255/2002 (ACommHPR, 2004).

[74] ibid, 50–52.

[75] *Tanganyika Law Society v. United Republic of Tanzania*, Applications nos 9 and 11/2011 (ACtHPR, 14 June 2013), 107.2 ff.

did not mention it again, and it certainly did not apply to the given case, simply ruling that a discriminatory treatment for exclusion from electoral lists cannot be justified by 'social needs'.[76] Similarly, in *Ingabire Victoire Umhoza v. Republic of Rwanda*, the respondent state repeatedly invoked its MoA in applying the Charter, but the Court did not mention it at all in its merit stage, concluding that the restriction to the applicant's freedom of expression was in violation of the Charter as it was to be considered not necessary in a democratic society.[77] Finally, in 2020, the ACtHPR in *Jebra Kambole v. Tanzania* expressed its view on the MoA. While acknowledging the merits of the doctrine, citing *Prince v. South Africa*, it ultimately concluded that

> while it is for a particular State to determine the mechanisms or steps to be taken for purposes of implementing the Charter, [the Court] retains the jurisdiction to assess and review the steps taken for compliance with the Charter and other applicable human rights standards. In particular, the Court's duty is to assess if a fair balance has been struck between societal interests and the interests of the individual as protected under the Charter. The doctrine of margin of appreciation, therefore, while recognising legitimate leverage by States in the implementation of the Charter, cannot be used by States to oust the Court's supervisory jurisdiction.[78]

In conclusion, the position of both the African Court and Commission towards the MoA is not well defined, struggling between an explicit endorsement and a rejection of the doctrine. Such an eclectic approach could in some respect both favour convergence and produce unexpected episodes of fragmentation, depending on the specific circumstances of the cases.

6.5 EXPLAINING DEFERENCE AND SUBSIDIARITY DIFFERENCES: THE POLITICS OF THE COURTS AND COMMITTEE AND THEIR RELATIONSHIP WITH MEMBER STATES

The striking difference in the approach of the four jurisdictions under analysis towards deference and subsidiarity may have a wide range of causes. Among them, as suggested throughout the chapter, the politics surrounding those bodies and their relationship with member states appear significant. This may seem obvious considering that subsidiarity concerns the relationship between the national states and the regional or international institutions.

[76] ibid, 119 ff.

[77] *Ingabire Victoire Umhoza v. Republic of Rwanda*, Application no 3/2014 (ACtHPR, 24 November 2017), 124–127, 145, 162.

[78] *Jebra Kambole v. Tanzania*, Application no 18/2018 (ACtHPR, 15 July 2020), 78–82.

As often recalled throughout the book, the African, European and Inter-American systems had different historical developments and were deeply affected by the politics and history of their continents.[79] These elements deeply shaped the adjudicatory approach of the courts and their perceived role in the international human rights law system.

The ECtHR is the oldest regional body and has benefitted from the democratic stability of several, and arguably the most influential, of its member states.[80] Although the forty-seven member states of the Council of Europe have had different historical developments in relation to human rights and the rule of law, a substantial group of them, such as France, Germany, Italy, the United Kingdom, the Netherlands and all the Scandinavian countries, just to name a few, emerged after the Second World War as strong democratic countries. This allowed the Court to rely increasingly on their cooperation to implement the judgments, acquire legitimacy, show effectiveness and lower its workload. Indeed, the success of the court in terms of number of complaints it receives every year and the pressure to continue to be effective in terms of domestic implementation of its judgments led the ECtHR to grant more and more deference to its member states. This, in turn, sparkled an even stronger demand for deference from some member states, especially in response to some sensitive cases such *Hirst v. United Kingdom*,[81] concerning prisoners' voting rights, and *Lautsi v. Italy*,[82] on the mandatory display of a crucifix in public school classrooms. As a response to this, the principle of subsidiarity and the doctrine of the MoA found explicit recognition in the Brighton Declaration[83] and deference to member states overall increased. Moreover, as demonstrated by a recent study by Stiansen and Voeten, this backlash and request for more deference led democratic

[79] Christof Heyns and Magnus Killander, 'Universality and the Growth of Regional Systems' in Dina Shelton (ed), *The Oxford Handbook of International Human Rights Law* (Oxford University Press, 2013).

[80] Mikael Rask Madsen, 'From Boom to Backlash? The European Court of Human Rights and the Transformation of Europe' in Helmut P. Aust and Esra Demir Gursel (eds), *The European Court of Human Rights: Current Challenges in Historical Perspective* (Edward Elgar, 2021).

[81] *Hirst v. United Kingdom*, Application no 74025/01 (ECtHR, 30 March 2004).

[82] *Lautsi v. Italy*, Application no 30814/06 (ECtHR, 18 March 2011).

[83] Brighton Declaration. For a more detailed discussion of the Brighton Declaration backlash at the ECtHR see Mikael Rask Madsen, 'The Challenging Authority of the European Court of Human Rights: From Cold War Legal Diplomacy to the Brighton Declaration and Backlash' (2016) 79 *Law and Contemporary Problems* 141–178; Mikael Rask Madsen, Rebalancing European Human Rights: Has the Brighton Declaration Engendered a New Deal on Human Rights in Europe? (2017) 9 *Journal of International Dispute Settlement* 2, 199–222.

governments to gradually appoint more restrained judges and the Strasbourg Court has become more reluctant to rule against democratic states.[84]

This close relationship between the ECtHR and its member states is not only evident in the application of the MoA, but is also reflected in its practice of preferential judicial dialogue with national legislation or to the bias towards member states found in some specific contexts, such as on migrants' rights.[85]

On the contrary, the IACtHR, although similarly old as an institution, experienced a completely different relationship with its member states, leading more towards a clash than a cooperation. Due to the political instability, dictatorships and military coups that affected several member states throughout the last half century, the IACtHR quickly established itself as a stronghold of human rights and rule of law in conflict with the national states.[86] Differently from the ECtHR case, backlash from member states not happy with the jurisprudence of the IACtHR culminated in their withdrawal from the jurisdiction of the Court, such as in the case of Venezuela, rather than with increased deference, further acerbating the conflict between the IACtHR and its non-compliant member states.[87] This understanding of its role clearly does not align with strong deference to member states and although the principle of subsidiarity is present in the Inter-American system, it is interpreted by the Court in the most protective way for the applicant.

As for the African Court, the situation is uncertain, due to the fact that the court is still young and in search of its own adjudicatory approach. The relationship with its member states has been more similar to the IACtHR than to the ECtHR due the withdrawal of several states, including Rwanda, Tanzania and Benin of their declaration allowing direct application from NGOs and individuals.[88] However, the ACtHPR is still exploring all its

[84] Øyvind Stiansen and Erik Voeten, 'Backlash and Judicial Restraint: Evidence from the European Court of Human Rights' (2020) 64 *International Studies Quarterly* 4, 770–784.

[85] See, for instance, Marie-Bénédicte Dembour, *When Human Become Migrants: Study of the European Court of Human Rights with an Inter-American Counterpoint* (Oxford University Press, 2015).

[86] For a more detailed discussion of the history and evolution of the IACtHR see Yves Haeck, Oswaldo Ruiz-Chiriboga and Clara Burbano Herrera (eds), *The Inter-American Court of Human Rights: Theory and Practice, Present and Future* (Intersentia, 2015); Cecilia Medina Quiroga, *The American Convention on Human Rights: Crucial Rights in Their Theory and Practice* (Intersentia, 2016).

[87] Ximena Soley and Silvia Steininger, 'Partying Ways or Lashing Back? Withdrawals, Backlash and the Inter-American Court of Human Rights' (2018) 14 *International Journal of Law in Context* 2, 237–257.

[88] See Nicole de Silva and Misha Plagis, 'A Court in Crisis: African States' Increasing Resistance to Africa's Human Rights Court', Opinio Juris, 19 May 2020, available at http://opiniojuris.org/2020/05/19/a-court-in-crisis-african-states-increasing-resistance-to-africas-human-rights-court/.

options and, as shown above, is circumspectly looking also at some deferential options.

Against the background of the regional human rights systems, the UN HRC emerges with completely different features.[89] Its international and universal standing and role, as well as the need to show independence from any specific member state or region, makes it very reluctant to fully accept a doctrine of deference. In addition to that, the fact that several of its cases concern countries where democracy and the rule of law are yet to be enforced makes it even harder to indulge in a deferential approach.

6.6 WHAT IMPACT MAY THE MOA HAVE ON FRAGMENTATION AND CONVERGENCE?

The previous sections showed a variegated picture of approaches towards deference and subsidiarity, ranging from the strong subsidiary ECtHR's MoA to the opposite CC doctrine at the IACtHR.

The question now is to what extent the differences or similarities in understanding deference and subsidiarity or the recourse to a 'regional consensus' may actually determine cases of fragmentation or convergence between the four jurisdictions. There is certainly a correlation between a similar use and understanding of these elements and convergence but not enough to establish a cause-effect link. This is mostly because there is not much case-law from the IACtHR and the African bodies on issues and rights where the ECtHR usually grants wide MoA, such as right to privacy, religion, assembly and association and expression.

The following sections will present some selected examples of cases where the doctrines on deference and subsidiarity played a key role in reaching convergence or generating fragmentation, in order to show how the use of the MoA doctrine can lead to fragmentation or convergence.

6.6.1 *Fostering Convergence*

When two bodies adopt similar approaches to deference and subsidiarity, it is logical to expect that this would ease the maintenance of convergence in their case-law. Notably, two paradigmatic examples will be presented to show this dynamic: the case-law of the ECtHR and the HRC on the restriction of

89 See, among others Helen Keller and Geir Ulfstein (eds), *UN Human Rights Treaty Bodies: Law and Legitimacy* (Cambridge University Press, 2012)

freedom of expression for the protection of public morals and the case-law of the four systems on defamation.

6.6.1.1 The ECtHR and HRC on the Restriction to Freedom of Expression for the Protection of Public Morals

The adoption of the MoA by the HRC in *Hertzberg*[90] was very much in line with the reasoning of the ECtHR in *Handyside*.[91] The HRC's case concerned the censorship of a broadcasting programme on homosexuality for the protection of public morals while the ECtHR's case, as recalled before, was related to the destruction of a book containing sexual and drug references for the protection of public morals as well. What makes the two rulings converging is not just the outcome, that is, finding no violation of the freedom of expression of the applicant, but the reasoning on what constitutes 'public morals' and how the ECtHR or the HRC should assess the proportionality of the restriction to the pursuing of the legitimate aim.

On the one hand, the HRC held that '[...] public morals differ widely. There is no universally applicable common standard. Consequently, in this respect, a certain margin of discretion must be accorded to the responsible national authorities'.[92] On the other hand, in a very similar formulation, the ECtHR held that 'it is not possible to find in the domestic law of the various Contracting States a uniform European conception of morals. The view taken by their respective laws of the requirements of morals varies from time to time and from place to place [...]. Consequently, Article 10 para. 2 leaves the Contracting States a margin of appreciation'.[93]

The two approaches are clearly similar if not identical, putting the two bodies precisely on the same page. A less deferential approach by one of the two bodies would have probably led to different reasoning and conclusions, ultimately triggering fragmentation. Even if the HRC has now changed its approach on the substantial matter of the prohibition of homosexuality as a threat to public morals, what matters is the method used for assessing the proportionality of the restriction, applying a highly deferential model. After *Hertzberg*, the HRC has never again discussed either the meaning of public morals or the way of assessing what fits within such a category, supporting the hypothesis that its understanding has not changed.

90 *Hertzberg*, HRC.
91 *Handyside*, ECtHR.
92 *Hertzberg*, HRC.
93 *Handyside*, ECtHR, 48.

This convergence of the two bodies in granting considerable deference to their contracting parties when dealing with a restriction based on public morals could be explained by the sensitive nature of what constitutes public morals. Indeed, if, on the one hand, there is the consistent approach of the ECtHR on the use of the MoA, on the other hand, there is the exceptional deference of the HRC to its member states. The latter could be justified by the desire of the HRC not to establish an ultimate definition of what is public morals, an assessment that is impossible to make without risking to uphold a culturally biased approach. This is particularly important for the HRC, which has jurisdiction over 168 countries with different cultural, historical, social and religious backgrounds. Without defining what constitutes public morals, the HRC decided to avoid entering the dispute, which could have likely been criticised as an imposition of some values over others. The MoA-like language is the solution that the HRC found in this situation in order to respect the state party's cultural identity. By doing so, the HRC fulfilled its universalistic mission of setting a very general and broad standard for everyone while respecting the relativist approach of each state party and fully converging with the ECtHR.

This situation of convergence is likely to last due to the continuous interest of the HRC in maintaining its cultural neutrality and the omnipresent MoA doctrine in the ECtHR. However, due to the limited number of HRC cases on the matter it is impossible to conclude that the Committee has a well-established approach to the issue and only future case-law will confirm such a hypothesis.

6.6.1.2 The MoA in Defamation Cases

Another example of how a similar approach to deference led to convergence is that of defamation against public figures. Here, one can observe a slightly different phenomenon – the agreement of all the bodies on not granting a margin of discretion but, rather, on limiting such discretion to certain specific situations.

Two cases in particular could be compared, *Canese v. Paraguay*[94] before the IACtHR and *Dąbrowski v. Poland*[95] before the ECtHR. Both cases concerned the conviction of a journalist for having published alleged defamatory articles against public figures. The IACtHR, in finding a violation of the freedom of expression of Mr Canese, held that 'democratic control exercised

[94] *Ricardo Canese v. Paraguay* (IACtHR, 31 August 2004).
[95] *Dąbrowski v. Poland*, Application no 18235/02 (ECtHR, 19 December 2006).

by society through public opinion encourages the transparency of State activities and promotes the accountability of public officials in public administration, for which there should be a *reduced margin* for any restriction on political debates or debates on matters of public interest'.[96] Similarly, the ECtHR held that 'it is in the first place for the national authorities to assess whether there is a "pressing social need" for the restriction and, in making their assessment, they enjoy a certain margin of appreciation. In cases concerning the press, the national margin of appreciation is circumscribed by the interest of democratic society in ensuring and maintaining a free press'.[97] Moreover, it later concluded that 'having regard to the above considerations, the applicant's conviction was disproportionate to the legitimate aim pursued, having regard in particular to the interest of a democratic society in ensuring and maintaining the freedom of the press'.[98]

The two cases show that, despite the IACtHR's apparent distance from the ECtHR on the deference doctrine, its approach in defamation cases significantly converged with that of the ECtHR. More precisely, the IACtHR did not recognise the theory of the MoA but agreed with the ECtHR on the point that, in certain circumstances, the 'margin of discretion' of the member states should be limited as for the restriction of fundamental rights. This could possibly suggest an implicit acceptance of the MoA doctrine by the IACtHR. However, even without delving into this realm of speculation, one needs to recognise that the two regional courts shared the same approach towards the latitude of discretion member states should enjoy in the given situation, ultimately leading to a full convergence of their case-law. The position of both courts has been confirmed by many other cases on defamation against public figures even without such an explicit reference to the margin of discretion, thus confirming their consistent approach.[99]

The same attitude towards the matter could be found in the case-law of the HRC and of the two African bodies. In *Rafael Marquez de Morais v. Angola* before the HRC,[100] *Konaté Issa v. Burkina Faso* before the ACtHPR[101] or *Kenneth Good v. Botswana* before the ACommHPR,[102] similar facts were submitted with almost identical reasoning and outcomes. The three bodies

[96] *Canese*, IACtHR, 97.
[97] *Dąbrowski*, ECtHR, 31.
[98] ibid, 37.
[99] cf *Bodrožić v. Serbia*, Application no 32550/05 (ECtHR, 23 June 2009); *Karman v. Russia*, Application no 29372/02 (ECtHR, 14 December 2006) and *Herrera Uloa*, IACtHR.
[100] *Marquez de Morais v. Angola*, Communication no 1128/02 (HRC, 29 March 2005).
[101] *Lohé Issa Konaté v. Burkina Faso*, Application no 004/2013 (ACtHPR, 5 December 2014).
[102] *Kenneth Good v. Botswana*, Communication no 313/05 (ACommHPR, 26 May 2010).

recognised the importance of freedom of expression as a key element for the survival of democracy and they upheld that, in cases of alleged defamation against public figures, a higher level of criticism should be tolerated, thus limiting the discretion of the state parties on the restriction of freedom of expression and the respective penalties. The three cases did not mention the MoA nor did they explicitly use the terminology of 'margin' or 'discretion', even though both the HRC and the African bodies proved to be in other circumstances more open to the MoA doctrine than the IACtHR.[103] Nevertheless, the underlying assumption could be considered similar. By stating that there should be higher tolerance for defamation against public figures, the HRC and the African bodies are, de facto, restricting the margin of discretion of the state parties in deciding when and how to pose lawful restrictions to the freedom of expression of their citizens. However, this remains at a hypothetical level, and only future case-law could confirm this interpretation or show that these bodies simply decided not to engage with the MoA. Nonetheless, what led to convergence in this case was not the common resort to a deferential approach but rather the decision of according less deference to the contracting states when defamation against public figures is involved.

The ultimate reasons behind this convergent attitude are hard to identify with certainty, but the increasing attention of the civil society and international organisations (IOs) to the matter of criminalisation of defamation may have contributed to its development, together with the campaigns of NGOs and other civil society actors in support of the freedom of expression of journalists who denounce abuses and wrongdoings of politicians.[104] As it will be addressed in detail in the following chapter, NGOs and civil society could have a considerable impact on human rights adjudication through lobbying and participation in litigation.[105] In general, considering the well-established jurisprudence on the matter across systems, I would argue with confidence that the convergence of the case-law on this matter is solid and meant to last, together with the understanding of a 'lower margin of discretion' to be accorded to the state parties.

[103] See, Section 6.4 on the HRC and Section 6.5 on the African bodies.

[104] See, for example, the work done by Pen International, MLDI, International Press Institute and Article 19, culminating in the Principles on Freedom of Expression and Reputation, first adopted in 2000 and then amended in 2015, that received the endorsement of the UN, OAS and CoE. See also Chapter 7 on the role of NGOs.

[105] See Section 7.7.1.

6.6.2 *Triggering Fragmentation*

The doctrine of the MoA and related subsidiarity and deference approaches can also trigger fragmentation, especially when two bodies adopt significantly different attitudes. Many scholars highlighted how the different attitude of the ECtHR on the one side and the IACtHR, HRC and African bodies on the other could hypothetically increase the likelihood of fragmentation.[106] However, few are the cases in which this threat becomes real and fragmentation arises.

The following two examples will show how a different use of the MoA triggered fragmentation in cases related to the freedom to manifest religion and the restriction to freedom of expression for the protection of public morals.

6.6.2.1 The ECtHR and HRC on the Restriction to Freedom of Wearing Religious Attire

The most significant example, for its relevance and number of cases involved, is the case of fragmentation between the HRC and the ECtHR on the restriction of the freedom to wear religious attire already presented in Chapter 2.[107] The three main issues at stake were the prohibition to wear the Sikh turban in official identification documents in *Ranjit Singh v. France* and *Mann Singh v. France*, the prohibition to wear the headscarf in educational premises in *Leyla Şahin v. Turkey* and *Raihon Hudoyberganova v. Uzbekistan* and *F.A. v. France* and the prohibition of wearing a full-face veil in *S.A.S. v. France* and *Yaker v. France*.[108]

In the *Mann Singh* case, the ECtHR ruled that the prohibition of wearing the Sikh turban in an identity photograph did not amount to a violation of freedom of religion because the restriction, justified by public order, fell

[106] McGoldrick, 'Affording States a Margin of Appreciation'; McGoldrick, 'A Defence of the Margin of Appreciation'; Legg, *The Margin of Appreciation*; Marjan Ajevski, 'Fragmentation in International Human Rights Law – Beyond Conflict of Laws' (2014) 32 *Nordic Journal of Human Rights* 87.

[107] cf Chapter 2, Section 2.2.2 for a detailed discussion of the cases.

[108] *Mann Singh v. France*, Application no 24479/07 (ECtHR, 11 June 2007); *Ranjit Singh v. France*, Communication no 1876/2000 (HRC, 11–29 July 2011); *Raihon Hudoyberganova v. Uzbekistan*, Communication no 931/2000 (HRC, 8 December 2004); *Leyla Şahin v. Turkey*, Application no 44774/98 (ECtHR, 10 November 2005); *F.A. v. France*, Communication no 2662/2015 (HRC, 16 July 2018); *S.A.S. v. France*, Application no 43835/11 (ECtHR, 1 July 2014) and *Yaker v. France*, Communication no 2747/2016 (HRC, 17 July 2018).

within the margin of appreciation granted to its member states.[109] On the contrary, in *Ranjit Singh*, the HRC did not afford any margin of discretion to France and went on assessing the proportionality and necessity of the restriction, concluding that it constituted a violation of the ICCPR.[110] The only element that determines a different outcome in the two cases is the different deferential approach of the two bodies.

Similarly, the determining factor for deciding *Leyla Şahin* and *Raihon Hudoyberganova* or *F.A.* differently was the opposite position on the granting of a MoA for justifying the restriction of the freedom of religion of the two applicants.[111] If, on the one hand, the ECtHR considered that it was within the MoA of Turkey to prohibit wearing a headscarf in a public university for protecting national security, on the other hand, the HRC ruled straight away that such an infringement of the freedom of religion amounted to a violation of the ICCPR.[112]

Although in *S.A.S. v. France* and *Yaker v. France*, what ultimately diverged was the interpretation of what legitimate aim was considered valid for the restriction of freedom of religion, the MoA played a key role anyway. One of the reasons why the ECtHR accepted France's justification for a full-face veil ban for protecting the 'living together' was a wide degree of subsidiarity to France in deciding what is needed to ensure the enjoyment of the rights of others and, therefore, what are the conditions for the 'living together'.[113] On the contrary, the HRC did not grant such deference and rejected France's claim altogether.

In addition, also in *Jasvir Singh v. France*, *Aktas v. France* and *Bikramjit Singh v. France*, the ECtHR and the HRC diverged by an opposite deferential approach.[114] The cases concerned the prohibition for pupils to wear a *keski* (a small hat similar to a turban) in schools. The first two applications, brought before the ECtHR, were declared manifestly ill-founded based on the Court's reasoning in *Dogru v. France* and *Kervanci v. France*.[115] Here the ECtHR argued that it was within the MoA of its member states to decide how to

[109] *Mann Singh*, ECtHR, 8.

[110] *Ranjit Singh*, HRC, 9.

[111] *Hudoyberganova*, HRC; *Leyla Şahin*, ECtHR.

[112] cf Tom Lewis, 'What Not to Wear: Religious Rights, the European Court, and the Margin of Appreciation' (2007) 56 *International and Comparative Law Quarterly* 395.

[113] *S.A.S. v. France*, Application no 43835/11 (ECtHR, 1 July 2014), 141–142, 153 and 157.

[114] *Jasvir Singh v. France*, Application no 25463/08 (ECtHR, 30 June 2009); *Aktas v. France*, Application no 43563/08 (ECtHR, 30 June 2009); *Bikramjit Singh v. France*, Communication no 1852/2008 (HRC, 4 February 2013).

[115] *Dogru v. France*, Application no 27058/05(ECtHR, 4 December 2008); *Kervanci v. France*, Application no 31645/04 (ECtHR, 4 December 2008).

protect religious pluralism, state secularism and national security and health. In light of that, such a restriction pursuing the legitimate aim of safeguarding health and security was not disproportionate and did not constitute a violation of Article 9 ECHR.[116]

On the contrary, the HRC in *Bikramjit Singh v. France* did not consider France to have provided an adequate explanation for restricting the freedom of religion of the applicant. It argued that the state 'had not furnished compelling evidence that, by wearing his *keski*, the author would have posed a threat to the rights and freedoms of other pupils or to order at school'.[117] The Committee imposed high scrutiny over the state and, on this basis, reached an opposite conclusion. While the ECtHR held a consistent approach towards a strong application of the MoA doctrine, the HRC decided here to adopt a completely different approach from that of *Hertzberg*. The reason for this different attitude may lie on the same rationale – the desire of abstaining from taking any position that could be perceived as culturally biased, especially from a western and Christian perspective. However, if in *Hertzberg* the adoption of the MoA was the way to avoid taking a side, in *Hudoyberganova, F.A.* and *Mann* the MoA would have meant taking the position of the member state and, thus, taking a clear stance against the freedom to wear religious (non-Christian) attire in specific situations. By ruling in favour of the applicant, the HRC reiterated its commitment to safeguard the freedom of religion of everyone and drove away any criticism about it being western-Christian centred, especially in a time when the relationship between the Islam world and the Western values was particularly tense. Regardless of the alleged hidden willingness of the HRC to embrace the MoA,[118] in this case, the HRC had to take into consideration its nature and role before adopting any MoA-like doctrine. Considering that more than half of the HRC's state parties are majority Muslim countries and that the issue of restriction of non-Christian religious attire in Europe was very topical at the moment, the HRC was under the spotlight, and a different ruling would have been welcomed with prejudice.

This situation of fragmentation, MoA-wise, is likely to continue and affect future cases with similar facts since the motivations behind the different deferential approach by the ECtHR and the HRC are still in place and are part of the core identity of the two bodies.

[116] ibid, 70–74.
[117] Bikramjit Singh, ECtHR, 8.7.
[118] See Bikramjit Singh, ECtHR, 4 and Shany, 'All Roads Lead to Strasbourg?'.

6.6.2.2 The ECtHR and IACtHR on the Restriction to Freedom of Expression for the Protection of Public Morals and Religion

An opposite approach towards deference and subsidiarity could be considered the triggering cause for fragmentation also between the ECtHR and the IACtHR in two cases related to the restriction of freedom of expression for the protection of rights of others. *Wingrove v. United Kingdom*[119] and *Olmedo-Bustos v. Chile*,[120] better known as the 'Last Temptation of Christ' case, share very similar facts, namely the licence denied to distribute a movie on the basis that it contained highly offensive scenes for a Christian public. Yet, the two courts ruled in opposite ways.

The ECtHR rejected the claim of the applicant, affording the United Kingdom a wide margin of appreciation in 'regulating freedom of expression in relation to matters liable to offend intimate personal convictions within the sphere of morals, or, especially, religion'.[121] Two were the main reasons adduced by the Court: the lack of a regional consensus on the matter and the 'better position' rationale of the state in solving such a conflict of rights.[122] In contrast, the IACtHR considered denying the licence a violation of the applicant's freedom of expression and, adopting the CC doctrine, it demanded a change of the Chilean law on prior censorship.[123] The decision of the IACtHR to apply high scrutiny and rule on the merit of whether the screening of the movie was offensive as to infringe the freedom of religion of others is perfectly in line with its position on the matter. Contrary to the 'better position' rationale of the ECtHR, the IACtHR opted for a more 'activist' approach, operating more like a domestic High Court rather than a supra-national body. Ignoring any concern about the existence of regional consensus on what offends morals and religion and looking exclusively at the Chilean case, the IACtHR ruled with the aim of rendering a final and clear judgment to the detriment of the principle of subsidiarity but to the advantage of the applicants and of the clarity and foreseeability of the law.

This case is, indeed, an example of the different approaches taken by the IACtHR and the ECtHR towards subsidiarity, leading to fragmentation when issues like religion or morals, where the ECtHR applies the MoA doctrine almost in any case, are involved. The reason why there are only a few

[119] *Wingrove v. UK*, Application no 17419/90 (ECtHR, 25 November 1996).
[120] *The Last Temptation of Christ*, IACtHR.
[121] *Wingrove*, ECtHR, 58.
[122] ibid, 58–63.
[123] *The Last Temptation of Christ*, IACtHR, 71–72.

examples of fragmentation is that the IACtHR has a very limited case-law involving restriction of the freedom of expression for the protection of morals or religion. However, there is a high likelihood that cases involving these matters will increasingly be brought to the attention of the IACtHR. In particular, it will be interesting to see whether the Inter-American Court will stick to its 'activist' and non-deferential approach, thus keeping fragmentation, or it will be convinced by the necessity to adopt a MoA-language and restore convergence.

CONCLUSION

The ECtHR, IACtHR, HRC and African bodies have dealt differently with the principles of deference and subsidiarity. Some institutions share similar attitudes while others have adopted fundamentally different approaches to the issue.

The use of a MoA or a CC doctrine significantly affects the reasoning of these bodies and the outcome of the cases. Indeed, the similar or different deferential approaches and the adoption or not of the MoA could be invoked as causes for both convergence and fragmentation. This is especially the case in the domain of freedom of expression and religion, which is subject to significant restrictions based on sensitive competing interests and rights, such as public morals or national security. How a judicial or quasi-judicial body decides to interact with its state parties and whether it is advisable to opt for a more or less deferential approach is a matter that intimately concerns that body, and it is strictly linked with its historical and socio-political context.[124] Considering the deep difference between the ECtHR's MoA and the IACtHR's CC, I would tend to argue that we still don't have much fragmentation only because the case-law of the IACtHR on the right to privacy, expression, religion and assembly/association is still limited.

As it has been observed in the case of the HRC, the MoA can be used or not according to the issues at stake, in order to fulfil a specific agenda or to maintain a certain neutrality. The MoA is a very useful tool to respect the diversity of the contracting parties and avoid taking one side on sensitive issues, but it has the drawback of limiting the action of the judicial body in improving human rights protection. Whether it should be advisable for all the institutions to adopt a MoA doctrine is a question that goes beyond the scope of this book. However, I would argue that a limited use of the MoA or any

[124] Ignacio de la Rasilla del Moral, 'The Increasingly Marginal Appreciation of the Margin of Appreciation Doctrine' (2006) 6(7) *German Law Journal* 611.

similar deferential approach is useful to deal with particularly delicate issues or in cases of strong differences among the state parties and should therefore be welcomed. Still, when the resort to the MoA is frequent, like in the case of the ECtHR, it can lead to adverse consequences such as struggles with domestic judges' compliance with the ECtHR's judgments and, more generally, a chaotic and inconsistent jurisprudence that may slow down and affect the advancement of human rights protection.

Yet, such an important element should be carefully monitored in a comparative perspective being a 'too important piece to be left out of any consideration of fragmentation [. . .] especially given the doctrine's unpredictability at the moment'.[125] Indeed, the extensive use of the MoA by the ECtHR and the unclear and inconsistent adoption by the HRC and the African Commission and Court significantly affects the 'convergence-fragmentation' picture by practically preventing an ultimate assessment of the two phenomena and a clear understanding of the regional and international approach towards a certain issue.

What is more, a strong doctrine of the MoA as adopted by the ECtHR, which is based on a case-by-case analysis, makes it harder to assess which is the ultimate position of the Court on a certain matter of law and how the Convention should be interpreted according to the European judges. Arguably, the ECtHR is increasingly applying the MoA doctrine and in a more and more robust way.[126] Such inflationary use results in inconsistencies in its application and a lack of clarity in the ECtHR's case-law. This will not allow the assessment of fragmentation, but rather maintain an uncertain seemingly convergence, with sporadic cases of fragmentation. As observed by Brauch, the MoA prevents the elaboration of a clear standard of interpretation of the ECHR and it does not allow a proper comparison of the ECtHR jurisprudence with that of the other bodies, leaving any assessment to a case-by-case one.[127] Such a blurred picture, complicated by the lack of clarity on

[125] Marjan Ajevski, 'Freedom of Speech as Related to Journalists in the ECtHR, IACtHR and the Human Rights Committee – A Study of Fragmentation' (2014) 32 *Nordic Journal of Human Rights* 118, 130.

[126] Spano, 'Universality or Diversity of Human Rights?', 497–502; Jan Kratochvíl, 'The Inflation of the Margin of Appreciation by the European Court of Human Rights' (2011) 29 *Netherlands Quarterly of Human Rights* 324.

[127] Jeffrey A. Brauch, 'The Margin of Appreciation and the Jurisprudence of the European Court of Human Rights: Threat to the Rule of Law' (2005) 11 *Columbia Journal of European Law* 113.

the definition of what constitutes regional consensus,[128] may prevent the establishment of proper fragmentation.

The contradiction within the case-law of a body coupled with the unpredictability that comes with an inconsistent use of the MoA inevitably affects the foreseeability of the law and ultimately leads to a chaotic case-law that may constantly swing between fragmentation and convergence. Due to the limited case-law of the HRC, ACommHPR, ACtHPR and in particular of the IACtHR on issues where a deferential approach could be applied, fragmentation is still very limited. However, the increasing use of the CC doctrine by the IACtHR together with new and diversified cases may, in the future, trigger fragmentation.

[128] Dzehtsiarou, *European Consensus and the Legitimacy of the European Court of Human Rights*.

7

Outside the Courtroom

The Role of NGOs and the Obstacles to Litigation

INTRODUCTION

The second part of this book has discussed a wide range of legal and non-legal factors that influence the adjudication of IHRL cases and could trigger fragmentation or maintain convergence. When analysing the outcome of a judgment, we often tend to look only at what happens inside the courtroom, forgetting that there is a whole world outside it that could potentially affect to a great extent the interpretation of the law and the adjudication of a case. Judicial convergence and fragmentation can be triggered only when a human rights body actually decide on a given case. Yet, there may be several reasons why a case does not reach that stage in the first place or has a different impact on the judges and commissioners called to adjudicate it. Throughout the previous chapters, the book has already discussed how the history and politics of regional human rights bodies, as well as their member states, have a huge impact on their case-law and inform the development and adoption of several legal techniques and tests. In addition to that, this last chapter explores two further factors: the role of non-governmental organisations (NGOs) and the obstacles for a case to reach the merit stage.

First, it briefly investigates the role of non-governmental organisations, suggesting to what extent they can lead to convergence or fragmentation through their litigation, advocacy and lobbying activities.

Second, it addresses the situations where fragmentation does not arise because the cases do not reach the merit stage. This may happen as a consequence of the resort to friendly settlement, or when the human rights body encourages the applicant to withdraw the case or, finally, when there is no NGO or other legal aid for bringing the case before the judicial or quasi-judicial body.

7.1 THE ROLE OF NON-GOVERNMENTAL ORGANISATIONS

It is well recognised by scholars and practitioners that non-governmental organisations play a fundamental role in promoting and protecting human rights and they do so also by engaging with regional and international human rights bodies.[1] The proliferation of human rights judicial and quasi-judicial bodies increased the possibilities and ways for NGOs to participate in the work of UNTBs and regional courts and commissions.[2] Such an expanding engagement also gives them the power to influence, directly or indirectly, the arising of fragmentation or the maintenance of convergence between the bodies. The goal of human rights NGOs should be the promotion and protection of human rights around the world and, therefore, they should benefit from a convergence among regional systems, since it makes their argument stronger in their lobbying campaign with national governments. Therefore, we can assume that non-governmental organisations are generally keen to achieve and maintain convergence among systems or to give rise to fragmentation only when it means setting a higher standard of protection (a sort of positive fragmentation). Several interviews with human rights NGOs involved in litigation and other activities with the bodies under analysis confirmed their willingness to contribute to the maintenance of convergence in IHRL. Yet, they all stressed that their main intent remains to ensure justice to victims of human rights abuses on a case-by-case basis.[3]

1 Heidi Nichols Haddad, *The Hidden Hands of Justice: NGOs, Human Rights and International Court* (Cambridge University Press, 2018); Mohamed Abdelsalam, 'Individual and Ngo Participation in Human Rights Litigation before the African Court of Human and Peoples' Rights: Lessons From the European and Inter-American Courts of Human Rights' (1999) 8 *MSU-DCL Journal of International Law* 377, 377–396; George E. Edwards, 'Assessing the Effectiveness of Human Rights Non-Governmental Organizations (NGOs) from the Birth of the United Nations to the Twenty-First Century: Ten Attributes of Highly Successful Human Rights NGOs' (2010) 18 *Michigan State International Law Review* 165; Myrinne F. Rietveld, 'NGO Participation in Regional Human Rights Systems. A Comparison of Europe and the Americas' (2015) (Master thesis, Leiden University); Shamima Ahmed, 'The Impact of NGOs on International Organisations: Complexities and Considerations' (2010) 36(3) *Brooklyn Journal of International Law* 817, 817–840; Ximena Soley, 'The Crucial Role of Human Rights NGOs in the Inter-American System' (2019) 113 *AJIL Unbound* 355–359; Laura van den Eynde, 'Encouraging Judicial Dialogue. The Contribution of Human Rights NGOs' Briefs to the European Court of Human Rights' in Amrei Muller and Hege Elisabeth Kjos (eds), *Judicial Dialogue and Human Rights* (Cambridge University Press, 2017).

2 Heidi Nichols Haddad, 'Judicial Institution Builders: NGOs and International Human Rights Courts Judicial Institution Builders' (2012) 11(1) *Journal of Human Rights* 126, 130.

3 Interviews conducted between January 2017 and December 2019 by the author with eight human rights NGOs (who wished to remain confidential) operating in Africa, the Americas

In light of this, we can assume that the more NGOs engage with HR bodies, the higher is the likelihood of convergence or of fragmentation that increases the degree of protection for the applicant the NGO is vouching for.

Although generally underexplored in literature, the engagement of NGOs with human rights bodies has recently received some attention by a few scholars, highlighting the important role they play in shaping international human rights adjudication.[4] In this section, I will only give some brief account of the modalities and channels available to NGOs for interacting with the four jurisdictions under analysis. The first section explores the way NGOs can engage with regional and international bodies by actively participating in the litigation stage in different capacities. On the contrary, the second section focuses on how these organisations can have an impact on regional and international human rights bodies through a wide range of other ways, such as providing technical or financial support, lobbying or monitoring activities.

7.1.1 *Litigation*

Non-governmental organisations play an increasingly important role in international litigation.[5] In line with the respective charters, conventions and rules of procedures, NGOs can, in general, participate in the litigation phase in different capacities: they may institute cases or intervene as parties, provide assistance for fact-finding or legal analysis, testify or present *amici curiae*.

A significant study carried out by Mayer in 2011 revealed that the NGOs involvement in the ECtHR and Inter-American system takes place primarily through the representation of alleged victims of human rights violations.[6] The study was limited to the period between 2000 and 2009 and analysed only the intervention of NGOs in cases decided on merit. However, it shows a development of the NGOs' participation in regional human rights adjudication and some differences between the regional systems. NGOs' participation has increased over time in all regional systems, thanks to the possibility of NGOs to intervene both as an applicant and as representative of the applicants

and Europe and focusing, in particular on freedom of expression, freedom of religion, right to privacy and enforced disappearances and torture.

4 See, in particular, Haddad, *The Hidden Hands of Justice*; Soley, 'The Crucial Role of Human Rights NGOs'; van den Eynde, 'Encouraging Judicial Dialogue'.

5 Dinah Shelton, 'The Participation of Nongovernmental Organizations in International Judicial Proceedings' (1994) 88(4) *The American Journal of International Law* 611, 611–642.

6 Lloyd Hitoshi Mayer, 'NGO Standing and Influence on Regional Human Rights Courts and Commissions' (2011) 36(3) *Brooklyn Journal of International Law* 911, 911–946.

and due to the increasing interest of these organisations in human rights litigation. Moreover, it highlighted how NGOs engaged with 78 per cent of the cases that the IACtHR considered in the merits, with 68 per cent in the case of the ACommHPR and with only 4 per cent in the case of the ECtHR. Considering the assumed position of NGOs on convergence and fragmentation, such a disparity could contribute to explaining the activism of the Inter-American and African bodies towards convergence, absent in the ECtHR, probably encouraged by NGOs. Bearing in mind that the low percentage for the ECtHR is largely due to the fact that it issued a significantly higher number of cases compared to the other two bodies during this period, a possible additional reason for this difference could be also the availability of legal aid in the European system. This financial support, not available in the Americas or Africa, 'makes representing alleged victims more financially attractive to private lawyers in Europe'.[7] Unfortunately, the study does not extend to the analysis of which are the issues or rights that see the highest intervention of NGOs, as it will provide insightful information for drawing further links with the existence of convergence and fragmentation.

As illustrated in the following section of this chapter, cultural, historical and political reasons may influence the decision of an NGO to litigate a particular case before a given body, encouraging convergence simply because any risk is carefully weighted, and controversial cases with a low likelihood of success are avoided.[8]

Moreover, interviews with the ECtHR judges showed that reliable and well-known NGOs bringing cases on behalf of the victims could be very influential for the final adjudication, thanks also to their reputation and the media and public opinion's attention they can bring on the case.[9] This has been further confirmed by the interviewed NGOs, which considered raising awareness on the case as one of their objectives when deciding to litigate a case.[10] As for the HRC, NGOs do not have standing before the Committee, but they can bring a case on behalf of the victims as their representatives.[11]

[7] ibid, 936.

[8] Considerations confirmed by interviews with several NGOs involved in litigation on a wide range of rights across the five bodies. Interviews held between July and December 2017.

[9] Interviews with judges of the ECtHR held in person in Strasbourg on 6 and 7 July 2017, and with members of the HRC in Geneva and Aarhus between July and September 2017.

[10] Interviews with NGOs involved in litigation before the regional and international human rights bodies held between May and October 2017.

[11] Anna-Karin Lindblom, *Non-Governmental Organisations in International Law* (Cambridge University Press, 2005), 227–229.

7.1.1.1 Amicus Curiae

Amici curiae are an advantageous, inexpensive and one of the most influential ways for a non-governmental organisation to take part in the proceedings before human rights bodies. Compared to bringing a case in representation of the victim, it is a less costly and time-consuming alternative, and it is a more flexible instrument that does not bind the organisation in the future.[12] Schachter defines them as 'lobbyist and advocate tools, vindicators of the politically powerless'.[13] *Amici curiae*, or third-party interventions, may provide additional legal arguments missed by the parties, supplementary and detailed analysis of some points of law or support for the judges in areas of novel and problematic litigation. When analysed in the context of judicial convergence and fragmentation, amicus briefs definitely encourage judicial dialogue, as they often include extensive references to international case-law on the matter, and, therefore, support overall convergence or fragmentation when it leads to a higher level of human rights protection.

The IACtHR makes a large use of this insightful tool that helps it to be informed of other possible perspectives on human rights law interpretation and extends its knowledge. Recent studies reveal that in the last thirty-five years the Court received more than 500 *amici* from NGOs, academic institutions, research centres and private individuals on more than 100 cases.[14] The impact of *amici curiae* on the IACtHR's adjudication is, though, very hard to assess.[15] Non-governmental organisations and other institutions submitted *amici* briefs in important cases such as *Loayza Tamayo v. Peru*[16] on the application of the principle of *non bis in idem*, *Bámaca Velásquez v. Guatemala*[17] on the right to truth and *Mayagna (Sumo) Awas Tingni Community v. Nicaragua*[18] on indigenous peoples' rights. However, the IACtHR rarely mentioned them in its reasoning.

Nevertheless, scholars agree on the increasing importance and influence that *amici* exercise on the IACtHR even besides the mere outcome of the

[12] Shelton, 'The Participation of Nongovernmental Organisations in International Judicial Proceedings'.

[13] Madeleine Schachter, 'The Utility of Pro Bono Representation of U.S.-Based Amicus Curiae in NON-U.S. and Multinational Courts as a Means of Advancing the Public Interest' (2004) 28 (1) *Fordham International Law Journal* 88, 89–91.

[14] ibid, 105–108.

[15] Shelton, 'The Participation of Nongovernmental Organisations in International Judicial Proceedings'; Lindblom, *Non-Governmental Organisations in International Law*, 350–359.

[16] *Loyaza-Tamayo v. Peru* (IACtHR, 17 September 1997).

[17] *Bámaca Velásquez v. Guatemala* (IACtHR, 25 November 2000).

[18] *Mayagna (Sumo) Awas Tingni Community v. Nicaragua* (IACtHR, 31 August 2001).

judgments.[19] Indeed, in addition to the immediate impact that they may have on the Court's ruling, *amici curiae* contribute to creating awareness of the Court's jurisprudence since they are distributed through local, national, regional and international networks and often help to promote the Court's activities through press releases, blogs and social media.[20]

To a lesser extent, Article 36 ECHR allows third parties to intervene in the proceedings before the Court.[21] In the majority of cases, NGOs are allowed to submit written interventions when they have specific legal expertise in the matter of the case. Non-governmental organisations mostly submit comparative studies of domestic or international legislation, in order to better inform the ECtHR about a current standard or trend of judicial protection across Europe or the world. In *Hugh Jordan v. United Kingdom*, the Northern Ireland Human Rights Commission underlined the importance of considering the case-law of the IACtHR and the UN principles and guidelines on the subject in the case at stake.[22] Similarly, in *Nikula v. Finland*, Interights submitted a comparative case-law survey with reference to the HRC and the IACtHR.[23] Even if the actual impact of *amicus curiae* is difficult to assess, it is worth mentioning that the ECtHR has actually often made reference to them in its final judgments, as in *Soering*,[24] *Brannigan and Mc Bride*[25] and *Chahal*[26] and, as shown by Van den Eynde, they are extremely important in encouraging judicial dialogue.[27]

The interviewed ECtHR judges confirmed that *amici curiae* are highly taken into consideration and provide important information that the parties may have omitted and suggest relevant case-law to look at. However, the opinions are discordant on this last point. According to some judges, the case-law from other regional human rights bodies or international bodies contained in the *amici curiae* is particularly inspiring and encourages them

19 Shelton, 'The Participation of Nongovernmental Organisations in International Judicial Proceedings', 638–640; Lindblom, *Non-Governmental Organisations in International Law*, 355; Francisco J. Rivera Juaristi, 'The Amicus Curiae in the Inter-American Court of Human Rights (1982–2013)' in Yves Haeck, Oswaldo Ruiz-Chiriboga and Clara Burbano-Herrera (eds), *The Inter-American Court of Human Rights: Theory and Practice, Present and Future* (Intersentia, 2015), 108–109.

20 ibid.

21 For a detailed analysis of NGOs amicus briefs before the ECtHR see van den Eynde, 'Encouraging Judicial Dialogue'.

22 *Hugh Jordan v. United Kingdom*, Application no 24746/94 (ECtHR, 4 August 2001).

23 *Nikula v. Finland*, Application no 31611/96 (ECtHR, 22 May 2002).

24 *Soering v. United Kingdom*, Application no 14038/88 (ECtHR, 7 July 1989).

25 *Brannigan and McBride v. United Kingdom*, Application no 14553/89 (ECtHR, 26 May 1993).

26 *Chahal v. United Kingdom*, Application no 22414/93 (ECtHR, 15 November 1996).

27 van den Eynde, 'Encouraging Judicial Dialogue'.

to engage in a more structured dialogue. On the contrary, other judges believed that *amici curiae* do not usually contain any additional external reference to that already researched by the registry.[28]

The submission of *amici curiae* is also allowed within the African system and could be of particular relevance due to the lack of an adequate secretariat and registry to support the work of the Commission and the Court.[29] Unfortunately, the use of *amici* is still low (only in five cases before the ACtHPR) but, when it happened, the two bodies issued groundbreaking judgments and views such as in *Endorois*[30] or Konaté.[31]

Contrary to the regional systems, the HRC does not allow any third party to submit *amici curiae* in its proceedings. As a consequence of the lack of time and the high number of activities to carry out, the Committee also limits its examination to the written submissions of the parties and does not have the possibility at all to hold oral hearings. Such a restrictive approach may significantly affect the conclusions of the Committee in the specific cases it analyses and all the HRC's members interviewed indicated this as a big obstacle for their work and a limit to their adjudication.[32] Furthermore, the impossibility to submit *amicus curiae* to the HRC does not favour the judicial awareness and dialogue with other international and regional human rights institutions, possibly increasing the risk of fragmentation. To this extent, it would be desirable for the HRC to introduce the possibility of receiving third-party submission in line with regional human rights bodies, to provide its members with more information and perspective on a given case and, also, to avoid triggering fragmentation only for the ignorance of the international case-law on the matter.

28 Interviews with ECtHR's judges held in Strasbourg on 6 and 7 July 2017.

29 Frans Viljoen and Adem Kassie Abebe, 'Amicus Curiae Participation before Regional Human Rights Bodies in Africa' (2014) 58(1) *Journal of African Law* 22, 22–44.

30 *Centre for Minority Rights Development (Kenya) and Minority Rights Group International on behalf of Endorois Welfare Council v. Kenya* (ACommHPR, 25 November 2009).

31 *Lohé Issa Konaté v. Burkina Faso*, Application no 004/2013 (ACtHPR, 5 December 2014).

32 Interviews with four current and former members of the HRC held between September 2016 and October 2017. The ACommHPR provides hearings as a compulsory step but they are not public and reserved to the complainant and respondent state. However, the African Court's Rules of Procedure establish that public and open hearing should be held for any case brought in front of the Court. Slightly different is the case of the IACtHR that, in addition to written briefs and affidavits from witnesses, holds public hearings of witnesses and experts in almost all cases but without any obligation to do so. The European Court occupies a middle position, providing, in limited cases, the possibility of public hearings. However, due to the high number of cases that the Court receives, public hearings are becoming less likely.

7.1.2 *Lobbying and Other Ways of Participation*

Non-governmental organisations can also engage with regional and international bodies in a wide range of other ways, including indirect ones.[33] Yet, lobbying is certainly one of the most common and impactful. As a human rights judge said, '[T]he role of NGOs in lobbying for certain conduct by states [has been] the main contribution that NGOs can make to the cause of international justice.'[34] The NGOs conduct lobbying activities through targeted advocacy campaigns either directly addressing the court or indirectly through the member states.

However, according to the empirical research conducted by Haddad, the NGOs working in the European system do not engage so much in lobbying, but they focus rather on litigation and consultation.[35] Such a difference, especially when compared with the Inter-American and African systems, could add to all the other explanatory factors of the tendency of the ECtHR to adopt its own approach, being less open to external references and to get inspired by other regional and international case-law.

Indeed, the context of the court proved to be determinant for higher or lower participation of NGOs in the judicial and quasi-judicial activities. For instance, the number and influence of the NGOs in the Americas grew in the 1970s and 1980s as many opportunities for engagement came up since 'the Court and Commission were perpetually underfunded and severely threatened or neglected by many member states of the OAS'.[36] The lack of autonomy, or better the limited autonomy, of the Inter-American institutions created the opportunity for NGOs to provide political support as well. Similar considerations can be made for the African bodies, and this explains the large presence of NGOs and the strong relevance they have in giving a direction to the African rulings.

In addition, NGOs provide technical support and represent the view of stakeholders, facilitating communication with different interest groups. This happens to be particularly true in the case of the UNTBs and the African bodies that do not benefit from the same secretariats of the ECtHR and IACtHR.[37]

33 Haddad, *The Hidden Hands of Justice*, 130.

34 Brandeis Institutes for International Judges, 'Civil Society and International Justice: Help or Hindrance?' (2015), 2.

35 Haddad, *The Hidden Hands of Justice*, 176.

36 ibid, 140.

37 As confirmed during interviews with NGOs involved in litigation before all the four systems.

As a general consideration, an overview on the NGOs participation in regional human rights systems shows how the picture changes significantly from one system to the other. While in Europe and the Americas there are few powerful and very well-organised NGOs[38] that undertake any possible activities inherent to the courts and commissions, in the African system the NGOs are smaller, more numerous and often less organised. Yet, the engagement of these NGOs across regional systems is very different; contrary to a very limited engagement in Europe, NGOs are an active player in the Americas and Africa. As Haddad argues, the participation of NGOs in the activities of the regional systems is influenced by several factors, including 'the extent of the court deficiencies of resources and legitimacy, the institutional history of NGO engagement and the NGO motivation and resource'.[39]

All these elements could be invoked as partially contributing to the behaviour of regional courts and, as a consequence, the reach of convergence on specific topics and the arising of fragmentation on others even though it is not possible to establish a direct and univocal cause-effect link.

7.2 WHEN THE CASE DOES NOT REACH THE COURTS

A perusal of the cases under consideration before the regional human rights bodies and the HRC shows that there is a significant difference in their subject matter, to the extent that some issues have been widely addressed within some jurisdiction and almost never within others.[40] The problem lies in the fact that cases concerning violations of certain rights or specific issues have never, or almost never, been brought before some international or regional human rights bodies or they never reached the merit stage. This asymmetry creates an apparent situation of convergence of case-law that should rather be considered lack of fragmentation.[41] Some examples are particularly emblematic of this situation. For instance, cases concerning the enjoyment of freedom of religion have been particularly scarce in the case of the IACtHR or the African

38 Stichting Russian Justice Initiative (SRJI), European Human Rights Advocacy Center (EHRAC) and the Human Rights Center 'Memorial' in Europe and the CEJIL in the Americas as reported by Mayer, 'NGO Standing and Influence on Regional Human Rights Courts and Commissions'.

39 Haddad, *The Hidden Hands of Justice*, 14.

40 Information available on the official case-law research databases of the ECtHR (http://hudoc.echr.coe.int), IACtHR (www.corteidh.or.cr/cf/Jurisprudencia2/index.cfm), ACtHPR (http://en.african-court.org/index.php/cases/2016-10-17-16-18-21#finalised-cases), ACommHPR (www.achpr.org/communications/) and HRC (http://juris.ohchr.org/en/Search/Documents), last accessed 10 February 2022.

41 See the definition of fragmentation and convergence in Section 1.2.

bodies.[42] Moreover, the very few cases that reached the merits concerned the violation of the freedom of religion only *obiter*, as a consequence of the violation of other rights such as the freedom of expression or the right to property.[43] The only exception was one single case before the IACtHR where freedom of religion was directly considered in its trade-off with freedom of expression.[44] In light of this, it would be impossible to argue that the regional systems are really converging on the interpretation of freedom of religion, especially on matters like the freedom to wear religious attire, the limitation to freedom of religion in work-related situations or the balance between freedom of religion and right to health or education.

Similarly, the lack of cases can concern a specific issue within the scope of a particular right. This is the case, among others, of the 'sexual orientation' cases before the African bodies. Neither the ACommHPR nor the ACtHPR has considered the merit of any case concerning the adverse enjoyment of rights by the sexual orientation of the applicants. This is particularly odd considering that homosexuality is a crime in thirty-two African states and in two of them, the death penalty is applied for such an offence.[45] Nevertheless, given the lack of any case-law on the matter, one should not make any conclusive assessments about the presence of convergence or fragmentation but simply acknowledge the lack of fragmentation, waiting for further rulings that will confirm one or the other possibility.

In light of this, it is necessary to investigate what could be the reasons behind such a difference in the subject matter of the cases before the regional and international bodies. Besides the always valid argument that, as living instruments and mirrors of society, regional human rights bodies reflect the realities and challenges of their own regions, which may raise issues different from one another, there can be other factors that may be invoked. The following sections will help to identify some of these elements, both internal and external to the human rights bodies under examination. The first section will investigate the use, and sometimes abuse, of friendly settlements. The second section will present some cases where the human rights bodies actively encouraged applicants to withdraw their applications. Finally, the third

[42] ibid. So far, the IACtHR has decided only three cases where freedom of religion was involved, the African Commission six cases and the African Court none. This is significantly different from the ECtHR with more than 400 cases and the HRC with around 50 cases.

[43] cf, for instance, *Endorois*, ACommHPR and *Olmedo-Bustos et al. v. Chile (The Last Temptation of Christ case)* (IACtHR, 5 February 2001).

[44] ibid.

[45] Information updated to June 2018, available on the website of ILGA, https://ilga.org/maps-sexual-orientation-laws, last accessed 10 February 2022.

section will discuss the instances where the lack of availability of NGOs to help the victim to bring their case prevent them from seeking justice.

7.2.1 *Use and Abuse of Friendly Settlements and Unilateral Declarations*

All regional and international judicial and quasi-judicial bodies have, among their functions, the possibility and the duty to offer their services for the reach of a friendly settlement between the parties.[46] Some controversial cases may be settled before requiring an examination on the merits, thus avoiding any risk of fragmentation. In these circumstances, the role of the adjudicatory body should only be to facilitate the settlement, without intervening in favour of one or the other party. Neutrality and impartiality are key and should also be maintained considering that only a partial study or investigation on the case has been made by the secretariat or by the court or commission. However, the extra-judicial resolution of cases can sometimes be used by human rights bodies to avoid expressing a sharp opinion on a matter that may trigger fragmentation.

The use of friendly settlements to solve human rights disputes is a widespread practice within the European system.[47] As highlighted by a recent study, for some countries the recourse to friendly settlements and unilateral declarations has become an established trend.[48] For instance, after the election of the new government of Georgia in 2012, the Minister of Justice openly stated that the government wanted to 'unburden the European Court from Georgian complaints and establish a culture of resolving human rights [disputes] inside the country, so that people are no longer forced to prove their truth abroad'.[49] As a consequence, the number of cases against Georgia solved through friendly settlements or unilateral declarations increased significantly, reaching twenty-one in 2013, forty in 2014 and twenty-nine in 2015 compared to the mere six in 2011.[50]

Friendly settlements can often be advantageous for the applicants as well, allowing them to receive compensation and redress in a shorter time than

46 Article 39 ECHR, Article 49 ACHR and Article 9 of the Protocol establishing the African Court on Human and Peoples' Rights.

47 Helen Keller, Magdalena Forowicz and Lorenz Engi, *Friendly Settlements before the European Court of Human Rights* (Oxford University Press, 2010).

48 Tamar Abazadze, 'Friendly Settlements and Unilateral Declarations at the European Court of Human Rights', I EHRAC Bulletin, Summer 2016.

49 Statement of the minister of justice available (in Georgian only) at http://goo.gl/u4xYWK, cited and translated in ibid.

50 ibid, 22.

waiting for the final judgment of the Court. Moreover, together with the unilateral declarations, they are very much welcomed by the ECtHR since they ease its huge caseload and speed up its work. As highlighted by some scholars, the registry of the ECtHR has adopted a very proactive approach in facilitating the friendly settlement of cases, to the extent that the case lawyer sends a proposal for the settlement together with the communication instead of simply informing the parties of the possibility of a friendly settlement.[51] However, the cases solved in such ways may often concern serious violations of human rights that do not receive enough attention from the national authorities. Moreover, the applicants may be induced to accept the settlements even if unfavourable to them, due to the weakness and inexperience of their legal representatives.[52] Regardless of the outcome for the parties, the resort to these alternative dispute resolution methods prevents the ECtHR from giving its interpretation of the ECHR and addressing the specific issues at stake. Some of the Georgian cases concerned alleged violations of the prohibition of torture and inhuman and degrading treatments that could have been controversial for the Court to assess and adjudicate. Similarly, also Turkey has become more and more willing to settle Article 2 and Article 3 cases (right to life and prohibition of torture), in order to avoid increasing its negative records of ECHR violations.[53] By encouraging friendly settlements and upholding the government's unilateral declaration, the ECtHR indirectly avoided any further risk of fragmentation, reinforcing an apparent convergence with the other human rights bodies.

Similar considerations on the use of friendly settlements have been made for the Inter-American Commission and Court. The Inter-American bodies went through a similar trend from reluctance to huge support for friendly settlements, significantly extending the types of alleged violations that could be settled.[54] Such an extensive practice in encouraging friendly settlement can have an impact on the assessment of convergence or fragmentation since it limits the range of cases that the courts consider in the merit and, thus, the

51 Keller, Forowicz and Engi, *Friendly Settlements*.

52 Abazadze, 'Friendly Settlements and Unilateral Declarations'. The author argued that in the seven cases it analysed solved through friendly settlement, the Georgian Young Lawyers' Association (GYLA), which was representing the applicants, was not able to adequately defend the claims of its clients, thus striking agreements that were mostly favourable to the Georgian government.

53 Keller, Forowicz and Engi, *Friendly Settlements*, 76.

54 IACtHR, *Impact of the Friendly Settlement Procedure*, 2013, www.oas.org/en/iachr/friendly_settlements/docs/Report-Friendly-Settlement.pdf, last accessed 10 February 2022.

basis for ascertaining one or the other phenomenon. This leads to a situation of absence of fragmentation that could be mistakenly seen as convergence.

As for the African system, although there are two procedures available for friendly settlements, one initiated by the court and one by the parties, friendly settlements have been used only in a handful of cases, and they have often been considered too defensive of the state.[55] Yet, as the case backlog increases and the court and commission gain more and more experience we may see changes in the two bodies' behaviour.

7.2.2 *When the Human Rights Bodies Induce the Applicant to Withdraw the Case*

In addition to favouring friendly settlements, human rights bodies can play a key role in preventing some cases from reaching the merit stage directly by inducing the applicant to withdraw the complaint.

A clear example of this comes from the ACommHPR on a case related to the criminalisation of homosexuality in Zimbabwe. In 1994, Mr Courson brought a complaint against Zimbabwe claiming that the prohibition of sexual contacts between consenting adult homosexual men in private was a violation of his rights under the African Charter, including the right not to be discriminated against on the basis of sexual orientation.[56] The Commissioner acting as a rapporteur for the case openly declared that 'because of the deleterious nature of homosexuality, the Commission seizes the opportunity to make a pronouncement on it. Although homosexuality and lesbianism are gaining recognition in certain parts of the world, this is not the case in Africa. Homosexuality offends the African sense of dignity and morality and is inconsistent with positive African values'.[57] Not surprisingly, after such declaration, Mr Courson decided to withdraw the application, and the Commission never ruled on the case.

In this circumstance, the African Commission did not give rise to fragmentation simply because it de facto prevented the case from reaching the merit

[55] Victor Oluwasina Ayeni and Tajudeen Ojo Ibraheem, 'Amicable Settlement of Disputes and Proactive Remediation of Violations under the African Human Rights System' (2019) 10(3) *Beijing Law Review* 406–422; Jorge Contesse, 'Settling Human Rights Violations' (2019), 60 *Harvard International Law Journal* 1.

[56] *William A. Courson v. Zimbabwe*, Communication no 136/94 (ACommHPR, withdrawn 22 March 1994).

[57] E. A. Ankumah, *The African Commission on Human and Peoples' Rights: Practice and procedures* (1996), 174, as quoted in Frans Viljoen, *International Human Rights Law in Africa* (Oxford University Press, 2012), 265.

stage. Otherwise, it would have most likely ended up with a view of the commission in favour of Zimbabwe and, hence, in contrast to the other regional and international case-law on the matter.[58] This confirms the fact that the absence of fragmentation does not forcibly mean that all the human rights bodies are convergent in their approach and understanding of fundamental rights.

That said, things have significantly changed from 1994 on this matter and there is no account of similar direct or indirect invitation to withdraw the case from members of regional and international human rights bodies. Therefore, it is not possible to draw any conclusion on whether this was just a single occurrence or the expression of the African bodies' attitude towards these kinds of cases, with a deliberate intent to avoid the matter for, *inter alia*, triggering fragmentation.

7.2.3 *Availability of NGOs in Bringing a Specific Case in Front of the Court*

Non-governmental organisations play a fundamental role in supporting victims of human rights violations by bringing their complaints before regional and international judicial and quasi-judicial bodies. They provide legal assistance and representation to people that otherwise would not be able to have their case heard before human rights bodies and therefore, as it was presented previously in this chapter, they could have a significant impact on fragmentation or convergence. Here it will be enough to highlight how they also may play a role in determining which kind of cases, that is, which subject matters, are brought before the court, indirectly avoiding or facilitating the rise of fragmentation.

First, NGOs working in litigation before regional courts mostly operate on a pro bono basis without charging any fee from the applicants.[59] Therefore, in accepting to engage with certain cases rather than others, they follow their own agenda. This may be dictated by many different reasons. The donors' indications and the reception of specific funds for fostering certain rights or addressing certain kinds of issues may greatly influence the choice.[60] Alternatively, the choice could be inspired by a strategic decision to focus on particular topics before specific bodies for either having a higher likelihood

[58] cf *Toonen v. Australia*, Communication no 488/1992 (HRC, 1994) and *Sutherland v. United Kingdom*, Application no 25186/94 (ECtHR, 1 July 1997).

[59] Abdelsalam, 'Individual and Ngo Participation in Human Rights Litigation'.

[60] Mayer, 'NGO Standing and Influence on Regional Human Rights Courts and Commissions', 911–946.

to succeed or visibility in the international arena. For example, an experienced litigator in the field of freedom of expression, interviewed for this book, confirmed that due to the well-established attitude of the ECtHR towards tabloid media, cases on this topic would rather be brought before the HRC.[61] In addition, sometimes the NGOs follow some hints and advice directly from the human rights bodies.[62] For instance, during an interview with a representative of an eminent NGO active in litigation before the Inter-American bodies, it emerged how the Inter-American Commission sometimes encourages relevant NGOs to bring cases concerning specific issues in order to develop its case-law on a new point of law or to provide an innovative interpretation of the American Convention on neglected matters.[63]

Second, specialised NGOs working on specific issues are not present everywhere in the world. They are set up to answer compelling problems and challenges of specific countries or regions, and they often focus their efforts at the local level. This situation, evident in the case of indigenous rights, could make it difficult if not impossible for a certain applicant to find an NGO available to help them bring a case before a certain regional human rights body, while such an opportunity would be very much available in other regions.[64]

Finally, interviews with NGOs involved in litigation before regional and international human rights bodies revealed that there are also political motivations behind the decision to bring a certain case before a specific body. For example, considering the existing case-law of the concept of *laicité* of the state before the Strasbourg Court, controversial cases concerning freedom of religion will be rather brought before the HRC.[65]

Similarly, it would not be wise to bring a case before the African bodies against a state that has high political influence in the AU, considering the low likelihood for the case to be successful or impactful on the life of the victim.[66] Likewise, NGOs proved to be very cautious in bringing cases before bodies they do not consider ready yet, that is, whose case-law on that subject is not developed enough to consider a given case properly. An example of this would

[61] Interview conducted with a European-based NGO specialised on freedom of expression and religion, June 2017.
[62] Mayer, 'NGO Standing and Influence on Regional Human Rights Courts and Commissions'.
[63] Interview with a US-based NGO, August 2017.
[64] For example, the NGOs specialised on indigenous rights focus only on the African or American regions and do not operate in Europe.
[65] Interview conducted with a European-based NGO specialised on freedom of expression and religion, 18 July 2017.
[66] ibid.

be a case involving discrimination based on sexual orientation, being premature to be brought before one of the African bodies.

CONCLUSION

This chapter sheds some light on other factors able to contribute to judicial convergence and fragmentation.

Human rights bodies are actors within a broader international system and, as such, are influenced by external factors that could contribute to shaping their adjudication. Among them, this chapter highlighted the role of non-governmental organisations and the different ways they interact with human rights bodies, being able to externally affect the course of adjudication through submission of *amici curiae*, victims' representation or other lobbying activities. However, there are many other actors that may significantly influence the human rights bodies' adjudication. For instance, member states may and do exercise both political and economic pressure on human rights bodies and can influence their adjudication.[67] However, proving such a relation is very complicated and goes beyond the scope and capability of this book.

Moreover, this chapter showed that, sometimes, those cases that are likely to trigger fragmentation are prevented from reaching the merit stage. This clearly leads to the apparent maintenance of convergence, avoiding in the first place the situation where two bodies may adjudicate in contrasting ways. Member states through friendly settlements, human rights bodies through open encouragement to the applicants or NGOs through the decision of not bringing specific cases forward are responsible for this. However, it should be remembered that the decision to avoid these cases from reaching the merit stage is not motivated by the desire to maintain convergence, as this is only a side effect of the pursuing specific political, institutional or identity agendas. Nonetheless, it is important to acknowledge the impact of these decisions on the fragmentation/convergence picture and how judicial convergence is sometimes the unintended result of choices made by the human rights bodies and other actors involved in human rights adjudication.

[67] cf Mikael Rask Madsen, 'Rebalancing European Human Rights: Has the Brighton Declaration Engendered a New Deal on Human Rights in Europe?' (2018) 9(2) *Journal of International Dispute Settlement* 199, where Madsen argues that the use of the MoA by the ECtHR is a sign of the acceptance of political pressure by its member states.

Conclusions

This book explored the issue of judicial convergence and fragmentation in international human rights law, focusing on the case-law of the African Court and Commission on Human and People's Rights, the European Court of Human Rights, the Inter-American Court of Human Rights and the UN Human Rights Committee.

The aim of the book was to answer two main research questions: is judicial fragmentation affecting international human rights law and what are the factors that may explain the current situation of fragmentation and convergence?

The first research question sprang from the active debate among scholars about fragmentation in international law and the possibility of this spreading into international human rights law bringing possible adverse consequences both for the system and the victims. Human rights norms are very broad and often vague, allowing a wide margin of interpretation and leaving significant power to the adjudicatory bodies to shape their content and application when called to interpret them in a specific case. Considering the value of the universality of human rights, the principle of certainty of the law and the need for coherence and consistency, and thus legitimacy, of the IHRL system, judicial fragmentation – if recurrent and on a large-scale – could certainly determine unpleasant situations of conflicting interpretations, which could ultimately lead to a lower level of human rights protection for the individuals.

However, contrary to the initial expectations based on the proliferation of human rights normative frameworks and monitoring and judicial institutions, the book confirmed what other scholars have argued, that fragmentation is not a significant phenomenon in IHRL, at the moment, and it only partially affects this branch of public international law.

Adopting a restrictive definition of judicial convergence and fragmentation focused on the outcome of the judgments, the examination of the case-law of the three regional systems and the UN HRC presented in Chapter 2 showed that much of the worries about fragmentation in IHRL were exaggerated. Complex topics such as the limits of the use of deadly force, the definition of what constitutes cruel, inhuman and degrading treatments, the application of the provisions on freedom of expression or freedom of assembly and even sensitive issues, such as the right to abortion and the prohibition of discrimination based on sexual orientation, received an overall convergent interpretation and application by all the bodies under analysis, if and when called to address them. Indeed, even if with some differences in the language or in the use of terms and standards, all the regional bodies and the HRC ultimately brought more convergence than fragmentation with their jurisprudence. Sometimes previous cases of fragmentation evolved to convergence over time, showing the commitment of human rights bodies to continuously review their approaches and interpretation, and the always changing nature of these phenomena.

Nevertheless, some sporadic instances of fragmentation were identified. In particular, the HRC and the ECtHR repeatedly adjudicated in significantly contrasting ways cases related to the wearing of religious attire, disagreeing on whether a restriction on the freedom to wear headscarves or Sikh turbans in educational premises or for document identification was a breach of the freedom of religion. Similarly, the ECtHR, on the one side, and the IACtHR and the ACommHPR, on the other side, adopted contrasting stances on the right to property over indigenous' ancestral lands, and the IACtHR and the ECtHR kept having a different understanding of the phenomenon of enforced disappearances and how this should be dealt with. Moreover, the substantial convergence found in this examination proved to be very fragile in some situations, easily leading to fragmentation under the right circumstances. This is the case of the Advisory Opinion of the IACtHR on sexual orientation and gender identity that ultimately triggered fragmentation with the ECtHR and the HRC on the right to marry for same-sex couples and the rights linked to gender reassignment and recognition.

All this prompted the need to answer the second research question of this book, aimed at understanding the reasons behind this unexpected situation of substantial convergence with only a few sporadic cases of fragmentation.

This book identified and discussed several legal and non-legal factors that can be considered as contributing both to the triggering of judicial fragmentation or to the maintenance of judicial convergence, depending on the circumstances. Yet, this is probably not an exhaustive list and further research could identify new factors behind these phenomena. Likewise, the versatility of these elements that until now mostly led to convergence requires a continual observation for any new element coming through that could possibly affect and change their effect on the IHRL system.

Among the reasons behind the limited fragmentation, as one could have expected, there is certainly the lack of many comparable cases before different jurisdictions.[1] As recalled several times in this book, in order to assess the existence of judicial fragmentation or convergence, it is necessary to have two cases with comparable facts and legal issues. However, very often the facts of the cases, the domestic legal framework or the conditions of the applicants are so different that two cases are not comparable and, therefore, no judicial fragmentation arises. This could be mistaken as judicial convergence on several matters but, in reality, it is merely an absence of fragmentation, since no two bodies have convergently adjudicated cases on those rights and issues.

The general theory of interpretation does not seem to be determinant in explaining the behaviour of regional bodies and the HRC. Although these bodies could have developed and applied different interpretative approaches, they all aligned with each other following the lead of the EctHR and fully embraced the principle of evolutive interpretation, which allowed them to go well beyond the strict letter of treaty provisions. However, differences in the interpretation clauses contained in their establishing instruments leave a door open to different interpretative approaches that may affect current convergence in the future.[2]

Judicial fragmentation in IHRL was mostly expected to be found in situations where an adjudicatory body is required to strike a balance between two or more competing rights or interests. The balancing of rights is one of the most complex operations in IHRL adjudication, and it is very easy to operate a different assessment, influenced by many elements and concerns of various nature. Nevertheless, this book highlighted how all the five bodies under analysis developed common balancing principles and tests, reducing to a minimum the instances of fragmentation springing from different balancing assessments. The two key safeguards for convergence in this field are the principle of necessity and the proportionality test.[3] Without providing any proper and clear definition and keeping a strategic vagueness and flexibility to both concepts, regional human rights bodies and the HRC managed to overcome textual differences in their provisions and apply these concepts in a convergent way to the given cases. This is how the apparent difference in what constitutes 'absolute' or 'strict' necessity or what is 'necessary in a

[1] Chapter 7, Section 7.3.
[2] Chapter 4, Section 4.1.
[3] Chapter 5.

democratic society', became just a language and stylistic variance without a contrasting practical implication.[4] Similarly, the completely judicial invention of the proportionality test, introduced in the human rights adjudication by the ECtHR, quickly spread in the adjudication habits of all the other bodies including those, like the HRC, that at first opted for a different balancing test. Maintaining the proportionality test as flexible as possible, all the bodies under analysis found themselves speaking the same language, despite sometimes meaning slightly different things.[5] This vagueness and flexibility, key for the success of necessity and proportionality, ensured mostly convergence so far. However, this probably also constitutes its main threat, considering that, under different circumstances, it may easily determine contrasting outcomes and, thus, fragmentation.

In the assessment of proportionality, a determinant role is played by the degree of deference that a given judicial or quasi-judicial body grants to its member states. This book showed how the doctrines of the margin of appreciation or the conventionality control could affect the adjudication and, thus, contribute to convergence and fragmentation.[6] Especially in situations concerning the restriction to freedom of expression or religion or the restriction to any right on the basis of national security or public morals, the decision to grant a certain margin of manoeuvre to the state parties can, depending on the conditions, trigger fragmentation or maintain convergence. The ECtHR created and fully embraced the MoA, making it one of the strongholds of its adjudication, so much so as to lure severe admonitions from scholars and practitioners on the allegedly excessive use of this doctrine that may ultimately undermine the individual's protection.[7] On the contrary, both the HRC and the two African bodies continuously swing between openly rejecting the MoA doctrine and silently adopting its language and standards, in line with the theory of subsidiarity.[8] On the other side of the spectrum, the IACtHR developed a completely different doctrine, the conventionality control.[9] Rightly considered the opposite of the MoA, the close scrutiny imposed by the CC might significantly increase the risk of fragmentation, requiring a uniform and universal implementation of the IACtHR's judgments in all the member states. Such contrasting approaches, highly due to the historical and political context of the different institutions, naturally increase the likelihood

4 ibid, Section 5.1.
5 ibid, Section 5.2.
6 Chapter 6.
7 ibid, Section 6.2.
8 ibid, Sections 6.4 and 6.5.
9 ibid, Section 6.3.

of fragmentation to arise. However, it equally increases the unpredictability of the position that a given body will adopt on a certain issue, preventing any final judgment on convergence and fragmentation. One of the reasons why fragmentation did not arise as expected due to the MoA versus CC between the European and the Inter-American courts is because the IACtHR did not have, so far, the chance to rule on many cases dealing with rights normally subject to MoA before the ECtHR. In particular, the case-law of the IACtHR on the right to private life and freedom of religion is extremely limited. Yet, if and when the IACtHR started to receive more cases on these issues, fragmentation could probably arise.

Another element that can significantly influence human rights adjudication is the resort to external references.[10] The phenomenon of judicial dialogue is increasing among regional human rights bodies, although differently embraced by each of them. If the African bodies and the IACtHR consider it a necessary step in the adjudication of each case, the ECtHR is still reluctant to look too much out of the European window. Nevertheless, they all engage in some form of dialogue, increasing their awareness about other bodies' case-law and reducing the likelihood of unwanted fragmentation. Still, this book showed that, even though judicial dialogue favours convergence, there is no strict causal link between them, since the former is not enough to ensure the latter. This is probably because it is almost impossible to ascertain the actual impact that a certain citation has on the judgment, as it may be just a nominal reference or, even without a proper citation, an external reference may have influenced the judges significantly in their adjudication.[11] Moreover, the African Court is increasingly limiting its reliance on external case-law, in particular on the ECtHR's one, likely putting an end soon to the 'judicial monologue' that significantly helped convergence so far.

Similarly, sometimes cases do not reach the merit stage for many reasons that do not belong just to the legal sphere.[12] For instance, the extensive use, and sometimes abuse, of the instrument of friendly settlement can prevent a certain case or type of cases to reach the merit stage and, hence, to present a possibility for fragmentation to arise. This book showed that this is the case of many applications concerning torture, cruel or inhuman acts and right to life against Georgia before the ECtHR, where possible instances of fragmentation could have been triggered but never did because the cases were settled before.

[10] Chapter 4, Section 4.2.
[11] ibid, Sections 4.2.3 and 4.2.4.
[12] Chapter 7, Section 7.2.

Alternatively, the applicants may be encouraged to withdraw the application before the judicial or quasi-judicial body has the chance to express itself on it, so as to avoid contrasting opinions. This is what the African Commission did in *Courson* on the criminalisation of homosexuality, a matter that was never since addressed by any of the two African bodies.

Finally, the absence of two comparable cases may be due to the lack of available NGOs or other civil society actors willing to help the applicant bring a given case before a certain body. This could be caused by the availability of legal aid, the cost of litigation or simply by the political agenda of the NGOs.[13] As confirmed by the interviews with NGOs and other actors involved in human rights litigation, all these organisations can have a significant influence on the adjudication of human rights bodies, ultimately contributing to fragmentation or convergence. Such an influence is exercised in several ways. The most obvious is the active participation in litigation, strategically choosing to bring only selected issues before each body, avoiding even the possibility for fragmentation to arise. Similarly, they can have a noteworthy influence through their third-party submissions, the *amici curiae*, where the inclusion of references to other human rights bodies encourages judicial dialogue and, ultimately, convergence between bodies. Finally, NGOs can impact human rights adjudication through lobbying activities. Especially well-known NGOs can successfully convince judges, commissioners and committee members in adopting new standards of protection and it is in their interests that judicial convergence among these bodies is achieved.

These non-legal factors were demonstrated to be very important in contributing to the understanding of judicial convergence and fragmentation, because the mere legal analysis proved to be sometimes limited for such a purpose. This is because all the five human rights bodies under analysis do not work in a vacuum, but are present in the international arena, subject to influences by and relationships with other actors. Moreover, these bodies are composed of people who, like any human being, bring with them their background and experience, which may have an impact on their adjudication.

Through a study on the educational and work experience background of current and former members of the five bodies under analysis, this book showed that part of the explanation of convergence and fragmentation could and should be searched in the individual profile of who adjudicates the cases.[14] Of particular relevance is the university educational background that revealed that the majority of the members of the African bodies and the

[13] ibid, Section 7.1.

[14] Chapter 4.

IACtHR received their legal education in Europe, thus assimilating the 'European' approach to human rights adjudication. Assuming that such a distinctive European approach exists, this finding would confirm an endogenous Europeanisation of the African and Inter-American systems and significantly reduce any relativism argument, contributing to the explanation of the overall convergence among regional systems. Yet, the changes between 2018 and 2021, especially in the composition of the ACtHPR, may suggest a shift in the trend, which could ultimately lead to more episodes of fragmentation in the future. Similarly, an academic background with a speciality in international or comparative law subjects or having served as a UNTBs' member or a SP mandate holder proved to correlate with the increasing use of external references and the attention paid to the development of other bodies' jurisprudence in their separate opinions. Moreover, all these human rights adjudicators share the feeling of being part of the same community, an invisible college of human rights experts, working together towards one common mission of promoting and protecting human rights. All these elements naturally increase the likelihood of convergence and decrease that of fragmentation.

Finally, one should not ignore the contribution of the organisational structure behind these bodies. Secretariats and registries could play a key role in facilitating convergence and avoiding fragmentation, considering their fundamental task of preparing cases, researching relevant jurisprudence and helping judges, commissioners and committee members in the final drafting.[15] Interviews revealed a very different organisation of the registries among regional courts, with the IACtHR having a specific section dedicated to dialogue with other human rights bodies and an explicit instruction to research the relevant case-law from all other regional and international human rights bodies for each case before the court. Likewise, the registry of the ACtHPR has also a consolidated practice of looking at the ECtHR and IACtHR case-law, as well as UN relevant sources, when preparing a case. On the contrary, the ECtHR's registry is very much focused on the European framework, with its preliminary case-law research oriented towards the domestic case-law of its member states and to the case-law of the European Court of Justice rather than other human rights bodies. The priorities of each body are then mirrored in the organisation of its registry and, resources and time permitting, they can influence judicial convergence and fragmentation.

[15] ibid, Section 3.2.

These legal and non-legal factors, examined throughout the book, can help understanding the predominant occurrence of convergence over fragmentation in IHRL but they all present limitations. First, most of them can be determinant for the occurrence of both phenomena depending on the circumstances, confirming the constantly changing and unstable nature of convergence and fragmentation in this field. However, the book showed that it is not imaginable to have a perfect causal link between one factor and one judgment, as the latter is always the result of many variables that are intertwined. Second, the analysis of all these factors is limited by the impossibility of assessing what is the reality behind the curtain of a judgment, meaning what really induces judges, commissioners and committee members to adjudicate in a certain way. There are many hidden elements that may influence their judicial behaviour, which the book could not address at length. Interviews with judges and with other relevant stakeholders contribute to providing a clearer picture, but the extent to which they actually revealed all the influences and elements that play a role in their adjudication remains unknown. This is the case, for instance, of the extent to which judicial dialogue actually means a desire to strengthen human rights universality or rather a simple matter of convenience or whether political interests and the wish to avoid a clear-cut fragmentation motivate the granting of the MoA to member states. All these questions remain unsolved and prevent this book from providing more conclusive explanations, yet they pave the way to future avenues of research.

This book also echoed what several scholars have recently increasingly shown: that a mere doctrinal legal analysis may not be enough in explaining legal phenomena. Indeed, political, sociological and behavioural approaches have informed the identification and analysis of some of the explanatory factors. The findings of this book leave the door open to further research, mostly sociology, politics and international relations oriented, which was not the focus and approach of this study. A political analysis of the behaviour of regional human rights bodies and the HRC, where the influence of member states and politics equilibria are considered in detail, may bring some additional interesting perspectives. Similarly, a review of judicial fragmentation and convergence under a postcolonial theory lens may provide an alternative picture of the relationship between human rights bodies and be able to justify some judicial attitudes and interpretations.

This book leaves another big question unsolved: the evaluation of the merit of judicial convergence and fragmentation for the IHRL system. Assessing whether we should aim for perfect convergence in human rights adjudication as a confirmation of the principle of universality or rather welcome any episode of fragmentation as an expression of legal pluralism and healthy relativism is a controversial matter that requires a separate and dedicated discussion. Although it was not the aim of this research, some considerations in this regard could and should be made. Judicial fragmentation has been traditionally seen as a threat to the coherence of any legal system and a dangerous consequence of the development and proliferation of frameworks and institutions. However, this book showed how judicial fragmentation can have a double value, depending on the specific circumstances. It can be triggered both for advancing the standard of protection for the victims or for departing from a higher standard and lowering it down to the advantage of the respondent state. This may lead to the identification of a positive and a negative fragmentation, according to whether the judgment triggering fragmentation sets a higher or a lower standard of protection for the victim. However, this definition has many problems starting from which standpoint one should adopt in making the assessment. Indeed, in most cases, judicial fragmentation arises in the context of balancing between different rights and interests. Whilst in the case before the supranational body there is always an applicant versus a state, the state at that moment is representing the rights and interests of other individuals. Therefore, simply stating that fragmentation is positive when it is in favour of the victim means taking the side of the applicant to the detriment of another individual whose rights the state is protecting and enforcing. A clear example of this is the *Handolsdalen* case on indigenous property rights before the ECtHR. Here the two contrasting interests are those of the indigenous people claiming their right to property over their ancestral lands and those of the private landowners who legally purchased a land and claim a right to property over it. One may conclude that the ECtHR was responsible for triggering 'negative' fragmentation because it ruled against the Sami's right to their ancestral land but, in doing so, they protected the equally important right to property of the individual landowners. It follows that it is almost impossible to label fragmentation as positive or negative and a careful assessment and balancing should always be attempted to avoid undermining the protection of the rights of all the parties involved, unless one wants to establish a hierarchy of rights.

Nonetheless, there are some instances where it is possible to state with more confidence that a situation of fragmentation is negative. This is the case, for instance, of the controversial headscarf rulings where the freedom to manifest religion by wearing religious attire allegedly clashes with issues of national security and public order. Except for those instances where a certain religious attire can actually pose a security threat, in the majority of the cases, one can assert that triggering fragmentation by ruling in favour of the state party is negative in as much as diminishing the standard of protection for the victims to the advantage of the state only. However, a case-by-case assessment is always required, as a sharp evaluation is impossible and, ultimately, dangerous. As a matter of fact, the often invoked convergence that certainly strengthens the universality of human rights and makes the entire human rights system of protection look efficient and coordinated may also have negative sides. If convergence simply means aligning its jurisprudence to that of the most influential human rights body regardless of the standard of protection set or of the specificity of the case, then this should be avoided. In the best-case scenario, one should vouch for maintaining judicial convergence to the highest standard and triggering fragmentation only when this is needed to increase the level of protection. Yet, the assessment of whose protection should be primarily considered remains problematic and susceptible to many different variables.

In conclusion, judicial fragmentation and convergence in IHRL remain complex phenomena always subject to change. Due to many legal and non-legal factors, the matter is very far from being settled, and any new judgment may change the situation. Considering that some bodies, such as the African ones, are just now evolving into more experienced courts and others, such as the IACtHR, are now receiving more differentiated cases due to the political evolution of its member states, it is reasonable to imagine that in the future these two systems will consider new cases on issues and topics that so far have been addressed only by the ECtHR. This increasing number of comparable cases will allow the assessment of judicial fragmentation or convergence and the legal and non-legal factors identified in this book should be observed carefully to assess which role they play towards one outcome or the other. Some of these explanatory factors are under the control of the judicial or quasi-judicial bodies while others are external and fall outside of their domain. Although judicial convergence is not always desirable and not desirable at all costs, it is certainly advisable for human rights bodies to reflect on the current international and regional standards on a given issue before triggering fragmentation. This means that judicial dialogue, or simple awareness of external jurisprudence, could be an easy and feasible safeguard for ensuring well-reasoned case-law, regardless of whether it feeds convergence or ultimately triggers fragmentation. An improved dialogue between institutions, which would also require additional and dedicated resources, registry and secretariat staff and willingness from judges, commissioners and committee members would definitely benefit IHRL and bring more coherence and legitimacy. However, other actors such as NGOs also play a key role and they should be aware of their influence and power and be taken into consideration in this debate.

APPENDIX 1

International and Regional Human Rights Instruments

INTERNATIONAL INSTRUMENTS

Binding Documents

- International Covenant on Civil and Political Rights (1966) and its two Optional Protocols
- International Covenant on Economic, Social and Cultural Rights (1966) and its Optional Protocol (2008)
- Convention on the Prevention and the Punishment of the Crime of Genocide (1948)
- Convention on the Elimination of All Forms of Racial Discrimination (1966) and its amendment (1992)
- Convention on the Non-Applicability of Statutory Limitations to War Crimes and Crimes against Humanity (1968)
- International Convention on the Suppression and Punishment of the Crimes of Apartheid (1973)
- Convention on the Elimination of All Forms of Discrimination against Women (1979), its amendment (1995) and its Optional Protocol (1999)
- Convention against Torture and Other Cruel, Inhuman and Degrading Treatment (1984), its amendment (1992) and its Optional Protocol (2002)
- International Convention against Apartheid in Sports (1985), the Convention of the Right of the Child (1989) its amendment (1995) and its four Optional Protocols (1989, 2000, 2000 and 2011)
- International Convention on the Protection of the Rights of all Migrant Workers and Members of Their Families (1990)
- International Convention for the Protection of All Persons from Enforced Disappearances (2006)

- Agreement establishing the Fund for the Development of the Indigenous Peoples of Latin America and the Caribbean (1992)
- Convention against Discrimination in Education (1960)
- Protocol Instituting a Conciliation and Good Offices Commission to be responsible for seeking a settlement of any disputes which may arise between States Parties to the Convention against Discrimination in Education (1968)
- International Convention against the Recruitment, Use, Financing and Training of Mercenaries (1989)
- Slavery Convention (1926) its amending Protocol (1953)
- Supplementary Convention on the Abolition of Slavery, the Slave Trade and Institutions and Practices Similar to Slavery (1956)
- Convention for the Suppression of the Traffic in Persons and of the Exploitation of the Prostitutions of Others (1949)
- Protocol to Prevent, Suppress and Punish Trafficking in Persons Especially Women and Children, supplementing the United Nations Convention against Transnational Organized Crime (2000)
- Protocol against the Smuggling of Migrants by Land, Sea and Air, supplementing the United Nations Convention against Transnational Organized Crime (2000)
- Convention on the Reduction of Statelessness (1961)
- Convention relating to the Status of Stateless Persons (1954), the Convention relating to the Status of Refugees (1950)
- Protocol relating to the Status of Refugees (1967)
- Statute of the International Tribunal for the Prosecution of Persons Responsible for Serious Violations of International Humanitarian Law Committed in the Territory of the Former Yugoslavia since 1991 (1993)
- Statute of the International Criminal Tribunal for the Prosecution of Persons Responsible for Genocide and Other Serious Violations of International Humanitarian Law Committed in the Territory of Rwanda and Rwandan Citizens Responsible for Genocide and Other Such Violations Committed in the Territory of Neighbouring States, between 1 January 1994 and 31 December 1994 (1994)
- Rome Statute of the International Criminal Court (1998)
- Geneva Convention relative to the Treatment of Prisoners of War (1949)
- Geneva Convention relative to the Protection of Civilian Persons in Time of War (1949), the First Protocol Additional to the Geneva Conventions of 12 August 1949, and relating to the Protection of Victims of International Armed Conflicts (1977) and the Second Protocol Additional to the Geneva Conventions of 12 August 1949, and

Relating to the Protection of Victims of Non-International Armed Conflicts (1977)

- Convention on the Rights of Persons with Disabilities (CRPD) (2006)
- Convention on Consent to Marriage, Minimum Age for Marriage and Registration of Marriages (1962)
- ILO Conventions:
  - Convention No. 169 concerning Indigenous and Tribal Peoples (1989),
  - Convention No. 100 concerning Equal Remuneration (1953);
  - Convention No. 111 concerning Discrimination (Employment and Occupation) (1958);
  - Convention No. 182 concerning Worst Forms of Child Labour (1999);
  - Convention No. 122 concerning Employment Policy (1964);
  - Convention No. 29 concerning Forced Labour (1930);
  - Convention No. 105 concerning the Abolition of Forced Labour and Convention No. 87 concerning Freedom of Association and Protection of the Rights to Organize Convention (1948).
  - Convention No. 138 concerning minimum age for admission to employment (1976);
  - Convention No. 123 concerning the minimum age for admission to employment underground in mines (1965);
  - Convention No. 112 concerning the minimum age for admission to employment as fishermen (1959).

Non-binding Documents

- Basic Principles and Guidelines on the Right to a Remedy and Reparation for Victims of Gross Violations of International Human Rights Law and Serious Violations of International Humanitarian Law (2005)
- Basic Principles for the Treatment of Prisoners (1990)
- Basic Principles on the Independence of the Judiciary (1985)
- Basic Principles on the Role of Lawyers (1990)
- Basic Principles on the Use of Force and Firearms by Law Enforcement Officials (1990)
- Body of Principles for the Protection of All Persons under Any Form of Detention or Imprisonment (1988)
- Code of Conduct for Law Enforcement Officials (1979)
- Declaration of Basic Principles of Justice for Victims of Crime and Abuse of Power (1985)

- Declaration of Commitment on HIV/AIDS (2001)
- Declaration on Race and Racial Prejudice (1978)
- Declaration on Social Progress and Development (1969)
- Declaration on the Elimination of All Forms of Intolerance and of Discrimination Based on Religion or Belief (1981)
- Declaration on the Elimination of Violence against Women (1993)
- Declaration on the Human Rights of Individuals who are not nationals of the country in which they live (1985)
- Declaration on the Protection of All Persons from Being Subjected to Torture and Other Cruel, Inhuman or Degrading Treatment or Punishment (1975)
- Declaration on the Protection of all Persons from Enforced Disappearance (1992)
- Declaration on the Protection of Women and Children in Emergency and Armed Conflict (1974)
- Declaration on the Right and Responsibility of Individuals, Groups and Organs of Society to Promote and Protect Universally Recognized Human Rights and Fundamental Freedoms (1998)
- Declaration on the Right of Peoples to Peace (1984)
- Declaration on the Right to Development (1986)
- Declaration on the Rights of Disabled Persons (1975)
- Declaration on the Rights of Indigenous Peoples (2007)
- Declaration on the Rights of Mentally Retarded Persons (1971)
- Declaration on the Rights of Persons Belonging to National or Ethnic, Religious and Linguistic Minorities (1992)
- Declaration on the Use of Scientific and Technological Progress in the Interests of Peace and for the Benefit of Mankind (1975)
- Durban Declaration and Programme of Action (2001)
- Guidelines for Action on Children in the Criminal Justice System (1997)
- Guidelines on the Role of Prosecutors (1990)
- Guiding Principles on Internal Displacement (1998)
- Principles for the protection of persons with mental illness and the improvement of mental health care (1991)
- Principles of international co-operation in the detection, arrest, extradition and punishment of persons guilty of war crimes and crimes against humanity (1973)
- Principles of Medical Ethics relevant to the Role of Health Personnel, particularly Physicians, in the Protection of Prisoners and Detainees against Torture and Other Cruel, Inhuman or Degrading Treatment or Punishment (1982)

- Principles on the Effective Investigation and Documentation of Torture and Other Cruel, Inhuman or Degrading Treatment or Punishment (2000)
- Principles on the Effective Prevention and Investigation of Extra-legal, Arbitrary and Summary Executions (1989)
- Principles relating to the Status of National Institutions (The Paris Principles) (1993)
- Recommendation on Consent to Marriage, Minimum Age for Marriage and Registration of Marriages (1965)
- Safeguards guaranteeing protection of the rights of those facing the death penalty (1984)
- Set of principles for the protection and promotion of human rights through action to combat impunity (2005)
- Standard Minimum Rules for the Treatment of Prisoners (1955)
- Standard Rules on the Equalization of Opportunities for Persons with Disabilities (1993)
- United Nations Declaration on Human Rights Education and Training (2001)
- United Nations Declaration on the Granting of Independence to Colonial Countries and Peoples (1960)
- United Nations Guidelines for the Prevention of Juvenile Delinquency (The Riyadh Guidelines) (1990)
- United Nations Millennium Declaration (2000)
- United Nations Principles for Older Persons (1991)
- United Nations Rules for the Protection of Juveniles Deprived of their Liberty (1990)
- United Nations Rules for the Treatment of Women Prisoners and Non-custodial Measures for Women Offenders (the Bangkok Rules) (2010)
- United Nations Standard Minimum Rules for Non-custodial Measures (The Tokyo Rules) (1990)
- United Nations Standard Minimum Rules for the Administration of Juvenile Justice (The Beijing Rules) (1985)
- Universal Declaration on Cultural Diversity (2001)
- Universal Declaration on the Eradication of Hunger and Malnutrition (1974)
- Universal Declaration on the Human Genome and Human Rights (1998)
- Vienna Declaration and Programme of Action (1993)

REGIONAL INSTRUMENTS

Europe

- Convention on Human Rights and Biomedicine (1997)
- Convention on Violence against Women and Domestic Violence (2011)
- European Charter for Regional or Minority Languages (1992)
- European Convention Against Torture (1987)
- European Convention on Human Rights (1950)
- European Framework Convention for the Protection of National Minorities (1994)
- European Social Charter (1961)

Africa

- African Charter on Democracy, Elections and Governance (2007)
- African Charter on Human and Peoples' Rights (1981)
- African Charter on the Rights and Welfare of the Child (1999)
- OAU Convention Governing the Specific Aspects of the Refugee Problems in Africa (1969)
- Protocol on the Rights of Women in Africa (2003)

The Americas

- American Convention on Human Rights (1969)
- Inter-American Convention on Forced Disappearance of Persons (1994)
- Inter-American Convention on the Prevention, Punishment and Eradication of Violence against Women (1994)
- Inter-American Convention to Prevent and Punish Torture (1985)
- Inter-American Democratic Charter (2001)
- Inter-American Convention on the Elimination of All Forms of Discrimination against Persons with Disabilities (1999)

Other Regional and Sub-regional Instruments

- Arab Charter on Human Rights (2004)
- ASEAN Human Rights Declaration (2012)
- Charter of Fundamental Rights of the European Union (2000)

- Organisation of Islamic Cooperation, Plan of Action for the Advancement of Women (Cairo Plan of Action for Women) (2008)
- Organisation of Islamic Cooperation, Covenant on the Rights of the Child in Islam (2005)
- Organisation of Islamic Cooperation, the Cairo Declaration on Human Rights in Islam (1990)

APPENDIX 2

Comparative Table of Leading Cases

	ECtHR	IACtHR	African bodies	HRC
Equality and Prohibition of Discrimination	Article 14; Article 5-Protocol 7 Case-law = *Rasmussen* v. *Denmark*; *Fredin* v. *Sweden*; *Belgian Linguistic Case*; *Cyprus* v. *Turkey*; *Dudgeon* v. *UK*; *Timishev* v. *Russia*	Article 1; Article 24 Case-law = *Advisory Opinion on the Proposed Amendments to the Naturalization Provisions of the Constitution of Costa Rica* (copious references to ECtHR Belgian Linguistic Case); *Advisory Opinion on Juridical Condition and rights of the Undocumented Migrants*; *Atala Riffo* v. *Chile*	Article 2; Article 3 Case-law = *Legal Resources Foundation* v. *Zambia*; *Jawara* v. *The Gambia*; *Purhoit and Another* v. *The Gambia*; *Egyptian Initiative for Personal Rights and Interights* v. *Egypt*	Article 2; Article 3; Article 26 Case-law = *Shrin Aumeeruddy-Cziffra et al.* v. *Mauritius*; *F.H. Zwaan-de Vries* v. *The Netherlands*; *Carl Henrik Blom* v. *Sweden*; *Ibrahima Gueye et al.* v. *France*; *Boreks* v. *The Netherlands*; *Zwaan De Vries* v. *The Netherlands*; *Nahlik* v. *Austria*; *Toonen* v. *Australia*
Right to Life	Article 2 Case-law = *McCann* v. *UK*; *V.O.* v. *France*; *Pretty* v. *UK*; *Al-Sadoon and Mufdhi* v. *UK*; *Ocalan* v. *Turkey*; *Jordan* v. *UK*; *Musayeva and others* v. *Russia*; *Kelly and others* v. *UK*; *Kaya* v. *Turkey*; *Osman* v. *UK*	Article 4 Case-law = *Monter-Aranguren (Detention Centre of Catia)* v. *Venezuela*; *Hilaire Constantine and Benjamin et al.* v. *Trinidad and Tobago*; *Artavia Murillo* v. *Costa Rica*; *El Amparo* v. *Venezuela*	Article 4 Case-law = *DRC* v. *Burundi, Rwanda and Uganda*; *Forum of Coscience* v. *Sierra Leone*; *Interights and Other* v. *Botswana*; *International Pen and Others* v. *Nigeria*; *SERAC* v. *Nigeria*	Article 6 Case-law = *KL* v. *Peru*; *Judge* v. *Canada*; *La Vende* v. *Trinidad and Tobago*; *Delgado Paez* v. *Colombia*

Prohibition of Torture	Article 3 Case-law = *Al-Adsani* v. *UK*; *Ireland* v. *UK*; *Chahal* v. *UK*; *Selmouni* v. *France*; *Soering* v. *UK*; *Saadi* v. *Italy*; *Tyrer* v. *UK*; *Aksoy* v. *Turkey*; *Henaf* v. *France*	Article 5 Case-law = *Miguel Castro-Castro Prison* v. *Peru*; *Mejia* v. *Peru*; *Loayza-Tamayo* v. *Peru*; *Caesar* v. *Trinidad and Tobago*; *Velazquez Rodriguez* v. *Honduras*	Article 5 Case-law = *Doebbler* v. *Sudan*; *Article 19* v. *Eritrea*; *Dobbler* v. *Sudan*; *Ouko* v. *Kenya*	Article 7 Case-law = *Sooklal* v. *Trinidad and Tobago*; *Osbourne* v. *Jamaica*; *Chaparro and others* v. *Colombia*; *Estrella* v. *Uruguay*; *Aber* v. *Algeria*
Liberty and Security	Article 5 Case-law = *Wintwerp* v. *Netherlands*; *Fox, Campbell and Hartley* v. *UK*; *Murray* v. *UK*; *Brogan and others* v. *UK*; *Novoka* v. *Slovakia*; *El Masri* v. *FYRM*; *A and others* v. *UK*; *Letellier* v. *France*; *Timurtas* v. *Turkey*	Article 7 Case-law = *Gangaram Panday* v. *Suriname*; *Pacheco Teruel et al.* v. *Honduras*; *Velazquez Rodriguez* v. *Honduras*; *Goburu* v. *Paraguay*	Article 6 Case-law = *Mouvement Burkinabe' des Droits de l'Homme et des Peuples* v. *Burkina Faso*	Article 9 Case-law = *Mukong* v. *Cameroon and Carballal* v. *Uruguay*; *Madani* v. *Algeria*; *Celepli* v. *Sweden*; *Karker* v. *France*; *Van Alphen* v. *Netherlands*: *Kulomin* v. *Hungary*
Fair Trial	Article 6 Case-law = *Airey* v. *Ireland*; *Allenet de Ribemont* v. *France*; *Othman* v. *UK*; *Incal* v. *Turkey*; *Zimmermann* v. *Switzerland*; *Axen* v. *Germany*; *Taxquet* v. *Belgium*; *Saunders* v. *UK*; *Gridlin* v. *Russia*; *Benham* v. *UK*; *Kononon* v. *Latvia*	Article 8; Article 9 Case-law = *Exception to the Exhaustion of Domestic Remedies*; *Chocron Chocron* v. *Venezuela*; *Durand and Ugarte* v. *Peru*	Article 7 Case-law = *Malawi African Association* v. *Mauritania*; *Egyptian Initiative for Personal Rights and Interights* v. *Egypt*	Article 14 Case-law = *Bahamonde* v. *Equatorial Guinea*; *Fei* v. *Colombia*; *Maleki* v. *Italy*; *Lubuto* v. *Zambia*; *Deisl* v. *Austria*; *Harward* v. *Norway*

(*continued*)

(*continued*)

	ECtHR	IACtHR	African bodies	HRC
Freedom of Religion	Article 9 Case-law = *X and Church of Scientology* v. *Sweden*; *Arrowsmith* v. *UK*; *W.* v. *UK*; *Chappel* v. *UK*; *Ahmad* v. *UK*; *Kokkinakis* v. *GreeceDahlab* v. *Switzerland*; *Leya Sahin* v. *Turkey*	Article 12 Case-law = *The Last Temptation of Christ (Olmedo-Bustos* v. *Chile)*	Article 8 Case-law = *Prince* v. *South Africa*; *Centre for Minority Rights Development (Kenya) and Minority Rights Group International on behalf of Endorois Welfare Council* v. *Kenya*	Article 18 Case-law = *Malcom Ross* v. *Canada*; *Singh Bhinder* v. *Canada*; *Paul Westerman* v. *the Netherlands*; *Yeo-Bum and Myung-Jin Choi* v. *Republic of Korea*; *J.v.K. and C.M.G. v. K.-S.* v. *the Netherlands*; *J.P.* v. *Canada*
Freedom of Expression	Article 10 Case-law = *Handyside* v. *UK*; *Vereinigung Bildender Kunstler* v. *Austria*; *Sunday Times* v. *UK*; *Socialist Party* v. *Turkey*; *Fluentes Bobo* v. *Spain*; *VgT* v. *Switzerland*; *Thorgeirson* v. *Iceland*; *Filatenko* v. *Russia*; *Giniewski* v. *France*; *Boldea* v. *Romania*; *Jacubowski* v. *Germany*; *Casado Coca* v. *Spain*; *Steel* v. *UK*; *Goodwin* v. *UK*; *Vajnai* v. *Hungary*; *Chauvy* v. *France*; *Garaudy* v. *France*; *Aksoy* v. *Turkey*; *Jersild* v. *Denmark*; *Gunduz* v. *Turkey*; *I.A.* v. *Turkey*; *Pfeifer* v. *Austria*	Article 13 Case-law = *Compulsory Membership case*; *Ivcher Bronstein* v. *Peru*; *Rios Case*; *Herrera Uloa case*; *Canese case*; *Kimel* v. *Argentina*; *Tristan Donoso* v. *Panama*; *Marcel Claude Reyes et al.* v. *Chile*; *The Last Temptation of Christ (Olmedo-Bustos* v. *Chile)*	Article 9 Case-law = *Konate' Issa* v. *Burkina Faso*; *Article 19* v. *Eritrea*; *Zimabwe lawyers for Human Rights and Another* v. *Zimbabwe*	Article 19; Article 20 Case-law = *Hertzberg and Others* v. *Finland*; *Faurisson* v. *France*; *Gauthier* v. *Canada*; *JRT and the WG Party* v. *Canada*; *Sohn* v. *Republic of Korea*

Freedom of Association	Article 11 Case-law = *Young, James and Webster* v. *UK*; *Sigurjonsson* v. *Iceland*; *Rafah Patyidi and Others* v. *Turkey*; *United Communist Party of Turkey and Others* v. *Turkey*; *Bukta and others* v. *Hungary*	Article 16 Case-law = *Advisory Opinion on Compulsory Membership in an Association Prescribed by Law for the Practice of Journalism*	Article 10 Case-law = *Jawara* v. *The Gambia*; *Lawyers for Human Rights* v. *Swaziland*	Article 22 Case-law = *J.B.* v. *Canada*; *Ismayilov* v. *Azerbaijan*; *Korneenko et al.* v. *Belarus*
Freedom of Assembly		Article 15 Case-law = *Advisory Opinion on Compulsory Membership in an Association Prescribed by Law for the Practice of Journalism*	Article 11 Case-law = *International Pen, Constitutional Rights Project, Interights on behalf of Ken Saro-Wiwa Jr and Civil Liberties Organisation* v. *Nigeria*	Article 21 Case-law = *Kivenmaa* v. *Finland*; *Gryb* v. *Belarus*
Right to Property	Article 1, Protocol 1 Case-law = *Avellar Cordeiro Zagallo* v. *Portugal*; *Lapinskaya, Kulikov, Kurkunov and Silka* v. *Ukraine*; *Chassagnou* v. *France*; *Bălăucă* v. *Romania*; *Mamidakis* v. *Greece*; *Chapman* v. *The United Kingdom*; *Jahn and Others* v. *Germany*	Article 21 Case-law = *Mayagna (Sumo) Awas Tingni Community* v. *Nicaragua*; *Yakye Axa Indigenous Community* v. *Paraguay*; *Torres Benvenuto et al.* v. *Peru*	Article 14 Case-law = *The Social and Economic Rights Action Centre and the Centre for Economic and Social Rights* v. *Nigeria*; *Malawi African Association, Amnesty International, Ms. Sarr Diop, Union Interafricaine des Droits de l'Homme and RADDHO, Collectif des Veuves et Ayants-droit and Association Mauritanienne des Droits de l'Homme* v. *Mauritania*	Case-law(linked with non-discrimination) = *Oló Bahamonde v. Equatorial Guinea*; *Ackla* v. *Togo and Diergaardt of Rehoboth Baster Community et al.* v. *Namibia*

(*continued*)

(*continued*)

	ECtHR	IACtHR	African bodies	HRC
Right to Private and Family Life	Article 8; Article 12 Case-law = *Niemietz* v. *Germany*; *X. Y. Z.* v. *The United Kingdom*; *F.* v. *Switzerland*; *A. B. and C.* v. *Ireland*; *Dudgeon* v. *UK*; *Rees* v. *UK*; *Christine Goodwin* v. *UK*; *Leander* v. *Sweden*; *Khan* v. *UK*; *Loizidou* v. *Turkey*; *Gillow* v. *UK*; *Powell & Rayner* v. *UK*; *Hatton* v. *UK*; *Klass* v. *Germany*; *Silver* v. *UK*	Article 11; Article 17 Case-law = *Morales de Sierra v. Guatemala*; *Atala Riffo* v. *Chile*; *Duque* v. *Colombia*	Article 18 Case-law = *Democratic Republic of Congo* v. *Burundi, Rwanda and Uganda*; *Kenneth Good* v. *Botswana*; *Egyptian Initiative for Personal Rights & INTERIGHTS* v. *Egypt*	Article 17; Article 23 Case-law = *Hopu and Bessert* v. *France*; *Toonen* v. *Australia*
Freedom of Movement and Asylum	Protocol 4: Article 2 and 3 Case-law = *Piermont* v. *France*; *WM* v. *Denmark*; *Sisojeva* v. *Latvia*; *Guzzardi* v. *Italy*; *Labita* v. *Italy*; *Paramanathan* v. *Germany*; *Ivanov* v. *Ukraine*; *Gochev* v. *Bulgaria*	Article 22 Case-law = *Municipio de Ituango* v. *Colombia*; *Barrios Family* v. *Venezuela*; *Juses Tranquillino Velez Loor* v. *Panama*	Article 12 Case-law = *Huri-Laws* v. *Nigeria*; *Institute for Human Rights and Development in Africa* v. *Angola*; *African Institute for Human Rights and Development* v. *Guinea*	Article 12 Case-law = *General Comment No.27*; *Chiti* v. *Zambia*; *Aboufaied* v. *Libya*; *Ory* v. *France*

Index

African Charter on Human and Peoples' Rights, 174
  interpretation clause, 103
  necessity, 172
African Commission on Human and Peoples' Rights, 35
  composition
    education, 142
  judicial dialogue, 115–119
  margin of appreciation, 211–213
  necessary in a democratic society, 182
  politics, 216
  proportionality, 192–193
  rules and procedures, 138
  secretariat, 163
  sexual orientation, 240–241
African Court on Human and Peoples' Rights, 35
  composition
    education, 142
    professional experience, 145
  interpretation clause, 103
  judicial dialogue, 119–121
  margin of appreciation, 211–213
  meetings with other bodies, 165–167
  politics, 216
  proportionality, 192–193
  registry, 163–164
  rules and procedures, 138
  separate opinions, 149–151
American Convention on Human Rights
  interpretation clause, 102
  necessity, 172
amicus curiae, 109, 232–234
  African bodies, 234
  ECtHR, 233
  HRC, 234
  IACtHR, 232
amnesty, 206
Arab Charter on Human Rights, 24
  equality, 25
Arab Court for Human Rights, 36
ASEAN, 36
assembly, freedom of, 57–58
association, freedom of, 179
authority, delegation of, 107
autonomy, 16, 174, 235

backlash, 38, 154, 198, 214–215
balance of rights, 183
better position, 198, 200, 207, 209, 219, *See also* subsidiarity

Cançado Trindade, Antonio Augusto, 151
citation. *See* judicial dialogue
civil society. *See* NGOs
coherence, 4, 16, 26, 29, 105, 121, 167, 244, 252–253
compliance, 29, 36, 76, 105, 108, 118, 121, 213, 226
composition
  ACommHPR
    rules and procedures, 138
  ACtHPR
    rules and procedures, 138
  education, 141–144
  Europeanisation, 144
  HRC
    rules and procedures, 138

composition (cont.)
IACtHR
rules and procedures, 137–138
postcolonial theory, 160
professional experience, 144–149
in academia, 147
in international organisations, 145
conventionality control, 196, 203–208
convergence, 121, 144, 167, 211, 216, 229, 244
judicial, 27–29
normative, 20
one-sided, 144
Council of Europe, 174
cross-fertilisation, 165
cross-referencing. *See* judicial dialogue

declarations, unilateral, 239, *See also* friendly settlements
defamation. *See* expression, freedom of
deference, 196–197, 214, 221, 247, *See* subsidiarity
democracy, 179, 204, 210, 216, 220
democratic society, 113

education, 141–144, *See also* composition
effectiveness, 33, 99–100, 214
elections, 120
enforced disappearances, 65, 130–132
equality, 120
European Committee of Social Rights, 33
European Convention on Human Rights
interpretation clause, 103
necessity, 171
European Court of Human Rights, 33
composition
education, 142
professional experience, 146
judicial dialogue, 78–80
margin of appreciation, 199–203
meetings with other bodies, 165–167
necessary in a democratic society, 178–179
necessity, 176
overview, 33
politics, 214–215
proportionality, 185–188
registry, 161–162
rules and procedures, 137
separate opinions, 154–158
European Court of Justice, 34, 135, 184
Europeanisation, 144, 154, 160
Europeanisation of human rights. *See* composition
expression, freedom of, 53–56, 209, 213, 247
ACtHPR, 54
defamation, 54–56, 205, 218–221
hate speech, 54
journalists, 117
judicial dialogue, 113–114
margin of appreciation, 200, 224–225
proportionality, 187, 191
protection of public morals, 65, 210, 217–218
protection of religion, 224–225
external sources. *See* judicial dialogue

fair trial, 119–120
fertilisation, legal. *See* judicial dialogue
fragmentation, 180, 182, 216, 221, 237, 245
actual, 24
in international law, 14–18
institutional, 17, 27
internal, 118
judicial, 27–29, 130, 244
normative, 16, 19–20
positive, 229
potential, 24
friendly settlements, 238–240

gender identity, 88, 132

harmonisation, 107, *See* convergence
history
of member states, 208
IACtHR, 203
indigenous rights, 87
of regional systems, 174
housing, right to, 118
Human Rights Committee, 32
composition
education, 142
judicial dialogue, 124–126
margin of appreciation, 208–211
necessary in a democratic society, 180–181
necessity, 177
politics, 216
proportionality, 188–190
rules and procedures, 138
secretariat, 164

ILO Convention No. 169, 77, 127
impartiality, 137–138, 238

independence, 137–138, 216
  from member states, 139
indigenous rights, 77–87, 245
  ACommHPR, 84
  ECtHR, 78–80
  IACtHR, 81–84
  judicial dialogue, 120
  lack of judicial dialogue, 126–128
  property, 77–87
influence, 229
Inter-American Commission on Human Rights, 34
Inter-American Court of Human Rights, 34
  composition
    education, 142
    professional experience, 145
  conventionality control, 203–208
  judicial dialogue, 110–114
  meetings with other bodies, 165–167
  necessary in a democratic society, 179–180
  necessity, 176
  politics, 223
  proportionality, 190–192
  registry, 162–163
  rules and procedures, 137–138
  separate opinions, 151–154
interim measures, 123
International Court of Justice, 15, 17, 32, 135
International Covenant on Civil and Political Rights
  necessity, 172
International Criminal Tribunal for the Former Yugoslavia, 17
International Law Commission, 15, 18
  2006 Report, 16

journalists, protection of, 113
  judicial dialogue, 117
judge-rapporteur. *See* Secretariats
judicial borrowing. *See* judicial dialogue
judicial dialogue, 103–134, 162, 164, 248
  ACommHPR, 115–119
  ACtHPR, 119–121
  ECtHR, 78–80
  false citations, 109
  HRC, 124–126
  judicial monologue, 121
  lack of
    freedom of religion, 128–130
    indigenous rights, 126–128
  legitimacy, 105
  same-sex marriage, 132–134
  state compliance, 106

Kalaydjieva, Zdravka, 155
Keller, Helen, 155

legitimacy, 1, 5, 29, 105, 107, 114–115, 118, 121, 183, 214, 236, 244, 253
legitimate aim, 179, 186
Lemmens, Paul, 155
liberty and security, right to, 51–53
  ACommHPR, 53
  ECtHR, 52
  HRC, 53
  IACtHR, 52
life, right to, 45–49
  abortion, 45–47
    ECtHR, 47
  American Convention on Human Rights, 25
  death penalty, 125
  use of force, 47–49
    absolutely necessary, 182
    ACommHPR, 48
    ECtHR, 48
    HRC, 48
    IACtHR, 48
lobbying, 235, *See also* NGOs

margin of appreciation, 89, 187, 196, 199–203
  African bodies, 211–213
  defamation, 218–221
  freedom of expression, 200, 224–225
  freedom of religion, 70
  HRC, 208–211
  IACtHR, 204
  origins and evolution, 199–201
  protection of public morals, 217–218
  same-sex marriage, 89
  wearing of religious attire, 221–224
Medina Quiroga, Cecilia, 152
migrants, right of, 64–65
migrants, rights of
  proportionality, 191
minorities, rights of, 209
Motoc, Iulia, 154
movement, freedom of, 178

necessary in a democratic society, 172, *See also* necessity
necessity, 169–184, 246
  absolutely necessary, 182

necessity (cont.)
ACHPR, 172
ACHR, 172
definition, 175
ECHR, 171
ICCPR, 172
in a democratic society, 172, 176, 179
ACommHPR, 182
ECtHR, 178–179
HRC, 180–181
IACtHR, 179–180
necessary in a democratic society, 201
pressing social need, 176
neutrality, cultural, 218
NGOs, 220, 229–236
amicus curiae, 232–234
African bodies, 234
ECtHR, 233
HRC, 234
IACtHR, 232
availability, 241–243
litigation, 230–232
lobbying, 235–236

Office of the High Commissioner for Human Rights, 30
opinions, separate, 125
Ouguergouz, Fatsah, 150

parallelism, normative, 20
Pettiti, Louis Edmond, 156
Pinto de Albuquerque, Paulo, 156
political participation, right to, 123
politics
of member states, 210
indigenous rights, 87
of the systems, 213–216
African bodies, 216
ECtHR, 214–215
HRC, 216
IACtHR, 223
private and family life, right to, 122
proportionality, 186, 191
professional background. *See* composition
professional experience, 144–149, *See also* composition
in academia, 147
in international organisations, 145
proliferation
of human rights institutions, 29, 229
of human rights instruments, 244
of international instruments, 21
of judicial institutions, 26
of regional instruments, 23
property, right to
ancestral lands, 77–87
proportionality, 192
proportionality, 113, 169, 178, 184–193, 246
African bodies, 192–193
ECtHR, 185–188
HRC, 188–190
IACtHR, 190–192
public interest. *See also* defamation

reasonableness, 188, *See* proportionality
regional consensus, 91, 112, 198, 202, 207, 210, 216, 224
Registry. *See* Secretariats
relativism, 143, *See* universality
religion, freedom of
ACommHPR, 117
burqa ban, 72
convergence, 117
feminist critique, 77
fragmentation, 65–77
headscarf, 68–71
in education settings, 68–72
Islam, perception of, 76
lack of judicial dialogue, 128–130
laicité, 75
margin of appreciation, 70, 221–224
proportionality, 187
reasonableness, 189
rituals, 117
secularism, 75
Sikh turban, 66–68
wearing of religious attire, 65–77, 245
Restrictive measure, adequacy of. *See* proportionality

Secretariats, 160–165
ACommHPR, 163
ACtHPR, 163–164
collaborations, 162
meetings, 165–167
ECtHR, 161–162
HRC, 164–165
IACtHR, 162–163
separate opinions, 149
ACtHPR, 149–151
ECtHR, 154–158
IACtHR, 151–154

limits, 158
sexual orientation, 237, 245
discrimination based on, 58–60, 133
African bodies, 60
ECtHR, 59
HRC, 59
IACtHR, 58
marriage, 87–92
ECtHR, 89–91
HRC, 91
IACtHR, 87–90
judicial dialogue, 132–134
regional consensus, 91
regional consensus, 208
survival pensions, 61–62
Sicilianos, Linos Alexandre, 155
subsidiarity, 196–198, 201, 204, 212, 221

Tchikaya, Balise, 150
third-party interventions. *See amicus curiae*
torture, cruel, inhuman and degrading treatments
judicial dialogue, 116
torture, cruel, inhuman and degrading treatments, prohibition of, 49–51
death row, 62–63
ECtHR, 49
enforced disappearances, 131
IACtHR, 50
judicial dialogue, 113, 123
travaux preparatoires
ACHR, 173
ICCPR, 173
treaty interpretation, 97–101, 246
clauses, 101–103
universal jurisdiction, 103
context, 98
evolutive, 99, 124
object and purpose, 98
pro homine principle, 100

UN Declaration on the Rights of Indigenous People, 77
UN Human Rights Council, 30
Special Procedures, 31
Universal Period Review (UPR), 31
UN Treaty Bodies, 31–32
UN Working Group on Indigenous Populations, 128
universality, 37–40, 109, 121, 211, 218, 244
transformative, 40

victim, 130
Vienna Convention on the Law of the Treaties, 17, 98

Ziemele, Ineta, 157